MW00806269

NO SURRENDER

True Stories of the U.S. Navy Armed Guard in World War II

NO SURRENDER

True Stories of the U.S. Navy Armed Guard in World War II

by

Gerald Reminick

The Glencannon Press

Palo Alto
2004

Published by The Glencannon Press
P.O. Box 341, Palo Alto, CA 94302
Tel. 800-711-8985
www.glencannon.com

First Edition, first printing.

Library of Congress Cataloging-in-Publication Data

Reminick, Gerald, 1943-
No surrender : true stories of the U.S. Navy Armed Guard in World War II / by Gerald Reminick.-- 1st ed.
p. cm.
Includes bibliographical references and index.
ISBN 1-889901-34-2 (alk. paper)
1. United States. Navy. Armed Guard. 2. World War, 1939-1945--Naval operations, American. 3. World War, 1939-1945--Personal narratives, American. I. Title.

D769.45.R36 2004
940.54'5973--dc22

2004055255

Acknowledgements

There are many people who have helped me compile this anthology of World War II United States Navy Armed Guard stories. I would like to thank Charles A. Lloyd, Chairman of the USN Armed Guard Veterans Association for his assistance; Dan and Toni Horodysky, creators of the *American Merchant Marine at War* website; Tom Bowerman and Agnes Bridger, creators of the *WW II U.S. Navy Armed Guard and WW II Merchant Marine* website. Both websites are treasures of information. I also thank Captain Arthur R. Moore for his indispensable reference, *A Careless Word ...A Needless Sinking.*

A great deal of what follows is due to Armed Guard veteran, Lyle Dupra, whom I thank for his encouragement and support; as well as: Robert Norling for his "stack" of stories; Harold Skinner for his stories and support; Naval Armed Guard poet, George Hurley, for his poems and poetic experiences; and Joe McKenna for prodding the Long Island Navy Armed Group of veterans for stories.

I especially appreciate the libraries of Suffolk County Community College and my colleagues therein for their support and the encouragement and my family, for their encouragement.

A special thank you is in order for Professor Joyce Gabriele, my colleague and editor, who has looked over my shoulder and guided me in all my writings.

And finally, a very special thanks to my editor, Bill Harris. His patience and support brought this anthology to fruition. Thanks, Bill!

Dedication

To the 2,085 Armed Guards who gave their lives,
To their families and friends,
And to those who survived.

Their motto was "WE AIM – TO DELIVER"

And they did!

Contents

Foreword

The stories in this book are told by those who experienced them, but they are really more than that. As was — and, sadly, still is — true of the merchant mariners alongside whom they served, the Armed Guard has never received the proper recognition and acknowledgment for its patriotic service and sacrifices. Lightly armed and manned, in circumstances of extreme danger, against the full might of the Nazis and the Japanese on the sea and in the air, they persevered in the crucially important task of protecting the critical supply lines. Without their valiant efforts none of the great historic battles, which command so much of the attention, could have been won.

"… In the beginning, the Naval Armed Guard was a volunteer group, and no sane insurance company would have given even a "fool's wager" on their life expectancy. These men repeatedly sailed, time after time, and whenever or wherever needed. There were no safe havens. Their ships were attacked, destroyed, or sunk far out to sea, close to shores, and even in some ports.

"The enemies were not the only causes of death, destruction, and maiming. Unbelievable rough seas claimed many. The frigid waters of the North Atlantic claimed a share of lives and loss of body parts from being frozen. Many were consumed in the fiery holocaust of burning tankers, and/or vaporized in the explosions of those ships which carried nitro and other explosives. Being sunk and forced to swim in placid seas was not a gift of prolonged life either. If one did not have a boat or raft to 'get on board,' the effects of body muscles being exhausted, soon succumbed them to drowning. Without a doubt, many lives were claimed by the sea predators. Many visual reportings by survivors have been recorded and documented by those who were more fortunate. Of those who made it to any floatation device, their days were also numbered. Fresh water, food and medicines were not endless. Depletion by rationed usage was inevitable. Depending on where their ship was sunk, the cold, the heat, or starvation was sure to claim them, unless rescued. More often than not, they perished under these hostile conditions."[1]

Each narrative in this compilation, therefore, is the story of an individual hero *and* stands for the stories and experiences of the hundreds of heroes who lived — and died — in the great campaign to make the world safe. In the annals of "the greatest generation," the U.S. Navy Armed Guard deserves a special ovation.

1

Before World War II

World War I

One of the turning points in World War I sea warfare was the Allies' success in blockading Germany's seaborne access to raw materials and food. Germany's reaction was a new kind of warfare — the submarine. At first Germany used restricted submarine warfare against merchant vessels. Then she made the decision to go against *any* type of Allied vessel. Beginning in February 1917, the Kaiser instructed his U-boats to sink all merchant shipping found in British territorial waters.

"Germany launched this all-out submarine *guerre de course* in the British Isles with multiple attacks conducted simultaneously with 'utmost energy' by about sixty U-boats. To minimize detection by Allied aircraft and submarines, and counterfire from merchant ships, and to take advantage of higher speed for escape, U-boat skippers attacked at night while on the surface. The results were spectacular: 540,000 tons sunk in February, 594,000 tons in March, and an appalling 881,000 tons in April. During April alone — the grimmest month of the U-boat war — the Germans sank 423 merchant ships, of which 350 were British.* Moreover, as anticipated, the campaign scared off most of the many neutral ships trading with Great Britain."[1]

This new tactic was in direct violation of Chapter 4 of the 1909 Declaration concerning the Laws of Naval Warfare:

> **Article 48**. A neutral vessel which has been captured may not be destroyed by the captor; she must be taken into such port as is proper for the determination there of all questions concerning the validity of capture.
>
> **Article 49**: As an exception, a neutral vessel which has been captured by a belligerent warship, and which would be liable to condemnation, may be destroyed if the observance of Article 48 would involve danger to the safety of the warship or to the success of the operations in which she is engaged at the time.
>
> **Article 50**: Before the vessel is destroyed all persons on board must be placed in safety, and all the ship's papers and other documents which the parties interested consider relevant for the purpose of deciding on the validity of the capture must be taken on board the warship.[2]

Because American vessels were being sunk, President Wilson sought congressional approval to arm U.S. merchant ships. However, a split in Congress denied his request. "A furious Wilson then exercised his constitutional powers and directed the navy to furnish guns, ammunition, and gunners to American ships clearing for ports in Europe and passing through German war zones."[3] The Navy brass were strongly opposed as they felt the directive would reduce the quantity of equipment and supplies available for the surface navy. But Wilson ultimately won out. And after the sinking of three American ships (*City of Memphis*, *Illinois*

---

* Total figures vary by source. Generally speaking, in this period the U-boats sank about 1,000 ships for about 2 million tons.

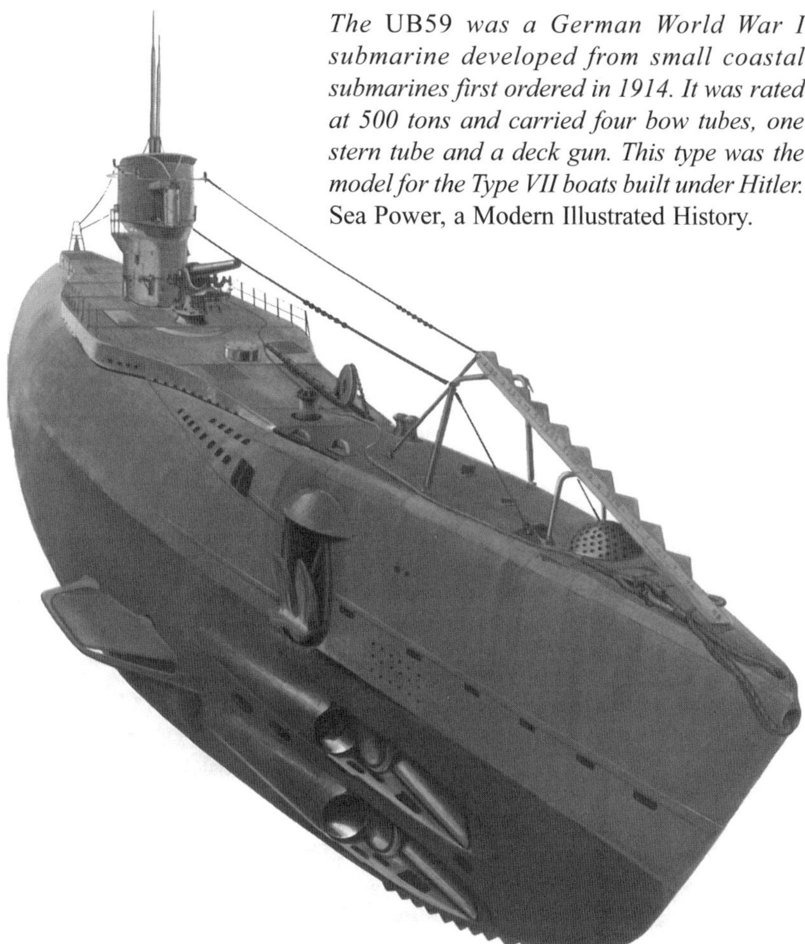

The UB59 *was a German World War I submarine developed from small coastal submarines first ordered in 1914. It was rated at 500 tons and carried four bow tubes, one stern tube and a deck gun. This type was the model for the Type VII boats built under Hitler.* Sea Power, a Modern Illustrated History.

and *Vigilancia*) in March 1917, Wilson and the United States Congress declared war on Germany on April 7, 1917.

At the outbreak of World War I in Europe in 1914, the U.S. had a shortage of merchant ships. This shortage created a dependence upon foreign countries to ship her exports, troops and war materials. "Much warning went unheeded until 1914: this country dozing in isolation with 90 percent of its overseas commerce in foreign bottoms. Quickly most of that 90 percent was withdrawn by its owners for war. The United States paid an 8 billion-dollar freight bill for what space could be had in three years to 1917. Mountains of goods piled up."[4]

Congress, realizing the need for U.S. flag ships, passed the Shipping Act of 1916. This authorized the newly formed U.S. Shipping Board through the Emergency Fleet Corporation to build ships. More than 2,300 ships were built under the auspices of that agency from 1918 to 1922 (Ironically, most were completed and delivered after the war was over). To defend the ships that were produced, the U.S. Navy realized the necessity of placing armament aboard U.S. ships and training men to handle the armament. These men became known as the Armed Guard.

Serving aboard 384 ships in World War I, the Armed Guard's main purpose was "to maintain the guns and ammunition, protect the ship, its crew and precious cargo from the enemy with orders to fire the guns as long as the ship was afloat. This was to keep the enemy from crippling the ship, then boarding it for provisions they needed to stay on patrol longer. In previous engagements, the enemy had been known to kill the crew before sinking the ship."[5]

> During 1917-18, the navy furnished a total of 30,000 men to the AG [Armed guard]. They compiled a record of 1,832 transatlantic crossings in AG status, 347 sightings of submarines, and 227 attacks by submarines, of which 197 were repulsed.
>
> Of 2,738,000 tons of American marine shipping on which they served, only 168,458 were lost. Attacks repulsed by the AG saved 1,140,000 tons. Not a single troop ship was lost, although over 300,000 men were transported to Europe per month.
>
> The AG gun crews, of fifteen to thirty-two men usually under command of a chief petty officer, served on practically every American vessel that plied the war zones, …
>
> Of the total of 384 ships carrying naval armed guards, 42 were lost – 36 sunk by enemy action, and 6 others lost through other causes such as internal explosion, fire, mines, and grounding. A total of fifty-eight AGs were lost.[6]

With the end of World War I, the Navy Armed Guard was disbanded.

America's Merchant Marine between the Wars

The Great Depression dealt ship construction a severe blow. The U.S. ships built in 1920 were becoming outmoded. "In 1936, our merchant marine was fourth among six leading maritime nations in tonnage, sixth in vessels ten years of age or less, fifth in vessels with speeds of twelve knots or more."[7] Not only were the ships deteriorating, so were the working conditions and wages for the mariners who crewed these ships. This deterioration caused constant friction among the unions, seamen, and ship owners.

However, as the threat of war became more and more evident, Congress passed the Merchant Marine Act of 1936. This became the cornerstone of a new American merchant marine — one capable of carrying its own trade, competing globally and providing transport for troops and war materials. It called for five hundred ships to be built over a ten-year period. The U. S. Maritime Commission was created to oversee this enormous program including the training of new officers and seamen to crew the ships.

Ship construction commenced but wasn't adequate by the time war broke out. However, eventually American know-how and determination were more than equal to the task. By the end of World War II, American industry would complete a building task that will never be duplicated. "Within a year-and-a-half after the United States entered the war in 1941, the shipyards were building ships faster than the enemy was able to sink them. From 1942 through 1945 United States shipyards built 5,592 merchant ships, of which 2,710 were Liberty ships, 414 were the faster Victory type, 651 were tankers, 417 were standard cargo ships, and the remaining 1,409 were military or minor types."[8]

When the war began, only 55,000 mariners manned our ships. There was an immediate need to train men to sail and remain on the new ships. The draft kept our armed services supplied with men but the Merchant Marine was different because these men were volunteers. By war's end 250,000 mariners would be trained and serve.

The Arming Merchant Ship Section of the Fleet Maintenance Division of the Office of Naval Operations took over the authority and management of the Navy Armed Guard. This section was called Op-23L:

> Op-23L gave general direction to the program. It formulated doctrine and issued directives. It kept elaborate files and records. It worked to improve training and to standardize all procedures in the Armed Guard Service. It worked to overcome the shortage of guns and trained personnel ... Working closely with the Arming Merchant Section was the Coordinator of Defense Installations on Merchant Ships in the Maritime Commission. The Maritime Commission War Shipping Administration, under the direction of the Coordinator of Defense Installations on Merchant Ships, had the responsibility for the installation of defense items in collaboration with local naval agencies at the yards. The Port Directors were entrusted with the execution of directives from the Chief of Naval Operations (Op-23L) and played a large part in the administration of the entire program. Theirs was the day-by-day responsibility to see that each ship which left port was properly armed, equipped, and manned with Armed Guards. They also arranged for necessary repairs and for replenishment of material when ships returned from voyages.[9]

The U.S. Navy Armed Guard would do its part in World War II.

2

TRAINING

Following the training of 100 reserve officers in the summer 1941 at the U.S. Naval Academy, a camp for Armed Guard gun training was created at Little Creek, Virginia on September 17, 1941.

FDR directed the Chief of Naval Operations, Admiral Harold Stark to appoint an officer in charge of the Armed Guard program. USNR Commander Edward Cleave was chosen. "By the end of November 1941 Cleave had supervised, under the Vice Chief of Naval Operations, the arming of fifty-five American-owned ships. By the end of January 1942 — one month later — the number totaled 112. By June 1942 it was in high gear with 1,064 merchant ships boasting some kind of defensive armament."[1] At first, the newest and heaviest armament was placed on the Navy's surface warships. As a result, many merchant ships carried fake guns made out of concrete until they received the real thing.

At Camp Shelton part of the training included handling 20mm guns at "The Shed." Courtesy of U.S. Navy Armed Guard WW II Veterans.

Soon there were three Basic Training Armed Guard Schools; Little Creek, Virginia (moved to Camp Shelton, Virginia in 1943), Gulfport, Mississippi (initially in Chicago and moved because of inclement wintry weather), and San Diego, California. In addition to these Basic Training sites, antiaircraft gun ranges were situated near: Dam Neck, Virginia; Shell Beach and New Orleans, Louisiana; Pacific Beach, Point Montara and San Francisco (Treasure Island), California and in Seattle, Washington, and Lido Beach, New York. These locations also served as centers for refresher courses.

Training was tough and demanding. The men learned how to load and fire many different types of armament.

> Although the 20-millimeter Oerlikon is coming into widespread use on cargo ships, there are many .50 caliber Browning and .30 caliber Lewis machine guns in use, and the men must be able to handle all of them. In the big-gun field, the major calibers found on merchant ships include the three-inch 50 (dual purpose), the four-inch 50, the five-inch 50, the five-inch 51, and the new five-inch 38 (dual purpose), as well as the three-inch 23 and six-pounder.[2]

In addition, the Armed Guard mission was taught:

At San Diego 20mm practice included firing live antiaircraft rounds out over the Pacific. San Diego Historical Society.

> There shall be no surrender and no abandoning ship so long as the guns can be fought. In case of casualty to members of the gun crew the remaining men shall continue to serve the gun. The Navy Department considers that so long as there remains a chance to save the ship, the Armed Guard should remain thereon and take every opportunity that may present itself to destroy the submarine.[3]

After Basic Training, an armed guard was sent to an Armed Guard Center. There were three Navy Armed Guard Centers: Brooklyn, New York; New Orleans, Louisiana and Treasure Island, California. "These Centers handled records, mail, and payroll along with administering discipline, furnishing recreation, health, legal problems, additional training ...."[4]

The Brooklyn Armed Guard Center opened in May 1941. On November 10, 1941, it received the first Navy Armed Guard Officers. Growth was rapid and it "became one of the largest military commands in the Navy ... By March 1944, 47,000 men and 2,800 officers with a payroll of over $2,000,000 a month. Over 5,000 men were fed each day ... By November 1944, 59,062 men were attached to the Center."[5]

The New Orleans Armed Guard Center, known as NOLA, was established in March 1942.

The U.S. Navy Armed Guard Center at 1st Avenue and 52nd Street, Brooklyn, New York, as it appeared in the winter of 1945. U.S. Navy Armed Guard WWII Veterans.

> *The purpose of the Center was to provide at one central location, facilities for receiving, berthing, messing, equipping and training men in the Naval Service assigned to duty as Armed Guard gun crews on Merchant ships. A program of training was begun in June 1942, in an enlisted barrack which was equipped with one 20 MM, one .50 caliber and two .30 caliber guns. Transient officers with combat experience were assigned to instructional work for brief periods between voyages.*[6]

The Treasure Island Armed Guard Center was established in December 1941 and rapidly expanded

> *... from zero to reach peak capacity of personnel of 46,817 on June 2, 1945. The Center had personnel on board 2,106 vessels. The men had to be cared for like those of the other Centers and Waves took over the duties of men as gunnery instructors in many cases... By the middle of 1945, the process of shifting battle tired veterans from the Atlantic to the Pacific center in the buildup for the Japanese invasion was well underway. Many of the crew were trained in Seattle, Washington, San Diego, California, Farragut, Idaho, and many more places, too numerous to mention...*[7]

Treasure Island, California in San Francisco Bay, as it appeared in 1945. Courtesy of U.S. Navy Armed Guard WW II Veterans.

From these training facilities came the Officers, Gunners, Radiomen, Signalmen, Medics and Radar men that made up the U.S. Navy Armed Guard.

~~~

Van C. Mills served in the U.S. Navy throughout the war, then graduated from Texas A &M in 1951 with a degree in Range Management and Forestry. The attack at Pearl Harbor brought the war into sudden and sharp focus.

Remembering Pearl Harbor

The attack on Pearl Harbor occurred sixty years ago, but I still remember it as if it were yesterday.

Following graduation from Athens High School, Texas in 1941, I volunteered to serve in the U.S. Navy for the duration of the National Emergency. I had been closely following the war in Europe and I believed that I was eventually going to be drafted. The Navy pay was $21.00 per month, which wasn't too bad for an East Texas farm boy.

My Boot Camp training was completed in San Diego on December 5, 1941, just two days before Pearl Harbor. I was in the 133rd Boot Company of 1941. Most of the personnel doing the training were in the US Naval Reserve and had been called up for active duty.
~~~

When the news of Pearl Harbor was heard, these reservists were angered, devastated and shocked. How could this have happened to one of the finest navies in the world? On the day of the attack, there were rumors that the Japanese might try to land troops down in Mexico or somewhere along the West Coast.

After the attack, firing pins were immediately put into our old World War I Springfield training rifles. For the next two nights we slept in our clothes alongside our rifles and bandoliers of ammunition. Soon after the attack, volunteers by the hundreds started pouring into the naval base. Within two to three weeks the base was out of uniforms. Recruits were drilling in civilian clothes wearing cowboy boots, tennis shoes or dress shoes. The training period for all available personnel was cut short. Even the USS *Saratoga* left soon after the attack with an initial troop shipment to Hawaii.

After graduating from a Navy Radio School in Los Angeles in early 1942, myself and about twenty-five other signalmen were sent to the Armed Guard Center in Brooklyn. Some guys in this group who had lived on the East Coast began referring to the Armed Guard as a "suicide squad." I wondered, "What had I got myself into?" When I first shipped out on the East Coast on 8 June 1942 some of the harbors looked like graveyards with the masts of ships sticking out of the water. It also seemed like we saw an empty life boat floating on the water every day.[8]

~~~

James Gailey's recollection of Armed Guard Training first appeared in the March/April 1993 issue of the Pointer, *the publication of the U.S. Navy Armed Guard Veterans.*

U.S. Navy Armed Guard WW II: Training

The Iraq war brought back many memories of my experiences during World War II. Most of this time was spent in a "special force" of the U.S. Navy called the U.S. Naval Armed Guard.

On Sunday morning, December 7, 1941 we learned that the Pearl Harbor Navy Base, in the Hawaiian Islands had been bombed by the Japanese Naval Air Force and that we were in a
~~~

state of war with them. I had been trying to join the service prior to this, but my mom and dad would not sign for me, as I was not old enough without the consent. The attack really set me on fire for a second time, but my parents still would not sign. I had not registered for the draft yet, but all nineteen- to thirty-year-olds were now required to do so. But I was only eighteen.

I went and signed up on Monday December 8, 1941. They gave me papers to carry home for my parents to sign and to come back on Friday for further examination, which I did. I was told to come back on Monday, the 15th to be sent to Raleigh, N.C. When I got to the recruiting office I met a bunch of men who were joining to stay out of the Army, as they were older and would he drafted anyway. We were all examined and sent to Raleigh for further examinations and to be sworn in. I actually entered the service on the 16th of December 1941.

On Monday night, I reported to the recruiting office where there were about fifty of us who were ready to go. They marched us all to the train station and we headed for Raleigh, N.C. When we arrived in Raleigh, around 11 PM, we joined hundreds of others who had come from all over the U.S.A. This was ten days before Christmas.

They marched us to the U.S. Post Office, located on Fayetteville Street, downtown. We went to the top floor, in the attic, which was unfurnished and unheated. We had to take off all our clothes and stand naked all the while until they finished with everybody's physical examination, both inside and out. About 3 AM they finished and let us put our clothes back on. Then they gave anybody that wanted to back out, a chance to do so. They swore in the rest of us and told us we were free until 7 AM. We were to be put on a troop train to Norfolk, Virginia for training. I was tired and sleepy so I lay down on a cold, damp, cement floor and tried to go to sleep, but it was too cold. I should have gone to eat with the other boys. We did not get anything to eat until that evening, but I did not know this then. Lesson one!

The train came in from Florida and was loaded with guys like us who had enlisted. We got into Norfolk around 2 AM. They met us at the station with trucks and buses to take us to the Naval Operations Base, which we soon learned to call "NOB." Some of the trucks were the tractor-trailer types which were named "cattle cars." We arrived at the Navy station and they took us to a chow hall and fed us. It was chipped beef on toast and I'll never forget that was my first meal in the Navy. They told us it was called S.O.S.

They took us to a supply house and issued us: soap, towel, washrag and bedding. Everybody with their "skinned heads" that had arrived before us were laughing and yelling to us about our hair, as if they were old-timers, but they had been there only a few days themselves. They marched us to a barrack. We had an air raid drill at 11 PM. We had to go outside for about half an hour, in our shorts. The next day, we paraded around in our birthday suit as the doctors really gave us another physical exam, "inside and out"!! If you had any modesty, it was soon gone.

After the physical we were taken to a supply store. They measured us and gave out our clothing and bedding, along with four suits of whites, two suits of blues, four skivvies and shorts, four pair of white socks, four pair of black socks, four white hats, one dress blue hat, two blankets, one pillow and pillowcase, one mattress and cover, two pair of shoes and two pair of leggings. We always had to wear the leggings while we were in boot camp. All of these items had to be rolled or placed a certain way with your name showing. We were issued a big bag called a "Sea Bag" to put this entire gear in, plus a hammock. All of this had to be rolled up to carry whenever you were transferred to throughout your Navy career if you survived. At this point I did not know if I would survive or not!

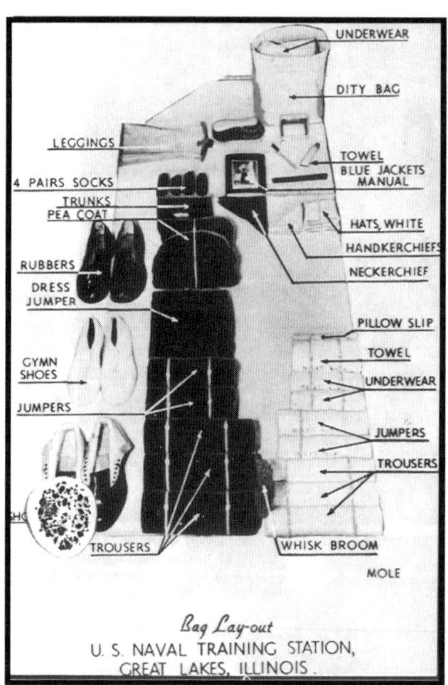

The bag lay-out was common throughout the Navy. Courtesy of U.S. Navy Armed Guard WW II Veterans.

The next day, we got our haircut, the same skinned head cut as those who were yelling to us when we arrived. Now it was our time to do the yelling to the new recruits. We were assigned to a platoon and a barrack. The barrack was built in the shape of an "H" and was two stories tall and a platoon was in each of the wings of the "H" with a hall through the middle. This area was used for the bathroom, showers, washer and dryer room. It was heated and it was nice to sleep in a warm bed and get up in the early morning to a warm room.

A platoon was about 100 sailors and we did everything together. We would drill all day together and marched everywhere we went. We would march to the chow hall, march to the movies and march to get shots. We drilled every day except Sunday. They would come around on Sunday morning and yell that all who wanted to go to church, to put on their dress blues and fall out in front of the barracks at a certain time to be marched to the services. I did not go, but they came back to make the rest of us put on our dress blues and stand at "Attention" until the others returned. So the next Sunday, I went to church. Sunday evenings, all of us would try to call home, and you had to wait in a long line to get a phone.

Every morning, before breakfast, we would have to run for about thirty minutes. We would have on nothing but our bathing suits and knickers. It was cold there in December but it did make our breakfast taste good. Most the time we had scrambled eggs or pancakes. Some mornings, we had baked beans and corn bread. The other meals were pretty good and I stayed hungry all the time.

About all we did was march, drill, get shots and more shots. We received shots many times and it made your arms so sore but you had to do push-ups and other exercises every morning, along with many other things. I shed a few tears at night in boot camp but I was not by myself. While in boot camp, we had to go to a pool and swim from one end then back. If you couldn't swim, they would tell you to jump in or they would push you in. If you were about to drown, they had a long pole that they would stick out for you to grab and you would have to go to swim classes at night to learn to swim fifty yards before you could graduate from boot camp. We were told this was necessary if our ship was sunk and had to get away from its suction. I swam the fifty yards the first time. They must have stopped requiring you to swim as I was with many afterwards who could not swim a lick.

We went to the firing range and fired our .30 caliber rifles we had drilled with all during "boots." Our drill chief was good, but a tough and mean old-timer. He never had a kind word and he never smiled. He just chewed you out for no reason. I guess this was to teach you take orders. There were a lot of CCC (Civilian Conservation Corps) boys in our unit and I guess they had been given the choice of service to join. I was still with my two schoolmates and this sure helped me a lot.

We had snow the last week we drilled. We moved to another barrack and we could go to the canteen at night as we could not before this time in our training. We would buy and sell candy bars to others who could not go, as everyone stayed hungry.

We graduated on January 6, 1942 after three weeks of boot camp. The "Boots" training usually was six to eight weeks, but they cut us short. Upon graduation, we were given the chance to go sign up for schooling in different trades, but I signed up for sea duty as did my two schoolmates. The scuttlebutt was that you had to work in mess halls if you wanted to get into schools. They went down the alphabet and they took sixteen men, including me, and they said, "You few lucky men are going to be in the Navy Armed Guard." Nobody knew what it was. The officer told us it was a "suicide squad."

There were a lot of platoons that graduated the same day we did and they got some extra men out of each platoon to put in the Armed Guard. They sent us to Little Creek, Virginia on Highway 60 which was out in the "boondocks" with just one building. One barrack was all they had ready. The cement floor was muddy from the construction going on and we just tracked the mud inside. We had been used to having clean, shiny, waxed floors. The bunks were cots lined up in a row and jammed together, with no room to walk between them. To get into your bed you had to crawl over one end to get to it. I shed a few tears here at night, too. I thought, What in the world have I gotten myself into.

We were put into a gun crew of eight men and given a crew number. I was in Gun Crew No. 106 along with some of the men

Taken in October 1941, these photos show the development of Little Creek, Virginia. Top, barracks foundation; center, completed barracks; bottom, barracks interior. Geo. J. Paquette.

I had trained with at NOB. We started going to classrooms learning to break down small weapons: pistols, rifles, machine guns and put them back together again. We had some "big guns" out in the back of the barrack that we practiced simulated loading and firing on with dummy shells. After about a week of training, we were taken out to the USS *Paducah*, a World War I gunship which had the big 3-inch 50 and 4-inch 50 guns, along with .50 caliber machine guns plus other small arms that each gun crew took their turn on and practiced firing into Chesapeake Bay. We stayed out for two days of training. At night, we strung our hammocks in a place like a porch on a deck. We had a roof overhead but no outside wall. They would drop a canvas down at night with no heating and it was in January. It was very cold and windy. You never got warm in bed and it was hard to sleep in a hammock. You had to sleep in one position — uncomfortable!!

The bathroom had a trough that water ran through all the time, so you did not have to flush it, as it would send the waste out the other end. Somebody was always wadding up toilet paper and lighting it and letting it float down under those who were seated and then standing back to watch them jump up.

We were sent back to Little Creek and stayed there only a few days. We were sent to Brooklyn, New York Armed Guard Center. We caught a cruise ship in Norfolk in the evening and made it to Baltimore, Maryland overnight, going up the Chesapeake Bay, bypassing Washington, D.C. on the way. We arrived in Baltimore around 7 AM and were taken to a cafeteria for breakfast. We were put on a train to New York and arrived around noon. We were put aboard trucks and carried to the Brooklyn Armed Guard Center at 1st Ave. and 52nd Street which had been a National Guard Armory. It was built as one big room. Everything was done in this room. You ate, slept, drilled and shipped out of here and very seldom went outside unless you had guard duty or had liberty. The liberty in New York is what we liked most of all.

The rear of the building was on the riverfront. The front faced to the street where people drove on, but it was blocked off in the front of the building and guard duty was set up to keep people off of it. We would march back and forth in the cold weather with a rifle on our shoulder and nearly freeze to death, as it was January. You could not stay out on guard but a few hours at a time. The local people would bring you coffee at night but I was afraid to drink it, thinking it might be poisoned, but I'm sure they felt sorry for us and wanted to do their part and help our morale.

We stayed in Brooklyn nearly a week going out on the "Big City" a few times. Our crew number came up to be shipped out. Our ship was in Galveston, Texas. We rode by Pullman on a train and we arrived in about six days in "Warm, Sunny Texas." There was snow on the ground almost all the way to the border. Everything was "free" and paid for by the Government. To a young man who had never been away from home, this was great! I did not know yet when I had gotten into!! ...[9]

~~~
~~~

Donald G. Kloenne, Radioman Third Class sent the following story, parts of which were previously printed in the "Letters to the Editor" section of the Summer 1991 issue of Naval History Magazine.

Training

On March 17, 1943, I was inducted into the United States Navy at Grand Central Palace on New York City's Lexington Avenue. After a week to get our affairs settled, we were herded on to dirty, decrepit cars of the "Creeping Crawler," sometimes known as the Lehigh Valley Railroad. Eventually the train pulled into an on-the-base siding at Sampson Naval Training Station on the shore of Seneca Lake in New York's Finger Lakes region. It was tough sleeping that first night in the barracks. I was a bit older than many of my fellow recruits and had done some traveling, but for many of them it was the first time they had ever been away from home and the barracks was the sight of a lot of sniffling and sobbing.

After we all got settled into the routine of basic training, some of the highlights that still linger in my memory are: the number of "brave" young men who were ready to die for their country but couldn't stand the site of a hypodermic needle. Every time we were inoculated for something or other, you could count on at least half a dozen swooning from the sheer terror. (I was O.K. as long as I kept my eyes focused elsewhere.) Another fear-inducing requirement was the Abandon Ship Drill, which meant donning a life jacket and then jumping from a high platform into the deep end of one of the base pools. I was a good swimmer and had no qualms about making the jump, but others simply 'froze' on the platform. I particularly remember one non-swimmer who was terrified of the water and refused to jump. Rather than being forcibly pushed into the water, he was simply told that the only way to get down from the platform was to make the required jump. He sat down and stayed. And stayed! Shortly before 'lights out' he straggled into the barracks having spent most of the day and missing two meals on that platform before finally finding the courage of desperation and taking the leap. Another of our trainees couldn't see the point of taking a shower each day. He didn't bathe daily at home and didn't feel the need to do it now. Fortunately "stinky" was at the other end of the barracks, so I wasn't personally affected, but a number of his nearby bunk mates were, and with the assent of the chief in charge of the barracks, ganged up on him, dragged him into the showers and scrubbed him down with a G.I. brush. He got the message.

As a break off the base, we were taken on a ten-mile hike, five miles out and five miles back. The first five miles there was a lot of enthusiasm; just to get out of the confines of Sampson was a welcome change. By the end of the second five miles it was a footsore, bedraggled bunch of sailors slogging their way "home" amidst a lot of grumbling about how, "If we wanted to be in the infantry, we'd have joined the Army."

It was during Basic Training that I got to fire a weapon for the first and only time during the War. We were taken to the firing range, given some instruction, and then allowed to fire five shots at a target. In all honesty, I can't say I was much of a marksman.

However, even some of the men who had had previous experience with rifles didn't do much better, so everybody decided that it just had to be that the rifles were worn and the sites were out of adjustment.

Basic eventually ended and it was time to move onto something else. Since I was a fairly proficient typist, I applied for either yeoman or storekeeper positions, but the Navy decided they had more need for my typing abilities as a radioman, so I stayed at Sampson to attend the base Radio School. As a new seaman second class (and later 3rd class petty officer) we were entitled to periodic liberty and could venture into the small town of Geneva, New York to mingle with the girls at the local USO or to eat an honest-to-goodness civilian meal in one of the restaurants.

After that "small town," it was off to the "big city." I was included in a draft of twenty-eight men being shipped to the Navy and Marine Corps Armory in Los Angeles for Armed Guard training. We had a Pullman car to ourselves, but there were only twenty-six berths, so each of the four nights en route we had to draw lots to see who had to double up, two to a berth. Happily, I was never "Unlucky Louie." In a typical government snafu, the railroad had been given incorrect directions and dumped us off at the Marine base, Port Hueneme, California, rather than Los Angeles. The Marines fed us, rounded up a bus, and sent us on our way to the proper destination.

The Armory was located at 15 Lilac Terrace (how's that for a war-like name?) in Chavez Ravine, not far from where Dodger Stadium now stands. The L.A. "Zoot Suit" war between service personnel and the 1943 equivalent of "Hippies" had just subsided and we were all required to pull occasional guard duty on the perimeter of the armory with .45 caliber automatics at our waist. At the armory, I was trained in Merchant vs. Navy radio procedures. Some of the symbols were different, and whereas Navy operators copied "Fox" schedules, Merchant operators copied "BAMS" (Broadcasts to Allied Merchant Ships). In the Central Pacific we copied Navy wireless stations NPG, San Francisco; NPM, Honolulu, and later in the war, NPO, Manila. In the South Pacific it was ZLD, Auckland, New Zealand, while in the Indian Ocean we copied a British station in Colombo, Ceylon (now Sri Lanka) whose call letters I can't remember. As an emergency backup for signalmen, I learned to read blinker light, semaphore and flag hoist. Blinker light was no problem, but let's just say it was a good thing that nobody had to depend on me to send a semaphore signal or to read a flag hoist.

One of the chief petty officers serving as an instructor was always telling us what "good duty" the Armed Guard was and how lucky we were. Then we would hear all the "loose lips sink ships" propaganda and on movie nights would see films like *Action in the North Atlantic* with torpedoed cargo ships sinking beneath the waves stern first and tankers totally enveloped in flames. The chief persisted in his "Good duty" claim after the film, but I'm afraid he was met by a raucous chorus of cheers. Cheers of the Bronx variety, that is. But, after six weeks, Armed Guard training came to its end, and I was off.... to prison!

The prison was on Terminal Island in Los Angeles harbor and was being used as a temporary barracks for sailors assigned to ships due shortly in a port. A few days later, mine came and I boarded the SS *John P. Altgeld*. The *Altgeld* proved to be a somewhat peculiar ship. At first glance it appeared to be a regular

Liberty ship, but it was, in fact, a tanker. Due to the tanker shortage in 1942-43, it had been fitted out with oil tanks where the cargo holds should have been.[10]

~~~

Harold E. Skinner forwarded this story which tells of his training period that would eventually lead him into the Armed Guard. The story occurred, "before I transferred into the Armed Guard and illustrates the tensions that develop when a group of young men with diverse backgrounds come together for a long time."

Survival in a Navy Service School

In late May of 1943 I completed boot camp training at Farragut Naval Training Station in Idaho and enjoyed a fifteen-day leave. Then I returned to the same base to begin communications training at Radio School. The Navy was in desperate need of trained personnel to man the ships of the expanding merchant and battle fleet. It was to be a twenty-week program of typing, Morse code, and fleet communications procedure.

Before joining the U.S. Navy I had completed a two-month course of railroad telegraphy during which I had also learned International Morse. Likewise, I had an excellent background in typewriting. Since the course was predicted on starting from zero in both code and typing, my progress was easily far in advance of most of the 120 member class.

It was in the Farragut Radio School that Milan LaMarche and I became good friends. Being from north Idaho, both of us tended to be on the defensive about our home region in the face of a barrage of derisive comments from men who claimed to hail from "more civilized" places. We stood together while being accused of having one leg shorter than the other because of running across the "hills of Idaho." Our bunkmates, of course, came from a cross-section of the many states, east, west, north and south, and most were assigned to Farragut against their wishes. From the parade ground in front of the barracks they could see nothing but distant woods and mountains, so their opinion of anyone native in the area was not too high. They even claimed
~~~

that Navy recruiters had to chase us down and put shoes on us before they could swear us into the Navy. We tended to shrug off most of this chiding as only good-natured heckling, but I would soon learn that I was the focus of pranks with a more sinister attitude.

Three unsavory bullies, one from the East Coast, one from San Francisco, and one from Seattle named Harris, decided to make life difficult for me, probably from jealousy about my excellent grades or possibly because I was dating a girlfriend and could visit my home town frequently. Their jibes gradually intensified, and I could hardly ignore their practical jokes.

One Sunday night when I returned from a weekend liberty to a darkened barracks, I discovered that my bunk was completely bare: no mattress or pillow, no sign that I had ever slept there. A friend who bunked nearby whispered that my seabag and personal belongings were in the corridor just around the corner at the entrance to the quarters. Sure enough! I found everything neatly packed in my duffel bag, as if I were about to ship out. Not a remark or giggle indicated awareness of my presence as I unloaded my seabag and made up my bunk.

A training class in marlinspike seamanship at Base Camp, Farragut, Idaho. Courtesy of U.S. Navy Armed Guard WW II Veterans.

Another weekend night when I came into the barracks late, I found a foamy mess of shaving cream and fragrant cologne smeared across my bunk and had to clean it up before I could go to bed. On another occasion one of the pranksters managed to steal the address of my girlfriend, most likely from a letter lying on my bunk, and wrote her a torrid love letter anonymously.

By that time I was reasonably sure who the culprits were but said nothing. I could somehow ignore this kind of harassment, but three obnoxious ones, domineering the younger and more vulnerable sailors, were becoming conspicuous to the point of developing a clique of like-minded overbearing and loud-mouthed individuals. Eventually their persistence in attacking me with insulting remarks could no longer be dismissed. One day, Harris' provocative comments in the barracks became downright insulting, and I angrily responded in kind. The result was that I challenged him on the spot. An instant excitement seized the barracks, and an electric tension filled the air. Suddenly all the harassment and practical jokes culminated in a choosing of sides. Men swarmed around me to promise their full support in the forthcoming grudge fight soon to be held in the drill hall. The opposing clan likewise formed around Harris's bunk. This was the usual accepted way to settle personal conflicts. I was to discover that I had friends among the younger, smaller sailors for whom the intimidation had become a way of life to be silently endured.

My friend Milan encouraged me because he knew I had no training in the art of boxing. He realized, too, that I fully expected to come out second best in the fight, since I was of average five-feet-nine-inch build and Harris was a long-armed six-footer. "Don't let him intimidate you," said Milan. "I was running alongside of him on the obstacle course, and he was slow and clumsy. Just get inside his reach and out punch him." Some of my buddies took me aside and put me through some punching exercises. They eavesdropped on the other "camp" and assured me that Harris had no fight training or experience. Signs appeared at the entrance of the barracks advertising the time and location of the great prizefight with caricatures of "Man-Mountain Harris." Men could even be seen arguing the fighting qualities to the two contestants, and some money bets were being placed.

The day of the big fight arrived. It would be in the afternoon after class time. A ring had been laid out and marked with ropes in the drill hall. We had a bell to signal rounds, and standard gloves were made available for our use. Thanks to my "seconds," some experienced boxers had already worked out with me and advised me on a few points of the sport.

In the first round we cautiously felt our way and probed for weak spots in each other's defense. I managed to land a few blows inside his arms while he managed a few grazing blows on my head. His counter-punching was effective enough that I had to cover up immediately after lunging close for a few punches. The fight dragged on, round after round, with no decisive blows landing. We were both shaken by a number of solid punches, but soon the greatest challenge was fatigue. Our brief workouts in no way prepared our arms and legs for the strenuous efforts and energy required for the endless minutes of dancing about the ring and swinging with all our might. After about the sixth or seventh round our amateur status showed up when we no longer came out slugging. After throwing an occasional punch our arms would simply refuse to respond. By the twelfth round we reached the point where we were simply standing, worn out, arms hanging loosely as we shuffled close and glared at each other, desperately hoping to find the extra ounce of strength to finish the other man. At one point I staggered Harris with an uppercut to the jaw but was too slow and tired to follow through and put him on the floor. By the thirteenth round we could muster only enough power to throw an occasional "roundhouse." It was then that I failed to dodge in time, and Harris managed to land a lucky blow, causing my nose to bleed. By then, of course, there was absolutely no fight left in either of us. There had been no knockdowns, and the bout was declared a draw as we were led from the ring.

After a shower and a quick massage by my friends, I returned to the barracks. That evening I learned how popular I had become among a number of men who had who had not known me personally before the fight. They filed past my bunk and thanked me for having fought in what they considered their cause against the bully. I learned a vital lesson that day which I never forgot. There are times when it is necessary to stand up for a cause, even when the risk is great. From that day forward no more taunts or insults were heard in the barracks, and for the first time a spirit of mutual respect prevailed among the men. The fight had indeed been worthwhile.

Radio school ended in November 1943, and I soon went to advanced training at "ComPool" (Communications Pacific Pool) for service on merchant ships in the U.S. Naval Armed Guard.[11]

~~~

Armed Guard Song

Armed Guard stand together
Don't give up the ship.
Submarines may stalk us
We won't give up, we won't give up our ship.
Friends and pals forever,
It's a long hard trip.
If we have to take a licking
Carry on and quit your bitching
Don't give up the ship.

Armed Guard of the Navy
On our Liberty ships.
Every darn invasion
Just another trip.
Shipmates on the ocean,
Comrades on the shore,
We are friends forever
Till we are no more.

Chorus

Friends and pals forever.
It's a long, long trip,
If you have to take a licking
Carry on and quit your bitching
Don't give up the ship.[12]
~~~

3

Not Without Problems

The newly graduated Armed Guard faced a series of problems before even boarding a merchant ship. The attitude of other members of his own branch of the service was enough to make him question the wisdom of his choice of duty. Lt. (j.g.) Robert C. Ruark: "... candidates for gunnery jobs aboard merchant ships were regarded and spoken of pityingly by their Navy comrades as 'fish food.' When a man was assigned to the Armed Guard, his roommates rolled their eyes in burlesqued horror, made strangling noises and drew their fingers slit wise across their throats."[1]

The foremost problem, at least in the beginning of the war, was the attitude merchant crews and officers had toward these young inexperienced Navy men. For the most part, they had never spent any time at sea. This created an attitude of contempt on the part of the merchant seamen.

Many of the older men had suffered through the terrible working conditions, low wages and outdated ships that made up our merchant fleet during the 1930s. As Felix Riesenberg explained:

> If you don't mind sleeping in a narrow bunk on a dirty mattress crawling with bedbugs and have no objection to crowding into a dark hole deep in the after peak of a ship, over the screw, where the fumes from showers and toilets permeate the air; and if lack of ventilation or light has no terror for you and you like to have your meals in a smelly messroom just off a hot galley, sitting at a narrow bench covered with a soiled oilcloth and facing a blank wall not too clean, with a slovenly mess boy shoving a plate of greasy stew over your shoulder – if these things please you and you are thankful for them and obedient, you are 100 per cent American seaman, a credit to your flag and to the United States.
>
> On the other hand, if you kick about such things, if you take part in "inciting to riot," join sit down strikes, and in that way interfere with the earnings of a rundown cargo steamer, you are a Communist. Living conditions, in brief, are the cause of much of the discontent and rioting we have had in the last two years along our waterfronts and on board ships of the United States merchant marine.[2]

It was only after the unions consolidated and began policing of their own members that conditions improved.

> Until the advent of the National Maritime Union conditions on American ships were appalling. The union has shortened hours, raised wages, and made considerable improvements in living conditions. Considerable improvements mean nothing more than war on vermin, clean sheets, extra sinks, and fairly nourishing food. The average fo'c'sle is crowded, unlit and unventilated, and very little can be done for the crew on most American ships until the old tubs are replaced by modern craft.[3]

Having lived through such conditions, experienced mariners naturally resented the young naval personnel coming aboard their ships.

In the bare beginning, the ensign or lieutenant who put to sea with the merchant marine could be reasonably sure of many unpleasant things. He could count pretty well on a hostile attitude from the merchant seaman, who resented the Navy's presence as a curb on their personal freedom, and who generally believed that the Armed Guard crews were but the first step in a Navy plot to take over the merchant service.[4]

From the perspective of the Armed Guard joining his first ship it was a bewildering situation, not at all like what he had been led to expect when he joined the Navy:

It is not surprising that the Armed Guard quickly became known as least-desired duty in the Navy. The Armed Guardsman was physically separated from his fellow Navy men; placed in a small group aboard a ship run by civilians. This single great dividing line automatically excluded him from the glamour, glory, and common experience of those who serve aboard a warship. It isolated him, took away from him the warm feeling of "belonging." It separated him, too, from the creature comforts which are an integral part of the Navy ships — services of doctor, paymaster, mail clerk, ship's store, recreational facilities, movies — and the fixed routine of a Navy vessel, which, in spite of their "gripes" it inspires, makes a sailor feel secure.

Most of all it took away from him, before he had ever known it, the feeling of pride in a ship which irrevocably binds many a man to Navy life. Looking at his carrier, cruiser, destroyer, or even his PC, the Navy man almost bursts with pride in exclaiming, "That's *my* ship!" He feels as if a part of him has been woven into the very metal fiber of her. He possesses and is possessed by her. What seagoing merchantman, even her master, would feel such fierce exultation over a rusty, streaked, disorderly freighter?[5]

The command structure aboard the merchant ships was another problem area. There were two sets of command: merchant and Navy. Typically, an inexperienced Navy Armed Guard officer, no older than a college student, was placed in charge of shipboard security and was in command during any combat situation. While at sea he shouldered a tremendous command responsibility with no superior officer to guide him:

> The Armed Guard commander must be at one in the same time a gunnery, communications, intelligence, supply, personnel, and (with a layman's apologies) medical officer, and chaplain. In addition to the broader departmental and corps responsibilities he must function as educational officer, first lieutenant, sensor, security officer, division officer, liaison officer, and chief specialist in charge of physical fitness. Here is a liberal education in naval duties for the young reserve officer.[6]

He was also responsible for overseeing the safety and security of the ship and cargo while in port.

> Most important perhaps of all the Armed Guard commander's duties is the field of minor diplomacy both aboard ship and on foreign shore. As liaison officer between the Navy and the ship's master and Merchant Marine, the young officer can perform valuable or discrediting service. It is a delicate mission which has been done both well and badly but fortunately more often well.[7]

Part of the difficulty was due to the fact that the captain of the ship could be overruled by the Armed Guard commander. Consequently, Armed Guard officers constantly walked a delicate tightrope concerning ship operations. The Armed Guard's charges also faced the daunting task of operating around the command of other ships' officers and crew.

The cause of the greatest friction between merchant and Navy crews was the supposed pay inequity between the two services. The people responsible for perpetuating this myth were the media. Two influential radio announcers heard by most Americans, Walter Winchell and Drew Pearson, were particularly negative about the American Merchant Marine. The columnist Westbrook Pegler caused the National Maritime Union to picket the World

Telegram building because of a negative article he wrote about mariners earning more money than the Armed Guard.

A study titled, "The Answer to the Supposed Inequity in Pay Between Merchant Seaman and Members of the Armed Forces in World War II" was conducted by the WSA (War Shipping Administration). Based upon this study a letter was written by Telfair Knight, Assistant Deputy Administrator for Training to Arren H. Atherton, National Commander, the American Legion, National Headquarters. The letter documented the pay differences between the two groups, proving that, overall, Navy men were better paid. Deputy Knight ended his letter by stating, "Your cooperation in dispelling the misconception in regard to merchant seaman's pay will be greatly appreciated." However, the letter and the American Legion did little to eradicate the misconception. The following table appears in the American Merchant Marine at War website and is based on a small part of the study:

Annual Income after Taxes (1943)

	Navy	Mariner
Seaman first class vs. Ordinary seaman	$1,886	$1,897
Petty Officer second class vs. Able seaman	$2,308	$2,132

Benefits

	Navy	Mariner
Permanent disability, merchant seaman, value		$6,290
Partial disability, Navy personnel, cash value	$11,000	
Death benefit,	$468	$5,000
Cash value, widow's pension	$15,350	0
	$26,818	$11,290[8]

Further important points in the study revealed that:

- Navy personnel were exempt from income taxes. Merchant mariners paid income taxes and "Victory" taxes.
- No allowances were granted for dependents of mariners.
- Navy personnel were paid twelve months per year with thirty days paid leave. They were also paid during periods of transfer and stand-by. The merchant seaman was paid only for such time as he served

aboard ship (average ten months). That stopped when he signed off or his ship was sunk.

- If a mariner was killed his dependents received a fixed sum of $5,000. The Navy man's dependents collected his base pay for six months and his dependants would be eligible for pensions for the rest of their lives on a varying scale. The wife would draw this pension for life or until remarried. Children drew the pension until their eighteenth birthday.
- Navy seamen could purchase additional national service life insurance that carried over after leaving the service. The mariner's insurance was much more expensive and was only applicable when he was aboard ship.
- Navy dependents received free medical attention and were charged nominal hospital expenses.
- Merchant seaman paid for their own clothing. Navy men received their initial clothing free ($133.00) and, after a year, received a quarterly clothing allowance.
- Career Navy men received pensions; seamen didn't have a pension plan.
- Miscellaneous benefits to Navy personnel included free postage, reduced furlough rates for travel, reductions on theater tickets and on meals while traveling and eligibility for the G.I. Bill. [9]

Consequently, there were many personnel problems involved in manning armed merchant ships. However, it did not take long for both sides to realize that victory and the safety of all aboard the ship depended on how well they worked together. This mutual cooperation improved as younger and better-trained merchant marine officers and crew came aboard the growing numbers of ships being built.

The following unedited letter from a Naval Armed Guard Crew appeared in the Tales of Hoffman: Hoffman Island Radio Association *newsletter. It appeared in a column entitled, "Relationships With the U.S. Navy Armed Guard."*

(Newsletter Editor: The letter is preserved here in its original form, complete with errors in typing, spelling and grammar. They show that it is a sincere expression of friendship and appreciation, not a "political" thank-you note. Ed.)[10] Courtesy of James V. Shannon, Editor.

Newsletter Editor: Many of us from time to time had enlisted men and officers of the Navy look down upon we Mariners for one reason or another. But the crew of the S.S. *Ralph Izard* was held in high esteem by her Navy Gun Crew.

Date: August 24, 1943
Subject: A Farewell Letter
To: Officers and Members of S.S. *Ralph Izard*
From: Gun Crew 651

For close to eleven months now, Gun Crew 651 has been stationed aboard the SS *Ralph Izard*, and for the most of us its been our first trip. In those long tiresome months we have joys, hardships, troubles of all kinds and seen action with the "Sailors in Dungarees". During our travels to many ports and foreign countries, its been not only quite interesting, but part of history as well.

Every bit of courtesy, kindness and respect has been shown us by these seadogs of fortune. They've cooperated with us at all times, taught us new ideas, new slangs, and there ways of life. In the estimation of the Gun Crew the Merchant Crew of the S.S. *Ralph Izard* are second to none in the world. We in the Gun Crew know we'll never sail with as great a bunch of guys, so we say hats off the Merchant Crew of the "Rudolph baby," every member including from the Captain right on down the line.

At the Battle of Sicily when things looked the blackest for all of us, when life was cheap as dirt, if it hadn't been for the Merchant Crew being with us one hundred percent, bringing our meals to the guns, passing and loading ammunition and in general keeping up our moral by their easy going ways, cracking jokes and etc. when the chips were down, we know we never would have got through those four endless nights and three terrorizing days alive.

Most likely we'll never see each other again, but that is beside the point. We know we have no way of repaying you, the Merchant Crew, for your fine ideals and manliness, so we're writing you this letter, just to show our gratitude. We want the Merchant Crew to feel that this one Gun Crew, that would go to

The Ralph Izard *fitting out at the Bethlehem-Fairfield shipyard before delivery.* Project Liberty Ship.

Heaven or Hell with them, if necessary. Also, we want to thank the Merchant Crew for the fine things they all said of our Lieutenant.

Sincerely yours,
Gun Crew 651

The S.S. Ralph Izard *survived the war and was scrapped in Panama City in April 1965.*[11]

~~~

It wasn't always easy even within your own gun crew. This letter submitted by Wendell Hoffman concerned his superior officer, Channing Reeves. It was written by Wendell at the request of Alice (Reeves) Botts in February 1994. Channing, Alice's father, was dying of cancer and she wanted to know about his Navy career. Channing Reeves passed away the day his daughter received this letter.

A Tribute to a Shipmate, Channing Reeves

February 20, 1994
Dear Alice:

In the spring of 1945, I had just gotten off a ship called the SS *Coastwise*. This old coal ship hauled coal from Newport
~~~

News or Portsmouth, Virginia to New Bedford, Boston, Chelsea or Lynn, Mass. Some were sunk by U-boats mistakenly taken for tankers.

A shipmate from Decatur, Illinois, Robert Keller, who I had gone through boot camp and sailed on two previous ships with, was with me, and we made up the Navy gun crew along with a Coxswain 3rd class and a signalman.

This old tub developed a leak and went into dry-dock in Portsmouth, Va. Keller wanted to see some friends from his hometown, stationed about 40 miles away. I agreed to stand his watch while he was gone. The leak was repaired 24 hours ahead of time and I had to go ashore to call Keller. I had stood my watch, Keller's watch and most of the coxswain's watch. He was in charge of us, but had a bad habit of goofing off when we in port and expecting Keller or I to remain on duty until he decided to return.

After standing over half the coxswain's duty, I went ashore and called Keller to come back. We were to sail within 24 hours. While gone, the Coast Guard checked and found no one on duty. While they were there, here came the coxswain. His name was on the duty roster but no one is supposed to leave his post until relieved. We were all in the hot seat!

Keller and I were taken off the ship and placed in the Armed Guard Receiving Station in Norfolk, Va.

We were assigned bunks inside a Quonset hut that was the office of the Armed Guard Center. We were assigned every menial task by the chief gunner's mate that he could think of, cleaning and painting the quarters, inside and out, a little landscaping etc. We considered this a breeze compared to what we had been through on our previous two ships. After approximately four or six weeks of this, the chief gunner's mate called Keller and me in and asked if we would like to sail with him. He explained to us that it had been his responsibility to determine if we should be sent to Brooklyn for disciplinary action or not. He explained that he and his assistant were due to go back to sea, along with a lieutenant from another office. They were looking for a handpicked crew, and a ship that was going to Europe. He also asked us to help him, because we were in direct contact with sailors at work and on liberty. We felt very proud of his confidence in us.

In the next week or so, the crew was put together and Channing Reeves was one of them. I had not met him before, but someone had picked him and a shipmate of his called Smitty, for part of this crew.

Upon taking our physicals prior to shipping out, the chief gunner's mate (a man in his thirties) was found to have a malignant lung tumor. He was hurriedly replaced by a coxswain. He proved to be very difficult to work with. He would do almost anything to advance his status with our lieutenant and had no consideration for the rest of the gun crew. He was however, a brave, hard-working sailor. Channing, as gunner's mate third class, was next in command. He was in charge of the big 5-inch, 38 gun on the stern and the 20mm machine guns close by. Keller and I were each on one of these guns. At times there was a conflict between Channing and the coxswain. Channing would ask his men to perform the duties assigned, and the coxswain would order his men. There was not a man on that ship that would not have gladly done anything Channing asked because it was always reasonable and necessary. And he was always there with us. The coxswain, however, would order his men to perform duties that were necessary but also things that would make him look good to the lieutenant and the inspectors. When this happened, I've seen Channing stand up for the crew and offer to slug it out with him, even though Channing stood 5-foot-ten or -eleven and weighed about 155 pounds and the Coxswain stood about 5-foot-eight and weighed about 190 pounds of solid muscle. The coxswain would start cussing, but would walk off talking to himself. He simply could not understand our loyalty to Channing!

One time, the lieutenant assigned Channing extra duty, chipping a gun for some minor infraction (probably reported or invented by the coxswain). This consisted of taking a chisel type hammer and beating on the deck until the rust was loosened down to the bare metal. It would probably have taken Channing at least forty hours of his free time to perform this task. The next morning after chow, every man not on watch, never said a word but went to work with a chipping hammer with a zeal that was unbelievable! Hearing the racket of about fifteen hammers on that deck, our lieutenant came back to investigate. He just looked, shook his head, grinned when he thought nobody saw him and went back to his quarters. Before sundown, that deck was not only clean, it was repainted, which Channing had not been required to do. We would have had to do it soon anyway, but we wanted to make a point and we did! Due to our watch duty, some of us worked around the clock to do the job.

The war at this time had just ended in Europe and we were scheduled to go through the Suez Canal. Since we were loaded with thousands of gallons of alcohol for hospital use, and just one torpedo would have blown us out of the water, our course was changed. It took us twenty-eight days to get to the Panama Canal, an easy safe trip. We went through the Canal and headed for Batangas Bay, which is about 50 miles from Manila.

We were now in a war zone without convoy. Two antiaircraft guns; 5-inch on the stern and 3-inch on the bow, with four 20mm machine guns each were on the port and starboard sides. Our duty was now four hours on, four hours off, with G.Q morning and evening, with all hands at battle stations for an hour. It was total blackout after sundown. We had all been through this before and had the confidence in each other's skill, yet there was still a great deal of stress involved.

Channing's quick wit and personality often times broke the tension. One time during a small surprise attack, I was left with an empty magazine. Quick as a flash, that long lanky redheaded daddy of yours jumped two tubs and came to my rescue! Another time, we took a coffee break from cleaning our guns; Channing went to the galley to ask the baker for some mincemeat pies, which smelled so good. The baker explained that all the Merchant Marine officers liked mincemeat pie so well they were sure to ask for seconds. There was just enough to allow for this. Channing thought his crew was just as good as any Merchant Marine officer. Our chow hall was right next to the ship's galley. Channing told us to line up outside the porthole and wait. As soon as the baker left (he went to the head, I think) all the mincemeat pies disappeared! We went to the after gun tub and ate one or two of the pies apiece! The baker was looking all over the ship, but by the time he found us we were all working on the big gun as if nothing had happened. We had seen him coming; the pies were gone but we had all those pie pans. Over the side they went!

At noon, Channing with that big grin on his face said, "Men eat as though you were really hungry." The baker went back and forth from the navy chow hall to the ship's crew mess hall to look for the culprits. We had fruit cocktail for dessert and we gobbled that up too! After that, we went back to the stern and threw up over the side. After fifty years, every time I smell mincemeat pie or see fruit cocktail, I think of this incident.

We encountered a storm on this trip and lost some life rafts. The waves were so large, they tossed us around like a feather on a pond. We had to sleep on our backs and put something between our shoulder and the rail to keep from rolling out. This was part of the typhoon that did so much damage in July 1945. Some days we only made 75 miles in twenty-four hours. We ran short of rations, and lived for a while mostly on boiled potatoes, cooked with grease and spices. Channing again came to our rescue. He persuaded the Army Security Officer to let him go into the holds and get some Army K-Rations, Spam and stuff like that for the gun crew. He had to be very discreet and we ate in our Navy quarters, because he was only allowed a certain percent shrink. The Army Major even came back and snacked with us at times! It sure beat those little boiled potatoes.

Shortly before the Japs surrendered, Tokyo Rose came on the radio naming our ship and accusing us of trying to outwit the Japs by not going through the Suez Canal. They were looking for us again and knew what we were loaded with. We were very glad when the atomic bombs were dropped. We were only a few days from Batangas Bay when we got word of the surrender. We fired all our guns like the Fourth of July!

We arrived at Batangas Bay after almost seventy days at sea. Upon arriving in the harbor, we dropped the anchor in the bay for further instructions. The coxswain immediately went to the stern and sold sheets, cigarettes, gum etc. that he had hoarded. We were allowed to purchase a certain amount of stuff from ships' stores every week. We were allowed two clean sheets every week and we would often times only use one and wad the other one up to look like two. A sheet would bring $20 in many foreign ports and the same for cigarettes. Often, we could not draw any pay and this was the way we got our liberty money.

About an hour after the anchor had dropped, a lot of natives were gathered around the stern and most of us were selling our wares. The coxswain then went to our lieutenant reporting us. Nevertheless, the only thing he could do was check out the report. We were all restricted to the ship for three days and you can imagine how we felt with the liberty launch loaded with the merchant marine only.

That night I was on ship's watch as our responsibility was to provide security for the ship at sea or in port. About 1 o'clock in the morning, I was on the after gun deck, where I had a pretty good view. I heard a noise below and it was our lieutenant and the ship's steward selling cigarettes and stuff. When they finished their transaction, I coughed a couple of times. Nothing was said but the next morning our restriction was lifted.

We were all mad at the coxswain, even though we did get off the hook. Going on liberty relieved this tension somewhat. Some of the guys thought we had put up with enough and were talking about ways to put him away. Channing had more reasons than any of us, but he talked us out of it, and came up with a better idea. On the way back home, nobody was to carry on a conversation with him. If he gave an order and it was in the line of duty, we did it. If it was not, we pretended not to hear him. If he came up to a group of guys and tried to participate in a conversation, we would all walk away and leave him standing by himself.

We all sat at the same place in our chow hall and if we were on detail, Channing always let one of us go early enough to sit in the coxswain's place. One time he ordered one of our more timid sailors to move. The kid didn't budge, but turned white and started trembling. The coxswain started cussing and threatened the kid. When that happened, Channing never said a word but stood up. When he did, we all stood up never saying a word, just looking at the coxswain, some picking up a Coke bottle. There were many empty seats but he was a stubborn cuss. He left and never tried that anymore. He ate cold cuts out of the fridge for three weeks and then broke down and apologized. Had it not been for Chan, a crime may have been committed and we could all have gotten into serious trouble.

We arrived back in Mobile, Alabama, in December of 1945. After going on liberty in Mobile, we received our thirty-day leaves.

Many other things happened on this trip, some funny and some not. Channing is the best friend I have ever had aside from Arlene (my wife) and he has been closer than a brother. When he passes on I'm sure there will be a special place in heaven for him. He made everyone feel like we were special when he was the one who was special. You have been truly blessed by having him for your Dad[12]

The SS John N. Robins *was scrapped in Osaka in 1964.*[13]

Left photo, Channing Reeves on left, Wendell Hoffman on right; right photo, Smitty on left, Channing Reeves on right. Taken on board. Wendell Hoffman.

4

First Voyage

There are major events in one's life that become etched in memory never to be forgotten. Such was the experience for the Navy Armed Guard who went to sea for the first time. One can just imagine the anxiety, excitement and even terror that accompanied these young men as they sailed on their first voyage. Danger and death lurked below the sea and in the air. Bravery was a commodity hard earned. "It has been said that 'If it were not for the U.S. Navy Armed Guard crews and other Armed Guard personnel, the ships and men of the Maritime would have been lost and so would the war.'"[1]

Edward Woods, a merchant seaman on his first voyage aboard a tanker at sixteen years of age wrote,

> At first, the Navy Armed Guard gunners were told not to fraternize with the merchant seaman. It was expected that we keep away from the gunners' sleeping quarters and they stay away from ours.

> We each had our own mess hall for eating and recreation. It took only a few days out to sea, however, before most of us became good friends and shipmates. We still respected each other's privacy, but we played checkers, chess and cards with each other. It was a gunner who taught me to play chess.[2]

~~~

James Gailey caught his first ship in Galveston, Texas beginning his worldly education as an Armed Guard.

My First Voyage

Our ship was in dry dock being worked on and wasn't prepared for us so we were put in the Panama Hotel to wait until we could go on board, again all-expenses-paid. We stayed here about two weeks with nothing to do but eat, sleep and go to the movies. We were enjoying this but we tried to get them to let us go home till it was ready, as we hadn't been home since we had joined. They did not let us and nobody had enough money anyway, as we were only paid $21 a month and drew only fourteen bucks after insurance was taken out.

After waiting about two weeks, we went aboard on February 10, 1942, a "rust pot" used in World War I owned by the Grace Steamship Company by the name of SS *Chipana*, but our quarters were clean with toilet and shower. They had just added them on. Our gunnery officer, Beattie, was an Ensign first-class, and was a pretty good person. We called him "Saddie" when he was not around. The crew all slept in one day room but officer "Saddie" had a room of his own.

The next day we sailed over to Houston where we loaded the ship with wheat and drums of oil and then we set sail to New Orleans, Louisiana that evening. We had been warned there were subs so we were worried about them all the way. We stayed there for about two weeks to finish loading our cargo to be shipped to the west coast of South America. The *Chipana* had a regular run down there. You did not have to be in the North Atlantic or South Pacific oceans to be in danger of being hit by a torpedo.
~~~

Shown at a San Francisco pier in 1935 is the Chipana, *which operated for Grace Line until 1946.* National Maritime Museum, San Francisco (Proctor Collection).

After the ship was loaded we headed out to sea alone. The water got rough and I got seasick stayed that way for two or three days and I could not do anything but stay in the sack. We received radio reports that ships were being sunk all around us. We were now in the Caribbean Sea. S.O.S. signals were coming in regularly. If the reports came in clear, we would steer away from them and it was not a day or night we didn't get reports. We did not dare to sleep in our bunks, or take off our clothes, as now you wanted to be out in the open, in case the ship was torpedoed as we were told it would take only three minutes to sink. We were not taking any chances of going down with her if hit.

The weather was warm and we had our cots on deck and slept with our clothes and our lifejackets on. We would have rain showers and you would just cover up your head and try to sleep. We held our watches, four hours on and four off. It did not take long to dry out after a cool shower and it felt good. If you had to eat a meal after watch hours, you lost that sack time. You had your laundry to do and cleaning the guns in the four hours off time so you never got four hours sleep at one time. I do not know how we made it to Panama but after about eight days, we pulled into Colon, a town on the east coast of Panama. We stayed a day and night before going through the Canal. The Canal was one way only and westward traveled one day and eastward the next. It took us all day to go through the different locks, lakes and Canal before getting to the area where you had go through more locks. The trip was pretty as it took you through the scenic lakes, jungle and mountains.

We pulled into Balboa, on the west side of the Canal and stayed just a few days. We went on liberty to town, a very pretty place but most of the people were black and spoke Spanish, which we could not understand. We rode a bus to town and they sat anywhere they pleased and I was not used to that, coming from the south in North Carolina. We were amazed as they drove vehicles on the left side of the road. The streets were very narrow and crowded. We took on fresh cargo in Balboa and the Panamanians did the dirty work on the ship, such as chipping and painting. They looked like the Aztec Indians that I read about.

Our merchant crew were older men and mostly "drunken sots" on this, my first ship. They were a better bunch on the other ships as younger guys were coming in. The food was good as we could go into the mess hall and order what you wanted from the menu. We would drag fishing lines from the fantail and catch some large fish. The cooks would clean the fish and hang them outside and "dry" cure them. They were really good. As we pulled into the Pacific Ocean side, we had Jap submarines to look out for, but they were not as plentiful and accurate as the Germans.

Our next stop was Buenaventura, Colombia. It took us a few days and we stayed one day so we did not get to go ashore. It was real pretty though and looked like the jungle we had read about. We would have these little rain showers every time a cloud would pass over but it didn't bother us much as it would dry out in a few minutes. It happened all the time we were in that country.

Our next stop was Guayaquil, Ecuador. It was about ninety miles up a river. They did not have a dock there so cargo had to be unloaded in the middle of the river into small, open boats that would take it to shore. We anchored in the middle of this river, which ran both ways. In the mornings, it would run one way, in the evenings, the other. The river was full of water lilies all the time and looked solid in low tide. The natives would take a big raft up the river in the morning and return late that evening with the flow of the tide using long bamboo sticks to guide them. These boats would be loaded with bananas. We caught a "Boat Taxi" to town. They had an earthquake not long before we were there. It still showed lots of damage. This is where the Panama hats are made. It is a poor looking country and vendors were selling fresh fruit, vegetables, hats and trinkets on the streets. We were scared to drink water or anything as it didn't look too clean. Most of the travel on shore at that time was by horse and buggy as there were few cars because of the dirt streets.

Our next stop was Tahar, Peru. It took a few days to get there and we had not heard of any subs being in the area. I think the Japs stayed around the west side of the canal with the few subs they had. The land around Tahar was barren, sandy mountains and this little town was on the side of the mountains, with lots of oil tanks. That is what we had in our oil drums for cargo. I did not get off here as the people did not look too friendly. They were in favor of the German way of thinking and anti-American.

Our next stop was Callao, Peru which took us four or five days to get to. Land was still barren mountains. This town was near Lima so we caught a bus there. It was a larger town and rather nice. Only four of our crew could leave the ship at a time. We took our turns. Four of us always went out together and one of our guys could speak Spanish, so we did pretty well getting around. The children followed us around town calling us "Americano" and begged us all the time. Our shipmate, who spoke Spanish always headed to a beer joint. I did not drink, but I was afraid to go by myself. I would drink some kind of cola. He would tell everyone I was his boy as he was around thirty-five years old. He drove the Greyhound bus out of Wilmington, North Carolina before he joined the service. The other two guys were from Florida and were in their twenties. The merchant crew unloaded rice and wheat here.

Our next stopover was in Arica, Chile and it took us about five days to get there. It was a smaller town with a nice park which we sat in. The kids in town wore uniforms to school. The town had dirt streets except on Main Street. The town was at the foot of a barren mountain just like the others we had visited recently. You could walk from one end of the town city limits to the other in a few minutes and outside of town was a desert. We tried to walk up the side of the mountain and you would become mired in the sand, like snow. There was snow on top of the mountains as they were high but really beautiful. We made a few more ports and came back to Arica to load ore as our cargo had come from Bolivia. There were three-masted ships sailing up and down the coast of South America. They were not pleasure boats. They hauled freight like we did in the holds.

We didn't have to worry much about subs in this area. We were always sailing alone on these trips. American sailors were in the towns and people treated us like "celebrities" in every town we visited. We visited Antofagasta, Chile for a few days and the town was just like the others. My buddies and I hired a horse and buggy taxi to find some girls but I didn't get one. Honest!! They picked up the girls and they took us to a beach club. We were sitting out on the beach at tables. They were ordering drinks, for everyone. Yes, even our taxi driver was still with us. They drank several more and decided to order lunch. All this time, I was sipping on my cola of some kind and decided to order some kind of sandwich. The girls were calling me "Chickatina." I didn't know what that meant but the guys started calling me "Chicken" from then on.

We decided to take the girls home and got ready to pay up the bill, as we had not paid anything to that point. And guess what? We could not come up with enough money to pay the bill so they called the police. The police sent the girls home and locked all of us up. It wasn't a very nice jail and we sent for the American Consulate. He got word to our Lt. (j.g.) on the ship and he came and bailed us out. We never got reprimanded for this but we had to pay him back. He was a good officer. We stayed there for a few more days. I did not go ashore with the boys here again.

They went back and looked the girls up again but I was broke and wanted to stay out of trouble.

We left there for one more stop in Valparaiso, Chile. It took about four days to get there. The landscape had changed now with trees on the mountains and it was a larger and nicer town. I was broke and scared from the last town and did not go ashore and guess what? They got into trouble here, also! They had picked up some women and went home with them. While they were inside the house, one of the women's husbands came home. The guys had to jump out the back window and run. He did not catch our boys but they didn't go back ashore as the husband was a policeman.

The ship's holds were emptied and we sailed back to Arica. I think we loaded up with tin ore. It took several days to load the ship as stevedores worked only in the daytime. I went ashore with a merchant seaman. He was one of the nicer ones and when the others headed for the beer halls, we took in the sights as this was a place I had never seen.

When they finished loading our cargo, the ship was low in the water so that the least little wave would come over our rails. We had to tie a line from one place to the other to hold on to when we had to go from one part of the ship to the other so a wave would not wash us overboard. I got wet many times trying to get to the "crow's nest" as we had to stand lookout watches up there too. We also stood watches on the bridge and we had two men on the stern at all times at sea. We were connected up by phone circuits and could talk to each other to stay awake. If the other person got quiet — you knew he was asleep. We left Arica and returned to Guayaquil, Ecuador where we loaded the deck with lumber. Just in case we got sunk, we had something to hold on to, for they were 4x4s, but were light as a feather. They were made out of balsam wood like you use to make model airplanes out of and life preservers. We stayed there a few days loading and sailed for Panama. I sure was glad to have the wood on the deck, as we would sink like a rock if we got hit by a torpedo. We still had the Japanese on the west side of Panama Canal with the Germans on the east to worry about. We stopped off again at

Balboa, taking on more supplies and waiting for our time in traffic through the Canal. All of the Indians we had picked up on the way down had to get off the ship at Balboa.

We went through the Canal and as we came out into the Caribbean, the Germans were sinking ships left and right now, and we had to travel alone, again. We didn't run in a convoy the first six months of the war. There was not a night or day that reports did not come in of ships being attacked and sunk. We would zigzag and hold our watches, four on and four off. The sea was rough and we were scared as our ship was low in the water. I never thought we would make it because the subs were so bad. I said my prayers every night and I am sure everyone else did. When you lay down at night, you wondered if you would wake up again. You couldn't see the submarines and you didn't know if they were around until after you were hit. They seldom came up to fight unless you were hit by a torpedo. We slept on the decks again with our clothes and lifejackets on and kept them with us during the day as we returned to the States.

On our way back to the States we came from Panama up through the islands and anchored out in shallow water every night. We ran only during the daytime following the coastline all the way to Texas City, Texas because of all the ships that were being sunk. We saw several ships sunk along the coastline. One night we thought we saw a sub on the surface and we fired two shots at it but missed and it didn't shoot back. The captain of the ship ordered us to cease firing to keep from giving away our position. You never knew if it was a friend or foe as a ship would pass you by in total blackout, total radio silence and you just hoped they didn't shoot. You had to walk around in the dark at all times. We made it to Tampa, Florida where we stopped for some reason or another. We stayed there for a day or two and I went home with another gunner who lived in Tampa. I called home about midnight and told them to write me in Texas City, Texas as this was where we going next. This was in May I think, and this was the first time they had heard from me in three months, and it was the first time I had called them since I had joined the service.

We still had not seen any Navy escorts and wondered where they could be. We later found out, all were tied up in the New

The .30 caliber World War I vintage machine gun, similar to that found on the Steel Engineer. Albert Lowe.

York area, protecting the eastern seaboard and the convoys to Europe. We made it to Texas City, Texas in three days without any trouble but I do not know how. The submarine terror was so bad that I had no idea of making it through the war. You just wondered when you'd get it. The ship was unloaded in about four days and we set sail to Houston to start reloading for the same trip previously taken. It was great to be back in the States again.[3]

~~~

Albert Lowe contributed several stories to this anthology. This story is of his first voyage aboard a lucky ship, the Steel Engineer.*

My Voyage on the SS *Steel Engineer*
September 24, 1942 – August 9, 1943

After gun school training at Little Creek, Virginia Navy Base, I reported to the U.S. Navy Armed Guard Center in Brooklyn and was assigned my first ship. The SS *Steel Engineer* was a Hog Islander launched in 1920. She was a coal running ship changed over to a steam turbine engine using oil. Her armament

* On June 28, 1942 the ship had been severely damaged by a torpedo. "… enroute New York/Capetown when one of *U-128*'s torpedoes hit amidships. Badly damaged, but still able to run, the freighter turned for Trinidad. June is a month of many rain squalls in the Caribbean and the captain of the *Steel Engineer* probably used one of these squalls to get away."[4]
~~~

The Steel Engineer *as she appeared after the war with her guns removed.* Albert Lowe.

consisted of: one 4-inch 50 aft – (Poop Deck) (This was a WW I vintage gun and I was the 2nd loader), one 3-inch 50 – Forward. (Bow), two .30 Cal. Colt Machine Guns – Wings of the bridge (These were WW I vintage and were belt fed), four 20mm. – (2) on the Bridge & (2) on the Poop Deck.

The ship was docked at the Bush Terminal in Brooklyn, N.Y. When I reported aboard the ship they had just finished unloading coffee from South America. The cargo hold had a definite smell of coffee! Now the ship was loaded with Army trucks, Jeeps, ammo, small arms, can goods and on the top deck, a locomotive. The cargo was marked: Russia!

On October 10, 1942 I went to my room to get some sleep because it was getting late and I was off duty. I was very tired as it had been a long day. When I awoke I went out on the main deck and to my surprise we were out to sea with no land in sight. We left N.Y. City on October 11, 1942 at 04:30 AM. We were sailing in a convoy of twenty-two ships. We had five escort vessels and local aircraft flew by. Our speed was 9 knots and we arrived in Guantanamo Bay, Cuba.

We left Cuba, 11:30 AM on October 23rd in a sixteen-ship convoy with seven escorts and fly-over aircraft. This was the first time I got seasick. I was on lookout duty near the 4-inch 50 gun on the stern. I got seasick, looking at the ship behind us. The sea was kind of heavy and while the ship behind us went up over the waves, we went down. The up-and-down movement got me seasick. The first time seasick and the last!

We arrived at Cristobal, Panama Canal on October 26th at 2100. While at Cristobal we had a day of shore leave and we left on October 28th to sail through the Panama Canal. As we went through the large locks we were pulled by an electric car called a "mule." We also had on board U.S. Marines with .45 pistols on their sides and some with rifles and bayonets. They were stationed in the wheelhouse on the bow and stern of our ship to prevent sabotage to the Canal locks, etc.

We left the Canal (Pacific side) with no convoy or escort. We sailed this time alone and we headed south to the Magellan Strait, which was the southern tip of South America. Our next port of call was Cape Town, South Africa.

After crossing the Atlantic Ocean and nearing Cape Town, a British two-engine aircraft flying only about ten feet off the ocean, signaled us for the I.D. of our ship. From our bridge, we sent up all kinds of flags for I.D. The British plane waved his wings (OK) and flew away. As we neared port you could see Tabletop Mountain. We arrived at the port of Cape Town, South Africa at 2030 on December 7, 1942 where we had liberty.

We departed Cape Town, South Africa on December 10 at 07:15 AM. Again we sailed alone as we headed north through the Mozambique Channel passing the Republic of Madagascar Island. Our next port of call was Abadan, Iran arriving in January 14, 1943. We traveled at 8 ½ knots and zigzagged all the way to the Gulf of Oman just as we had done approaching Cape Town, South Africa.

We started to unload in Khorramshahr. It was said that the temperature in the holds was 150 degrees. We had local Iranian and Indian men unload the ship. You also saw a large number of dhows (native sailboats) on this river. While the ship was being unloaded we had liberty. Some of our gun crew, including myself, took a ride on a paddleboat up the Tigris-Euphrates River to Baghdad, the capital of Iraq. There we slept in a local Y.M.C.A.

and did some sight-seeing. Meanwhile, the cargo of our ship went overland to Russia.

We departed Bandar Abbas, Iran at 1500 on March 22, 1943. We sailed in a convoy of twenty-seven ships and three escorts bound for Karachi, India doing 9 knots arriving there March 26 where we went on liberty. It was then off to Colombo, Ceylon on April 2nd sailing alone at 11.4 knots where we arrived on April 10, 1943, but not before we were attacked!

This Confidential report was filed concerning the attack.

Notice: Printed Matter June 21, 1943

Confidential

Report to: Navy Department
Office of the Chief of Naval Operations
Washington, D.C.

Subject: Summary of Statements Pertaining to Attack on S.S. *Steel Engineer*, U.S. Freighter, 5687 GT; Owners Isthmian S.S. Co. New York

1.) The *Steel Engineer* was attacked without warning on April 3, 1943 at 1345 GNT, approximate position 20.51N – 69.38E. Vessel sailed from Karachi India on April 2, 1943 for Colombo, Ceylon loaded with 3100 tons of U.S. Army cargo. Ship was not damaged and safely made port.

2.) The freighter was on course 132 degrees true; speed 10 knots in 34 fathoms; zigzagging, 10 mile 30 degrees zigzag course; blacked out; radio silent; 10 lookouts – 4 on bridge, 4 in gun bucket, 1 crows nest, I flying bridge. Weather clear; sea smooth; no wind; no moon; visibility good; no other ships in sight.

3.) At 1345 GMT two torpedoes were fired at the vessel, by a submerged Sub believed to be 150 yards distant, and, bearing 90 degrees from the ship. Both torpedoes missed, one passing 6' from the ship, the other 100'. Vessel executed a sharp zigzag. The sub subsequently came to the surface, 150 yards from the ship. Upon sighting the sub, the freighter was maneuvered so as to bring the enemy craft astern. The

Armed Guard opened fire at 800 yards, shooting three rounds at the sub.

The first shell fell in the U-boats wake. Other results have not been reported.

Distress message was sent and acknowledged; confidentials were retained aboard.

4.) Ship was not abandoned. Total complement on board was 58; no casualties.

5.) The sub was last seen at 2020 GMT when she dove on a course of 020 degrees. No description of the sub was available.

6.) The Armed Guard officer did not actually see the sub but did see some sort of track while the Master claims that he definitely recognized both the submarine and torpedo tracks.

R.G. Fulton
Lt. (jg,) USNR

From Colombo, Ceylon we left at 1200 sailing alone and arrived in Calcutta, India, at 1445 Apr. 16th. The ship unloaded some of the army cargo. We docked on the Hooghly River and

The 4-inch 50 gun in action on the poop deck of the Steel Engineer. *Albert Lowe was second loader on this gun.* Albert Lowe.

the dock was surrounded by an iron pier and a lock. Because the tide goes down, the ship remains floating behind this iron pier.

In Calcutta, I was also on liberty seeing the sights. I bought a statue of a family of elephants — one large elephant and two smaller ones. They all had ivory tusks and each leg had ivory toenails. The elephants were made of ebony wood.

We departed from Calcutta on April 25, 1943 at 2400 sailing alone at a speed of 8.7 knots. We arrived at port called Visakhapatnam on April 29th on the East Coast of India off the Bay of Bengal. Our ship was loaded with hemp and ballast. The ballast was put on board to keep our screw in the water. The ballast was put on board by a line of women that had large baskets on their heads. The loaded ballast (in baskets) was put on the head of these women by two men. Even with this ballast in our ship's hold the screw still shot out of the water in heavy seas!

We departed Visakhapatnam on May 1st 1943. Our next ports of call were: Colombo, Ceylon; Fremantle, Australia; and Wellington, New Zealand.

We departed Wellington, New Zealand June 20, 1943 and sailed alone arriving in Balboa, Panama Canal 1430 July 20, 1943. When we sailed across the Pacific Ocean, we spotted some whales spouting some water and a large tail that hit the surface and slapped the water. In the Pacific we spotted flying fish, some flying onto our deck. We spotted a shark, a ray fish and at one time, a very large turtle. We hit heavy seas in some seas and others that were smooth as glass. We arrived in Balboa, Panama Canal Zone on July 20 and left Cristobal Canal Zone on July 23rd in a convoy of seven ships and aircraft. This was our first convoy in a year. We arrived in Cuba in a convoy of twenty-seven ships. We left Cuba in a seventeen-ship convoy with five aircraft overhead doing 8 knots arriving in New York City August 4th at 0900 1943.

The U.S. Navy Armed Guard gave me the "Order of the Shellbacks Certificate" for crossing the equator aboard the S.S. *Steel Engineer* on the 15th day of July 1943 — on a Secret Mission of War, and having been initiated, then and there, into the Honorable Ancestors of the Shellbacks is and will be recognized as a Trusty Shellback.[5]

~~~

Joe Webb, Radio Operator, wrote about his first voyage.

America the Beautiful

It was about 11 PM when I joined my first ship in Hampton Roads, Virginia, in early February 1944. The night was dark. Ship, wharf, and the surrounding city were all blacked out. A very heavy fog drifted in slowly from the sea. There was no sign of the moon. The wet fog clung to my hair and clothes.

My ship, the Liberty ship S. S. *Benjamin Huntington*, looked like a ghost ship in the fog. I was filled with foreboding as I viewed the dim outline of the ship silhouetted against the dark sky. I had never been to sea in my life. In fact I had never even seen the sea before joining the Navy a little more than a year earlier. Still, I was nineteen years old now plus one month so I had no fear. It is that way when you are nineteen. I joined the Navy on the day I turned eighteen, eager to do my part for my country. Boot camp, radio school, and Armed Guard school had taken just over a year before the Navy felt that I was ready to go to sea. Now I had my chance.

I walked up the gangplank, presented my orders to the officer in charge, saluted and asked for permission to come aboard. A Navy boatswain welcomed me aboard and led me to my quarters at the rear of the boat deck. He showed me to my bunk, and to the locker where I could store my sea bag and hammock. (I never could figure out why I had to carry that damn hammock around wherever I went. It was heavy and bulky, yet every time I reached my assigned ship or station, the Navy had a bunk ready for me. Still, for three years I lugged that damn hammock around all over the world, wherever I went.)

After taking the train from the Armed Guard center in Brooklyn to Cape Charles, a ferry ride from Cape Charles to Little Creek, and finally a bus and taxi ride to reach my ship, I was tired, dead tired. I went straight to bed after that. When I woke we had already sailed to the mouth of Chesapeake Bay where the water was very rough. I didn't go to breakfast that morning, but
~~~

woke up vomiting. I vomited everything I had eaten and drunk for the last twenty-four hours, including a generous supply of beer, drunk on the trip by train from Brooklyn.

I continued to vomit for the next five days. When there was nothing to vomit, I had the "dry heaves." I couldn't even drink water without vomiting. After the first few hours, I vomited only green bile. I was sick in body, but happy in spirit. I have heard stories of sailors being so sick that they wanted to jump overboard. I was very sick; I never had any desire to jump overboard. Sometimes I drank water just to wash out my stomach. I gargled to refresh my mouth and throat.

There were two Merchant Marine radio operators already aboard. I was the only Navy operator. We got together and agreed on four-hour watches. The other operators urged me to allow them to take my shifts until I felt better. But that would mean that each of them would be on duty half time, day and night, and that was unfair to them. I expressed my gratitude but refused their offer. From then on for my entire tour of duty I was always there, and always on-time for my watches. I found a bucket and placed it next to my chair in the radio shack. I used ropes to lash my chair and bucket to tie points on the legs of the radio console. I found other tie points along the walls to secure the other side so that neither bucket nor chair moved when the ship rolled from side to side and pitched up and down in the swells. When I was relieved at the end of each watch I took my bucket with me, washed it out, and stowed it for the next watch.

We sailed along a southeasterly course towards the Sargasso Sea. Before long I found out from the captain that we were headed for Casablanca in North Africa. We were carrying supplies for the troops there. We had aircraft engines in the holds, and a deck cargo of trucks and tanks. All were lashed firmly to the deck, but I felt from the way the ship behaved that we were somewhat top-heavy. I shuddered at the thought of sinking due merely to someone having miscalculated the distribution of our load.

After a few days the sea calmed. I don't know if it was that or the fact that my seasickness had run its course, but one day I stopped vomiting. I was hungry. I went to the galley looking for something to eat. There I found a jar full of stuffed green olives.

I ate half a dozen of them and they stayed in my stomach. I suppose I could have eaten anything at all at that point, but from that day to this I have always loved green olives. I am sure it is due to that incident. Soon after that I ate normally and felt much better. There's something about the sea and that salt air that is exhilarating. I was so happy that I had chosen the Navy in preference to the other services.

Our captain was Norwegian. Soon after we sailed I asked him for the position of the ship, four hours in advance. I was taught in Armed Guard school that we radio operators must have that information with us while on duty, in case we are required to send a distress call. (The Merchant Marine operators had not been doing this, but I have no idea why). The captain was a friendly man, easily approachable, and he was happy to comply with my request. Thereafter every four hours, twenty-four hours a day, the captain sent a message from the bridge to the radio shack giving the projected position of the ship over the next four hours. For my own personal interest I plotted our position on a chart that I found in the radio shack.

I posted our hourly position on the console in front of me on my watch. We were receiving periodic warnings of German submarines spotted in our vicinity, so I did not wish to take any chances. I knew exactly what to do if we were torpedoed. If I were on duty at that time I must place the code books in a weighted bag that was always in place next to my chair, tie the bag, then throw the bag overboard. Then and only then could I go to my designated lifeboat station. If I was not on duty at the time I must first make my way to the radio shack and do exactly the same before proceeding to my lifeboat station.

When general quarters sounded I must proceed immediately to my battle station at a 20mm antiaircraft gun on the foremost starboard side of the bridge. If I was on duty at the time I must first wait for a Merchant Marine operator to relieve me before I could proceed to my battle station.

The Sargasso Sea looked like a giant lake, smooth as glass. No waves rocked the ship, and there was no breeze except for the ten-knot breeze created by the ship's progress. We sailed on for days like this, with the sun shining brightly. During my off-duty hours I often went to the bow of the ship to enjoy feeling the wind in my face. Dolphins were our constant companions, riding our bow waves. I enjoyed watching them play. It must be fun being born a dolphin.

I was born in January 1925. I remember only vaguely the good times in the 1920's. By the time I started to school the Great Depression was in full swing. In addition to the Depression, or maybe because of it, Europe was in turmoil. The rise to power of Adolf Hitler had already cast a great shadow over the future not only of Europe, but our own future as well.

My father was a World War I veteran, having served in the front lines in France for the entire war. As a result, he was keenly interested in European politics. When I was barely school-age I remember him saying over and over, "We're going to have to fight those *** Germans once again. Thank God you boys (my younger brother and I) are too young to fight." He was right in one sense, but he got the timing wrong. It was to be many more years before Hitler built his armed forces to the point where he would attack the West.

But America was an isolationist country in the 1930s, and we were to remain that way throughout the 1930s. There was little sympathy in public opinion for America to become involved in yet another European war. Besides, we had plenty to worry about right here at home, with high unemployment and business prospects poor. The Depression seemed to never end.

Japan was not even considered a threat to America. Most Americans viewed Japan as a cute little Third World country building little dime store trinkets to sell to us. Nobody seemed to view Japan as a serious military threat. After years of war in China, Japan had failed to conquer even that impoverished country. How could they possibly be a threat to us? If necessary, we felt quite confident that we could conquer Japan within ninety days or less. Our problem was Germany.

Finally, and without further incident, our ship approached the African coastline. How beautiful, I thought. Rolling hills along the coast made the landscape look just like the coast of California.

The sky was cloudless as we approach the city of Casablanca. We could see the city directly ahead, with low white buildings blending in with the desert landscape. The main streets were extremely wide, with a park-like, grass-covered median strip lined with palm trees.

Near the shore we were besieged by a flotilla of Arab row-boats. All wanted to trade cigarettes and sheets, in exchange for cash. Some trading took place, but we had outrun most of them by the time we neared Casablanca harbor.

Casablanca harbor was a mess of dead ships. I soon learned that they were all the Vichy French ships, sunk by the American Navy during our landing in North Africa. We had notified the French in advance of our plans to invade, and we had asked them not to fire on us. Ignoring our warnings, Admiral Darland, Vichy French commander in North Africa, ordered them to fire. Now we could see the results. Cruisers, destroyers, and other vessels all rested on the harbor floor with large holes in their sides. As the harbor was relatively shallow, all were partially above water. On several of these vessels we saw Arabs sitting on small rafts, pounding rivets around repair plates. They sat there all day long, hammering.

The ship's crew was called together and told what to expect going ashore. We were told to stay out of Medina, the native quarter of Casablanca, which was off-limits to American military personnel. We were paid in specially printed "gold seal" dollars and were told to accept no other currency while ashore, but we were not told why. I had never seen a gold seal dollar, nor had anyone else. As far as we could see, a dollar is a dollar, so everybody ignored that order. We were all patriotic at that time, but we were given no reason for that order. In retrospect I believe that we would all have obeyed the order had we been told why. After the war I discovered that this was because the Germans had forged American dollars so cleverly that even the experts could not tell the forged dollars from the real ones. Gold seal dollars were printed to thwart the Germans from using counterfeit dollars to procure material from abroad.

Interestingly, some of the Merchant Mariners on board told of going to Argentina on an earlier trip, where they could buy

American dollars at a fraction of their real value. When asked to explain why, their explanation was that the Argentines felt America would lose the war against Germany. We all knew that Argentina was highly supportive of Hitler's Germany, but for anyone to think that America would lose this war was beyond my own ability to imagine.

I went ashore several times during the ten days or so that we were in Casablanca. I always traveled with other sailors for protection. Arab adolescent gangs stalked the streets constantly; sometimes rushing forward and snatching anything lose such as a wallet or even a handkerchief sticking out of the sailor's vest pocket. We were warned not to challenge such youth gangs, since they would attack us in force. At the same time we noticed that these gangs ignored the French sailors, although I never knew why.

French sailors and French civilians were sullen. Shopkeepers were willing to sell their wares, but they were not friendly on any other level. They also seemed to have a dislike for speaking English. Looking for a friendly face, a friend and I found a little Jewish girl at a public park who was very friendly and spoke perfect English. She also spoke Hebrew, Spanish, German, and French, all fluently, and she cursed like a sailor! She said she was twelve years old but she looked more like an American eight-year-old to us.

Our little girl told us that there were no German Armed Forces in that area when the Americans landed. She said there was one German liaison officer in Casablanca, but very few other Germans. We were fighting French soldiers house to house to establish our beachhead there. That was a shock to me, since I had considered the French to be our allies. After all, Norway was a conquered nation, yet we were sailing with Norwegians all the time, and we could trust them completely. Why were we at war with the French?

Soon it was time to leave Casablanca and head home for another cargo. This time we sailed a more northerly route, and soon we were in rough waters. I was seasick again, and again it lasted for about four to five days before I recovered. This time the weather had not improved, but I had. Now I could go to the galley and eat anything, provided that it would stay on my plate. Eggs served at breakfast were particularly hard to keep on my plate. I solved that problem by balancing my plate in my left hand while I held a fork and ate with my right hand.

The weather went from bad to worse, and we were running into squalls. I was issued foul weather gear that I wore whenever I was out on deck. Nights were dark and dreary, and to my Navy issue leather bottom shoes the metal deck was as slick as glass. When I got up alone for midnight or 4 AM watch I was concerned when the ship rolled, for fear I might start sliding down the deck and over the side. I worked at a plan. If I started to slide I would slide on my back and hold my hands straight out so that I could catch hold of the steel cable surrounding the side of the ship. I knew well that, should I go over the side in this weather, there would not even be any effort to rescue me.

Submarines were stalking us once again. One night while I was on watch I picked up a distress signal transmitted by a lifeboat. It must have been very close since those transmitters had a very low power output, and the signal was very dim. I notified our Norwegian captain immediately, and he relayed my message to the senior officer of the escort by flashing light. I was told later that of the seventy ships in our convoy, only two of us had managed to pick up that signal, and mine was the only complete and coherent copy. We sailed on, but I felt good that someone had without doubt been assigned to look for that lifeboat.

The weather was very stormy, and our empty ship was bobbing around like a cork. The screws spent more time out of the water than in the water, speeding up and vibrating madly when pumping air. I noticed on my plot of ship's position that we had not moved at all over one twenty-four-hour period! Our ship was not able to make progress in such heavy seas. Our Norwegian captain stayed in constant contact with a Senior Officer of the Escort (SOE), a U.S. Navy trained, and no doubt inexperienced, seaman. We were trying to get to a rendezvous point off the East Coast of the U.S, but the two of them could not agree on the course to take to get where we wanted to be the next day. Finally the SOE used his seniority to direct our course. Next day he sent a message to our captain confessing that he was wrong. He further confessed that had he taken our captain's recommended course we would be exactly where the captain predicted! I admired both men more than ever for their integrity. We made it back to New York without further incident.

A few days liberty in New York and we were ready to sail once again. Once more the deck was crowded with deck cargo by the time we were ready to sail. We also had 500 American soldiers with us this time. Down the Hudson River and out to sea again and again I was very sick! This time the sea did not get better, but after the first four to five days I did. A day or two at sea I learned that we were headed for Naples. Submarines stalked us once again, but this time we were accompanied by an "Escort Carrier," with a few airplanes to keep watch for submarines. The Atlantic was constantly stormy, but not as bad as it had been on the trip back from Casablanca. Eventually we reached Gibraltar.

We sailed through the Strait of Gibraltar and anchored on the northern coast adjacent to the town of Gibraltar, where we stayed overnight. Our American escort left us and disappeared westward into the Atlantic mist. The next day British destroyers took over escort duties as we weighed anchor and headed eastward. Several ships launched barrage balloons, trailing them along on the journey to Naples. The Mediterranean Sea was like a giant lake, smooth as glass.

We sailed to Augusta, Sicily, but were forbidden to go ashore. I was told that this rule was for the benefit of the British services, to protect them from the inflation caused by Americans. Augusta harbor was beautiful, with Mount Etna towering directly overhead. The mountain was smoking, but quietly without eruption. We could stand on deck and admire the view for about three days without going ashore.

From time to time I had looked at the soldiers on board, sympathizing with their fate. They were not allowed on the deck where we spent most of our time. They also had separate dining and sleeping arrangements, which I understood were much more basic than our own. I felt so lucky being in the Navy, wondering how many of the soldiers I was looking at would never make it back home. The Germans were still holding Monte Casino, just to the north of Naples.

Several days later we sailed north for the Strait of Messina and on to Naples. After waiting in the harbor for a few hours we were allowed to dock. We pulled up to a waiting wharf, and started unloading our cargo. The soldiers we were carrying marched off the ship and out into the city. We never saw them again. I felt a touch of sadness, but we had our own war to fight.

I was allowed to go ashore almost immediately. As I walked down the side of the wharf with a couple of friends, we saw several other liberty ships, but one caught my eye because its bow was missing! I mean totally blown off! As I walked past in wonder, a radio operator I knew yelled at me from the main deck. "What in hell happened to you," I asked?

"We ran into a mine in the Strait of Messina a few days ago!" he replied.

"Where do you go from here?" I asked.

"Back to the states for repair, just as soon as they weld a big piece of steel over our bow!" he replied. I have no idea why that ship didn't sink to the bottom!

We had a visit that first night by the Germans shortly after curfew. We were all at general quarters, standing at our silent guns. We had orders not to fire, for fear of hitting someone on shore. The shore batteries were firing constantly, and the sound of flak raining down on our steel hall was deafening! They must have been putting a lot of steel in the air, but I didn't see any airplanes going down. Bombs in the city flashed, followed by a booming sound a few seconds later.

Suddenly I saw a very bright light directly overhead. It just hung there, shining so brightly that it was like daylight all over the harbor, and it looked like the light was directly over our ship! I wasn't frightened, but I sure felt like I should do something. Why couldn't we fire directly overhead at whatever it was that was lighting up the harbor? Next day I learned that it was a flare. The Germans were on a reconnaissance mission, photographing ships in the harbor. We were told to expect an attack on the ships next day, but it didn't happen.

Naples was a bombed out city, and it was hard to find a building that was intact. The San Carlos Opera House looked intact when viewed from the harbor, but it was totally gutted. We wandered around the city for the few days we were there, picking up a few bottles of wine and storing them in the ship's locker. We knew this was against Navy regulations, but the officer in charge of the Navy crew, a lieutenant, was quite liberal.

On our last day ashore three of us were walking down the streets of Naples when we saw three very friendly young ladies standing on a balcony above us, waving. We quickly found a stairway leading upstairs and sat down to talk with the ladies. We had just purchased a big bundle of cherries that we took with us. As we ate the cherries together and talked, one sailor tried to maneuver one of the ladies into an adjacent bedroom. She objected in a very friendly way, and made it quite clear that she was unavailable that day, but if he would just come back tomorrow, everything would be fine! He agreed, and soon we were away.

Once back out on the street and clear of anybody else, I turned to my friend and said, "You stupid ass! You know that we sail at dawn tomorrow!" He replied, "I know, but I wasn't going to say that to her!" Now I knew that I was not the only one aboard who remembered our briefing to keep our mouths shut when we were ashore! The enemy was close at hand, and we could never mention the time of sailing and destination of our ship!

Soon we were sailing north along the Italian coast towards Rome. Rumor was that our destination was Anzio, but when we were out of sight of land, we turned west. One or two days later we were told that we were heading home to pick up more cargo. Suddenly that peaceful Mediterranean turned sour, and for the next few days we were in a very intense storm. It was hard to see any land in the storm, but I knew from my charts that we had sailed southwest towards the northern coast of Africa.

One day while on watch I received a very strange signal that I was unable to decode. The signal was composed of four letter groups, but all our coded signals were made up of five number groups. We used a two-step process. First we looked up four letter groups in a book, and then encoded them into five number groups. I decided to try to see if this message had been done in one step. It worked!

The message identified a Liberty ship, giving its exact position, speed, port of departure, and destination. I looked up the position on my map. To my surprise that ship was sailing north, just off the west coast of Greece! At that time Greece was under German occupation! I shuddered! To begin with, I had orders never to transmit unless our ship was sinking, or if we were in port. Secondly, the one step coding of this signal was a dead giveaway to any German listening to our channel, as it gave position, speed, and destination of the ship! Either that radio operator was exceedingly stupid, or it was a clever trick. From what I had seen so far in this war, I decided on the former explanation.

At last the storm cleared and we could see the northern coast of Africa on our port side. Africa looked like one big sandy desert! I received a coded report about that time saying that we could expect an air raid from German aircraft based in Corsica and Sardinia. However, the report continued, once past Algiers we would be safe, since the Germans did not have wing tanks on their aircraft and they would be out of range should they go past Algiers.

About 2 PM that day we sailed past Algiers. An alabaster city nestled in sand dunes; the city was strangely beautiful lying there in the desert. We were making good time now, and soon we would be safe at Gibraltar. We were past any danger of air raids by the Germans. Besides, it wouldn't make sense to raid us now that we were empty. My signalman friend and I calculated that our cargo was worth about ten times the value of the ship, so why raid us while we were empty? It didn't make any sense at all. What value was a big empty steel hull with a small steam engine attached? The sea was calm and we were making steady progress to the west. I was confident that the threat was over.

That evening about 7 PM general quarters sounded and we all rushed to our guns. I was on watch at the time, so I had to wait to be relieved. As soon as my relief arrived I rushed to my gun position on the bridge. By that time our escort was busy sailing round and round the convoy covering us with smoke screen. It was hard to see anything, even the ship next to us. We didn't have to wait long though for things to start happening.

Gunfire from the 40mm antiaircraft guns on the British Corvettes broke the silence. Suddenly it looked as if all seventy merchant ships opened fire at once with 20mm guns and 3-inch guns. We had two 3-inch guns and one 5-inch gun. The 3-inch guns opened fire but the 5-inch gun was a surface gun, incapable of elevating its sights high enough to fire against aircraft, so it remained silent.

My shipmate was at our gun, while I was busy loading and putting tension on magazines. Soon I got caught up and I tried spotting planes for him. The planes were flying directly overhead, at mast level. Several planes flew directly overhead. I kept pointing and yelling at my shipmate to fire. He constantly failed to see the plane coming. Over and over again I could see the planes many seconds before he could. I asked to take over the gun myself, but he refused and held on.

Suddenly one of the planes burst into flame on our starboard side, struck the water, bounced and struck the water again, leaving two spots of burning plane on the sea. Then I saw a parachute descending through all that flak in the sky. One of the British vessels picked up the pilot. Incredibly he was uninjured! Next a plane on our port side went down in flames. Again the pilot bailed out and was rescued uninjured!

I couldn't see any ships in distress so it looked as if we were all okay. From the positions that the planes fell, I felt sure they were downed by our escort, rather than by our Liberty ship guns. Besides, the British were better gunners. Most of our sailors were first time out, with little or no experience in action. I could have been wrong. Our sailors were eager, but there was no substitute for experience.

Next day my signalman friend told me he had been briefed from the SOE. Twelve Stuka dive-bombers were in the initial attack, retrofitted to launch torpedoes at low level. British Spitfires shot down eight of these before they could reach the convoy. Two were shot down over the convoy, leaving only two to return to their bases. We hadn't lost a single ship in the attack.

The ship adjacent to us on our port side had been dragging torpedo nets since we left Naples. These were heavy wire nets draped over the side and extended from the ship's booms fore and aft. The morning after the attack they started to haul in the torpedo nets. As they lifted the net on their starboard side they found a torpedo stuck securely in the mesh. The SOE ordered them to return to Malta immediately and have it removed. We proceeded to Gibraltar one ship short. We were well aware that the torpedo had been dropped over the top of our ship, striking the water directly between our two ships. We did not have torpedo nets on our ship.

After exchanging escorts at Gibraltar, we moved into the Atlantic once again with an American escort. Almost immediately the sea became rough, but this time I did not get sick. The farther we moved out into the Atlantic the rougher the water became. We were on northerly course once again. Waves crashed over the ship and the wind lashed out at us, slowing progress to a crawl.

Submarines were once again tailing us. Soon we received orders from SOE that we must stand radio direction finder (RDF) watch. That meant me, the only Navy radio operator aboard. Although this was in addition to my regular radio watch, it wasn't that bad. Since RDF duties were rotated around the convoy, I only had to stand watch 4 hours a day. We were to listen for submarine transmissions, and we were given a brochure describing signal characteristics.

I read the instructions carefully and started my RDF duties. I would spin the dial across the low-frequency band, listening for any transmissions. I would then identify each transmission as not a submarine. It sounds boring, but in actual fact it seemed like fun, checking and identifying every transmission source.

After a few days I picked up a very peculiar call signal. Instead of CQ or other identifiable call, this one in Morse code was **..-..** but I knew we had no such call signal in our Morse vocabulary. Further transmissions identified it definitely as German. I quickly took a bearing, determined direction sense, checked my bearing, and checked direction sense a second time. The German was not stupid, as he was only on air maybe twenty seconds, but that was sufficient for me to catch him. I turned my information over to the captain, who immediately transmitted it to the SOE via flashing light. I returned to my duties and thought nothing further about it for the moment.

Next day my signalman friend called my attention to his log, and in particular to a flashing light signal he had just received from SOE that morning. It read, "Congratulations on your RDF bearing." The message said nothing more. Had they found and sunk that submarine? I have no proof one way or the other, but I knew that I had done my part.

My ship continued through that North Atlantic storm to New York. This time I was replaced by a third Merchant Marine radio operator. I was sent back to the Armed Guard Center in Brooklyn for reassignment, eventually ending up in the Pacific. But that is a totally different story.

Throughout all of my experiences in the U.S. Navy, I was extremely grateful to my country, since they were totally behind our operations in every way. There was nothing like the cooperation that we had during the Second World War, when the whole nation was focused on victory above all else. We were not alone![6]

The SS Benjamin Huntington *went to the Reserve Fleet after the War and was scrapped in Santander, Northern Spain, in 1971.*[7]

~~~

Bob Norling forwarded this story as well as many others in the chapters that follow. After the war, Bob worked forty years as a newspaper reporter and editor. His last stop was twelve-plus years at The Boston Globe *as head makeup editor and late night editor.*

Shooting Back

The World War II role of the Armed Guard was strictly defensive. But we only barely had that capability on my first ship.

The tanker *Gold Heels* was well-armed when built and commissioned as the Italian Navy oiler *Brennero* – four 4.7–inch .45 caliber surface guns and two 3-inchers for AA [antiaircraft]
~~~

Taken in November 1943, this photo shows the Gold Heels *ex-*Brennero *in drydock at Todd Shipyard, Brooklyn, having added armament installed. Note the unusual "torpedo blisters" below the waterline.* Bob Norling.

protection. But, looking back twenty years later, thank goodness we never had to fire a shot in anger.

She had been interned, taken over by the U.S. and renamed *Gold Heels.* The Navy found an old 4-inch 50 somewhere to mount on a stern gun platform. Scuttlebutt was that it dated from the Spanish-American War. At the bow was an empty gun tub.

For AA armament, we had two 30-caliber Lewis machine guns. If you had to use them, they had to be hand-held and fired from two empty gun tubs on the bridge. To protect gunners from serious burns, they had leather-covered asbestos grips. They looked like what the Lafayette Escadrille used in aerial combat with the Red Baron and Co. in World War I.

The one and only time the old 4-inch was test-fired while I was aboard everyone not assigned to the gun moved well forward to be out of harm's way. Blam! It went off. Grease squirted from all the fittings. The concussion produced a shambles of loose gear and a mighty cloud of dust below decks aft. The pointer and the trainer stood up and their seats fell to the deck.

Contrast this with my next ships, two Liberty ships. The *Abner Nash* had a dual-purpose 5-inch 38 aft, a 3-inch 50 forward and eight 20-millimeter guns. The *Benjamin Ide Wheeler* was similarly armed except that it had a 3-inch 50 aft.

We also had two Enfield rifles on the *Abner Nash*, for plinking at floating mines in the Irish Sea and en route to and from Murmansk in North Russia. We didn't explode any mines and we used a lot of ammo on the Murmansk run, but scored no kills. On the *Wheeler,* we painted five Rising Sun planes on the stack and got credit for 12 assists at Leyte in the Philippines.

My next ship, the *Admiral Halstead*, like the *Gold Heels* had an old 4-inch 50 aft, plus a 40-millimeter in the bow, four 20s and two water-cooled 50-cailber MGs. We got into some action at Morotai and Leyte, but no kills or assists.

My last ship was the *Kansan*, an old freighter homeward bound in 1945 from the Southwest Pacific. The war was almost over and we had nothing to shoot at with a 5-inch 51 (quite possibly as old as the *Gold Heels* 4-inch 50), a 3-inch 50 and four 20s. Just maintenance all the way from Sydney to San Francisco.

A nice quiet way to end Armed Guard duty in WW II.[8]

~~~

Harold E. Skinner describes his first voyage which went to the west coast of Central America.

The Banana Cruise

It was a sunny afternoon, January 22, 1944, and the seagulls were circling overhead as this nineteen-year-old sailor made his way along the Wilmington pier of Los Angeles Harbor. My seabag, in which all my worldly experiences were carefully packed, seemed a bit lighter as I walked expectantly alongside the docks. My orders in my pocket assigned me, S1/c (RM) Harold E. Skinner to the S.S. *Sagua*. The suspense and pent-up emotions were all related to my first sea duty in the U.S. Naval Armed Guard of World War II. After seven months of communications training, I was anticipating the excitement of new shipmates, life at sea, and the lure of foreign ports.
~~~

A few more paces and suddenly a tall, slender smokestack could be seen rising above the level of the pier. As I approached, the outlines of a small coastal vessel took shape. My reaction was one of disappointment. I thought that such a small, fragile craft could hardly be the proud cargo ship I dreamed of.

A Navy gunner in dungarees was washing clothes on deck as I came up to him. Noticing the confusion on my face, the gunner remarked, "Yes, sailor, this is the SS *Sagua*, but don't expect any exciting cruise in this old grease bucket. Our mission as Armed Guard is terribly important, though, to maintain civilian morale on the home front. We hardly ever lose sight of land. They sail for the United Fruit Company and we make a round-trip about once a month to Costa Rica. We bring back a load of bananas, and it's the Navy's job to protect those bananas."

Suspecting some exaggerations and omissions, I decided that danger on the high seas was not the only stuff of which high adventure is made. Actually, the ship's primary mission was to carry supplies and equipment for the construction of the Pan-American Highway through Central America. The 3,299 ton ship had an international crew of Latin Americans, an English captain, a Danish first mate, and a Yugoslavian chief radioman; the latter being my immediate superior. The Armed Guard contingent included seven gunners, one signalman, two radiomen and a gunnery officer. The principal armament consisted of a 4-inch 50 stern gun; then there were two gun tubs with 20mm machine guns amidships.

I studied the communications equipment, and the chief radio officer explained the operation of the transmitter. Actually, an operator almost never broke radio silence at sea except when under attack. On watch I constantly monitored the international distress frequency, 500 kHz, and periodically copy coded messages transmitted to all merchant ships in that zone. At any time the ship's secret call sign might appear in the heading of a message, so alertness was required.

At last the heavy equipment was stowed in the holds, and on February 5, 1944, the *Sagua* proceeded independently toward the open sea. Life picked up a rhythm of its own as the merchant seamen and Navy personnel started their watch schedules. My four hours on duty in the radio shack and eight hours off were calm and relaxing. Occasionally land swells rocked the ship, and flying fish frequently landed on deck. Navy gunners standing watch in the aft gun tub combined duty with pleasure by rigging an ingenious trolling line to fish for tuna from the stern. When a fish struck, a light restraining cord was yanked loose, tripping a bell and stopping snugly at the point of total resistance.

The gunnery officer, an ensign, was young and affable but assumed the fatherly figure and uncomfortably lectured the two new sailors on the ever-present danger of venereal disease in foreign ports. A sailor so afflicted might suffer serious consequences for lost duty time ensuing, including a reference in his permanent service record.

When off-duty, I occasionally wandered to the bow and exchanged a few remarks in Spanish with the lookout. There I first noticed playful porpoises swimming swiftly towards the bow the ship, looking very much to a novice like torpedoes moving on a deadly course. In only a few minutes, however, I caught a serious sunburn, unaware that exposure to the sun in that latitude must be reckoned with. The visits to the bow soon ended when the first mate advised off-duty personnel to avoid distracting the lookout.

At twelve knots of speed S.S. *Sagua* reached port in Manzanillo, Mexico on February 10. The Armed Guard crew went ashore briefly, looking for bargains in jewelry and cosmetics and eyeballing girls who were walking about on the plaza. At 11:15 PM the ship sailed for Corinto, Nicaragua, where it docked five days later. Soon vital equipment was being discharged for the highway construction. I performed the routine duty of standing gangway watch. All at once a tall, imposing official, dressed in a gold-braid uniform befitting an admiral, stepped to the top of the ramp. He saluted pompously and released a torrent of Spanish. Not understanding a word, I returned the salute and hurried off to inform a bilingual merchant marine officer that official business was waiting at the gangway.

On February 16 the *Sagua* left Corinto, arriving the next day at Puntarenas, Costa Rica. Within three days the cargo was unloaded. Ashore once again, the Armed Guard crew enjoyed the carnival atmosphere of the lively little port. They bought leather goods, trinkets, and handcrafted articles. Senoritas were prevalent at every corner, waiting to approach and steal the wallet of any unwary seaman.

On February 20 the *Sagua* sailed south to a long pier in Quepos, Costa Rica. Its arrival had been anticipated, and for a good reason. Mounds of green bananas were piled high on the long pier like so much lumber. Once the loading operation got underway, however, it was amazing how quickly the fruit disappeared into the holds. I joined a few of the gun crew who, at the last moment, hid stalks of the green fruit in a deck locker.

The *Sagua* sailed north on February 21. One immediate change in the galley menu noticed by the crew was an unusual variety of banana fritters, baked bananas, fried bananas, and banana pudding at mealtime. The return voyage was uneventful, and on March 7, the old ship entered the channel of San Pedro harbor. The first concern of the Navy crew was to remove their illicit supply of fresh bananas, now yellow, while avoiding United Fruit Company officials. Under cover of night they slipped away with their prizes to the great satisfaction of local friends and relatives; fresh bananas were generally scarce, being reserved for military centers.

The pleasant duty of my first cruise ended abruptly on March 9 when I was detached from the *Sagua*, and within a week I was in San Francisco awaiting assignment to another ship. The banana cruise had been an incredibly relaxing interlude for a young sailor, as well as an amazing first seagoing adventure. It was not my fate to continue this idyllic life of a peacetime cruise, for soon I would sail into the far reaches of the Pacific war zone.[9]

5

The Gulf of Mexico

Although the Gulf of Mexico and the Caribbean were successful hunting grounds for German U-boats, this area of conflict never received the same level of notoriety as the North Atlantic. From February 19, 1942 until August 13, 1942, forty-one ships were sunk, damaged or mined by U-boat action in the Gulf of Mexico and twenty-two Navy Armed Guards were killed along with 413 merchant seamen.[1] From February 7, 1942 through December 14, 1942, 145 ships were either sunk, damaged or mined in the Caribbean with 172 Navy Armed Guards killed along with 1,186 merchant mariners. In addition, there were seventeen passengers, forty-two Army personnel, three Navy men and twenty-three stevedores killed in this area of action.[2] The tankers, with their precious cargos, were the primary targets of the U-Boats.

The carnage stopped in August 1942 as the Allies started using defensive tactics:

Actually the month of July was to see the virtual end of the Gulf of Mexico campaign. The defences in this landlocked sea were now far too strong for U-Boats to survive.[3]

With the shutdown of the U-Boat playground in the Gulf, the United States Navy had finally achieved control of its coastal waters. They had paid an awful price for the prewar neglect.[4]

~~~

This first story is from J.W. (Bill) Janes who spent four years and nine months in the Navy.

S.S. *Meton*

My first ship, the S.S. *Meton*, was an oil tanker. It was 425 feet long and J.W. George was the only signalman aboard. He was from the state of Mississippi. There were a total of eleven Navy personnel on board, with a boatswain's mate 2/c in charge. The S.S *Meton* was equipped with a 5-inch 38 caliber gun on the fantail and four .30 caliber antiaircraft guns. I think the .30 caliber guns were water-jacket cooled. We had plenty of 7 x 35 binoculars to use on watch. Her load capacity was 66,000 barrels and she was built in 1919.

The night I went on board, the *Meton* pulled out, and headed for the Panama Canal. For one who has never been more than thirty miles from home, this particular night was memorable. Here I was traveling through the San Francisco Bay area, passing Alcatraz and under the Golden Gate Bridge. Everything was all lit up like a Christmas tree and it was quite a sight.

After arriving and unloading at the south end of the canal, we spent a day traveling through the Canal locks to the Gulf of Mexico. It was quite a sight!

We traveled in convoy, across the Caribbean, transporting oil to and from places such as Galveston, Texas; San Juan, Puerto Rico; Kingston, Jamaica; Guantanamo Bay, Cuba and two Dutch Islands of Curaçao and Aruba. On one occasion the convoy pulled into the mouth of the Mississippi River so the *Meton* had to drop anchor until a convoy was going her way. While anchored, the
~~~

ship's boatswain had the deck crew painting over the side on the port bow. While they were scrapping and painting, they had plenty of company to watch them, visit and joke with. One joker, on the scaffolding, told a very funny story, and a ship's fireman, who was hanging over the rail like the rest of us were, busted out laughing and his teeth fell out and went to the bottom of the river. The skipper had to call for an appointment at the dentist in New Orleans. He was the only one aboard that got to go ashore while we anchored there. He (the fireman) was the only one aboard the *Meton* that died when the ship was later sunk.

After a number of trips across the Caribbean, we took a load of oil at Curaçao. On the night of 4 November 1942 the *Meton* joined a convoy for Cuba. She was the lead ship of the outside starboard column. At 3:10 AM the morning of 5 November, 1942 the *Meton* was torpedoed with three torpedoes in quick succession. At the same time, a British tanker (*La Cordillera*) and a Norwegian tanker (*Astrell*) were torpedoed. One was loaded with gas and it was set on fire. A number of fellows went down with the one on fire.

I was asleep on an army cot on the boat deck next to the navigation room, with my life jacket under the cot. When the first torpedo went off, it flipped me and the cot over onto the deck, the life jacket washed over the side and everything and everyone was totally blackened with oil. Moments later, all but one fellow showed up and the captain gave the order to abandon ship. My cot was within feet of the only life boat that had not been damaged. As the second mate was in charge of this particular boat, he lowered the boat, and unrolled the rope ladder. The second mate's name was Schroeder and he sure had a German accent. An engine room fireman, who was on duty in the engine room at the time, did not show up until the lifeboat was pulling away. Schroeder held an oar out for him to grab onto, but he could not hold onto the oil-covered oar and he went under. He did not resurface. This fireman had just received word, a few days before, that one of his two sons had been killed in action.

The *Meton* was taking on water very slowly now. We rowed out a safe distance and watched the other two ships go under.

The one with the gas fire was out of sight and the surface gas was still burning. An hour or so later, we could hear the Dutch torpedo boats coming to pick us up long before we could see them. One fellow and I got to lay up on the bow of the boat as we headed back to Curaçao. That was the greatest, and the most memorable boat ride that I have ever had in my life.

Compiler's note: The following is from the Royal Netherlands's Navy Warships of World War II website. The Artillery-Training Sloop Van Kinsbergen*, launched in January 1939, came to the rescue of* Meton *and the Norwegian tanker* Astrell *after they were sunk by* U-129 *(Witt) while in the movement of Convoy TAG-18 off Curaçao.* Van Kinsbergen *assisted in rescue of the tanker crews from both ships and was unsuccessful in hunting down* U-129. Astrell *was sunk by* Van Kinsbergen *because she was beyond repair. "The sloop continued her search until evening. The Dutch* Van Kinsbergen *saved a total of 69 men from both tankers (49 of* Meton*, 20 of* Astrell*).*[5]

"At 0710 GCT, a torpedo struck the ship at No. 4 tank, a second struck at No. 6 tank, just aft of the midship house, and a third hit at No. 9 tank just forward of the poop deck. The first two torpedoes started fires, but the third put them out. The ship settled on an even keel until she sank about ten hours later. Her complement consisted of thirty-eight crew members and twelve Naval Armed Guard. One fireman (Theodore R. Cowing) was killed in the explosion. The U-129 *(von Harpe) was scuttled in Lorient, France on August 18, 1944."*[6]

Bill Janes continues:

Shortly after sun up, we were back at the dock at Curaçao. The first thing we were given was a detergent that would get the crude oil out of our hair and off of us. Then we were given a complete outfit of clothing, along with a small amount of money. Because of an ingrown toenail, the first thing I bought was a pair of scissors, which I still have. My biggest problem the following night was trying to sleep, with the continual thought of not what happened, but what could have happened, and the aching from the concussion, which wore off after a day or so. A few days later, we got to fly out of Curaçao on an Army C-46 that took us to Guantanamo Bay, Cuba.

Our transportation from Cuba to New York was on a Navy sub chaser. It was escorting a convoy that traveled near the Cape Hatteras area. A storm hit the Cape as we were traveling through the area, and it tossed that 130-foot vessel around like it was a cork. They estimated the groundswells to be as much as thirty feet. It is the only time I was bothered with seasickness. One morning, when the water was so rough, I was sitting in mess hall having coffee, along with a few of the ship's regular crew. Apparently, they were eating early lunch before going on watch, for they had their mess trays with food. Suddenly, the ship took a sharp dip in then up in the air. The trays slid to the end of the table and onto the deck. Some of the food was still on the trays when they picked it up.

Arriving at the Armed Guard Station in Brooklyn, we knew we would be on leave soon. The second morning at muster, everyone was to report to the indoor swimming pool to pass the swimming test. I never could swim, and still can't, so I soon got my first lesson. I had orders to report back at the pool the next morning, but at muster, we were notified our leave papers were ready, so we picked them up and headed for Grand Central Station. Thirty days later, we were to report back to the Armed Guard Base at Treasure Island.[7]

~~~

This story from Van Mills describes a little-known Armed Guard facility. According to Van, "In all of the literature, letters, publications I have ever read, I have never read anything about the AG at Key West."

Key West, Florida – Hell Hole of the Navy

In 1942, Key West was considered the hell hole of the Navy by Armed Guardsmen who served there. An old warehouse on one of the docks had been converted into a barracks and offices for AG personnel and other US Navy personnel.
~~~

The only fresh water available at Key West was through a two- or three-inch pipeline from the mainland of Florida. The pipeline was always breaking down and we had to take quite a few saltwater showers.

The Navy had a canteen where you could buy soft drinks and play a jukebox that had two records. One of these records was, "Send Me One Dozen Roses." I can't remember the other one. The town at Key West was off-limits to service personnel and there was one small beer-joint at the edge of town.

In the early part of the war, the Navy escorted the merchant ships from the East Coast to Key West. The convoy would then split up at Key West and the merchant ships were on their own. Armed Guard personnel would be taken off the ships by the Navy and taken to Key West or to the USS *Seven Seas*. The *Seven Seas* was anchored off Key West in an area protected by antisubmarine nets. She was once owned by heiress Barbara Hutton. *Seven Seas* was a three-masted schooner and could be powered by sail or motor. The Navy however had cut off the masts. The early coastal convoys had only Navy radiomen and signalmen on the ships. The only weapon on the first ship I was on was a submarine gun.

You could spend a month or more on the base at Key West before you caught another ship. I served temporary duty out of Key West on the USS *Seven Seas,* USS *PC-640* and *488.* While I was on *PC-488* we had two sub contacts. On one contact we dropped all of our depth charges but the sub got away. The other sub also got away.

On a four-hour watch you stood one hour each in the crow's nest, bridge, sonar and on the wheel. It took twenty-one days to go from Trinidad to Recife, Brazil. We escorted 5- to 6-knot convoys and we always ran out of fresh water except for drinking.

In early November 1942, about fifteen radiomen and signalmen who had been stuck or stranded at Key West were sent to Miami, Florida for some R&R and retraining. We stayed in a hotel that had been taken over by the Navy. We were living on subsistence and drawing sea pay.[8]

6

THE ATLANTIC OCEAN

On September 3, 1939, the Battle of the Atlantic began with the torpedoing of the British liner Althenia. *It continued for five and-a-half years, making it the longest battle of World War II; it would take the Allies three-and-a-half years to turn the tide.*

At the beginning of World War II, naval strategy continued the theory of World War I: whoever controlled the seas dominated. Consequently, Britain blockaded German ports and the Germans used their deadly U-boat fleet to disrupt Allied movement of foodstuffs, fuel oil, gasoline, munitions and heavy equipment.

A wartime memorandum to the German military staff read: "Germany's principal enemy in this war is Britain. Her most vulnerable spot is military trade ...The principal target of our naval strategy is the merchant ship, not only the enemy's but every merchantman which sails the seas in order to supply the enemy's war interests ..."[1]

After France fell in 1940, direct access to the Atlantic via the French ports and submarine pens was available to the German navy. The U-boat force was free to roam the Atlantic using wolf-pack tactics to wreak destruction and terror upon ships transporting vital goods to Britain and Russia. After the U.S. declared war on Germany in 1941, Hitler sent his U-boats against the east coast of the U.S., and in January 1943, a U-boat offensive called Operation Kettle Drum Beat was executed. The results were devastating to U.S. merchant ships, their crews, and the U.S. Navy Armed Guard who protected those ships.

The following was compiled from the American Merchant Marine at War website. The totals indicate the devastation in this theater of action. There are a number of ships in which the death total is unknown for merchant and Armed Guard crews. The table does not include Murmansk, Normandy or the Approaches to the Mediterranean.

Theater	**Ships Sunk/ Damaged**	**Deaths**				
		Crew	**Armed Guard**	**Pass.**	**Troops**	**Army**
U.S. East Coast	169	1,347	140	39	-	1
North Atlantic	166	2,053	674	18	770	4
N.E. Atlantic & No. European Ports	105	314	155	18		12
	440	3,714	969	75	770	17[2]

It wasn't until 1943 that the tide of battle changed in the Atlantic. New defensive measures involving air support, convoys, radar and the mass production of over 2,700 U.S. Liberty ships bridged the supply line to Britain, Russia, and our other Allies.

~~~

Dr. Leonard Amborski's brother, Norbert, was a Cadet-Midshipman in the Class of 1942 at the United States Merchant Marine Academy. Norbert lost his life on his first voyage, aboard the SS Stone Street. *The SS* Stone Street *had twelve Naval Armed Guard on board (two perished), and forty crew members (eleven perished).*
~~~

Heroes of the S.S. *Stone Street**

This is the story of heroes in the crew of the S.S. *Stone Street* which was sunk on September 13, 1942 by the *U-594* by (Fredrich Mumm), a member of the thirteen U-boat wolf pack called "Vorwarts." The *Stone Street*, in ballast, was in convoy ON-127, consisting of thirty-three merchant vessels sailing from Liverpool to the United States. After a three-day running battle with the wolf pack, the S.S. *Stone Street* was forced to leave the convoy due to excessive "smoking." This sitting duck was torpedoed with a loss of thirteen lives about 800 miles east of Newfoundland, a short distance from which airplane cover could have offered protection.

The first three torpedoes missed the vessel but the fourth hit it amidships. The S.S. *Stone Street* (6,131 GT) was the ex-Italian freighter S.S. *Clara*, built in 1922 in Monfalcone, Italy. It was seized in Savannah and assigned by the War Shipping Administration to the Waterman Steamship Corp. and sailed under the Panamanian flag. The poor condition of this vessel was reflected in its "smoking."[3]

The following excerpt is of the report made by the Naval Armed Guard officer Granville C. Geisert Lt.(jg):

> … At 2100 in accordance with the Commodore's orders, due to our smoking and continuous straggling, we left the convoy going twelve miles to starboard. As we turned to leave the convoy, the engine fires went out causing a twenty-minute delay. When we got underway, again there was a tremendous shower of sparks from our funnel, which was not controlled for fifteen minutes. This spark throwing was not an unusual condition on the *Stone Street.*
>
> September 13, at 0130, there was a terrific explosion and we saw snowflakes in the direction of the convoy. We altered course another twelve miles to starboard.
>
> At 1045 and [Lat.] 48:18 N and [Long.] 39:43 W, we were struck by a torpedo amidships on the port side. Another torpedo

---

* Taken from *The Last Voyage: Maritime Heroes of World War II*, by Dr. Leonard Amborski.

just missed our bow. The submarine was not sighted. The weather was clear but the sea rough. An attempt was made to send a radio S.O.S. but it was very doubtful if it was transmitted because our antenna was knocked down by the concussion. The ship immediately listed about 45 degrees to port making it impossible to train the gun or get around on deck and the ship continued under way as the engines were not stopped. First Assistant Engineer Kelly was on watch at the time. Captain Andersen gave the order to abandon ship and the forward starboard lifeboat was safely lowered although Boatswain A. Hendrickson was crushed between the ship and the boat. The after starboard boat was lowered but the forward motion of the ship swamped it and crushed it against the side. I threw my briefcase containing confidential papers in this boat. When it was swamped the case washed out and the last I could see it was rapidly sinking. The forward port boat was smashed by the explosion and the after port boat was thrown up on the boat deck and hooked in such a position it could not be lowered. We attempted to launch the after starboard raft but it was jammed; however we succeeded in launching the after port raft and ten men and myself boarded it, being the last off the ship. The lifeboat with Captain Andersen in charge picked up the men floating in the water after leaving eleven volunteers on a raft with Cadet R. Vetter in charge. Robert Calvin Makin, AS, U.S.N. drowned when he could swim no longer. He did not get a life jacket because he had stayed at the boat station helping to lower a boat, which he was unable to reach after it was in the water. McDonald, Sea2c, U.S.N.R. was washed over and struck by the screw which mangled his legs. Although he had on a life jacket, he drowned before he could be picked up. Cox. J.J. Chatterton, U.S.N.R. was in the water with these men when they died.

According to the deposition given by Messman Joseph T. Watt, Engine Cadet Norbert Amborski

...had got caught between the ropes that hold the lifeboat, and was thrown in the water. The ship was still making headway, and the

suction of the propeller was starting to draw him towards it when he called for help. I saw my brother (John Watt) leave the lifeboat and jump in and try to rescue the engine cadet. I did not see my brother get to him, because at the time a heavy sea came, which took our boat up and was bringing it down, but during that time I believe that the propeller drew the boy to it and what I saw then was where he was tossed up in the air by the propeller. I saw nothing further of my brother or the engine cadet. The only two men that I actually saw killed were the Bosun and the engine cadet...[4]

At 1200, the periscope of the submarine passed within twenty feet of our raft but did not stop.

At 1215, the *Stone Street* sank and a submarine surfaced by the other raft asking for the captain and the chief engineer. Cadet R. Vetter directed them to the lifeboat. This was a very small submarine and in the opinion of my men was French-built with German guns.

At 1225, a very large submarine surfaced and began signaling to the smaller one, which went to the lifeboat and made inquiry concerning the two officers. My Coxswain and other Armed Guard crew members who were in lifeboat reported that the submarine was told that the chief was killed and that the captain was the boatswain. Third Mate Stokke and Captain Andersen were taken aboard the submarine and it pulled about 100 yards away from the lifeboat. In a few minutes it returned, capsized the lifeboat, and took the occupants, who had fallen in the water, aboard. They could not tell if this was deliberate or accidental. Captain Andersen's briefcase floated out and he was forced to admit he was the captain after the submarine commander had decided to take the third mate prisoner. They also reported that the captain was asked why he lied and he replied that he had done it for the men because they thought he might be able to navigate the lifeboat to Newfoundland; the submarine officers asked where we were going, what we were carrying, our tonnage, and many other questions which were answered by Captain Andersen. They asked if the convoy formed west of Scotland; what zigzag course we were steering, and when told none did not believe it because they had missed with three torpedoes before they hit with the fourth.

They asked if this were the smoking ship and were extremely provoked when told that it was because they said we had sunk one of their flotilla; references were made to the admiral on the large submarine. Upon request for good treatment, the men were given whiskey, food, cigarettes, and matches (French). The submarine commander also said he would advise London about position.

After attempting unsuccessfully to right the lifeboat, seventeen men were placed on two rafts. The submarine then left with Captain Andersen prisoner. My Coxswaln Joe Chatterton, and others reported that the age of the crew of the submarine ranged from eighteen to thirty; they were well-trained and seemed happy; the commander was in his early thirties and spoke very broken English. He used as an interpreter the second officer, who appeared to be about seventeen years old, and spoke fluent English with an American accent.

Before leaving, Captain Andersen placed Third Mate Stokke and Cox. J.J. Chatterton, USNR in charge of the rafts. These rafts were attached to each other by a line and drifted away together. I was on the other pair of rafts with eleven men on each which were secured together and Chief Officer Pedersen was in charge. We rationed out provisions for thirty days.

There was one swamped lifeboat with seven men aboard. We could maneuver the raft enough to go to their assistance. From this boat, we rescued one man three days later.

September 14, at 2200, we sighted signals and a flare in the distance. We learned later these were from the other pair of rafts.

September 15, at 1000 we sighted a capsized lifeboat about 1000 yards away. We spent two hours propelling our rafts to it. It was capsized but we righted it, baled it out, and found it in usable condition with almost all of the supplies and provisions remaining intact. This was the boat the Germans had capsized. We took the provisions from the rafts on to the boat, cast one raft adrift, and secured the other to the boat. We began rowing in a southwesterly direction. While we were righting the boat, a submarine was standing by at about a mile.

September 16, at 0500, we sighted a mast and flag about four miles away toward the west. We altered course toward it.

At 1350, we arrived at a swamped lifeboat with W. Atkins, A.B. and the body of P. Joel, 4th Asst. Engineer aboard. Atkins told us that H. Williamson, chief steward, Gordon Davis, 2nd asst. engineer, C. Clower, oiler, M. Kahn, deck engineer, and R. Evans, fireman had died or gone overboard. We took Atkins on the raft along with the provisions from his boat and started rowing southwest. Mr. Pedersen made a sail out of flags, which we used in conjunction with the oars.

And 2100, we now knocked off rowing because of the good speed we were getting out of the sail.

September 17th at 0200, we sighted lights in the distance so we set off a flare and gave S.O.S. signals with our flashlight. The Very pistols would not work.

At 0230, the lights pulled away.

At 0430, we sighted a masthead light and began sending distress signals and lighting flares. We set out course toward this light and soon could see running lights of a ship. We received a signal "O.K." from blinker.

At 0600, we were picked up by the S. S. *Irish Larch*, at [Lat.] 48:50 N. and [Long.] 40:00 W. The seventeen men on the other pair of rafts had been rescued at 0130 that morning. They told Captain Horne that there were others so he searched until we were found. Upon assurances by Chief Officer Pedersen that there were no more survivors, Captain Horne picked up our lifeboat and proceeded to his destination where we landed. We were given first aid and the best of treatment on the rescue ship ...[5]

Coxswain Joseph J. Chatterton distinguished himself and received a commendation from the Secretary of the Navy for his outstanding courage and aggressive fighting spirit during the encounter with the enemy from September 10, 1942 until September 13, 1942.

Captain Harald Andersen was taken prisoner by U-594 *and spent the remainder of the war in the Milag POW camp for merchant seaman.* U-594 *was "Sunk 4 June, 1943 west of Gibraltar, in position 35.55N, 09.25W, by rockets from a British Hudson aircraft (48 Sqdn.). 50 dead (all hands lost)."*[6]

~~~

James Montesarchio's first story concerns the North Atlantic.

I never told my C.O. that …

In September 1942, after my father had given his consent, I went down to White Hall Street, Manhattan, New York City. I was sworn in with my father right at my side. We were all thinking about Newport, Rhode Island; Norfolk, Virginia or Treasure Island, California, where we might be sent for training. Instead they gave each of us a nickel and marched us to the nearest subway for a ride to the Brooklyn Armed Guard Center. My father was still beside me. When we got there my father finally had to leave me. Just think of your own father marching with you so you could get into the Navy. I did sprinkle a little tear as I saw him slowly disappearing from me.

When we got into the domed building, it was a madhouse. At least 2,000 guys were walking around, some in uniforms and some not. We found out very shortly thereafter that the fellows out of uniform were survivors just torpedoed right outside the three-mile limit. They were only on their ships but for a very short time. We were there to take our "boot" training for thirty days.

We were bunked on an old World War I cattle boat, the U.S.S. *Newton* which was tied up along the pier at the Armed Guard Center. We took our training out in the open fields across from the *Newton*. I must say we had very good training from two old World War I chief petty officers named Millen and Gross. We learned a lot from them and at times they treated us like they were our fathers. I've never forgotten them.

After "boots" I applied for Ship's Company and got it. So I was at the Armed Guard Center for a while aboard the U.S.S. *Newton* watching gun crews come in and out and also survivors. I finally decided I had to go to sea so I volunteered once again and got it.

I received a call to pack my sea bag and hammock and off I went to my ship at Pier 5 Brooklyn, right under the Brooklyn Bridge. The ship was the *William H. Webb*.
~~~

The USS Newton *docked at the Armed Guard Center, Brooklyn, New York was used as a training ship and brig.* Courtesy of U.S. Navy Armed Guard WW II Veterans.

When I got aboard they were insulating the bulkheads and somebody said that was because it was headed for very cold weather. Some of the merchant crew signed off and we had to get new men to take their place.

We left New York for Gourock, Scotland and along the way we picked up quite a few ships going there. It took us about twenty-five days to get there with all the zigzagging.

From Gourock we sailed to Oban, Scotland and formed a new convoy. We left Oban with about sixty-five ships, still not knowing where we were going. The seas were really rough and the freezing waters were brutal. I'll never forget my first 12-to-4 watch up in the crow's nest with the Atlantic in all its fury beneath us. Climbing up to the crow's nest I looked down and all I could see was water beneath me because the ship took quite a roll. It was scary, but I managed okay.

I never told my C.O. that I didn't have any gunnery training and they were getting ready to position us on the 5-inch 38 gun. When I told him he couldn't understand how I managed to get aboard without gunnery training. So he made me the hot shell man. I had to catch the shells as they were ejected from the breach of the gun. I wore asbestos gloves as the shells were hot coming out. I'll never forget that initial explosion that gun made. It took me off the gun deck about a foot and I couldn't hear a thing for quite a while afterwards. I managed to get through it but I learned to open my mouth when the shell would explode to take the pressure off my ears. I was already starting to become an old salt. We were just test-firing the 5-inch 38 at the time.[7]

~~~

This is Louis V. Ritter's first story. It ended in England and according to Lou, "The experience is one I will live with and remember all my days. As they say, you can leave the service but it never leaves you."

The First of Four Trips Across the Atlantic

I enlisted in the United States Navy Reserve in November, 1942. I still remember the recruiting place. It was Broad Street, Manhattan, New York. I was then sworn in December 13, 1942, into the Navy. I went on active duty in January 4, 1943. I was sent along with others by train, to Great Lakes Naval Station for the "boot" camp. I spent eleven weeks at Camp Green Bay. After "boot" camp we got a seven-day leave. After leave I returned to Great Lakes and then went by troop train to Gulfport, Mississippi. We were there about a month in gunnery school, and then sent to New Orleans, Louisiana, to a place called Algiers.

We then received orders to report to Mobile, Alabama where we boarded the Liberty ship S.S. *Samuel Moody*. We proceeded up to New York City to load cargo. They loaded bombs and parts of planes. This is one of four trips across the Atlantic Ocean. As in all trips, we experienced severe storms and high waves. At times we had submarine alerts and all ships would scatter. Then back to formation.

On one trip we came across a floating mine. An escort vessel fired at the mine blowing it up. On another trip we came across a
~~~

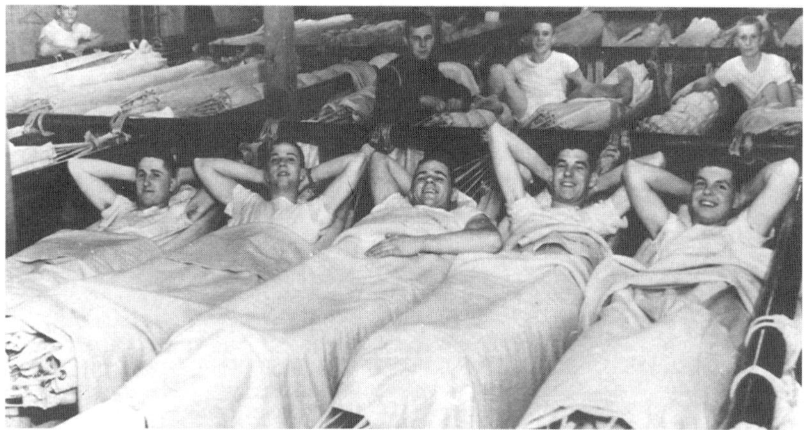

Boot training at the U.S. Naval Training Station, Great Lakes, Illinois included learning the intricacies of sleeping in a hammock. Courtesy of U.S. Navy Armed Guard WW II Veterans.

ship with all its lights on. This was a neutral ship, like Portuguese or Swedish. We had to go out of our way to avoid being silhouetted against its lights. There was a blackout all the time. At times we had porpoises swim under our bow making like a torpedo.

On another trip two different fights broke out. One involved a man being cut on the arm with blood spurting out from an artery. In another instance a cook and the mess boys were throwing glasses and pitchers at each other. All had to be restrained. They were taken off in England never to be seen again. In a third instance a merchant boatswain's mate fell into the Manchester ship canal and drowned. He was laid to rest in England.

While in England I saw buildings destroyed in London. I saw the searchlights playing into the night sky while bombing was going on. I saw people living in the underground (subway), being used as a bomb shelter. This experience is one I will remember all my days. As they say, you can leave the service but it never leaves you.[8]

The SS Samuel Moody *was scrapped in Richmond, California in May 1964.*[9]

~~~
~~~

In 1943 the Navy Armed Guard crew of the Samuel Moody *(in striped shirts) played a soccer game against the R.A.F. (Royal Air Force). Pictured with Lt. Boyer, center, are Marigiliano, Ransom, Rieglemeyer, Riley, Triplett, Mastandrea, Ravotti, Patton and Ricci.* Courtesy of U.S. Navy Armed Guard WW II Veterans.

Franklin H. Pearce tells of his experience on the Esso Baton Rouge. *Prior to "F. H." shipping out, this ship "was torpedoed by the German submarine U-123 (Hardegan) at 0248 EWT on April 8, 1942 about 13 miles off Brunswick, Georgia... Three men on watch in the engine room were killed..." After repairs in two shipyards, the ship was made ready for sea again on November 30, 1942.*[10]

Then Everything Broke Loose

I enlisted on October 11, 1942, and had three weeks of "boot" camp at Great Lakes, Illinois. I had a nine-day leave and then it was out to sea on the *Esso Baton Rouge.* This ship had previously been torpedoed and was raised and refitted at Baltimore. She made a couple of shake-down trips to Texas picking up oil for Boston.

During the last few days of December 1942 we left New York City to form a convoy at Halifax. We started to leave there early in January 43. The first ship reported to have been torpedoed was right after leaving the nets at Halifax.

The Esso Baton Rouge *as she appeared before the war. Built in 1938 at Bethlehem's Sparrows Point Yard, she measured 12,950 deadweight tons with a length of 463 feet and breadth of 64 feet.* U.S. Navy Armed Guard WW II Veterans.

We had about seventy ships in this convoy including the troop ship *Dorchester*. Axis Sally identified our ship by name one night and said, "Yank, go back home and we will not sink you." A tantalizing thought! The weather was very cold and the ship's crew had to keep busting ice off the rigging and the seas were

Taken from aft looking forward, this photo shows the damage done to the Esso Baton Rouge *when she was torpedoed the first time.* U.S. Navy Armed Guard WW II Veterans.

very high. It was rumored we had only four Canadian Corvettes as escort. This was entirely possible because I only saw one of them briefly from between the waves.

We arrived Belfast, Ireland and what a beautiful sight; beautiful green grass separated by wood fences and very small fields. Then we went to Swansea, Wales, where we unloaded and then formed a convoy to sail to Curaçao off the coast of Venezuela. We finally reached beautiful weather about 400 miles southwest of the Azores and then everything broke loose on February 23, 1943. We were under attack by wolf pack and numerous ships were sunk and damaged.

I was off watch lying on an Army cot on the starboard side of the bridge when, for lack of a better word, the BLAMS started. The ship right ahead of us got hit, we started around it and we took a hit on the starboard side from the *U-202* just under the No. 5 20mm gun tub which was my buddy S1c Gilbert Esham's station. Norman Gabrielsen on No. 3 saw him enveloped in flames and he was no more.

General quarters had rung when the ship ahead got hit, and I ran toward my gun station as trainer on the 3-inch 50 on the bow. I reached the ladder, climbed up and just when I was about to swing my leg over into the tub it hit us dumping me off-balance and I tumbled, I think, into the gun tub. The ship shook violently and I do remember coming out of it sitting on my butt trying to see why my right knee was hurting so bad. It was knocked to the outside a little and I tried to bang it back into place, but to no avail. Then I stood up and it popped back into place and it hurt an awful lot. As the ship was listing to starboard already, I remember Gun Captain Zelewski trying to talk to the bridge to see if we could abandon ship. No luck.

I looked toward the rear, all was afire and the stack was falling away amidst the smoke and flames. We all managed to get back to the bridge hanging onto chains alongside the catwalk. Here there was a lifeboat but I didn't ever want to get into water, and at this time I was confused to say the least. I did manage to let myself down the rope ladder but fell the last few feet banging my knee again. After we all got into a lifeboat it was really full and some joker reported that land was only three miles away.

Everyone fell for it. Then we started rowing and this guy just stood there pointing with his thumb straight down and we almost threw him out of the boat. Not funny!

Then a shape appeared in the water and I remembered it was about dusk about this time but we couldn't distinguish for sure what it was. The officer in charge told us to, "Shut up and don't make a sound!" Well, I had it figured out that I wasn't going into the water and if I had to die I was going to die in the DAMN BOAT. It turned out to be the HMS *Totland*, at one time the Coast Guard cutter *Cayuga*. F.D.R. gave ten of these cutters to England before our part of the war and this was one of them. They had already picked up many survivors. I made it to the top of the rail, and a British sailor grabbed me as I was about to tumble back into lifeboat. He asked, "Had a bad night, Yank?" I don't remember my reply and then we were all gathered into a room. All of a sudden it became so very quiet. We heard three torpedoes go by, two alongside, one underneath and I may add when you've got about three seconds to live there isn't any time for life review.

We did have sweet revenge as the *Totland* sank a sub (confirmed) a day or two later. We then proceeded on to Curaçao, where we got some food and rest. The wounded were put on a plane heading to San Juan. We then went on a seaplane with the blisters on the side. I think it was a Catalina flying boat and I spent all my time near a hole in the rear as I was airsick for sure.

We arrived in Miami and they took us immediately into a basement of this huge hotel and told us not to speak to anyone. Here there were a few very good looking females in swimsuits. I am sure every one of us broke those silly rules right away. Then a Red Cross lady with those famous small green bags containing a razor, soap, washrag and towel came up and gave us each one. They asked for three dollars each and needless to say every one of those bags ended up on the floor. I suspect they're still there.

We flew into New York City in a drafty old clunker with seats alongside each other. We had been issued only white uniforms and very light denim jackets from the Navy. We arrived in Philadelphia cold, miserable, etc. When the door opened there stood a Salvation Army Lady with hot coffee and donuts. We told her that we didn't have any money. She said with a tear or two we could never take your money. I tell you I don't think I will ever have a cup of coffee and donuts that will ever taste that good! God bless them! We finally reached New York City and I went home on survivors leave …[11]

The SS Esso Baton Rouge*'s "complement was forty-three crew members and twenty-five Navy Armed Guard. Of this number, two crew members (1st Engineer Joseph M. Cooper and F/W Howard Landis) were killed in the engine room, one Navy man (S1c Gilbert C. Esham) was lost, and four men were seriously burned from flaming oil. The* U-202 *(Posner) was sunk on June 2, 1943 South of Greenland with 24 lost and 30 captured."*[12]

"One of the merchant crew, Galleyman Russell O. Wirtz, bravely assisted a Navy Armed Guard and others, and received the Merchant Marine Distinguished Service Medal."[13]

~~~

This is a continuation of James Gailey's experiences as an Armed Guard.

Ice Fields and Fog

After a couple of days of getting checked over and paid, we received our leave and delayed orders to New Orleans with fifteen days to get there. Gas was scarce during my stay at home and I caught a train to NOLA (New Orleans, Louisiana) where my records were kept. At least, I was still going south and to warmer climate. I took the exam for coxswain and passed.

They were looking for coxswains to sign up for "Lighter than Air" service. This was duty on blimps that searched for subs. Training was at Lakehurst, New Jersey, but I was turned down due to damaged eardrums from gun blasts, so I could not stand high altitudes. I stayed at New Orleans a couple weeks as I waited to catch my ship. The weather was nice and we'd go out to Lake Pontchartrain where there was an amusement park and we had good duty and got to see all of the sights.

When I was assigned to another ship, we had a crew just out of "boots," except for another coxswain. We had to catch a train to Mobile, Alabama where we went aboard the SS *Mormacrey*
~~~

owned by the Moore-McCormack Lines. It was a nice ship with a 3-inch 50 on the bow, 5-inch 38 on the stern and four 20mm on the bridge. We soon caught a convoy to New York but we were loaded in Hoboken, New Jersey. I met a nice girl there and wrote her until the end of the war. We took on more war materials; tanks, trucks, our ammo and food. We caught a large convoy and sailed up the coast near Boston where other ships joined us. Others joined us off Newfoundland; Labrador and Greenland and then it was on to Belfast, Ireland and Liverpool, England.

It was early spring of 1943 and we encountered heavy fog. You could not see midships from back aft much less the ships in the convoy. We pulled a paravane attached to a long cable in the water trailing astern which caught the water and would shoot a spout high in the air for the men on watch on the bow of the ship astern to see.* Ships were blowing their foghorns all the time and we slowed to a lower speed. Then, the waters started to get really rough and the ship's propeller would come out of the water and would vibrate the ship terribly. You learned to get your sleep holding on to your bunk railing to keep from being thrown out. We slept in our clothes and to get to chow hall amidships, you would have to go down a deep shaft back aft and walk along the propeller shaft, to the engine room, always afraid of being caught down there in that place, in case of an enemy attack. Now you know how merchant seamen must have felt in the engine room and as they kept the shaft oiled and ship going. A heavy line had been strung from the aft quarters to amidships, but the danger of being swept overboard was extremely high so we chanced the shaft. The ships in the convoy were running a zigzag course every seven minutes. We were lucky that we did not ram each other. One good thing was that the subs couldn't see us either, so they couldn't attack.

When we ran out of the fog, we ran into an iceberg field. They were so thick; you could almost walk from one to another. The ship could not dodge them all and you could hear them rubbing on the side of the ship and you had to go real slow to keep from knocking a hole in the side of the ship. We did not have to

* This device was commonly referred to as a fog buoy.

worry about subs here either for they couldn't run in these waters either. Soon, we were out of the icebergs and the wolf pack was waiting and they attacked. One submarine got in among the rows of ships and sank two ships. This was not near us but the escort ships were running up and down the convoy trying to locate the subs. We sailed on as the escorts stayed back, dropping depth charges for a couple of hours and were also searching for and picking up survivors. They would then catch back up with us. Two days before reaching the British Isles, the ships put up their barrage balloons in casc of an aerial attack. The balloons were attached to the ship with a very long steel cable in hopes to keep the enemy aircraft high enough to miss their target and also to give the gun crew a better shot at the planes. (They were soon discontinued, because the planes would shoot down the barrage balloons, fouling up the ship's propeller). Some ships left the convoy and sailed for Iceland while some went to Great Britain. We went to Belfast, Ireland to unload. It had taken over two weeks to get there.

Belfast was a pretty place and everything was so green and people were very nice and friendly. I only got to go to town one time as we stayed just one day. The horses looked like Budweiser horses and reminded you of home. Liverpool, England was our next port-of-call which was a larger town and was nice but they had suffered a lot of war damage. The British people suffered a lot and had it real tough during this time. I really felt sorry for them. They did not have any luxuries such as cosmetics, stockings for the ladies, no sweets, and many were without decent shelter as many of their homes had been "blown" to bits from the German air raids. We went home with some of the girls and they made coffee, but had no sugar or cream. We hated to drink their coffee as we knew they couldn't afford but they insisted. They were real nice girls. We could not be in town at night as that was when they would have their aerial raids but there was not one while we there. It didn't get dark till after 10 PM and then we would be back at the ship.

We unloaded and as they did not have cargo to ship back to the states, we took on sand as ballast. We joined our convoy and headed towards Iceland where we picked up more ships. Then we headed back to the ice fields and the fog, for protection, and it took us about two weeks to return to New York. The crew of the SS *Mormacrey* and the ship will be one of my fondest memories. How lucky we had been to survive! We were taken off and replaced by another crew. We wish we could have stayed on, for she was loading to go to Brazil.[14]

~~~

Alvin T. Kemble, Jr., submitted this harrowing story of survival.

Thirty-four Days

I was a seaman, first-class, in the United States Navy for three years during World War II from 1942 until 1945. I enlisted in the Navy in October 1942 and was sent to Bainbridge, Maryland for my basic training. After only being in basic for about three weeks, we trainees were asked to volunteer for service in the Armed Guard. Naturally, we asked what the Armed Guard would entail, and we were told that we would find out what we needed to know after we got there. If we volunteered, we were told that we would go home for eight days first. So, I volunteered.

Upon returning from my eight-day leave, I was sent to Little Creek, Virginia for gunnery school. Here, we were trained in the maintenance and proper use of shipboard guns that we would be using later. Upon mastering the training, I was then sent to the Armed Guard Center in Brooklyn, New York. I was only there a very short time until we were transferred to a shipyard in Baltimore, Maryland, where we were to pick up a new Liberty ship (SS *James W. Denver*) and prepare it to get underway. We sailed the ship to New York where we were to pick up 10,000 tons of general cargo for the armed forces.

On April 1, 1943, we sailed out of New York to meet up with a convoy that was headed to Casablanca and North Africa. But as we got underway, and the fog closed in around us and we were not able to locate the other ships of the convoy. Our captain decided that we would continue on our own without the company of the convoy. We were only a few days out of port when a bearing
~~~

in our line shaft broke and we lay dead in the water for what seemed to be a long period of time. Eventually, repairs were made and we were back under power again.

However, on April 11, 1943, while lying in my bunk, our ship was hit by two torpedoes at about 1700 hours. The Liberty ship rolled onto its starboard side while the alarms sounded for general quarters. It wasn't long until the command to abandon ship was given. I jumped off the fantail and floated in the water for some time. My life jacket had a little red light attached to it. After floating for a while, I heard someone call out and a lifeboat appeared out of the mist and I was pulled out of the water.

There were five lifeboats full of survivors, so we decided to try to keep them altogether. But a storm developed during the night and by daylight we discovered that our boat was left alone. Our boat had eighteen men aboard and we realized that we needed to ration our supplies. However, when we checked those supplies we found that there was no food included and limited amounts of fresh water. We limited the amount of water per man to just three ounces in the morning and again at night.

During our first whole day in the lifeboat the weather was rainy, windy and cold, so we spent the entire time soaked to the skin. During the second day, all our efforts were focused on looking for passing rescue vessels. On the third day, as evening was approaching, someone said that a ship was nearing us. It nearly ran over us, and our lifeboat ended up on the wash of the stern of a submarine as it passed by. It had to be the German sub that sank us only three days before.

The captain of the sub emerged to talk to us survivors. He told us that we had sailed out of New York where the big ballplayers lived, and he wanted to know what cargo we were carrying. He also asked if we needed any medical attention. He then told us to sail 300 miles due east and that we should come to the African coast. There we would be spotted by shipping and should be rescued. The German captain then wished us "God be with you," and submerged and sailed off leaving us alone.

For the next several days we suffered severe storms. The seas were running exceptionally high with huge troughs and crests. Each wave would practically fill the lifeboat with seawater and we bailed constantly. But if it wasn't storming, then the weather and sea was dead calm. There would be no breeze and the sun was relentless. To pass the time and take your mind off the conditions we would talk about the food your mom would make at home, like the best pies that she would bake. Even with the searing heat each man still only received six ounces of water per day. For food, we tried to capture live fish but we weren't very successful.

After about three weeks in a lifeboat, one of the guys yelled at a large boat approaching which appeared to be the *Queen Mary*. It passed close enough to us that we could see men walking about on her decks. We shot a flare from my rescue pistol, but the ship never altered its course and left us all alone again. We knew that she couldn't stop to pick us up but we all hoped that she would radio our location to someone who could. But after a few days we realized that wasn't going to happen either.

Day after day, we continued to just sit in the boat. It was too crowded to even lie down. We were sitting up constantly and getting weaker by day. We drifted into a pod of whales and we were afraid that they would capsize the boat and we knew that we were too weak to get ourselves or others back into the boat again.

Going into the fourth week of our ordeal we were sitting as usual, when out of the blue, two flying fish landed in the boat. We divided the fish into eighteen pieces and we finally had something to eat for the first time. A few nights later, a slight breeze came up and one of the men, who was from the western part of the U.S., asked if anyone felt a stinging sensation on their skin. He said it felt just like the sandstorms that he was used to back home. The next morning, everything in the boat was covered by sand. We got excited thinking that maybe there was land close by. But our eyes were getting weaker, and we couldn't see any sign of rescue.

On a thirty-fourth day one of the guys thought he saw a little boat out on the horizon but none of us could see it and we said that it was probably just a mirage. But eventually others of us saw it too and we realized that it was a small sailboat of some sort. It approached us and sailed around us briefly. But it would not come near us and it turned and sailed off, leaving us all badly depressed.

It was gone only a short while when a bigger boat sailed up and the occupants called to us in Spanish. Luckily, we had a sailor aboard from Puerto Rico and he answered them in their native tongue. They came alongside and we saw that it was a 75 ft. fishing boat out of Los Palmos of the Canary Islands. They took us to a Spanish fort on the edge of the Sahara desert where we rested for four days. A supply boat came and picked us up and took us to the Canary Islands. During our seven days there, we could shower for the first time since the sinking and we were provided with fresh clothes.

Then we were shipped to Cadiz, Spain, where we rested for about three days. We were told that we must be ready to ship out at any time. We were loaded onto a truck and were being taken to the Rock of Gibraltar, but on the way one of the survivors was struck in the head by a tree branch and seriously injured. We worked hard to keep him alive but it took a whole day to reach the Rock by truck. Unfortunately, he died three days later and we buried him in the Strait of Gibraltar.

While in Gibraltar, we were debriefed by the US Naval intelligence where we were shown pictures of German subs so that we could identify the one who sunk us. To my surprise, on the way up the steps to the debriefing, I was approached by a mass of large monkey-like primates which seemed to have the run of the place. Not knowing what to do, I retreated and tried to find another way into the building. Upon being delayed for my meeting, I apologized for my lateness and explained the monkeys. I was told that local superstition believed that if the monkeys ever leave the Rock, the British will lose the Rock as well.

So eventually I was aboard the USS *Lakehurst* and heading back to the good old U.S.A. I would be granted a short leave for R&R and then back to the war. I would make a couple of trips across the Atlantic to Normandy and also a trip to Okinawa, Japan before I returned to New York. I was then told that the war was about over, and that I had too many points to go back to sea. I finished up stateside until my discharge from the Navy in October 11, 1945.[15]

Alvin Kemble, Jr,. U.S. Navy Armed Guard WW II Veterans.

The submarine was the U-195 *(Buchholz). The five lifeboats were either picked up or landed on April 18 with eleven survivors, April 24 with fifteen survivors, May 4 with ten survivors, May 6 with fourteen survivors (including the captain), May 16 with nineteen survivors (including Alvin Kemble). Miraculously, only two men perished in this horrendous ordeal.*[16] *Kptlt. Heinz Buchholz met his fate on 6 Feb. 1944 as his U-boat* U-177 *was sunk in the South Atlantic.*[17] U-195 *survived the war to only to be turned over to the Japanese becoming* I-506. *She was surrendered and finally broken up in 1947.*[18]

~~~

Joseph McKenna, Jr., is co-chairman, along with James Pellegrino, of the Long Island, New York Chapter of the U.S. Navy Armed Guard Veterans. They have a large group and this author has had the fortunate experience to speak before them on three occasions. Joe has worked tirelessly to get his men to submit their stories for this anthology. I am deeply grateful for his assistance. His World War II buddy, who has since passed away, was also deeply grateful for Joe's assistance.

"Thank God for Joe McKenna …"

I enlisted in the Navy in October 1942. My "boot" training was at Sampson, New York. I then volunteered for the Armed Guard. U-boats were not the only danger to merchant ships, but we had to contend with mines, aircraft, surface warships, and armed raiders. They all had to be combated. We slept fully clothed with our life vests close by. The nights were not a happy time for us, for it was then that danger was more likely to strike!

My first ship was the tanker SS *Panam* off the North Carolina coast. On May 4, 1943 we were torpedoed and sunk in fifteen
~~~

minutes. I was on watch and saw the torpedo coming toward us. My Lieutenant, Arley Zinn came up to the bridge for a roll call and he said, "Let's go back to the gun deck." When we got there, he noticed that S1/c Earl Mayle was missing. He knew that we were buddies and he said, "Go find Earl!"

I quickly went to our quarters and found that the door was jammed. I started kicking in the door panel on the bottom. After quickly breaking through the panel I had to crawl through the water on my hands and knees to get to Earl. The top bunk had fallen on top of him and he couldn't move. So, with all of my 132 lbs., I put my shoulders under the bunk and somehow with the help of God, I lifted the bunk off Earl. I then dragged him out to the gun deck and my shipmates started to clap.

Just then another torpedo hit and we started to go down fast. This is when I was injured by shells to my right leg and knee. I helped Earl to the only lifeboat and somehow we lowered the lifeboat to the water and we rowed away from the suction of the ship. After we got away from the ship we were picked up some six hours later by the U. S. Coast Guard cutter USS *SC664*.

"On May 4th at 0100 the Panam *developed engine trouble causing her to become a straggler from the convoy thereby allowing the* U-129 *the chance to attack.*

"At 0825, a torpedo struck on the port side in the engine room completely wrecking it and demolishing the engines. Flooding in that area became simultaneous. About 8 to 10 minutes later another torpedo struck on the port side amidships, wrecking the pump room. The Panam *sunk at 0855 EWT on May 4, 1943... The Master ordered abandon ship following the 2nd torpedo. Three boats were launched. Some crew members jumped overboard and were picked up by the boats. 49 survivors were rescued... Two crew members were killed when the torpedo struck in the engine room..."*[19]

Joe McKenna continues:

After fifty-six years I finally located Earl Mayle and his wife Shirley. She said he had passed away in October of 1993. She told me that all he ever spoke about was my saving his life. He would say, "Thank God for Joe McKenna. If it wasn't for him I wouldn't be here!"

I risked my life to save my shipmate Earle Mayle and I feel I should have been acknowledged for heroism and beyond the call of duty. My Lieutenant, Arley Zinn put me in for an award while at N.O.B. base in Norfolk, Virginia. He said that, "I risked my life facing certain death to save my shipmate." It seems no one followed up on it.[20]

Joe has written his Congressman to this effect.

~~~

The following letter (based on the original submission) was submitted by William Hicks, Jr. His letter was published in the 2002 January-March Pointer, *but Bill's name was incorrectly listed as William H. Howard. This letter contains what he originally submitted. He is still trying to get more information concerning the attack.*

Dear Chairman Lloyd:

I note with interest on Page 2, Jan. 2002 *Pointer* that no mention is made of an Armed Guard – Merchant Seaman having destroyed a submarine. In early 1943, I was assigned as a deck cadet to an old Hog Island freighter, the S.S. *Del Mar.* I made two voyages; one in February 1943 was from New York to Casablanca and back. We encountered several sub attacks en route and a hurricane on the return trip. Our gun crews were busy and I served as a 20mm loader for the port station on the fantail.

The second trip, May 6, 1943 was to Liverpool, England with many sub attacks and an Armed Guardsman named Jaworski and I manned the 20mm. One evening, we were under attack and during the battle, the conning tower of a sub appeared on our port side. Perhaps it was brought up by the depth charges dropped by our escorts. The gun crew from a ship on our port side began firing and thank God for tracers. Jaworski and I hit the deck of the gun mount and watched the tracers over us. Then the gun captain of the five-inch gun aft yelled for ammo passers. We jumped from the gun mount and passed ammo for what was the last of the sub. There were no further sightings. We returned to Boston with the traditional
~~~

broom at the masthead designating a "clean sweep." This should have been noted in the ship's log and the report from the Armed Guard Gunnery Officer. I believe his name was Fred Jung, USNR... Sometime ago I was the guest speaker at Wayte Huffer's Armed Guard – Merchant Marine group in Richmond, Virginia, and I made two points: The first was that we hoped the sub we sank was "one of theirs." The other was that my bride, Mabel Claire Billings saved my life. Had I not departed from the *Benjamin Bourn* when I did in September 1946, I would have been aboard when she struck a mine at Leghorn, Italy the next trip. I wish I could confirm the facts about the S.S. *Del Mar* gun crew. My fellow cadet in the engine room was Christian Nelson but I have no idea of his whereabouts. It is my earnest prayer that the action of that evening be confirmed. Being seventy-eight years of age now I wish I had kept better records.

I thank C.A. Lloyd and all involved in the groups for their work and devotion to causes, and pray God will bless them in their retirements...

William H. Hicks
Chief Mate, U.S. Merchant Marine
Lt (jg) USNR Retired[21]

~~~

Bob Norling was a Signalman 3/c on the SS Gold Heels *from February 1, 1943 to August 13, 1943 and the SS* Abner Nash *from August 31, 1943 to June 15, 1944.*

The Captain's Dead

Captain Jensen was a crusty old Dane. He wasn't easy to make friends with, even after I made it a point to tell him my father also was from Denmark. To him, I was just the signalman, one of the Armed Guard crew assigned in early 1943 to his tanker, the *Gold Heels*.

She was named for a one-time speedy racehorse. But her best speed when I was aboard never exceeded 8 knots, unless she had following seas and favorable currents. She logged 10.9 in sea trials after she was built in 1921 as the Italian Navy oiler *Brennero*.
~~~

In March 1941 she was in New York, the wrong place at the wrong time as American relations with Mussolini went from bad to worse. So the U.S. government placed her in "protective custody."

After Pearl Harbor she was made a prize-of-war, given to the War Shipping Administration, renamed *Gold Heels* and operated by Keystone Shipping Co. of Philadelphia. She didn't come close to looking like a tanker, with stack and engine room midships, plus torpedo blisters the Italians called Pugliesi bulges *(submarine blisters)*.

Captain Jensen had a sense of humor, but kept it masked behind the seriousness of his command. It came out once in a while; especially when our gunnery officer decided to study navigation and once plotted our position as just west of Cleveland — as we were sailing across the Gulf of Mexico from Key West to load in Galveston.

Gold Heels wasn't a spit-and-polish ship and by March 1943 was infested with cockroaches and rats. After a run from Galveston to Norfolk with a load of Navy Bunker C oil, it was decided to fumigate the ship with cyanide gas while at anchor in Hampton Roads.

One morning everyone, merchant crew and Navy, was taken ashore to NOB Norfolk and told to remain off the ship for thirty-two hours, after which *Gold Heels* would be gas free. We returned to the ship the following afternoon at eight bells and resumed our duties.

Everything was fine until the next morning when, about 6 o'clock, the second mate woke me and said, "Flags. The captain's dead. Lower the flag to half-staff." A pocket of gas had formed over Capt. Jensen's berth. He turned in, and that was it.

The navy investigated, we missed two convoys and Keystone Shipping promoted the first mate to command of the *Gold Heels*. The first thing he did was bring his pet cocker spaniel aboard. That resulted in hazardous night watches topside as both wings of the bridge became slippery and smelly.

Capt. Jensen didn't live to see *Gold Heels* become the USS *Carondelet* about a year later for service as a Navy station tanker in New Guinea and the Philippines. And I failed to spot her when a Liberty ship I sailed on in 1944 had business at Milne Bay, where the old *Gold Heels* performed her naval duties.[22]

Action in the North Atlantic

Not the movie — just the story of the most personal hygiene-conscious Armed Guard gunner I ever sailed with.

His innovative way of performing a necessary bodily function provided rousing entertainment for his shipmates aboard the Liberty ship *Abner Nash*, and also for sharp-eyed lookouts on nearby ships in convoy with us.

For this story, his name will be Paul Johnson. The two Armed Guard gunners whose contamination pushed Paul over the edge, you might say, will remain nameless.

It so happened that the two guys had picked up goodly cases of what we sometimes called mechanized dandruff or, more commonly, crabs. Their condition was the result of messing around with the wrong girls in Liverpool in that fall of 1943.

The problem came to light after the ship sailed November 6 and joined a convoy homeward-bound for New York. Paul bunked aft in the deckhouse below the five-inch 38 gun platform, sharing the same head with the two gunners and a number of other Armed Guard crewmen.

Poor Paul was frantic. He didn't want to go forward in rough seas or on cold wintry nights. And he surely didn't want to take any chances in the head the two gunners used. For him, there was but one solution, and he told no one of his plan.

The North Atlantic, most will agree, is a pretty rough place in November, and was living up to its reputation the next morning. A gunner on bridge watch looked aft and gave a gleeful shout. Everyone who heard him looked in the same direction. And what they saw probably was a major moment in Armed Guard history.

There was Paul, pants down, hanging onto the stern rail and leaning outward in a sling-like harness, doing his business in a grand display of daring. For Paul, it mattered not if the stern shot upward or dipped deep in a trough as the *Abner Nash* pitched into the seas.

This went on for several days, and in extremely rough seas he damned near got a free wash on numerous occasions. On signal watch I could see guys on nearby ships also enjoying the show.

When the two gunners got rid of their infestations, Paul came back inside.

He was a brave, determined sailor. He took everything the wild North Atlantic threw at him.

And he gave something back in return every time he hooked himself up to his perch back there over the roaring seas.[23]

~~~

The following poem was written by Joseph V. Wagner and the twenty-five man Armed Guard crew of the SS Abraham Baldwin *in 1943.*

The Cruise of the *Abraham Baldwin*
Or
Twenty Ways Not To Cross The Atlantic

Listen, Sailors, and you shall hear
A tale that is very long and drear,
An account of a voyage that broke men's hearts,
A tale of woe from the Northern parts.

The men who designed this type of ship
Figured to cut the percentage of slip,
But they never figured the screw would keep dry
As it missed the sea, and spun in the sky.

We left Boston on a late summer's day
And headed north where the submarines play.
The wolf pack struck, and the wind did howl,
The seas were high, nasty and foul.

They rolled 'cross the boat deck, and down the galley stack,
The side door was lifted, and tore off with a crack.
~~~

The bulwarks split as she pitched and tossed;
The lifeboats broke loose and they were lost.

For sixteen days she rolled and pitched
While the crew below swore and bitched,
'Til the Irish Sea some relief did give,
And we thought once more we would live.

We took over Union Street, invaded her pubs,
And after hours we sought the clubs.
We took all their women — took all their drinks
And left with their curses, sailed with their jinx.

They told us the weather was going to be bad;
They sent us to sea, we were driving them mad;
They gave us no ballast and took all our oil
And sent us to act as submarine foil.

We headed north and gave her full steam
'Til we broke her back where the Northern Lights gleam.
The bow did pitch while the stern lay still;
She was hinged like a door on a windy hill.

Put the sea on her quarter to ease her shell
And headed for St. John's – straight into Hell.
Ran up a lee-shore, wind one hundred and ten
And prayed to God to please say when.

Both anchors down, full steam ahead;
Eighteen fathoms was read by the lead.
That the anchors would hold we all did pray,
For the Navy's a million miles away.

But we rode her out and took her in,
And they patched her sides that were so thin,
And said, "At Torpedo Junction you have a date,
So put to sea, or you'll be late."

We joined a convoy which was very slow,
And creeping westward we did go.
From here on out all was smooth sailing –
Except for that now I am wailing.

"Winches, Capstans, Pumps that fail,
Icebergs, Ice-Fields, Growlers and Gales,
Convoy Collisions, Depth Charges and Fogs,
For downright misery we sure are hogs.

"Fuel oil is low, and the grub's about out;
The crew from their quarters are beginning to shout;
Some have the scurvy, and some have the itch;
We doubt if we live to fill out this hitch.

When off our bow 'The Lady' does stand,
(The one with the torch held high in her hand),
At us she may look as we're inward bound –
If she sees us again, she'll have to turn 'round.[24]

The SS Abraham Baldwin *survived the war and was scuttled as an artificial fish reef off Horn Island, Mississippi on April 30, 1976.*[25] *This is a National Park area known as the Gulf Island National Seashore and is a wildlife preserve.*

7

Northern Russia

The most difficult and hazardous duty encountered by the Armed Guard in World War II was aboard ships traveling to Murmansk and Archangel, Russia. This route was shorter than going through the Persian Gulf, the only other route available to supply Russia, but was far more treacherous for several reasons.

First, the "Hellish" winter weather — ships sailed across the Barents Sea through snowstorms and gales while on constant watch for icebergs and German mines; second, the almost constant darkness, and, third, Hitler was determined to control the waters leading to these ports.

> … during the spring of 1942 the situation profoundly changed. The Germans, having failed to conquer Russia at the first dash, realized how important were Anglo-American supplies in stiffening Russian resistance, and they determined to do what they could do to stop

them. A flotilla of submarines was sent north and soon rose to a strength of twenty. More aircraft was sent to northern Norway, particularly long range dive bombers and torpedo aircraft...[1]

For the merchant convoy, the situation was nerve-wracking:

For eight days and nights, the Focke-Wulf Condors have been circling the convoy, hovering in the horizon clouds tantalizingly beyond gunshot. Their mission is reconnaissance, and they have the patience of vultures waiting for the kill. Sooner or later, attack planes are bound to show up, but no one knows when. The men who man the guns on the merchant vessels can do nothing but stand by and wait, taking turns on lookout, while their ships plough deeper into the Barents Sea.

On the ninth day, when nerves are frayed to the snapping point, new signal hoists flutter up on the Commodore's halyards. The time for action has come. This is it! ...[2]

Being within range of the Luftwaffe, Russian harbors were constantly attacked while ships were being discharged.

American ships were almost constantly in North Russian waters either en route, in harbor, or on the return to the United States. They were under almost daily attack .... The Navy made every effort to give ships for Murmansk the best possible armament and large quantities of ammunition. These efforts began to pay off as expert Armed Guard crews gained experience in gunnery.

While some of the early crews went to Russia with improper winter clothing, every effort was made to remedy the situation in 1942. The advice of Admiral Bird's expert on winter clothing was sought on the best available clothing for the North Russian climate and before 1942 ended these crews were being furnished with the best and most complete sets of winter clothing which could be obtained.[3]

By the end of the war the U.S. Navy Armed Guard had protected approximately forty convoys that delivered goods to Russia. These ships "…. carried more than 22,000 aircraft, 375,000 trucks, 8,700 tractors, 51,500 jeeps, 1,900 locomotives, 343,700 tons of explosives, a million miles of field-telephone cable, plus

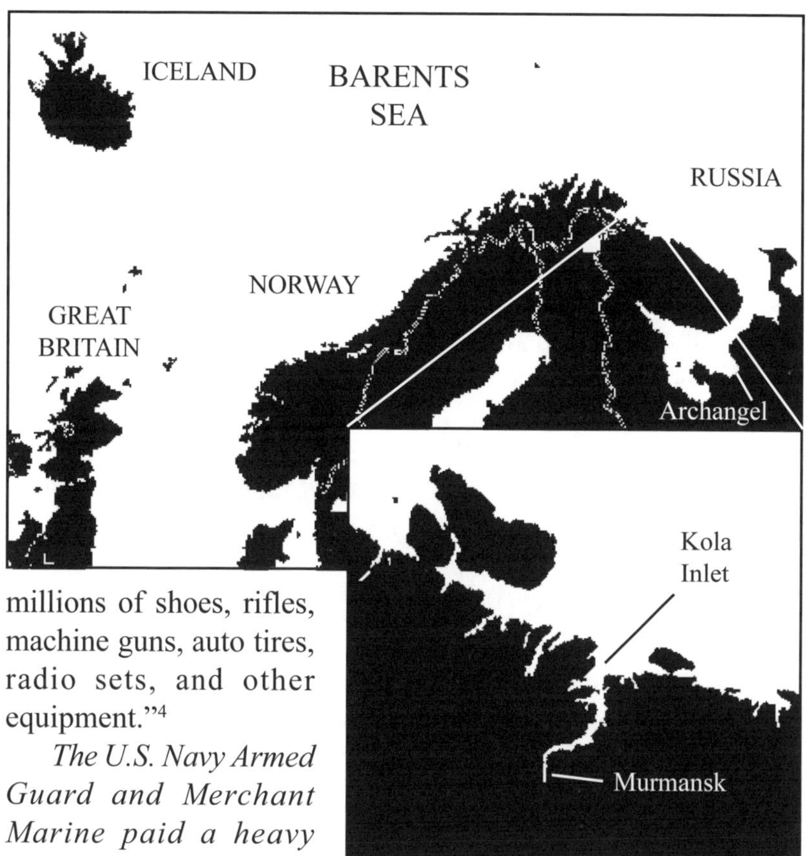

millions of shoes, rifles, machine guns, auto tires, radio sets, and other equipment."[4]

The U.S. Navy Armed Guard and Merchant Marine paid a heavy price to get the goods to Russia. The total of ships sunk or damaged on the Murmansk Run was "83 ships, 458 merchant seamen and 139 Naval Armed Guard were killed. In 1942 alone, 63 ships were in this category."[5]

~~~

Charles J. Hayes, radioman 2/c, never forgot his Murmansk experiences. Two ships went down under him.

Murmansk Experiences
Part 1 – S.S. *Alamar*

The SS *Alamar* was a member of Convoy PQ-16 to Murmansk in May 1942. *Alamar* left Philadelphia in March with stops in New York and Halifax en route to Iceland.
~~~

We stayed at anchor in Reykjavik harbor for about two weeks until a convoy was formed and left for Murmansk in late May, evidently waiting for the ice floes to break up before proceeding to Murmansk.

Early on, the seas were calm with dense fog and poor visibility. Some ships came so close it was possible to have a conversation with their crew. Ice floes were constantly banging against the ships' sides. When the fog cleared, ships were scattered out of position and destroyers and corvette's escorted merchantmen back to their positions and the convoy was reformed.

There was no enemy contact for the first week and we enjoyed bright sunlight — although very cold. The Arctic in May has twenty-four hours of daylight and "nighttime" is a sort of gray haze, but still with good visibility.

One bright day a plane showed up and circled the convoy out of range of our guns. (Which in the *Alamar*, consisted of .30 caliber and .50 caliber machine guns). Once in a while, an escort vessel would leave the convoy and head in the direction of the plane, which would just fly off and no shots were fired. We were told by the older merchant marine crew that the plane was taking pictures of the convoy and would return to German bases in Norway where the pictures would be studied and ships could be targeted according to the importance of their visible cargo. Each ship had supplies and equipment lashed on deck. Some had tanks or trucks or dismantled planes, etc. The *Alamar* had hundreds of 55-gallon drums of hi-test aviation gasoline topside. A wooden walkway provided access from bow to stern.

One day, a flight of planes showed up and started what would be a constant harassment of the convoy. The Luftwaffe used the

The Alamar *was built in San Francisco in 1916 and was operated by Calmar Steamship Co.* Mariners Museum.

continuous daylight to their advantage and came in at all hours of the day. One result of this constant air-raid was no chance of the Armed Guard getting any sleep, other than a quick nap at their gun station in the interval between raids. Food consisted of sandwiches and coffee eaten at your battle station.

Once in a while, a squall would come up with blowing snow and poor visibility. This gave a respite from the planes. But the U-boats were always prowling around and the escorts were dropping depth charges both during and between raids.

As I remember, it was May 26 when we saw the first ship go down. (*According to Captain Moore, SS* Syros *was torpedoed by* U-703 *(Biefeld). "...she sank within one minute. The ship sank so fast it was impossible to launch any boats."...*[6] There was a tremendous explosion and she went down in what seemed like seconds. There were no planes at the time, so we figured a sub took her down.

May 27, 1942 was the day I guess the Germans picked to wipe out the convoy. They came in waves overhead. Stuka dive-bombers joined the heavy bombers in the attack. We were closer to Norway and were now in range of the lighter Stukas.

I was a radioman third class at this time. However, there was nothing for me to do. The *Alamar* already had a radio operator and there was just no sense to having both of us sitting in the radio shack monitoring the frequency for messages. (Transmissions were not allowed, as subs could zero in on the radio signals.)

So, I became a volunteer loader on one of our .50 caliber machine guns. I teamed up with a young gunner's mate I'll call "Georgia" because that is where he hailed from. We had practiced in the quiet times before the planes came and we got to be a pretty good team. (I should mention that this early in the war — spring of 42 — there were not enough weapons. *Alamar* had 30s and 50s and not enough men. There were six Armed Guard enlisted and one ensign aboard.) So there was no formality — everyone pitched in wherever needed, especially during any air aids. It was not unusual to see a merchant sailor manning a .30 caliber machine gun, for instance.

Georgia was an excellent gunner and very well-trained. We didn't actually knock down any planes, but did manage to turn them off several times in their approach to our ship. But on this particular day — May 27, 1942 — they came in such numbers it was impossible to keep your eyes on them all. The Stuka dive-bombers used the bright sun to their advantage. They came down from the sun and we usually couldn't see them, but fired at the sound they made in their dive. (Stukas made a piercing, screaming sound when they dived to drop their bombs and it could really unnerve you.)

Our gun station was located amidships on the starboard side. There were ships on either side of us in the convoy and bombs were dropping between the ships. The noise was deafening between the planes, the bombs dropping and the antiaircraft guns firing from the ships.

While we were firing up at the Stuka coming in overhead, I bent down to get another load to keep feeding the gun. I looked back over my shoulder and saw a German JU-88 bomber approaching us from starboard aft. I pounded on Georgia's shoulder and hollered at him. He swung the gun around to meet the plane, but it was too late.

We didn't hear the bombs coming down, but there was a tremendous explosion. The noise was unbelievable. The *Alamar* leaned way over to starboard. The sea came up into the gun tub and both Georgia and I were picked up and carried over the side when the ship came back up and the wave of water went back down to the sea. I remember falling through what felt like a waterfall and then hitting solid water and going down like a rock below the surface.

I came back up into the sunlight and there was Georgia a few feet away, hollering at the top of his voice. I looked back and saw the *Alamar*, still afloat and listing to starboard. There was a lot of smoke coming from her deck and we could see the crew letting down the boats. Georgia was trying to let them know we were still around, but we were so far away I didn't think they could see or hear us.

The next time I looked, the *Alamar* was gone. As far as we could see, there was nothing but water. The ships and planes were all gone and it was just two of us bobbing around in the ocean. We looked at each other and kind of nodded our heads. We were sure that this was as far as we would go.

I don't know how long we were in the water. The cold Arctic water has the effect of putting you to sleep. I vaguely remember seeing a lifeboat and the face of *Alamar*'s first mate as he pulled me into the boat.

When I came to, I was in a bunk on a British corvette. It was crowded with survivors. All of *Alamar*'s crew, both merchant and Navy had survived. Georgia and I were the only ones who got wet.

The air raids continued for the remainder of May 27 and for several days afterward until Russian planes were able to come out and provide air cover for the convoy. All we could do on the corvette was to try not to get in the way of the ship's crew who were busy at their battle stations.

We finally reached Murmansk, safe and sound on Memorial Day, May 30, 1942.

Part 2 – Murmansk – June 1942

Memories that stand out:

1. Our first meal ashore after three days aboard rescue vessel: Hungry Navy Armed Guard spread globs of "jam" on the slices of black bread. Bread was tasty, but "jam" turned out to be caviar, which tasted like raw fish. Manfully eaten so as not to offend our Russian hosts.

2. Navy survivors were sheltered in a crude wooden barracks located on a hill overlooking Murmansk harbor. This location provided an overall view of the harbor as daily air raids by German planes from bases in Norway dropped bombs on ships, docks and buildings in the city.

Outmoded Russian planes slowly climbed up to meet the modern German Stukas and heavy bombers. Navy Armed Guard sailors watching a parachute floating down and standing and cheering as a Russian flyer is pulled from the water. Later, watching quietly as a slow, stalling outboard motor boat finally reaches downed German pilot. Even though they know he is the enemy who cost them so much, the young Armed Guard men feel relieved as he is finally taken aboard.

3. The Navy survivors were taken on an escorted tour of the city across the harbor. Buildings were demolished, windows broken, roofs caved in and streets in rubble. But, the work went on as ships were unloaded twenty-four hours a day and reloaded onto flat cars for the rail trip to Leningrad and inland Russia. (The Murmansk Railway was the vital link to Leningrad and to the front and remained open throughout the war in spite of repeated German efforts to destroy it.)

The most memorable part of the tour was the visit to the hospital where Allied survivors of Arctic sinkings and Russian soldiers and workers, injured in air raids, were being treated. Seeing the importance of medical supplies and equipment to the overworked staff under threat of constant air raids, made us realize how very important the Murmansk convoys were to the Russian people. The Navy Armed Guard crews were sobered at the sight of so many young men of various nationalities who had suffered loss of their arms or legs due to prolonged exposure in the cold waters of the Arctic; only their good fortune at early rescue saved them from a similar fate.

(Personal note:) The British Corvette that had rescued some of *Alamar*'s crew had provided me with the Royal Navy uniform as my own clothes had been ruined by the oil in the water. When we visited the hospital, a British sailor who had lost both arms and both legs, thinking I was a fellow Britisher kept pleading with me to please come back with a gun and shoot him, as he couldn't face going back home in his tragic condition. He kept up this incessant pleading as long as we remained and finally I had to leave and wait outside for the rest of the party. I was not yet eighteen years and was horrified by the sights in the hospital.

4. Young Navy Armed Guard sailors, standing on deck of aged American vessel, waving to the crew of a huge, modern Russian freighter passing by and realizing with surprise that many of the Russian crew members waving back are women.

5. U.S. Navy Armed Guard sailors voluntarily standing at attention on deck of SS *Massmar* (*The next ship Hayes was assigned to)* and saluting as Royal navy unit in a motor whaleboat

conducts memorial service over their corvette that had been sunk while at anchor close to *Massmar* during the previous day's air raid.

6. The most lasting memory of living ashore in Murmansk in 1942 is the courage of the Russian people who lived in the city. They were under constant attack, lived in primitive conditions, and had no luxuries and small comforts. Yet, they shared their meager rations, provided us with shelter, protected us from enemy aircraft and tried to keep us entertained. Their living conditions were abysmal with shortages of basic needs: food, clothing, etc. But, they never complained and never doubted that they would be victorious eventually. It was a rare experience — a privilege — to have lived amongst them for awhile. We all learned lessons of courage and fortitude and, I'm sure that those of us who have survived have been better men for the experience.

Part III – S.S. *Massmar*

The S.S. *Massmar* was one of the merchant ships to survive German air and sub attacks on convoy PQ-16 and arrived safely at Murmansk on May 30, 1942. Once the *Massmar* was unloaded and assigned anchorage in Murmansk harbor, the ship's crew and Armed Guard crew of the S. S. *Alamar*, all of whom survived the loss of their ship on May 27, 1942, were assigned to S. S. *Massmar* for return voyage to the States, via Iceland.

The return trip was uneventful. The Luftwaffe and U-boats showed no interest in the convoy, which was assigned number QP-13. The ships were all empty of war material and the Germans were probably saving their efforts for loaded Murmansk-bound convoys.

Built in Kobe, Japan in 1920, the Massmar *was operated by Calmar Steamship Co.* SSHSA

En route to Iceland, we met an outbound convoy, PQ-17 headed for Murmansk and as we waved at them as they passed, we could not have known that twenty-three of them would be sunk after their escorts left them on July 4th to chase after the German battleship *Tirpitz*, which was thought to be en route to the convoy. Following this terrible loss, PQ-17 would be the last convoy to Murmansk for several months. Meanwhile, *Massmar* and the rest of the convoy proceeded peacefully on their way to Reykjavik harbor. During the voyage, the *Alamar's* Armed Guard crew was assigned to lookout duty aboard the *Massmar*.

The night of July 5, 1942 was very cold with dark clouds, strong winds and heavy seas. My assignment as lookout was on a hatch cover just forward of the bridge. I felt certain that with the size of the waves, no sub could possibly fire a torpedo with any chance of success, although we took nothing for granted and still kept a sharp watch.

When I was relieved of my watch, I went to my bunk which was just off the main deck. (Of course, at this time and in these waters, we had learned never to be without our lifejacket – eating, sleeping or whatever.)

I had just laid down when there was a horrendous explosion that shook the ship. The noise was louder even than that on the *Alamar* when the bombs hit. I hit the deck and started for the hatch when another powerful explosion sounded. When I reached the main deck, it was already only three or four feet above the water. I looked down midships and saw a crew member trying to get a lifeboat free. The water was coming up so quickly the boat was already floating in the water before they had time to unhook the davits.

When I next looked over the side just in front of me, the deck was only a few inches above the surface. There was someone standing next to me — I don't remember who it was — and we both just stepped over the side into the water.

The sea was running high and those of us in the water would ride up to the top of a wave and then ride down into the trough, something like riding a small roller coaster. When you rose to the top of a wave you could see many people floating in the water and when you dropped down, you could see nothing but huge waves overhead. An overturned lifeboat floated by but I was unable to get to it.

Later, a lifeboat sailed by with a Navy Armed Guard sailor standing up in it! He had a big smile on his face as he sailed by. Some people called out to him from the water, but he didn't respond. He seemed to be in some state of shock and didn't seem aware of his situation.

All of a sudden, an overturned lifeboat came over the top of a wave, directly at me. There was a merchant seaman clinging to it and I noticed a line wrapped around the upturned bottom. The merchant sailor tried to reach me, but he was exhausted and wasn't able to pull me out of the water. I was able to grab the line that was wrapped around the boat and with some help from him, I was finally able to climb onto the boat. We both were able to secure our arms under the taut line and this kept us from falling off. Then, as happened when the *Alamar* went down, I fell asleep from the cold.

When I woke up, I was in the hospital at Reykjavik. I have no idea of the time that passed between the lifeboat and the hospital. I was told that we had been rescued by a Free French corvette. There were other survivors in the hospital, some in bed and some walking around. I looked around for my Armed Guard shipmates from the *Alamar.* There was just one other with me. He was the one who rode alone, standing in the lifeboat. He had no memory of that, although many others told of seeing him go by them while they were in the water.

My partner, the gunner's mate, "Georgia" was gone, as were my other mates, whose names and faces I still remember, but have not mentioned here. For years afterward, I wondered how a sub could be so accurate in that storm and thought perhaps I could have been more vigilant at my lookout watch. [*Capt. Moore writes: "The Freighter, SS* Massmar *was one of four American flag ships that were mined and sunk ...Her compliment was 38 merchant crew, 13 Naval Armed Guard and 36 survivors of the torpedoed SS* Alamar. *Seventeen crew members, including the captain, plus 23 crew members from the* Alamar, *including her Captain were lost. Nine navy men were lost."* [7]

However, many years later, the official report shows that our lead ship, HMS *Niger* sighted a rare, large iceberg and in the fog, mistook the iceberg for the coast of Iceland and ordered a course change. When she realized her error, she signaled back to the commodore, then struck a mine and sank with all hands lost. By this time, the convoy was in the minefield and *Massmar, Hybert,*[*] *Heffron,* and *Rodina* struck mines and sank Those who survived the loss of their ships owe their lives to the crew of the French Corvette *Roselys*, who stayed in the mine field picking up survivors for six hours, at great risk to their own lives.

Although it has been a lifetime since the *Massmar* went down, I still remember those young men of the Navy Armed Guard — seventeen, eighteen, nineteen years old — who fought against an overwhelming enemy and survived only to lose their lives in an Allied minefield.

However, in the poor conditions of storm and fog, we can understand the mistakes the *Niger* made and sympathize with their loved ones over their loss. And we can never repay the courage of the French ship *Roselys*, who so bravely saved so many lives at great risk to their own.[8]

~~~

Louis Paessun forwarded his story which gives his view of the Armed Guard and what life was like on the notorious Murmansk run.

The Secret Navy of World War II

I was eighteen years old when Pearl Harbor changed the history of the United States and my life. I decided to join the Navy in August of 1942. I received my "boot camp" training for about three weeks at Great Lakes, Illinois. After graduation from "boots" we were given the opportunity to volunteer for the Armed Guard

---

[*] George Bean's account of the SS Hybert being mined can be found in Vol. II of *Patriots and Heroes: True Stories of the U.S. Merchant Marine in World War II*, by the same author.
~~~

The Queen Elizabeth *arriving in New York in 1945 with 14,000 troops on board. Imagine how she looked with 24,000 cramming her spaces.* Publisher's collection.

branch of the Navy. We were not told what the Armed Guard did in the Navy and I thought it must be a job guarding warehouses or some sort of patrol duty. I didn't know that it was dangerous and devoid of any traditional glamour or recognition that was accorded to fighting vessels. We were regarded by most Navy personnel as draft dodgers or outright cowards trying to avoid combat duty. The general public thought we were a quasi-military outfit assigned to assist in guarding merchant marine ships while they were stateside. I had a rude awakening of our real duty, beginning December 1942 and it came just months after leaving "boots" at Great Lakes.

Training lasted only two weeks when we were sent to board the *Queen Elizabeth* to go to Europe along with some 24,000 troops. The *Queen* had been stripped of all her luxurious fittings and was so crowded that you had to sleep in shifts. Fortunately – the *Queen* was very fast and did not require an escorting squadron of sub chasers. No submarines could possibly catch her and my only wish was that later on — our own merchant vessels could have had that kind of speed.

As members of the Armed Guard we learned we were to man deck guns on slow merchant ships. We left Scotland on December 14, 1942. I was on the ship SS *Executive*, which was built in 1920. We arrived New Year's Eve of 1943 in Murmansk, Russia. We traveled in a convoy through storms, high winds and a snow blizzard. The normal daily temperatures were thirty to forty below zero. We could only stand lookout duty for twenty minutes at a time. We had no arctic clothing, hats or gloves. Bucking enormous seas and wind kept our mileage to two to three miles on some days. Our fastest speed was eight knots. We delivered "Boston Bombers" to the Russians along with enormous supplies of food, munitions, barbed wire and God only knows what else.

We thought that the Russians were our Allies and would be grateful for all those supplies brought under terrible sailing conditions and horrendous danger. The Russians treated us more like the enemy rather than their benefactors. We were severely restricted as to where we could go, could not talk to any Russians and we were virtual prisoners on our ship.

We were bombed every day by German airplanes, which could reach us very easily. One plane came in every day at very low altitude and I shot at him with our 20mm cannon and brought

Built at Hog Island in 1920, the Executive *was operated by American Export Lines.* SSHSA

him down. The Russians came over and wanted to know who had done the shooting since they had known the shots came from our ship. They were just curious since they had tried to bring him down for some time with no luck.

We were running desperately low on food and we were not allowed to bring food from one of our ships to another. I was sick most of the time and couldn't eat much even when we had a small meal.

On March 1, 1943 we headed out for home in convoy RA-53. We had to run through a heavy ice pack for five days. There were thirty ships to begin with and three were sunk by torpedoes and aerial bombs. My ship *Executive* was attacked by the German sub *U-255*. We sank at 8:30 AM on March 5. A torpedo missed us but hit the ship next to us, the *Richard Bland*. The second torpedo hit us and we were doomed to sink. We had a desperate time launching the lifeboats since all the falls were frozen in the minus thirty-degree weather. We had to jump into the lifeboat when huge waves brought it up to our deck level and it would immediately sink into a deep trough. You had to have been a pretty good jumper to make that leap! Our Signalman S1/c Neo "Anthony" Caponi was killed.

We were in the boat for six hours before we were picked up by a British fishing trawler. I was thrown into a bunk that belonged to a fisherman and he came back to sleep. I was very near death and they told the guy who owned the bunk to leave me alone since I was going to die anyway. I lived to spend the next four years on four other merchant ships.[9]

(The Executive *had "a cargo of 1,520 tons of Potassium Chloride. Of a complement of 38 merchant crew and 25 Naval Armed Guard, 8 crew members and 1 Navy man were lost, (five killed in the explosion and 4 by drowning)."*[10] *The* Richard Bland *was hit for the first time by* U-225 *(Reche) on March 5. The next day the disabled ship got lost in a gale and had to sail alone. On March 10, she was again struck by* U-225. *"Her complement was 41 merchant crew and 28 Naval Armed Guard. Of this number, 19 crew members, including the captain, and 15 navy men, including the ensign in charge were lost. There were 35 survivors."* [11]

~~~

Joseph Benedetto of the Long Island Naval Armed Guard chapter sent this, his first story.

Murmansk

In January 1943, my liberty ship, the *Ezra Cornell*, left for Murmansk, Russia. Our route was the North Atlantic to Scotland. The convoy formed up at anchorage in northern Scotland. It consisted of eighteen ships. Our cargo was a mixture of foodstuffs, bombs and explosives of many kinds, airplanes, tanks and on deck, four steam locomotives. These were welded, chained and tied down with steel cables. After lying at anchor for about seven days, we left one cold windy morning. The waves were breaking over the bow with such force that the ship would disappear and slowly rise above the waves. If one of these chains or cables had broken loose, I think the locomotives would have come through the Navy sleeping quarters.

The convoy proceeded north to Iceland and six more ships joined the convoy. The convoy headed east into the North Sea and at these latitudes in the winter, we had twenty-one hours of darkness and three hours of light. The convoy then headed for North Cape located at the most northern part of Norway, with Bear Island located about one hundred miles further north. This island was occupied by the German Air Force.

Two days out of Scotland we had our first General Quarters alarm. I was assigned to the 3-inch 50 on the bow. The entire gun crew ran forward to man the gun. At that moment, a German bomber appeared out of the clouds. He was so low we could've waved at the pilot. I'm sure he was as surprised as we were. The plane proceeded down the center of the convoy dropping several bombs. No ships were hit during that first encounter. For the next ten days, it was air attacks during the three hours of daylight and submarine attacks at night. Our convoy escorts were a mixture of cruisers and destroyers, a total of twenty-eight. One of our Navy crewmen had an attack of appendicitis, and while in his bunk one day counted 126 depth charge explosions. Sleep was in short supply. One morning, a British cruiser on our starboard
~~~

The Ezra Cornell *underway with a full cargo during World War II.* National Archives.

beam appeared to be signaling with his lights. They were too many flashing lights and it turned out he was firing at a spotter German aircraft. He would come out at first light and locate the convoy for the subs. The plane would dive and then would come up in a steep climb to avoid the antiaircraft fire from the cruiser. One of the bursts caught him at the right moment and we could see black smoke from the plane. When we finally reached the Russian coast, Russian fighters appeared and escorted the convoy to the city of Murmansk. The city was pretty well bombed out.

We finally got to the dock and the crew got shore leave. There wasn't too much to see or do. There was one building for all Allied personnel, officers and enlisted personnel, and merchant seamen. Entertainment consisted of a Russian official making somewhat of a propaganda speech, an old Shirley Temple picture and a ration of one glass of vodka. On occasion, a small sandwich was available. The Russian government gave all crew members, both military and merchant seamen, three hundred rubles. There wasn't much to buy, so we had "crap" games on the mess hall tables. Unloading was slow, so after a month, we finally headed for home.

Our port of return to the States was Newport News, Virginia. The crew members could not wait to go ashore to get some good old-fashioned American whiskey. Before leaving on this trip, my father had made some whiskey from bootleg alcohol. He filled an old Wilson bottle and told me to take it with me. I had it in my locker for three months and then I gave it to the crew members. As they passed it around, they could not get over the fact that I had this bottle for three months. I kept hearing, "Boy, you can sure tell this whiskey (in the Wilson bottle) was good old-fashioned American rye!" I never let on that my father had made it at home.

When all the details of the trip came in we learned the convoy had sunk two submarines and shot down three planes. The Russian government gave a medal to all military personnel for participating in the delivery of war material to the Russian people in their great need during the war. The convoy lost three merchant ships.

For an eighteen-year-old fresh out of high school, this was quite an experience. Today, after some sixty years, the details of this trip are still fresh in my mind.[12]

~~~

The next story is from George X. Hurley whom I have designated the U.S. Navy Armed Guard poet (his poems are found throughout this book). This is George's story about his experience going to Murmansk.

**I vowed if I ever came back,
I'd never go near Murmansk again!**

I was in the Armed Guard from 1942 till 1946 serving on five ships. My first trip was around the world with five guys from my hometown on the famous ship S.S. *Henry Bacon* on her maiden voyage. This was right after "boot" camp. Upon arriving on the *Henry Bacon*, I was told, "This is a 20mm gun and now you're a gunner." I learned fast!

My trip to Murmansk was the worst. On the way up to Murmansk JU-88's followed us and a wolf pack trailed us to the mouth of the river leading in. I was there at the dock Christmas of 1943. We underwent 103 air raids as we were only five minutes from the German airfields. Our life jackets reminded me of fireflies on a summer night. I vowed if I ever came back, I'd
~~~

The Henry Bacon *under way with signal flags flying.* Courtesy of Pete Lyse.

never go near Murmansk again!" I wrote a poem "Saga of the Murmansk Run (1943)" on paper bags to keep track so I'd never forget. (See Appendix for poem) After eleven months we limped into New York leaking water in the forward hold after traveling all around the world.

I made France and then the Philippines. It was interesting, but nothing will ever compare with the Murmansk run. So far Russia, the Philippines and France have sent medals, but our government should award all who participated in the Murmansk Run a medal. It was separate war fought by a few, the Armed Guard and the Merchant Marine.[13]

~~~

Here are Bob Norling's experiences in Murmansk

Stuka

We took on the last of our deck cargo in Weehawken, New Jersey, right across from New York City: four huge locomotives.

It was December 1943. Destination for the Liberty ship *Abner Nash* was Murmansk, with stops en route at Gourock and Loch Ewe in Scotland.

I stayed aboard the night before we sailed, and was awakened about three in the morning when something hit my bunk with a thud and a whimper. A couple of gunners, Terry Connelly and Walter Beeman, had decided we needed not one, but two pet mascots for the voyage.

Connelly had brought his own dog from home, a spitz named Margie. The dog I woke up with was a German Shepherd pup.
~~~

Considering his canine lineage and what we might encounter en route to Murmansk, he just had been named Stuka.

We sailed three days before Christmas. Stuka got along well with Margie and the rest of the crew and stood signal watches with me on the bridge. He got underfoot once in a while and would slip around when decks iced up. But on the whole, he became a real salt. He soon found the galley and mess halls and grew by leaps and bounds.

Enroute to Gourock, he tolerated three U-boat attacks on our convoy and depth charge counterattacks by Navy escorts.

We sailed for Murmansk to Loch Ewe on January 22, 1944, in Convoy JW56B. Stuka showed no fear as we ran a U-boat and Luftwaffe gauntlet for six days and nights, January 27 to February 1. The Germans were still furious about the loss of the battleship *Scharnhorst* a month earlier off North Cape, and made us the main target for a fifteen-U-boat wolfpack with the code name Werwolf.

We didn't get much sleep, but brave Stuka got his, curled up on my bunk through many attacks. German bombers targeted Murmansk seven times while we were there, and that didn't bother him either.

In Murmansk he often joined crew members on jaunts ashore, romping through snow banks and really enjoying something other than a steel deck under his paws.

One day he went ashore but didn't return. He wandered out into a Murmansk Street and was struck by a hit-and-run driver.

Brave sailor that he was, that was no way to die — ashore in a foreign port at the hands of a careless Russian soldier driving an American-made jeep. I wanted to find that guy and deliver some payback for what he did to Stuka. But that wasn't to be.

We sailed for home a couple of days later in Convoy RA57, short one dog in the crew – R.I.P. Stuka, USN, 1943-44.[14]

~~~

According to John Sheridan, "In 1944, the Liberty ship Owen Wister *was being fitted out for the run to Murmansk. This is my account of her two trips to that Russian port. I was one of the*
~~~

gunners and I kept a diary. I had almost two years of sea duty before I boarded the Wister *having spent most of this time in the North Atlantic. I joined the Navy when I was seventeen and was trained at Little Creek, Virginia. I had already seen some ships torpedoed, sunk, and some of the men I trained with, lost. So I had a little knowledge of the hazards to be faced while at sea. Like a few others on the* Wister, *I was a bit of a hell-raiser getting into trouble from time to time, but I always regarded my Navy years as the best years of my life."*

S.S. *Owen Wister*
Shipping Out

"Now hear this, now hear this, all men assigned to the *Owen Mister* will report to Gate 1 at 0700."

The loudspeaker broke the still of the predawn. Here and there men dropped out of their hammocks and felt around the floor trying to locate shoes and other loose gear. By 0600 I had dressed, tied up my seabag and had myself a cup of coffee. Then it was back to get my gear and off to the gate. I laid my gear aside and read names going to the *Owen Wister*, I found two that I knew.

At the supply window, each man was issued a couple pairs of thick socks, heavy long underwear, a full length lined coat and a face mask. Next we were lined up and out the door to a waiting Navy bus. The gear was piled into a truck that was to follow. A soon as we were all aboard the bus started up and headed for the bridge to New York. It was then that the bos'n announced that the ship was at its shipyard in Newburgh, New York, and that the trip would take a couple of hours. The ship was still being worked on and the men would have to stay in a hotel until the work was completed.

Arriving at the shipyard, it was discovered that the *Wister* was one of the newer liberty ships and had just returned from France. One good thing, she was riveted construction instead of being welded. I had heard of some of the welded ones that had broken up during storms, and it was sure to be rough waters around the Norwegian coast. My last ship had been welded and in rough weather I had heard her creaking and straining.

It didn't take too long to get to meet the commanding officer. Within ten minutes, he was out on deck along with the bos'n. The men were lined up and he started reading the orders.

The navy orders were the same regulations most of the men had heard before, but the ones he made up for the hotel stay were something else.

1. Three men assigned to each room.
2. No girls permitted in the rooms.
3. Men to clean the rooms and make the beds each morning.
4. Lights out at midnight, all personnel to be accounted for.
5. Men to pay for any damage to room or furniture.

Newburgh looked like a pretty good liberty town. The *Wister* was the only ship there and there were plenty of bars and a few pretty good-looking restaurants. The men were soon into the tailor made uniforms and setting out to find the action.

The next few weeks were spent working on the ship, cleaning the guns, painting the crews' cabins and gun tubs. The crews of the 3-inch and 5-inch guns were put through gun drills to keep from getting rusty. I and the other 20mm gunners played around with our guns, changing barrels and had our loaders practice changing magazines. Each night we were free to go out on the town.

Shipyard workers were busy installing a four-inch layer of insulation around the cabin, bridge and any exposed pipes. The *Wister* was 441 feet long and armed with eight new 20mm guns and she had a 3-inch gun on the bow. The stern gun was a beauty, a new 5-inch 38 equipped with a diesel engine to speed up pointing. I had seen one of these guns before when I was at a range in Guantanamo Bay, Cuba. All the new destroyers had this type of gun; it could spend out 5-inch shells fast.

By the end of October, work on the ship had been completed. The ship was pulled away from the dock and headed down the Hudson towards New York. It was a pleasant trip along the mountain side and past West Point and under the Bear Mountain Bridge. Soon they were passing ships anchored in the lower river waiting for convoys. Then around the Battery where they were all met by a waiting tug and nosed into a pier in Greenpoint.

At 0800 muster, the lieutenant made a list of men scheduled to attend a gunnery school out on Long Island. I was put in charge of the eight men who were to go. It was at this time that the Lt. expressed a desire to have the men win a ship's award. It would look good as he explained it, for the ship's record. The truck arrived before noon and the men piled into it for the two-hour ride to the range.

Arriving there, the men went through classroom studies and then headed out to the waiting guns strung out along the beach. I passed up the newer type guns with the Polaroid sights, settling for one that had the same open sights I was used to. I had tried the Polaroid sights once and found them too slow to focus. Along came the Navy plane towing the 20-foot sleeve, flying low over the water.

As the target came into range, the guns opened up on it. I saw my tracers hitting the target and I was getting a good score on this run. Re-loading, I waited for the next pass and again led the target, slowing down a little to let the sleeve fly into the tracer stream. After the firing was completed, scores were tallied up and the *Wister* crew was awarded a ship's certificate, the score was 3.23. This was the only ship's award for the day. Some of the men received good scores and were awarded individual certificates. My final average was 3.9 and that made me feel good as not many men ever got that score.

The Hudson was pretty well filled with heavily laden ships, mostly Libertys and tankers with a few old Hog Islanders thrown in. This should be a fairly large convoy, though all the ships wouldn't be going the same way. The *Wister* was riding low in the water, the locomotives making the ship top heavy. Along with the six locomotives were a score of big tanks. The men hoped the cables would hold the deck cargo in heavy seas sure to be encountered. If one of those locomotives broke loose, the ship might turn over.

The *Wister* was positioned in the outer column behind another Liberty ship, forward of a tanker assigned to the coffin corner. Just then the General Alarm sounded, bringing the men out on deck running to the guns. After all the guns had been checked, the General Quarters was secured and the men went down to have a cup of coffee, leaving the 4-to-8 watch to finish the sea watch. The response time had been pretty good; at least the Lieutenant was smiling as he left the bridge.

By the end of the 4-to-8 watch, all the ships were in position with escorts around them. The convoy had sixty or so ships, with eight escorts in sight and perhaps a few others ahead over the horizon. With that many escorts the convoy would be pretty safe.

Checking with the first mate, I learned that the ships would probably take fourteen days to make the crossing. The four or five ships scheduled for Russia would drop off at Scotland and the others would proceed to various English ports. No doubt we would be going ashore in Scotland as it took a while to form the Russian convoy. Also, some two dozen escorts had to be assembled. The Murmansk convoys always had strong support as these ships were prime targets for the German forces.

Into the Arctic

Finally the day to sail came and it was a cold rainy morning when the anchor was raised. The ships slowly passed through the submarine nets protecting the harbor. Picking up speed, the *Wister* fell in behind another liberty. After much signaling, the four rows of heavily laden ships were formed. There were to be only sixteen ships in this convoy. Escorts were already out waiting for them and soon had the merchantmen in line. God, where did all those destroyers and corvettes come from? There were twice as many of them as there were cargo ships. None of us had ever seen so many guardian angels in a convoy, especially a convoy this small.

Most of the convoy ships were either Liberty ships or tankers. Each of the tankers had some sort of catapult on the bow with a fighter plane sitting on it. These were probably the expendable fighters that were launched during an air attack. Once in the air there wasn't anywhere to land. The plane had to try to make it to land or else ditch alongside a destroyer and hope to be picked up. It sure was risky business but they sure as hell would come in handy if bombers showed up. The trip was bad enough but you could also look forward to sub attacks all along the route.

A convoy making up in New York. Note the Liberty ship backing out of the slip to join the vessels forming up in the distance. Meanwhile, other Libertys await their turn. Courtesy of U.S. Navy Armed Guard WW II Veterans.

The Germans knew where we were at all times as they had bases along the coast of Norway. It was getting colder now and the heavy weather gear was broken out and even the itchy long johns were put on.

The second day at sea saw the General Quarters alarm rung six times. The escorts were getting sub contacts and were dropping depth charges quite frequently. The water in the tubes holding the extra water for the 20mm froze and had to be chipped out. There was no need for water anyway; the hot barrels would cool off fast enough without it. The men were spending more time at the guns than inside. The wind was something else; it whipped around the gun shields causing one's eyes to water.

"God it's cold up here," said the bow lookout followed by, "I can't wait until we get over the Arctic Circle." The lieutenant told us to, "Knock it off and keep your eyes open." All conversation ceased. The alarm went off again as I finished my watch. I had just climbed down the ladders and was about to go inside. Up the ladders I went again to put in another hour in the cold.

On the third day the seas picked up with the wind spraying the lookouts with sheets of water. They were reassigned to the bridge where it was drier. Sub contacts picked up; some quite close to the *Wister*. One of the destroyers cruising through the columns made a contact just in front of the *Wister* and started dropping depth charges in the *Wister*'s path. The *Wister* swung out to give the escort room to maneuver. Some deep set depth charges went off just as the *Wister* passed. The concussions shook the *Wister* causing those inside to come running out on the deck, thinking the ship had been hit. A corvette came up to join the destroyer and the two ships saturated the area with depth charges. They must have finished off a sub because soon both escorts left the scene with whistles blowing and pennants flying. The corvette was taking a beating from the waves. She looked too small to be out there, but she was doing a great job.

The further north the convoy traveled the shorter the days got. Soon visibility was only half good five or six hours each day. The rest of the time was spent in semi-darkness. This was why the convoys were now set up for only the winter months. All signals were sent by Aldis lamps or else pennants were raised on the convoy commander's ship. Even the light messages were kept short; less chance of a sub lookout spotting it. It was about this time we started hearing planes. They were above the clouds, no doubt searching for the convoy. Sooner or later it was bound to clear up and then they would be spotted.

Temperatures started dropping and it was now 30 degrees below. With the wind, it felt much colder. The watches were changed to four hours on and four hours off as the planes worried the lieutenant. It was impossible to get any sleep; the alarms kept the men off watch running to their guns. Yet, the worst part of the trip was said to be up ahead; the Norwegian North Cape.

Corvettes were the workhorses of convoy escort duty accounting for many submarine "kills." Pictured is the Vancouver. Publisher's collection.

I was informed by one of the ship's officers that we had crossed the Arctic Circle the day before. It had started snowing on my last watch and showed no sign of letting up. The winds kept most of the deck clear, but the gun tubs were now starting to fill up and there was almost a foot of snow in them. It was cold standing in the snow and our feet were also wet. Soon the shovels would have to be broken out so the men could move around better. I asked over the phone if any of the men wanted to make a snowman. The answer I received from the freezing men was quite raw.

It became a problem climbing up the ladders with all the heavy clothing on; it was an effort to even walk. The ship's roll had to be timed just right to make any headway. Visibility was only a few feet in the heavy snow that was falling. The only good thing about it was the fact that the ships would be hard to locate in this mess. No doubt they were having the same weather ashore as no planes could be heard for some time now.

The next day saw the end of the snowstorm. The gun tubs were shoveled out but were now slippery as hell. Visibility improved bringing more sub contacts. The escorts were all over the place dropping depth charges. The concussions could be felt on the hull of the *Wister* making the men more nervous than before. The steward took a count of the charges going off and counted over 200 in one day. We were getting closer to Russia and we were now off the North Cape. Another day or so and we would be near the Kola Inlet. Another day after that and we would be going up the river into Murmansk.

The men were at battle stations the next morning watching two destroyers that had a sub located. They were saturating the area with depth charges when shooting could be heard and the next minute the call went out; "Aircraft Off the Starboard." All the guns swung in that position waiting for a fix on the planes. Suddenly they were spotted near some shell bursts, coming in low over the water. Most of the ships let go at them though others didn't. Suddenly the planes pulled up revealing a red star under their wings. They were Russian planes. They circled the convoy for a while until they were sure they were recognized. Then they started buzzing the ships, pulling up at the last possible moment. There were nine P-39 Air Cobras in all. These were American made and had been given to the Russians. One plane spotted something in the water, dived and sprayed the spot with gunfire. The nearest destroyer sped to the spot and began dropping half-a-dozen shallow set depth charges. A sub's bow was seen for a few seconds and then was swallowed up by the sea. The destroyer ran up her pennants; another sub had been sunk.

Just outside the Kola Inlet was a spot with exceptionally deep water. This was where the main body of subs was said to be waiting. This proved to be true as one of the lead ships took a torpedo in the bow and was causing a flurry of action by the escorts. There were depth charges going off all over the place and the *Wister* shook from the pounding on her hull. Just ahead gunfire was heard as one of the destroyers had forced a sub to the surface and was pounding her at close range with her forward guns. The bridge blew off the sub and the area was covered with a large oil slick. This brought the sub kill to six (later learned after talking to one of the officers). A short time later land was sighted off the port bow. Russia at last.

Murmansk

The convoy started to work into a single line following a Russian destroyer that was an old-timer. Someone mentioned that paint was probably holding the damn thing together. A tug passed heading seaward, to try to tow the ship that had been hit. She was seen to be smoking and was still afloat. Perhaps her cargo had taken up most of the force of the torpedo. Up the river filed the line of ships passing the snow-covered land. Soon we were passing gun emplacements along the river's banks. After a while the river widened and we were in Murmansk harbor.

For the next two days the ships laid at anchor in order to get the escorts a chance to refuel and load up with depth charges. By now they must have been about empty as it had been a busy past few days for them. The following morning the *Wister* was towed to a dock to where a large crane awaited to remove the heavy locomotives. Lines were thrown ashore and the ship tied up.

The dock workers looked all alike, dressed in knee boots, heavy coats and fur-rimmed hats. Some of them appeared to be women, their round faces and short heights the only difference. Russian soldiers were seen here and there with tommy guns slung over the shoulders. The first person up the gangway was some sort of high-ranking Russian officer. He was accompanied by an interpreter who translated for him. After a few minutes talking to the captain and the lieutenant, a set of orders for the Americans to follow was handed over and posted in the mess hall. After reading them, the men wondered if this was a friendly port.

There were only two places the Americans were allowed to go; the Inter-club and the Tourist Hotel. Everywhere else was off limits. There was to be no contact with the women and we were to speak only to the employees of the two places we were allowed to go. The men were to be back on the ship by 10 PM. Anyone found ashore would be arrested and outside of the ship's jurisdiction. No drunkenness would be tolerated. God, what a place this was and I wondered how many men would get into trouble in this dump.

At each scheduled liberty, men would be given chits to buy two drinks of vodka. Lucky, some of the younger gunners didn't drink, so they might be talked into swapping their chits for packs of cigarettes. We were warned against trading with the Russian civilians. This was considered a serious offense and might bring a jail term. The lieutenant also stressed that if any of the men got into trouble ashore, he wouldn't be able to help them.

With drink chits in hand and pockets loaded with cigarettes, we headed down the gangway past the unsmiling Russian guards. Near the sheds along the dock, the men started out what served as a road towards the town said to be over the hill.

We had to walk in the road and dodge many trucks going back and forth to the docks. The ground was snow-covered and filled the many craters along the roadside. The wind blew loose snow around and at times it was hard to see. Russian kids were seen to be hiding in the bomb craters watching the sailors. A few of the older ones came out offering orange colored paper to the Americans. Seeing no soldiers around, I accepted one giving the kid a pack of cigarettes. The paper turned out to be a twenty ruble note. He knew I couldn't buy anything with it, but at least it would be a souvenir to bring back home.

Next we passed what looked to be a row of army barracks. These turned out to be where the civilians lived; each of the families had only one room. The people we passed didn't seem too friendly as none of them even waved back to us. We were not used to this because everywhere we had been in the past, people were glad to see us. We passed some bombed out buildings and we reached what was to be the hotel.

Hanging across the front of the building were huge pictures of Lenin and Stalin. Entering, we found ourselves in the lobby with a flight of stairs leading up to where some music was coming from. At a landing halfway up, stood a huge brown bear, its arms upraised which was supposed to be a greeting. At first it looked alive; whoever stuffed it did a good job. Well at least the bears up here looked friendly. Upstairs we found a large room with tables occupied by sailors from some of the other ships. There were three Russians playing mandolins. They sounded pretty good too.

This room was supposed to be the restaurant, although the only things you could order here was tea, vodka and a hunk of black bread to eat. There was a waitress to take the orders. I knew a little Polish, so I tried it out on her, receiving only a blank look in return. Vodka was ordered and what a drink that turned out to be. Each drink was a large glass full. Guess those Russians knew what they were doing only allowing two drinks a man.

It was cold even on the ship. The only warm place was down in the engine room. Even the shower room was cold until the hot water warmed the room. At least the men got to take showers and get into clean clothes. They hadn't taken off the clothes they had left Scotland wearing until they had reached Murmansk. Our clothing had been wet the whole trip. Skivvies were washed and hung to dry in the engine room.

The lieutenant had given us permission to let our beards grow. This had helped keep our faces warmer. By now some of the men looked pretty good. I hadn't shaved since leaving Greenpoint and I had a mess on my face about as much as any nineteen-year-old would have. So I shaved it off and the next day. The moustache came off too.

A Russian soldier was brought on board to guard the top of the gangway. After he was there most of the day, it was discovered that he could speak English pretty good. He had studied it before the war. A lot was learned from him because he liked American cigarettes; though he had to sneak a puff now and then when the other soldiers on the dock weren't looking.

He told me a little about what life was like in the Russian Army. He had been in for six years and had lived in a small town outside of Moscow, though he hadn't been home in five years. He liked when he was sent on a detail to guard a ship because he got a chance to try out his English.

The Russian soldier refused all offers of packs of cigarettes, explaining that he would be searched when he returned to his base and punished if anything American was found on him. He gave us a Russian cigarette that had very little tobacco in a long empty tube. I gave him a few oranges which he hid and ate when it was dark. He gave me his red emblem, a star on a porcelain button. As friendly as he had become, as soon as his relief showed up, he went back into the cold disciplined Red Army soldier act.

The next time the Russian soldier came on duty I learned a little more about him. He said that if any of the soldiers were found asleep on duty, it was back to the front for them. He didn't want that to happen as life at the front was hell. There never was enough food to eat and they had to look around the countryside for food. All transportation to the front was taken up by war materials.

The next day, *Wister* was towed to another pier. There the tanks were unloaded and placed with another 100 already on shore. The place looked like a tank parking lot. Next the canvas was removed from the hatches and the hold cargo began to be lifted out. The first couple of decks of the No. 2 hatch contained hundreds of depth charges. We didn't even know they were aboard as they must have loaded them at night. They would have blown the *Wister* sky high if she had been hit in that area. We were all relieved when the last of them were unloaded. The escorts needed these charges for the return trip home.

Regular four on and eight off gun watches were kept while at anchor as there was always the threat of an air raid. We were sitting ducks out there in the river. The dock area had a bunch of barrage balloons to keep any planes from coming in low. One of the gunners remarked that those balloons would make nice targets to shoot at.

About this time I was wondering if there were any fish in the river. It was real deep and there must be something on the bottom. So I decided to give it a try. I had fish line in the bottom of my seabag along with a couple of hooks and sinkers. A piece of bacon was used for bait. Soon I was pulling up small codfish, a pound or two a piece. There seemed to be plenty of them and before long I had a pail full to the delight of the steward. I was told to keep catching them. The cook would clean them and they would be the next day's supper. The steward hadn't been able to get any fresh food ashore for almost two months. I felt it would be a good way to make up to the steward for the watermelon I stole in Scotland. In all, I pulled in more than sixty fish and they sure tasted good.

The fish dinner was more than enjoyed. The cook split them, rolled them in corn flour and deep-fried them. He also peeled a mess of potatoes and made French fries. Even the lieutenant saw it in his heart to thank the fisherman, suggesting I fish again next day. I didn't have the previous day's luck. This time I caught only a dozen or so before the bitter cold got to me in spite of all the hot coffee the steward kept sending me.

We went through a few more gun drills for the next week or so. One by one the ships were unloaded and were joining the *Wister*. A few escorts arrived and tied up to the ammo docks for refueling and ammo. Soon all the cargo ships were at anchor and another score of destroyers came up the river to join us. Next came a small carrier with six corvettes as escort. I was glad to see the carrier as it had double-winged Swordfish planes on deck. These were deadly against the subs as they circled the convoy being able to see any subs not too far beneath the surface. They had depth charges below their wings to drop on anything they saw. The captain and lieutenant went ashore for the convoy conference and returned the next morning. Some of the escorts were already leaving and soon the anchor was raised. The *Wister* slowly turned and headed down river. We were on our way back home.[15]

~~~

John Starkey submitted this story which begins with his volunteering for "special duty."

My Trip to Russia

It all started the last week of "boot camp" at Great Lakes, Illinois. We had muster on the grinder and the C.O. addressed us and asked, "If there were any volunteers for a special duty?" Me, being all gung-ho at the ripe old age of seventeen, raised my hand. Guess what? I was congratulated and told to fall in with a "few" others. We still didn't know what we had volunteered for.

We got on a train, which I called a cattle car, and got off at the Armed Guard Gunnery School in Shelton, Virginia. We were told very little about the Armed Guard except we were all going to be gunners aboard a Liberty ship. Destination was unknown to us at that time.

After finishing Gunnery School which consisted of 3-inch 50, 5-inch 38, 5-inch 50 and our main baby was the 20mm. These were to be our life-savers. We boarded another train for the Brooklyn Armed Guard Center. Mine was the Liberty ship, S.S. *James Smith.* We were all a bunch of "greenhorns" except for our signalman, radioman, and a GM/3 whose name was Cox. I don't
~~~

remember his first name. I don't remember the name of our C.O., who was a Lt.(jg), but he was a fine man.

We were assigned our duty station. Mine was a 20mm on the aft port side. We carried a 5-inch 50, eight 20mm, and a 3-inch 50. We armed for bear! Ha!!

It was March 1944, and after two days out of New York, "which wasn't far because we had a top speed of about 8 knots," our C.O. called us to quarters and read our orders. We were going to Murmansk and Archangel, Russia. Then he told us what we faced. And I volunteered for this? To make it clear, I am not a bit sorry.

I am not sure how long we sailed before we met up with the rest of the convoy in the North Atlantic, but we were not bored. Every day we cleaned and oiled our gun. I mean we tore it down and put it back together and you did it right because your life and the whole ship's crew depended on it. We also had a great crew of merchant marine. They were a top bunch of men.

As we moved up north in the Atlantic it got cold each day and when we crossed the Arctic Circle it was absolutely freezing. At night, being this far north, the Northern Lights were really a sight to remember.

We were getting our "sea legs" and getting used to our duties. We had four hours on and four hours off watches plus General Quarters every sunset and sunrise, and any time our destroyer escorts located a German U-boat. Sometimes the escorts would drop depth charges so close to us you would think the ship was going to break in two. The whole ship would vibrate and shake.

After we crossed the Arctic Circle, I don't believe we had one day or night that a U-boat wasn't chasing our convoy.

We had two oil tankers in the convoy and they were stationed in the middle of the rest of us because those were the ships the Germans wanted to sink the most. However, if they couldn't sink a tanker, they would go ahead and attack one of us. One ship off our port side got a direct torpedo hit. We heard the explosion and before the smoke had cleared, there was just an empty space.

We carried very heavy cargo. We had a locomotive on our decks and holds were loaded with bombs and flour. When you have that kind of weight on board, you don't stay afloat very long.

I remember being very scared on this run. There were many nights we had orders to sleep in our life jackets. It was uncomfortable but we got used to it. Outside was bitter cold. The spray came over the bow and froze as soon as it hit the rails or deck. We had parkas and face masks on and the only thing sticking out was our nostrils and it was still cold.

I am not sure how many ships we lost. "One was too many," but to survive in that water was impossible. Forty-five seconds was the life span for one in the water. I consider our convoy as being lucky. We could have lost possibly seventy-five percent of it if it hadn't been for this one snowstorm. This storm was very weird; one period we were in a hard driving snow and all of a sudden it would clear up. At one point we looked up and there was a German bomber directly overhead. It must have been on a reconnaissance mission and we went on G.Q. immediately for the rest of the day figuring the German Stukas would soon be upon us. To our surprise we never encountered anything.

We finally made Murmansk and left part of the convoy there and we proceeded on to Archangel through the White Sea. This was a good name for it because it was white with solid ice. We needed two icebreakers to get us through. We had a lot of Russian children come out on the ice when we got stuck. Our C.O. asked if we didn't mind giving the kids some of the chocolate candy bars we had stored in the ship's store. We really enjoyed watching the kids getting their Hershey Bars that we were throwing over the side to them. This was probably the first candy they had since the war began.

We finally got to Archangel and since all the men were at the front, the women unloaded our ship. Talk about strong women. They would go down the ladder into a hold and throw a sack of flour over their shoulder and come up out of there like it was a piece of cake. I don't believe I would have wanted to argue with one of them. There was one male and he was assigned as a guard at the gangway and had orders to shoot any Russian trying to steal food. I never saw him shoot anyone but I imagine he would have.

We stayed in Archangel for three days and missed our convoy. We had to sail a day-and-a-half alone eventually catching them. The Germans didn't bother us on the return trip and I still don't know why.[16]

~~~

John York was the merchant marine radio operator aboard the S.S. Benjamin Schlesinger. *He made two trips to Murmansk. The following is from the Naval Armed Guard report and his log of the brutal action that took place between March 18-20, 1945 in Convoy JW 65.*

Action on the Murmansk Run: Diary

Armed Guard Report:

At 1410 on 18 March 1945 one of the planes (?Avenger?) crashed into the sea near column #1 of the convoy, (approx 7500 yds. off our port beam) — cause unknown.

Continuous air coverage was offered by carrier planes. The number of aircraft, at any one time, ranged from 2 to 6. Carrier types seen were Avengers, Wildcats and Swordfish. The first tree [sic] or four days out Catalinas were sighted patrolling in the distance. Upon approaching Murmansk area Russian PE-

Shown is the YAK-3, successor to the YAK-1. Both were considered extremely capable dogfighters with very high maneuverability and a high rate of climb. Production of the YAK-1 was 8,721 and ceased in 1943 with introduction of the YAK-3. Imperial War Museum.
~~~

2s and YAK-1s patrolled the vicinity. Port of arrival: Murmansk, Russia. Date 20 March 1945 at 1600.

John York: "The Armed Guard held daily training drills of various types. One of the drills was to have instant plane recognition. They were pretty good at it, as I watched them."

Armed Guard continued:

Contact with enemy: Off Kola Bay, at 0945 on 20 March 1945, a ship on the port side of the convoy hoisted Pennant 2 (Sub on port). General Quarters was rung and all hands reported to battle stations. Shortly thereafter the same ship hoisted XF-1 (hit by 1 torp.). When last seen the ship appeared to be settling as a destroyer attempted a tow. About 1015 the wreckage of a Corvet was sighted 9000 yds off the starboard side of the convoy. The Corvet had been blown apart – the bow floated in a vertical position; another part floated nearby the bow. A lifeboat was making its way to the destroyer that was standing by.

At approximately 1210 the ship astern of us (*Thomas Donaldson*) was hit by two torpedoes (hoist XF-2). At this time the ships were practically in a single file for entering Kola Inlet. The ship astern after being hit veered to starboard and came to a stop. When last seen it appeared to be settling by the stern. This ship did not fire at anything as no targets were sighted. The weather during this period: Snow flurries permitted a variable visibility from 600 to 9000 yds. the sea was choppy with many small white-caps. The wind was fresh and steady.

After entering Kola Inlet a tanker veered to the port and ran ashore or into an iceflow – reason unknown.

All Navy enlisted personnel performed their duties in a manner befitting men of the United States Navy. A complete list of Navy personnel aboard this ship at the time of action is included in this report.

The Merchantmen all reported to battle stations and augmented Navy lookouts.

Naval Armed Guard Report:

General resume of the voyage: All Navy hands manned their battle stations at Dawn and Dusk during the entire voyage. Two floating mines were sighted by Convoy 17-18 March 1945. Adequate gun; fire & boat drills were held. Blue stern lights and fog buoys were shown in convoy from time to time, during adverse weather conditions.[17]

~~~

My Snowstorm

by George X. Hurley

The snow fell all that day
No one went out, there was no way
The drifts were like a storm at sea
A plow looked like a ship to me

Memories of the Russian run
Murmansk City, my faithful gun
It snowed there almost every day
But still, the Germans came out to play

Every year, when it gets cold
I think of when I was young and bold
We fought the foe in forty-three
To keep the Russians free

Now, to keep this memory alive
We're getting a medal number five
For the battle of the Arctic Ocean
I'll receive it with deep emotion

God picks the souls, he takes away
I lost a lot of friends in that fray
I wonder what's left for me
I fought to keep the Russians free.[18]
~~~

8

The Mediterranean

In November 1942 American and British forces landed in French Morocco and Algeria to begin the North African campaign. To capture Italy and attack Germany from the south, a massive invasion supported with ammunition, equipment, food, and supplies was required. This was no easy task because of philosophical differences among the Allied powers. After being refortified Russia was holding her own, but needed some of the pressure removed from her western front. The Americans wanted an all-out assault across the English Channel. The British desired a new southern front in what Churchill referred to as the "soft-underbelly" of the Mediterranean.

At the Casablanca Conference in January 1943 Churchill and Roosevelt agreed that Germany must be defeated before Japan and that a southern front was necessary to aid Stalin while diverting attention from the cross-channel invasion, which was at least a year away. Success on the southern front would rid the

Mediterranean Sea of Axis influence. The campaign would include North Africa and the capture of Sicily and Italy.

By May 1943, the Mediterranean was considered safe for the massive shipments needed in support of the offensive. Of course, first these ships had to convoy across the submarine-infested Atlantic. Once in the Mediterranean, the Axis submarines lost the safety of deep water. However, there the German Luftwaffe dominated; the Mediterranean was well within range and hundreds of attacks were made by German planes. In addition, Allied ships had to cope with mines and sabotage by Axis frogmen.

The southern front was an enormous undertaking.

> A census of dry cargo ships and tankers in the eastern Mediterranean during the fourth week of October 1943 indicates how enormous the supply task was, even though the Italian campaign was now north of Naples and Bari: 59 merchantmen sailed into Oran; Algiers 75; Augusta 9; Bizerte 39; Bone 26; Bougie 4; Brindisi 16; Catania 7; Malta 41; Naples 52; Philipville 6; Sousse 2; Syracuse 4; Taranto 18, and Tunis 5 (a total of 363 merchantmen).[1]

The U.S. Navy Armed Guard, merchant ships and crews paid a heavy price in reaching their objectives. A total of 279 ships were sunk or damaged in the Mediterranean-Black Sea and the approaches to the Mediterranean. Besides 456 merchant crew killed, 230 U.S. Navy Armed Guards lost their lives. In addition to these statistics, 504 Army-Air Force, 152 Army, 100 British Army and 264 Italian POWs lost their lives on these ships.[2]

~~~

Samuel J. Pitittieri, was a Navy Armed Guard gunner aboard the Liberty ship James Ford Rhodes. *His ship was No. 5 in the fifth column in a convoy which left Gibraltar in early November 1943.*

On the afternoon of November 11, the commodore signaled us to change position to column one, fifth ship and a Dutch ammunition ship took our place. That evening, all ships were ordered to start a smoke screen.
~~~

The James Ford Rhodes *under way in World War II.* Publisher's collection.

It was a partly cloudy sky and the escort on the starboard side flashed a yellow caution light. We were already at our battle stations while the smoke screen was on. The D.E. [destroyer escort] flashed a red light. I saw three German planes fly by the moon when all the ships started firing. I was on the port side on my 20mm gun and firing toward the bow, when I saw the "Dutch ammo ship" go up. It just blew from bow to stern and sank within minutes. When I looked around, I could see tankers on fire on the starboard side toward the shore. Other ships were being hit and falling back. We had to avoid hitting them. The attack lasted ten to fifteen minutes. We later heard that the planes were on a bombing run to Philipville, North Africa. We were lucky that they didn't drop all their bombs on the convoy.[3]

~~~

George A. Peak joined the Navy in 1942, following in his father's footsteps, a Navy veteran from World War I.

"What a small world!"

I was sent to Samson Naval base for boot camp training. While there, they were looking for volunteers for the Armed Guard, so I volunteered not knowing what the Armed Guard was. However
~~~

since I was a young eighteen-year-old raring to go and this was a voluntary effort, I joined — it ended up the best move.

I was sent to Gunnery school in Virginia, and I must have done well because I was recommended to be a pointer on the 5-inch 51 gun.

From there I was sent to the Armed Guard Center in Brooklyn, which became my home base. This was perfect for me because my home was in Brooklyn.

I caught my first ship, a Liberty ship, the *Caleb Strong* at a pier in Manhattan early in 1943. Our destination was Casablanca. It took about thirty days to get there since we were in a fairly large convoy. We lost no ships, but our escorts were quite busy. When the convoy got close to Africa, three ships and mine left the convoy and continued on to Casablanca. Being in Casablanca was a tremendous experience for a boy from Brooklyn. I had never seen palm trees that lined the main avenue. At the end of this street was the town pub where we spent most of the time while the ship was being unloaded.

When I was first assigned to the ship, we had a 20mm machine gun as a bow gun, four .50 caliber machine guns on the bridge and a 5-inch 51 on the stern. When we were ready to sail again, they had equipped us with a 3-inch 38 bow gun, eight 20mm machine guns and a 5-inch 51 gun.

This time our first port in the Mediterranean was Mostaganem [Algeria]. After unloading our cargo, we reloaded vehicles, ammunition and troops. In a convoy of about twelve ships our mission was to shuttle these troops to Naples, Italy. The problem was that our troops in Italy had not yet captured Naples so we delayed by going to Malta and then back to Sicily. All this time the troops we had on board were quite restless. Finally, six ships of the convoy headed for Naples. The timing was good because our army had just gotten past Naples, about three miles. We could see gunfire over the hills north of Naples.

Now that we were there we couldn't unload our cargo because the Germans had blocked all the piers by scuttling every ship in the docks. The troops disembarked on a makeshift pier. The vehicles and troops were unloaded, but we had to take the ammunition which was in the rear hold back with us to Africa to pick up more troops and vehicles. We shuttled three times between Africa and Naples.

Between shuttles we anchored off Gibraltar for a couple of days. This was interesting because we had to keep dropping depth charges all night to discourage the German swimmers from tying explosives to the screws of our ships. If we were not aware of the explosives when we started up the booby-traps would explode.

When we were in the port at Naples, we were attacked by air every night at dusk, precisely at 6:20 PM. The Germans were trying to play mind games with us.

During the trips from Africa to Naples, the German air power attacked us with high level and dive bombing. They also threw torpedo planes at us. These planes would come in using the African coastline as cover to make it difficult to see them.

This is where I had the most challenge as I was the pointer on the 5-inch gun. I had binoculars and scanned the horizon for torpedo planes. When I spotted one, I had my trainer train our gun toward the African Coast and I watched through the gun sight. The pilot in the plane knew we had seen him and took off. We played this game and kept scaring off the torpedo planes that saw the length of our gun. If they only knew we could hit them only by luck, they probably would've continued at us. That's why we only showed the gun and never fired it.

We were in the Mediterranean for about eight months and when we ran out of food, the purser tried to buy food from the Italians. The food didn't look appetizing to him so we settled for Army K-rations, etc.

It was now November, and we finally headed back to the U.S. The chef had saved a turkey for Thanksgiving dinner. That was great. So all's well that ends well.

When I returned to the Armed Guard Center in Brooklyn after a week's leave, I was sent to rest camp for two weeks. The camp was in De Land, Florida. What a life! When I returned to the Armed Guard Center, I was assigned to my next ship, the *Samuel Griffin*. It was now early 1944 and we headed to Manchester, England.[4]

George Peak was lucky not to have been on the Samuel Griffin *in May 1943 because she "was bombed by German aircraft at 2155 on May 19, 1943 while moored in Oran, Algeria. One bomb struck the ship in No. 5 hold causing a fire that was extinguished with great difficulty about 4 hours later... Her complement was 41 crew members and 33 Naval Armed Guard. Twenty of the Navy men were wounded.*[5] *The* Samuel Griffin *survived the war and was scrapped in Baltimore in November 1961.*[6]

~~~

This is a continuation of J.W. Janes' story from Chapter 5.

S.S. Ezra Meeker

Before the *Ezra Meeker* left New York, the Navy Armed Guard crew was increased to thirty-one. We left New York on 14 May 1943 in a convoy to Oran, North Africa. We arrived there, unloaded and reloaded for the invasion of Sicily. While the cargo was being changed the captain had himself a birthday party. He and a friend invited two nurses that they had met in Oran aboard to have dinner in the captain's quarters. The captain already knew of the impending invasion of Sicily and had dinner arranged. During dinner the captain must have talked of the plans because the nurses talked about them when they got back to shore.

The Provost Marshal heard about their discussions and questioned them about it. We didn't hear anymore until we returned to Oran from the invasion at Gela Beach, Sicily. As our ship tied up to another Liberty ship at the dock, several Provost Marshall officers were standing on the dock. Soon the lines were secured and these men came aboard our ship and went up the ladder to the captain's quarters. The captain in full dress uniform left the ship with the officers following him to an automobile that was waiting on the dock. They drove away never to be seen again. The next thing we had was a new captain.

At Gela Beachhead on July 10, 1943, the day of the invasion, we had a ringside view of the action on the beach. With field glasses, we could see the large German tanks coming down along a mountain pass and heading for the beach. When they were
~~~

sighted, a large Navy cruiser that was nearby, pulled in near the beach, turned its heavy guns onto the German tanks and destroyed seven or eight of them before they could get to the beach.

The *Ezra Meeker* had to unload onto a barge and it took the cargo of mostly ammunition to the beach. When unloading was completed we went back to Oran and loaded for Palermo, Sicily. While tied to the dock at Palermo, we were awakened every morning about 4:10 by the German dive-bombers. One of the barrage balloons flying overhead from the ship caught fire from a tracer bullet and came down in flames landing on the guntub rail. The 20mm gun operator who was fastened in the gun harness got so scared he couldn't stand up straight for a while.

After four days at Palermo, we went to Casablanca, North Africa for a load of supplies to take to Anzio Beachhead, Italy. Before we got to the Rock of Gibraltar, German torpedo planes attacked us. This occurred about a half-hour before sunset. The formation of planes came in skimming over the water with the sun directly behind them making it very hard to see them even though we could hear them. When they dropped their torpedoes they were set to run too deeply as the torpedo wakes all went underneath the ships. Not one ship was hit. With sixteen planes flying around us, they really drew a lot of antiaircraft fire. Very few of them made it back to their base. At the same time the planes were drawing all the fire, a submarine periscope appeared between our ship's column and the next column over. The escort vessel was notified and he made a run over the area dropping depth charges. No one knows if the submarine was damaged or not. Looking out across the water and seeing that periscope only a few hundred feet away was the most exciting moment of all.

At one time when we tied to the dock at Oran, some German prisoners were loaded on the ship next to ours and they had to walk across the main deck of the *Meeker*. Most of them looked to be teenagers.

Another time while we were in the Mediterranean area, the ship's deep freezer got so low the captain had to buy additional supplies to last until we returned to the States. A few days after restocking the freezer, our mess-cook asked the navy gun crew if they knew what kind of steak they were eating. Most of us thought it was beef. But believe it or not, he said it was horsemeat.

In October 1943 we joined a convoy and headed for the States. As we were pulling into Baltimore, the captain ordered a supply of groceries sent out to the ship by water taxi. We were each given a quart of fresh milk; the first fresh milk since we left the States.

When it comes to memorable sights, the best was the afternoon we arrived and passed by the Statue of Liberty. What a sight![7]

~~~

Dante Nieri finished Gunnery school in Gulfport, Mississippi in April 1943. He was sent to NOLA and then picked up his first ship the U.S.S. Wayne *which brought him to the Brooklyn Armed Guard Center. He was then assigned to the* John M. Clayton *on May 16, 1943.*

S.S. *John M. Clayton*
May 1943 - December 1943

Our bow gun was a 20mm and we had a 3-inch 50 aft. On our first day out we joined a convoy in heavy fog and headed for England. Early one morning on the 4-to-8 watch I was in the 3-inch 50 gun tub aft. I heard a swishing noise but I couldn't see any ships or bow wakes. I looked straight down and saw a big chunk of ice rubbing against the port side of the ship. As I turned to report it, there sat an iceberg taller than the bridge of our ship. We had sideswiped an iceberg and the bow watch never saw it in the heavy fog. We remained in that fog all the way to England. There we unloaded and went back to the States.

On our next trip we loaded and went straight across to Gibraltar. We started zigzagging through the Mediterranean all by ourselves. One day we saw wave after wave of Allied bombers and planes. These planes were flying from North Africa to bomb European targets in Sicily or Italy as we could hear the explosions. We continued on to Port Said, Egypt and a couple of days later we went through the Suez Canal to Port Suez. We anchored there while the captain went ashore for whatever captains go ashore for.
~~~

A motor launch came alongside and a couple of sailors came up the ladder. They were Italian sailors. An Italian-American merchant seaman was asked to translate and they still couldn't understand each other. Someone asked me if I could translate and to make a long story short, I did. They wanted to know if we wanted to go on board their ship, which was also anchored at Port Suez. Their ship was the *Eugenio Di Savoia* (Eugene of the House of Savoy), an Italian cruiser. They had surrendered to the British at Malta some ten or eleven months before. The British had left the ship intact and had put three signalmen on board to handle communications. Meanwhile, the *Eugenio Di Savoia* now patrolled the seas for the British.

Our Gunnery officers said, "O.K." but we had to do it in a "military fashion." Our officer had our signalman signal the cruiser for permission to go on board. They said, "O.K." and sent the captain's gig over and picked up our gunnery officer and took him to the cruiser. One hour later he came back in a whaleboat (lifeboat) rowed by a dozen Italian sailors. They came on board our ship and we, the Armed Guard crew, were dressed in military fashion; white pants, tee shirt, white hats, and shoes. We proceeded to get in their boat and were rowed over to their cruiser.

Later in the war the John M. Clayton *was taken over by the U.S. Navy and renamed USS* Harcourt *IX-225.* Photo: V.H. Young/L.A. Sawyer.

We assembled on the fantail of their ship and were given a "welcome aboard" speech by their captain. They broke us up into two groups and gave us a "cook's tour" of their ship. One group went forward and worked their way aft. I was in the other group, which started from the stern and worked forward. They took us into a gun turret and showed us how their guns were loaded, mechanical rammers, etc. On leaving the gun turret I got separated from the group by two Italian sailors who gave me a private tour of their ship. First they took me to a barbershop and got me a much-needed haircut. Then they took me to their gunner's mess hall and I had something to eat.

At one point an officer came and asked me to make an announcement over the loud speaker in English. They were looking for a British sailor. It seems the British would put three signalmen on board to handle communications and only two went ashore. One was lost on board and could not be found. As far as I know, he's still missing.

That evening, refreshment (wine) was served and a band gave us a little concert on the fantail. We had a good time and some of the guys were feeling good. We then boarded their whaleboat and rowed back to our ship where we disembarked and the Italian sailors rowed back to their cruiser.

... After unloading at Kharamsha, Persia, we retraced our trip back to the States. Our gun crew had been together since Gunnery School. They sent us home on leave and when we returned they sent us to a rest camp in De Land, Florida. From there we were all sent to different ships.

I have souvenirs from the Italian cruiser; two small 1943 calendars, an anchor pin and a medallion with the name of the ship on them, *Eugenio Di Savoia.*[8]

~~~

The following excerpts are from the Log of the SS William Patterson *covering the period of August 18, 1943 to April 5, 1944. Albert Lowe S1/c was one of the Armed Guard aboard the ship and was kind enough to send me this information. Al said, "Some*
~~~

action — we lost four ships in our convoy from England to Italy. Also, we were attacked while at anchor in Italy."

The S.S. *William Patterson* Liberty Ship

To: The Vice Chief of Naval Operations
Via: The Port Director, Swansea, Wales
Subject: Report of Voyage, SS William Patterson
From New York, N.Y. To Swansea, Wales
Reference: (a) General Instructions for Commanding Officers of Naval Armed Guards on Merchant Ships #4301
1. In accordance with reference (a) the following information is submitted:
(A) Type of Vessel Liberty.
Type of cargo: U.S. Army Supplies and Personnel.
Owner of vessel: U.S. Govt. represented by W.S.A.
Chartered to: U.S. Army Transport Service
Ship owned by U.S. Government Represented by War Shipping Administration and operated by A.H. Bull & Co.
(B) Port of departure New York City Date: September 22, 1943
Convoyed or independent: Convoyed
Speed: (aver.) 9.5 knots
No. of ships in Convoy: 64
No. of escort vessels or aircraft: 8 vessels
Port of Arrival: Swansea, Wales (England) Oct. 6, 1943
(C) Resume of Voyage: There were no contacts with the enemy. A routine voyage was made. The incidents out of routine were as follows:
Sept. 23, 1943 - On orders of the Convoy Commodore, all 20mm guns were test fired.
Sept. 26, 1943: Due to a failure of the ships engine's it was necessary to "STOP" the ship. Due to the fact that it was necessary for the ship to fall behind the convoy while the necessary repairs were made and that the ship could not be maneuvered in the event of an attack, Condition I was set. Ship stopped at 0600 and was underway at 0730. Secured from Condition I and set Condition II after ship was underway and set Condition III at 1430 when ship was approaching convoy.
Sept. 28, 1943 on orders from Convoy Commodore, test

fired all 20mm and 3"50 guns. Rounds expended: 20mm – 150 – 3"50 – 2AA

Sept. 30, 1943 Escort joined by aircraft carrier.

Oct. 4, 1943 – Twenty one (approx.) depth charges dropped by escort at a considerable distance from the ship.

Speed of the vessel averaged 9.5 knots. The only lights which were shown was the stern light during heavy fog and the breakdown lights during breakdown. These lights were necessary for the safety of the ship and its cargo and personnel. Ship followed zig-zag instructions as far as could be ascertained.

Commercial radio operator followed wartime instructions.

20mm ready boxes are found to be rather poorly located.

Wartime instructions for U.S. Merchant vessels were carried out.

C.A. Mac Mackin

On Nov. 12, 1943 – 1800, A German reconnaissance aircraft followed our convoy just before night fall – the aircraft was flying so high, our escort opened fire, but could not reach his altitude and got away.

To: The Vice Chief of Naval Operations
Subject: Report of Voyage …
From: Swansea, Wales England to Algiers, Algeria…

(A) Port of departure… Date: Oct. 25, 1943
Convoyed, Speed (aver.) 7 knots
No. of Ships in Convoy: 81
No. of Escort vessels or aircraft: 7 vessels, 3 aircraft
Port of Arrival Algiers, Algeria Date: Nov. 12, 1943

(B) Contact with the enemy occurred on Nov. 11, 1943 in the form of an attack on the Convoy by enemy aircraft. Time: 1813. Position: Lat.36 17N., Long.00 05W.

Condition of the sea: Slight Sea, Weather: Clear with low, scattered clouds and full moon. Opened fire at 1813 and ceased fire at 1915. Estimated firing range: 3000 yds. and less. 3"50 gun on bow was used to engage aircraft at long ranges and 20mm were used at 1200 yds. and less. There were no casualties in the Navy gun crew. One member of the merchant marine crew received a piece of shrapnel in the shoulder and two British sailors received minor cuts from shrapnel. The number of enemy is not known, however there were six twin motored planes in the first wave which approached on our port bow. Low and medium level bombing, torpedo attacks and some strafing of ships was observed. After the first wave, the attack appeared to break up into several simultaneous attacks from various directions by small groups. It is believed that four ships were lost from the Convoy, one of them exploding on our port beam in the next column. At least three planes and possibly more were destroyed, one of which was knocked down on our starboard bow apparently by fire from this ship. The only damage to this ship was a small hole on the starboard side between decks and apparently made by a 20mm projectile. One bomb was dropped on our starboard bow about 50 yds. away and a torpedo crossed our bow about 50 feet ahead of the ship.

(C) Resume: Other than the action described above a rather routine voyage was had. In cooperation with DEMS, 3"50 gun and 5"51 gun was fired at Milford Haven…

To: …
Subject: Report of Voyage …
From: Algiers, Algeria To: Oran, Algeria…

(B) Port of Departure: Algiers, Algeria Date: Nov. 30, 1943
Convoyed, Speed (aver.) 8 knots, No. of ships: 26
No. of escort vessels or aircraft: 6 vessels, 4 aircraft
Port of arrival: Oran, Algeria

(C) No contact with enemy…

To: …
Subject: Report of Voyage…
From: Oran, Algeria to Bari, Italy

(B) Port of Departure: Oran, Algeria Date: 23 December, 1943
Convoyed, Speed (aver.) 7.3 knots No. of Ships in Convoy: 27 ships
No. of Escort Vessels or aircraft: 6 vessels, 3 planes
Port of Arrival: Bari, Italy Date: 10 Jan. 1944

(C) Contact and action with the enemy occurred on 31 December 1943 while ship was at anchor in Augusta Harbor,

Sicily when town and harbor were attacked by planes. Time: 1900 ...Smooth sea and clear weather. Opened fire at 1905, ceased fire at 1930. Estimated range 1500 yds. Heavy barrage by 20mm and 3"50 gun used at longer range. Raid carried out by approx. 10 Junker 88s and was directed at shore installations rather than the harbor. Our barrage balloon caught fire and fell into the sea at our stern. One plane was seen to dive at ship while balloon was burning. 3"50 out of action when on eighth round, projectile lodged in bore of gun. Several jams occurred in 20 mm's, - Projectile lodged in barrel of #6 gun and exploded injuring gunner. Personnel casualties: - Everett Carl Johnson,... S1/c, injuries to right wrist and to lower right leg, and multiple cuts to face and body – caused when projectile exploded in #6 gun. Arthur D. Jones, ... GM3/c burns to left hand. Leslie V. Wanons ...S1/c cuts on 3rd and little finger of right hand. No official results learned. Two planes were shot down by shore installations. Some damage was done ashore and one shore battery was knocked out.

(D) Remainder of voyage was routine...

(E) Lack of experienced help and heavy rain slowed loading of the vessel...

The William Patterson *subsequently sailed from Algiers, Algeria to Augusta, Sicily and then to Taranto, Italy arriving there on February 15th. She sailed back to Algiers, Algeria arriving on February 28, 1944, then returned to New York.*

To: The Chief of Naval Operations...
Subject: Report of Voyage, S.S. *William Patterson*
From Algiers, Algeria to New York

(B) Port of Departure:... Date 5 March 1944
Convoyed, Speed (aver.) 9.0 knots, No. of ships in Convoy: 82 Ships (55 to New York)
No. of escort vessels or aircraft: 10 vessels – (8 to New York) 1 plane

(C) No contacts or action with enemy

(D) A routine voyage. Some rather rough weather encountered causing the ship to roll and pitch. Smoke was made by vessels in the convoy and by the escort on 5 March. Numerous flares and flashes from gunfire were seen on 8 March, after convoy passed Gibraltar. These were seen astern of the convoy on the horizon. Speed of vessel was 9.0 knots (Average). Only lights shown were dim blue lights during change of course.

(E) Vessel was not delayed in port to lack of port facilities

(F) Commercial radio operator appeared to carry out wartime radio instructions for merchant vessels.

(G) Ready boxes at No. 1,2,5 and 6 are rather low in gun tubs making it difficult for loader to obtain magazines readily.

(H) Master and Officers carried out "Wartime Instructions" for U.S. Merchant Ships

2. Report of outward voyage forwarded from abroad. (USNLO), Cardiff Wales)

C.A. Mac Mackin[9]

~~~

On the night of December 2, 1943, about fifty ships lay waiting for their cargos to be unloaded in Bari harbor. So many ships were in the harbor that they almost touched each other. Some had unloaded and were waiting to depart through the breakwater entrance.

Late that afternoon, a convoy of American ships entered the harbor, their way lit by lights from shore side cranes. Destroyers and mine sweepers darted in and out of the harbor protecting the ships and making sure the entrance was clear of mines. Security should have been tighter, but the British had become lackadaisical about defending the port. They felt Germany was retreating and no longer considered an offensive threat. Their primary concern was to rid the port of mines left behind by the Nazis. These still created havoc with the arriving freighters.[10]

This was the scene the week before the attack. The American Liberty ship Louis Hennepin *sent one of her lifeboats to take part in a heroic rescue of a mined ship. The following diary excerpts are from Armed Guard Bernard L. Anderson GM3/c to his wife. Anderson took part in the rescue:*
~~~

Darling what an exciting day I had today. This morning at about 11:00 I had to lay down as I had a headache when all of a sudden a depth charge or mine went off right at the entrance to harbor ... Well, when I heard this big boom that shook the ship from one end to the other I jumped up and grabbed my hat and coat and ran to the bridge, and there right near the entrance to the harbor was a mine sweeper that had been hit by a mine ... There are four mine sweepers always at work and sometimes more outside the harbor as German planes and subs are always dropping mines. There was Mannie Maloney and three or four other fellows on the bridge when I got there. The chief mate was there and he said, "Let's go," so we all ran and got our life jackets and jumped into the lifeboat that we have been using to get to the dock so we can walk to town. We started out for the wreck as we could see the fellows jumping into the water. One of the mine sweepers was blowing a siren for ships to come out. We were about the first boat to get outside the break water and behind us came about six or eight torpedo boats and big motor launches. They passed us going like heck. We got out to the wreck about five minutes later and the mine sweeper had already sunk and it went down in twelve minutes. The torpedo boats wouldn't go in to where it had sunk because the water was covered with an inch of oil and they were afraid their propellers would get fouled up in the wreckage that was floating around everywhere. There were three other small boats besides us and we went right in where it went down. The oil and steam was coming up in a gusher and my knees were really shaking by then. We picked up six fellows and were they ever greasy. You could hardly get a hold of them as they would keep slipping. We finally got them in the boat and pulled to where one of the torpedo boats was and we put them on board. The water was pretty rough and it was a job as the fellows were pretty banged up. One fellow's leg was broke in two places and he sure was bleeding bad. The other fellows had cuts all over them. They didn't have but shorts and undershirts on. They must have been sleeping at the time. They were all so shocked they couldn't talk ... We looked around for more survivors but we couldn't find any. By this time the oil was two inches thick on the water and it was so rough the water was breaking over the side and we were getting soaking wet with water and oil. There were 8 of us fellows in the lifeboat. We circled around poking at every piece of wreckage to see if there were any more fellows in the water, but we didn't find any more. We headed back to the ship covered with oil and plenty scared from what we saw. I was covered with oil and I still stink from the smell of it. Tonight our officer came back to the ship and said that out of 125 fellows on the minesweeper, only eighteen were saved. It sure was awful and everyone was thanking us for picking up those six fellows that were just about ready to sink. They were just like an oil soaked rag. They were so shocked they couldn't hold a cigarette in their mouth. They sure have a dangerous job. The mines are magnetic and only go off when a ship doesn't have a degaussing machine on board. The machine makes a ship repel a magnetic mine. They explode about nine or more every day since we have been here. About an hour after we had tied up the day we got in they exploded two right where we had passed over to enter the harbor. It sure makes a fellow realize that we are in a war.[11]

Bernard Anderson and nine others earned a commendation letter for their efforts.

On the night of the attack the German Luftwaffe thundered down out of a clear evening sky, skimmed along just above the ships and laid waste to the busy port. It was 7:30 PM. In the span of twenty minutes, the raid became the worst bombing of Allied shipping since Pearl Harbor two years earlier. In fact, this attack became known as Little Pearl Harbor. A total of seventeen Allied ships were destroyed. Five were U.S. Liberty ships: the SS John Bascom, *the SS* John Harvey, *the SS* John L. Motley, *the SS* Joseph Wheeler, *and the SS* Samuel J. Tilden.

The attack and subsequent destruction were only preludes of the horror to come. A U.S. Liberty ship (John Harvey) *laden with a top-secret cargo of mustard gas bombs received a direct hit and exploded, killing the entire crew (thirty-eight merchant, twenty-eight Navy Armed Guard, and ten Army) and spreading the toxic chemical across the water and through the air of Bari.*

The success of the attack was stunning. The Allied invasion of Europe suffered a major setback. The loss of life was appalling. More than one thousand Allied servicemen and more than one thousand civilians were killed. In addition, many survivors of the initial bombing later died from toxic contamination but their deaths were not attributed to the attack.*[12]

On the day of the attack (December 2) Bernard Anderson wrote in his diary:

> Returned to ship about 5:15 and at chow was playing cribbage. At about 7:30, all of a sudden the guns on shore started firing. I went out and all the ships were opening up. I ran to my gun tub and was knocked down a couple of times by the concussion of bombs. We were having an air raid and bombs were hitting everywhere. They were over us before anyone knew it and dropping bombs before I even got to my gun. We were tied to the dock here and one bomb hit about thirty feet from the bow and my gun tub. It was about 500 lbs. The water and mud were thrown up and I got soaking wet. Another hit the dock about fifty feet from the ship. The buildings were flattened. After I shot all my ammo I went over to Mannie's gun tub and helped him. Parachute flares were dropping all around us and everything was all lit up. The smoke and fumes from the guns were so bad you could hardly breathe. Ed Leahy and another fellow were hit by shrapnel. They took Leahy to the hospital. I believe he will be all right. In my gun tub I found a 40 mm from one of the shore batteries and a bunch of shrapnel. I am bringing some home if I ever get home.[13]

On December 3, Anderson wrote:

> We are getting all ready for them tonight, but most of the ships that weren't hit are pulling out. All together eighteen ships were burning and sinking, the ammunition in them going off and shrinking you out of your shoes. The air raid was about

---

* For a full account of the attack on Bari, see *Nightmare In Bari: The World War II Liberty Ship Disaster and Cover-up* by Gerald Reminick.

The Armed Guard crew of the SS Louis Hennepin. *Bernard Anderson is second from left in second row of left photo.* Courtesy of Bernard L. Anderson.

one hour and we kept shooting. The ships are still burning this morning and the air is covered with smoke. Two of the fellows on our ship were blown into the water by the bomb concussions. They are unloading us today ... It is 2:30 and honey I will close for now and write later ... Darling 5:30 and everyone is sure nervous. I ate chow but didn't have much of an appetite. We are ready for them planes tonight. Gee I sure hope they don't come. I can't put in words how terrible it was last night. There's things darling I couldn't possibly write or ever explain. It's awful. We have the ammo greased and ready to load in the magazines when they run out. There are only three ships here now. The rest have left. Last night about five planes were shot down of about forty-five. They dropped about 130 bombs, some over 500 lbs., and some 250. They sure done what they set out to do. Eighteen ships were sunk all over the harbor and the fires are still burning. There is shrapnel all over and there are pieces on deck as big as an apple box side and as jagged as hell. There was a German plane that flew over today probably to see how much damage they had done. I sure wish we were out of here. They are trying to get us unloaded first so we can go.[14]

December 4:

The town here, which has a population of sixty to eighty thousand, was bombed too and every window in the city is broken. The roads leading from the town are full of people moving out. We can see the buildings from the ship that were bombed and there isn't much left of them. Ed Leahy, the fellow that got hit or thrown against his gun by the concussion of the bombs during the raid, is supposed to have a broken back, but they haven't taken x-rays yet. I sure hope he will be ok. We are the only ship in the harbor that hasn't been hit.[15]

December 6:

Everyone is leaving town. Mannie and I walked uptown today and every building in the town has nearly every window broken, even the window frames. About two bombs or more hit the city and they are still digging bodies out of the debris. The people here sure don't like the Americans. They blame the raid on us and they sure give us a dirty look ... The ships that were sunk are still burning. They have been trying to put them out, but they are oil fires and are hard to put out. Poor Ed Leahy - we packed his sea bag today and I guess we are going to leave him here.[16]

December 7:

... today is 2 years since Pearl Harbor and we just about had another Pearl Harbor here. This raid was the worst major disaster since Pearl Harbor. More ships were sunk here in one raid than any other since Pearl Harbor ...[17]

December 10:

I went ashore this afternoon ... Boy this is a dirty town. The buildings are made of chalk and they are digging out bodies from the air raid last week.[18]

December 11:

We were moved to another pier where we took guns and torpedo tubes off an English destroyer that hit a mine. They are stripping everything off it ... I don't know whether I should write this or not. Yesterday and today the bodies of the fellows that died during the air raid we had here are coming up. A fellow who drowns comes up about a week later. They pulled up about thirty. It sure is awful to see the water here in the harbor full of debris and oil and you can't help but see a body when you look. I found out a few days ago one of our ships had mustard gas on it and a lot of the fellows are dying from it. Gee, are we ever lucky the wind was blowing out to sea.[19]

December 12:

We are now on our way to Augusta, Sicily. We left two fellows behind. Leahy has a bad back, but it isn't busted. They flew him to Africa. He will probably beat us home. The other guy got his nose busted and was at the hospital getting it set when we sailed unexpectedly because of the raid last night ...[20]

~~~

These two stories are from Joe Benedetto. The first occurred before Bari was bombed and the second afterward.

"Well done, Guisseppe!"

In the summer of 1943 my ship (SS *Ezra Cornell*) sailed for the port of Bari, Italy, located on the Adriatic Sea. Before leaving New York, my father insisted I take along the address of his brother who lived in a small town of Gioia del Colle, about twenty miles south of the city of Bari. I took the address just to humor him; not knowing our destination was that city.

About a week after we reached Bari, I went to my commanding officer and explained about my uncle living not too far away.
~~~

He gave me a two-day pass. I hitched a ride on an Army truck going south and the driver let me off in the center of this town. I noticed an Italian policeman standing nearby and in my limited Italian I showed him the address my father had given me. He looked at the address and name and indicated he knew where the family lived. I followed him for several streets until we came to a house. It turned out that my uncle was the owner of the house, but he didn't live there, but had a farmhouse about three kilometers outside of town. I was offered a ride by horse and cart to the farmhouse.

After a two-hour journey we approached the farmhouse. A man with a black moustache and a dark blue vest walked to the cart and said to me in Italian: "Guisseppe, I have been waiting for you." I had no idea what he was talking about. I had never met this man before in my life. We spoke for a while and I finally realized how he came to know me. My brother Luke was serving with the 36th Division in Italy. The American army had been held up at a town called Cassino for three months and my father, in one of his letters, had sent him our uncle's address. Eventually, my brother found his way to our uncle's house. Apparently, he too had shown him a picture of me in a navy uniform. My cousin George was a gunner on a B17 operating from a former Italian airfield of Foggia. He had also found his way to our uncle's house. Apparently, he too had shown him a picture of me in a navy uniform. This was the reason for my uncle's greeting of "Guisseppe, I have been waiting for you."

My uncle asked me if I wanted to meet my maternal grandmother. Without hesitation I said yes. The town she lived in was about two hours away by horse cart. My uncle said we must return before dark because the road we had to travel on went through an American military airfield and if we didn't pass through before dark we would have to use another route which would take much longer.

I spent that Sunday with my grandmother and many other relatives. We did stay longer than we should have and it was dark. As we approached the airfield, an Army M.P. stopped us. The soldier approached our cart with a flashlight. The next thing I heard was "What the hell is an American sailor doing out here?"

I explained my ship was in the port city of Bari and I was visiting relatives in the town of Santeramo. We spoke for a while and he said he was from New Jersey. He let me continue. My uncle thought I knew the soldier because we had spoken for a while. I explained he was from another state.

In 1968, my wife and I returned to Italy and spent many wonderful days with my uncle and his family. Several years ago, his son and family came to the United States on vacation… My father came to America in 1916. Who would have thought that a family relationship would survive through two wars? I am sure my mother and father are looking down from heaven and are saying, "Well done, Guiseppe!" This was a great experience for me. In the middle of a war, I met my family in a foreign country.[21]

Reunion

In July of 1944, the *Ezra Cornell* had been on the Mediterranean Sea for about four months when we were ordered to dock in Torre Annunziata, a small town located south of Naples. After docking, the mail came aboard and in this mail call were several letters from my brother Luke. He was serving with the 36th Infantry Division, which had been set up on the Anzio Beachhead. In one of his letters he said if my ship ever came to Italy, look for his division. It was a Texas outfit with an insignia with a "T" which stands for Texas.

About four days later, I got shore leave so I hitched a ride up to Naples, which was about one half hour away. At that time the harbor was full of ships, I would guess several hundred. After arriving in Naples, I noticed all kinds of American soldiers with the "T" patch insignia. I asked one fellow where they were located. He said the division had been pulled off the line and they were going to be re-equipped and they would be part of the invasion force going up to Southern France. They were located up in the hills above Naples. This soldier said, "Stay here because a truck comes by every half hour and I could ride up to the staging area."

When I got there, there were three divisions, the 3rd, 45th, and the 36th, a total of about sixty thousand men. When I finally located my brother Luke's group, they were bivouacked in a peach grove. My brother and I talked for the rest of the afternoon and I asked him if he wanted to come back to my ship and spend the night. He got permission and we got back to the ship in time for chow. After we ate, I introduced him to some of my shipmates. One of them, Charlie Brady, gave him a box of cigars, which he appreciated very much.

The next morning my brother left. My next liberty ashore was three days later, so I went up to the staging area. When I got there, with the exception of a few army personnel, the three divisions were gone. I assumed they were loaded on the ships in the harbor.

One morning about three days later, I came up on deck and found the ships were gone.

About six days later, the radio announced the invasion of southern France had taken place.[22]

Named after the inventor who founded Cornell University, the Ezra Cornell *survived the war. On December 22, 1967 she was "abandoned sinking after developing leaks 200 miles west of Luderitz. 23-12-67: Sank south of Walvis Bay…*[23]

~~~

This story is a continuation of Lou Ritter's first story.

Three Dynamite Sticks

My second Liberty ship was the SS *Patrick Henry*. She was the first Liberty ship launched.

In 1944, we sailed out of New York across the Atlantic to Capetown, South Africa.

An AWOL sailor from an aircraft carrier turned himself in to our lieutenant. He later was taken off in Dakar, West Africa. There we picked up one replacement and another sailor got off due to illness.

We were loaded with mahogany logs and in Dakar we were restricted to the ship because of bubonic plague. From there we sailed north and entered the Mediterranean Sea. We eventually anchored at Gibraltar and they dropped depth charges all night long. They sounded like an echo through the hull of the ship.
~~~

Shown just after launching, the SS Patrick Henry *was the first ship launched in the 2,710 Liberty ship building program.* Project Liberty Ship.

We left Gibraltar and proceeded to Naples, Italy. We passed Sicily and the Strait of Messina. We saw the volcano Stromboli spewing lava and smoke into the air. In Naples there were sunken ships all over the harbor. Every kind of soldier and sailor seemed to be there.

From Naples we proceeded up the coast to Piombino and Livorno (Leghorn). In Leghorn we docked next to a mine field that was surrounded by tape. That was meant to stay out of the area. One night while there, I was on watch on the aft gun tub when something exploded. The ship rocked back and forth like a cradle. I rang General Quarters and all hands went to their battle stations. I thought it was the Germans firing their crack 88 mm guns.

We later found out that soldiers had thrown three dynamite sticks into the water as a precaution to kill any enemy frogmen who might be trying to sabotage the ships. We were the third ship in there and there were sunken ships all over the place.

I went on a Jeep ride with two soldiers up to the Arno River. The town there was wrecked by heavy fighting including a horse which had its stomach blown out. On the way I saw the Leaning Tower of Pisa.

We unloaded the logs we were carrying and then proceed to Naples where we loaded a group of German POWs. From there it was on to Oran, North Africa where I got to visit the Kasbah (Market Place). After that, we left in convoy for New York where we unloaded the POWs.[24]

~~~
~~~

The Armed Guard gun crew of the SS Patrick Henry *in 1944. Courtesy of U.S. Navy Armed Guard WW II Veterans.*

Bob Somers who was Lou Ritter's friend and shipmate aboard the Patrick Henry *in 1944, sent this Air Raid Report filed by Ensign Chester Kasica, Armed Guard Officer on the SS* Patrick Henry. *This is Part C of the Report and it indicates the edginess of the gunners when they couldn't see a target.*

(C) During our first stay in Naples we had two air raids. The first one occurred on the evening of October 21, 1943, while we were anchored in the harbor outside the breakwater with a number of other ships and destroyers. At 1900 two white flares were seen 4000 yards away at the port bow, and several further off on the starboard bow. This was followed shortly by fire ashore and antiaircraft fire from several ships and shore batteries. A bomb fell less than 50 yards away on the port bow and Albert H. Sobal, S1/c, who was climbing into the forward machine gun nest on the port side fell to the deck and suffered a bad contusion of the left foot.

By this time planes could be heard, but it was only now and then that I believed I saw a plane at high altitude. Most of the machine gunners fired in too large a volume and I told them

Left, Bob Somers in 1944, and right, standing, in 1991. The person seated in the right photo is Lou Ritter. Bob Somers.

not to fire unless they had something within range to fire at. When the first bomb dropped, the gun captain got excited and expended forty rounds at the 3"50 on the bow before I could contact him since the sight-setter wasn't wearing the phones. At about 1915 three bombs dropped on our starboard bow, the closest one being about 200 yards away. I directed fourteen rounds of 3"50 ammunition set at eight seconds when on four occasions I believed I saw targets. The range at all times was 3500 yards and the scale was set at 500. About 3000 rounds of 20mm ammunition was expended. No ship was hit. Activity lasted till about 1940... The next day we learned that there were about 12 enemy planes and that four were shot down. An army base had been bombed ashore...

Ens. Chester C. Kasica, U.S.N.R.,
Armed Guard Officer

~~~

Bob Hassard was a member of the U.S. Naval Armed Guard crew aboard the Liberty ship SS Houston Volunteers.

A Message to a Friend

While forming a convoy off Norfolk, Virginia, the SS *Houston Volunteers* was the commodore ship of the convoy. A U.S. Navy DE (Destroyer Escort) 220 came alongside to deliver orders to the convoy commander. I was off watch and was observing orders
~~~

Bob Hassard in 1944, left, and in the trainer's position aboard the SS Jeremiah O'Brien *in 1995.* Bob Hassard.

being cast over. Seeing the number 220, I realized that someone I knew from home (Long Island, NY) was on that ship. I could not recall who it was.

The DE then moved ahead of the convoy on station. About an hour later, I realized who the person was that I remembered at home. I then went up on the bridge and asked the Navy signalman if he could get a personal message to the DE. He said they might only answer the light once because we were the commodore ship. He told me to write down what I wanted to say and to whom. I wrote it down and they did answer the light. He sent my message to my friend (Bill Siegel, Soundman 2/c aboard the U.S.S. *Frances M. Robinson*).

My friend received the message from me and sent his regards. The ships then went to Oran, North Africa. The navy ships went to the dock and the merchant ships anchored out in the harbor. I found out after the war that the Navy ships had gotten liberty to go into town, where Bill met another friend from home (Nick Esposito, a storekeeper stationed in Oran). When Bill found him in Oran, Nick was sleeping on a cot and Bill flipped him over onto the deck. They had a short visit while the convoy was in Oran. If my ship hadn't anchored out, we would have all been able to see each other. This was the talk of all the families for years.

My friend Bill Siegel passed away in 1965, and I ended up marrying his widow, Audrey, in 1969. We had all known each other from childhood, since we had all gone to school together.[25]

The SS Houston Volunteers *was scrapped in Oakland in 1966.*[26]

9

D-Day and Northern Europe

The invasion of northern Europe was delayed from 1943 to 1944 as the Allies built up the massive preparations for the one-chance-only invasion. During this period the Allies focused on their southern offensive: ridding Africa of the Nazis, gaining control of the Mediterranean Sea and forcing Italy to surrender. With each victory they moved closer to their goal of reaching into German air space from the south and bombing their cities and industries. Of special importance was crippling the supply lines from the German-controlled Balkans and cutting off the flow of the natural resources upon which Germany was so dependent.

Germany was forced to divert manpower and war materials from other theaters of action weakening her position against Russia. However, she still had a formidable Army and tank corps under the command of Field Marshal Erwin Rommel with which to defend herself against the coming Allied invasion.

The major question was where the invasion would take place. The Germans thought it would be at Calais, the narrowest point in the English Channel, and that an attack on Normandy — or anywhere else on the French coast — would simply be a diversion.

Normandy was indeed the location but two major obstacles faced the Allies: the absence of natural ports and how to unload the vast amounts of armament, equipment, manpower and supplies required to breach "fortress Europe." To achieve these objectives artificial harbors called "Mulberries" were constructed. They were sheltered by breakwaters named "Gooseberries." These were made up of ships and floating caissons ("Phoenixes") which were sunk off shore. An ingenious transport system was thus created with road and rails laid on top of the Phoenixes. Over these roads traveled some 150,000 men and 7,000 vehicles during the first few days of the invasion. By the end of June this number swelled to almost a million men, over 100,000 vehicles and over a half million tons of supplies. The magnitude of the invasion was incredible. "Over 1,300 warships, 1,600 merchant ships, and 4,000 landing ships were available for the liberation campaign together with 13,000 aircraft (including 5,000 fighters, and 4,000 bombers) and 3,500 gliders."[1]

Emory Land, head of the Maritime Commission wrote:

> ...32 American ships were to be sunk off the beachhead. They were manned by more than 1,000 merchant seaman and officers who volunteered for the hazardous duty. These ships, many of which had previously suffered severe battle damage, were charged with explosives for quick scuttling. They sailed from England through mined waters, filed into position off Normandy beach under severe shelling from German shore batteries, and were sunk by the crews to form the artificial harbor. Behind this breakwater, prefabricated units were towed in to handle the subsequent debarkation of men and equipment, to make invasion of Fortress Europe possible... This project stands as one of the most remarkable waterborne accomplishments of all time...[2]

The mulberry harbor at Arromanches. Note the breakwater created by sunken ships and the causeways to the beach. Publisher's collection.

The U.S. Navy Armed Guard was there guarding the breakwater ships and ensuring the invasion's success. It was a daunting task, accomplished under heavy enemy fire:

> Armed Guards on some 22 merchant ships which were scuttled [deliberately sunk] to make a breakwater played a vital role in the operation. For days they endured the early fury of the German counterattack and helped give fire protection to the forces ashore from their partly submerged ships. This was a task which required courage and the ability to do without sleep...
>
> The men aboard the 13 ships scuttled at Omaha Beach and the 9 ships scuttled off Utah Beach had much the same experiences. Crossing the [English] Channel there were the [enemy] mines and the E-boats [small fast German motor torpedo boats also known Schnellboote or S-Boats; similar to American PT-boats]. By day German 88mm guns fired at the block ships, and by night enemy bombers came over.[3]

Then began the logistical nightmare: supplying the invasion force once a foothold was gained, not only with supplies but new manpower. The attacks in various forms continued on our merchant ships and Navy Armed Guard:

> Armed Guards on merchant ships making trips between Britain and Normandy experienced just about every form of attack. Submarines and planes were supplemented by new "V" bombs [the German V-1 missiles — the "buzz bomb" — an unguided cruise missile launched from bases in France to hit targets in England] which passed over many ships on their way to England. Mines were a constant menace, and they took a heavy toll of ships. E boats were active .... German artillery continued to shell the anchorages [off the Normandy landing beaches] for some days.
>
> Fortunately, there was excellent [Allied] air cover and ships required to anchor off the beaches for only a few days before returning to England for more cargo. While the number of planes destroyed by Armed Guards at Normandy is not large, their guns made excellent records on the few occasions when they fired.[4]

In preparing for the Normandy invasion and thereafter through December 1945, a total of seventy ships were either sunk or damaged. Thirty were deliberately sunk. The others were either torpedoed by planes, hit by submarines or mined. A total of eighty-seven Army personnel, twenty-four merchant crew and ten U.S. Navy Armed Guard were killed. In addition, there were fourteen ships on which Armed Guards were wounded.[5]

~~~

Harlan P. Ross describes what it was like working on tugs at the D-Day beaches. This article first appeared in the May and June 2002 issues of Sea Classics *magazine.*

The Tug of War

This is the story of a year I spent as an eighteen-year-old U.S. Navy Armed Guard Signalman aboard a U.S. Army Transport Service tug boat, the *LT 130.* The tug was just 123 feet in length, rather small for the adventure it was about to embark upon. The crew totaled twenty-three men, mostly merchant seaman,
~~~

along with an Army radioman, two Navy Armed Guard gunners, and me. We were in Charleston, South Carolina. It was February 1944. In a matter of a couple of days we were directed to join up in a small convoy designated CK-1 comprised of six similar tugs and eight small Army tankers. Our escorts were two U.S. Navy Destroyer Escorts.

The winter North Atlantic lived up to its nasty reputation as the convoy plowed its way to Bermuda and then through heavy seas, to the Azores and from there to the British Isles where the *LT 130* was directed into Newport Wales. From there we were sent to Plymouth, England which became our base of operations and where we got a new captain; a Norwegian named Arvin Heiberg. Captain Heiberg's family was still in Oslo under the

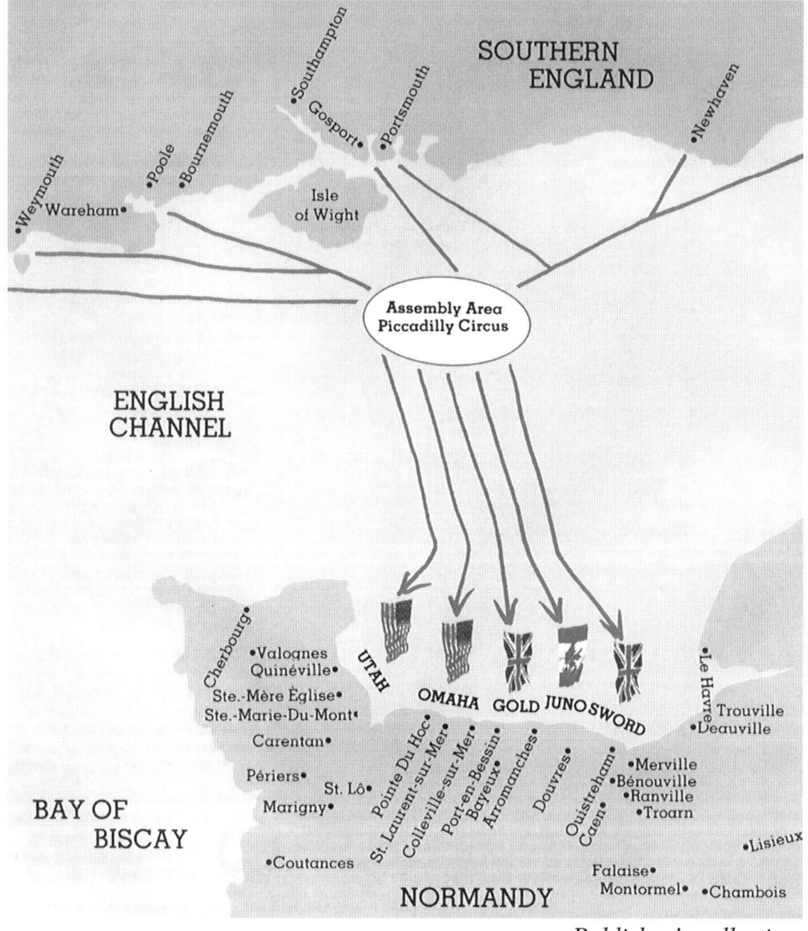

Publisher's collection.

Omaha Beach on the coast of Normandy, shortly after D-Day. Note the barrage balloons and number of ships in the background. National Archives.

control of the Nazi occupation and he was determined to do all he could to hasten the end of the war. As a result the *LT 130* hardly ever cooled down as he took on assignment after assignment towing and deploying equipment and war material from one port to another in preparation for the big push which everyone knew was approaching but no one knew when. We were in and out of the English Channel ports of Fowey, Falmouth, and Southampton among others and Bristol channel ports such as Cardiff, Bristol, and Barry Docks. Although our shore leave was usually very brief, one or two nights, the crew did get to see and enjoy a great variety of seaport towns.

About 3:00 or 4:00 o'clock in the dark morning of June 6, 1944 we were towing two barges and headed east along the north shore of the English Channel when Captain Heiberg suddenly ordered the helmsman to swing the wheel a hard right. A hard right meant south and south meant the coast of France; Normandy to be more precise. It was then we knew the "big push," the attack on Hitler's Fortress Europe was about to happen and we were to be in it.

The two barges we were towing in tandem were loaded; one with small arms ammunition, and the other with 5-gallon cans of gasoline. Our job was to follow in the first wave of the invasion as close to shore as we could get and swing the two barges around in a "crack the whip" fashion so that they would drift ashore for the GI's already on Utah Beach. Shells from the beach were raining down indiscriminately among the thousands of ships and boats in the armada. Once we accomplished this assignment we went back to England and were hooked up to a huge concrete caisson which we towed back to Omaha Beach for the artificial harbor, code-named Mulberry.

Le Havre and Antwerp were captured in the summer and late fall. We were assigned to tow heavy equipment into Antwerp just as the "Battle of the Bulge" unfolded. Hundreds of German V1 and V2 "buzz" bombs were showered on the city and docks causing a great amount of damage. It was Christmas of 1944.

When the "Bulge" was contained and things quieted down a bit we were surprised to be told that, after practically a year, the navy gunners and signalman were to be relieved of duty aboard the *LT 130*. The emotional reaction to this was a fascinating mixture of sheer joy and the sad realization that I would part with not just acquaintances but friendships of unique depth. From the captain down to the lowliest oiler or deck hand we had shared and weathered experiences, which would probably never be matched in any of our lifetimes. I believe that somehow I knew this. Now that I look back through the passage of over half a century that premonition has proven to be true. Not just the danger, fear and excitement, but in terms of meaning and purpose, that year is unmatched. Though I served aboard two more ships as far away as the Philippine Islands, that tugboat had developed in my mind a soul and a personality with which I identified and which I shall never forget. The ever-brightening light of history reveals what I didn't, and actually couldn't have known at the time; that I and twenty-two others aboard had been an integral part of the *Greatest* amphibious assault in history. This battle was the turning point, which led to the final victory in the greatest war the world has ever known. And we were in it aboard a lowly tugboat … The Tug of War![6]

~~~

This story is a continuation of James Montesarchio's earlier story.

D-Day

We left New York on the S.S. *William H. Webb* in April 1944 in convoy to Great Britain. They were forming up convoys in Great Britain and we finally ended up in Southampton. We missed the June 6th invasion of Omaha and Utah Beaches but we finally made the invasion two weeks later at both beaches. We carried supplies, munitions and about 500 men of General Patton's 3rd Armored Division. We delivered into both Omaha and Utah beaches a total of five times. In the process, we were rammed by another ship putting us out of commission. We were forced to return to Belfast, Ireland for a temporary plate and sent back to the States.

I have never been sorry of my service in the U.S. Navy. It taught me to appreciate the simple things in life. To understand that we must all get along with one another in order to survive![7]

On a voyage from Philadelphia to Murmansk the S.S. William H. Webb *ran ashore on a reef near Kildin Island [off Murmansk] on January 15, 1946. She broke in two and was a total loss.*[8] *According to James, all members of the crew were rescued.*

~~~

The first part of John Lucarelli's story appears in Chapter 12, "Storms and Weather." After the bow of his ship broke off in a storm, they abandoned ship and were picked up by an English fishing trawler and taken to Liverpool. From Liverpool they were sent to Londonderry for training in plane recognition and spent Christmas 1943 there. Afterward, the NAG crew was sent back to Liverpool where John finally boarded the Panamanian freighter S.S. Audacious. *The* Audacious *was the former Italian ship* Belvedere *and was to be scuttled at Normandy.*

The Next Morning the Harbor was Full of Ships

Soon after we boarded the *Audacious* a crew came on board and removed anything that a small crew could do without. We then sailed around the British Isles for quite some time. The only time we went ashore was in Falkirk, Scotland for fuel. Liberty was short.

Finally we anchored in Southampton. Crews came aboard and welded plates on the inside of the hull and installed large batteries with a lot of wiring.

> The 22 block ships were carefully prepared for their assigned operation. The heavy [deck] gun aft was removed and four 20mm [antiaircraft guns] and a 40mm [antiaircraft] were generally substituted. The ships were stripped of all unnecessary gear. About eight explosive charges were placed in the holds and large openings were cut in the traverse bulkheads. Necessary food supplies and ammunition had to be moved topside, for the decks of some of the ships were to be underwater at times.[9]

The next morning the harbor was full of ships and the sky full of planes. When we set sail, they told us that our ship was purposely being sunk for an artificial harbor. When they blew the charges, our ship did not sink on her keel, but rolled on her side, where we ended up standing. Several ships came alongside and righted us. We manned the guns for what I thought was twelve

Some of the sunken ships at one of the gooseberrys at Normandy. Robert Milby.

days. We were finally picked up and brought to Southampton where they told us that they expected only 10 percent of the crews to come back.[10]

Albert Lowe, left, and his brother, Irving in 1944. Albert Lowe.

~~~

The following is an Official Report concerning a ship that Albert Lowe S1/c was on during the invasion of Normandy. Al came aboard the Liberty ship SS Clara Barton *on May 25, 1944 along with two other men who were assigned to the Naval Armed Guard crew. Al had previously been aboard the SS* Edmund Fanning. *While the* Fanning *was unloading in England, he went to see his brother, Irving, a parachute rigger stationed nearby. He returned to the ship four hours over leave.*

"I hadn't seen my brother in years because he had joined the Navy in the 1930s. I had joined in 1942. We did see each other and we had a great time. When I got back to my ship my Lt. (jg) Bertrand B. Prince, reported me as being AWOL."

Al was subsequently transferred to the Clara Barton.

The following report was filed on June 11, 1944 by Ensign Ralph M. Zink, USNR, Commanding Officer, Naval Armed Guard aboard the SS Clara Barton *concerning the action from June 6 to June 11, 1944 and Albert Lowe was there.*

CONFIDENTIAL

June 11, 1944

To: The Chief of Naval Operations

Via: (1) U.S. Naval Port Officer, Southampton, England
(2) The Commander U.S. Naval Forces in Europe

Subject: Cross Channel Operations, S.S. *Clara Barton* From June 6, 1944 to June 11, 1944.

Reference: (a) General Instructions for Commanding Officers
~~~

of Naval Armed Guards on Merchant Ships, 1943, Third Edition, paragraph 4301.

1. In accordance with reference (a), the following information is submitted:

(a) Type of vessel, Liberty, EC2-S-C1. Cargo and personnel, 550 troops, U.S. Infantry and Field Artillary [sic] and train. Owner of vessel, WSA. Chartered to Coastwise, Pacific and Far East Line.

(b) Port of departure, Barry Roads, Wales. June 6th. Convoyed. Port of arrival, Utah Beach, France June 8th. Departed Utah Beach, June 10th. Arrived Southampton, June 11th.

(c) Enemy action. At 0200, June 8th while in convoy cross channel, and aerial bomb exploded about 800 yards off starboard bow. The plane was heard, but not seen. It was not engaged with gunfire. Escort vessels operating on the horizon, both port and starboard, engaged surface targets with 20 mm fire and light guns between the hours of 0200 and 0430. At 1100, June 9th, concealed enemy guns from the shore began shelling the area in which the vessel was anchored. By 1300, two near-hits exploded on the starboard quarter of the Liberty ship 500 yards on this vessel's port beam, and three shells exploded within 200 yards of the *Clara Barton*'s bow. The vessel moved to a safer anchorage. About 2030, June 9th, the 20 mm guns engaged a low-flying aircraft identified by the ROC spotters aboard as a Messerschmidt 109F. No hits were scored. At about 0400, June 10th, an unidentified aircraft circled the ship above the clouds and dropped an aerial bomb on the S. S. *Charles Morgan* which lay at anchor about 1500 yards off the starboard quarter of this vessel. A direct hit was scored in # 5 hold. A few moments later, an aerial bomb exploded about 300 yards off the stern of the *Clara Barton*. On the morning of June 11th, while in convoy to Southampton, escorts engaged surface targets within 2000 yards of the starboard beam sporadically between the hours of 0100 and 0400.

The Liberty Ship, SS Charles Morgan *was bombed by German aircraft at 0400 local time on June 10, 1944 while lying at anchor in 33 feet of water about ½ mile off Utah Beach, Normandy, France, having sailed from Newport, Wales June 6 in Convoy EBM-3. The ship had completed discharge and was awaiting orders. She was flying a barrage balloon from the aftermast. Her complement was made up of 45 merchant crew, 27 Naval Armed Guard, 64 U.S. Army Port Battalion, the British Convoy Commodore and staff of three, and 2 Royal Navy plane observers. Of this number, an Able Seaman and 7 U.S. Army men were killed.*[11]

(d) From Barry Roads to Lands End, Condition III sea watches were maintained. From Lands End to Area Zed, Condition II, and cross channel, Condition I. While in the Utah Beach area, Condition II was maintained during daylight hours, and Condition I during the night. Cross channel to Southampton, Condition I was re-assumed. [sic]

(e) Unloading delays were as follows: It was impossible to establish the exact location of a Beach Commander from this vessel. Control seemed to shift from one landing craft to another. This resulted in delay in securing barges for unloading. On June 8th, the vessel was unable to secure barges after 1800 and thus more than

The Charles Morgan *with her after end resting on the bottom after being bombed by the Luftwaffe.* National Archives.

four hours of daylight unloading were lost. The barges were also unwilling to unload a cargo of 5 gallon tins of gasoline and of water. Point blank refusal came from two American and one British unloading barge. Finally, about 2200, June 9th, a British barge unloaded the tins in the dark. This was about five hours after the vessel had otherwise been unloaded. The unloading operation might also have been speeded up had more of the heavy vehicles aboard been stowed in # 2 and # 4 holds where jumbo booms are available. Too many light jeeps were stowed in these holds. Time was lost in removing many light loads with the jumbo booms which operate comparatively slowly. Finally, experienced Army winch operators and stevedores who were supposed to be aboard with the troops were not placed on the vessel. The Merchant crew did most of the unloading, but could have operated more efficiently had additional experienced personnel been assigned to the ship as was originally promised.

(f), (g), (h). Satisfactory

(i) On the evening of June 9th, visibility was poor. It was noted from this vessel that the small amphibious craft in the Utah Beach area opened fire indiscriminately with 20mm guns upon all aircraft sighted. In two instances, seen from aboard this vessel, planes definitely identified as friendly Spitfires by the Royal Observer Corps spotters were fired upon by these small craft. The contagion then spread to two ships in the center of the harbor who opened fire with 20mm's and heavier guns. The Spitfires were fortunately out of effective range and none were seen to be hit. A quicker, more definite system of identification seems to be indicated for the assault area. The amphibious craft apparently need some sort of central control to advise whether planes are friendly or enemy before they fire. The larger vessels who fired upon friendly aircraft may not have had ROC spotters assigned to them. If all ROC spotters are capable as the ones assigned to the *Clara Barton*, they are to be highly recommended. They are able to positively identify aircraft long before they become a threat to the ship should they prove to be hostile and while they are still well out of range. This Gunnery Officer feels that there is still time to effectively open fire once the ROC spotter has made positive identification.

On the morning of June 10th, Commodore Meek and his signal staff came aboard. He was able to take the Southampton bound convoy in charge upon receiving orders from a control ship. Commodore Meek spent the better part of the day attempting to contact control for his orders. No orders came through. Both the U.S. Signalmen and the Commodore's signal staff were on the bridge at all times. Late in the afternoon, a Coast Guard vessel came alongside and stated that the Commodore should have sailed four hours earlier, that he had been sent his orders, and that he had missed his convoy. The vessel finally sailed with another convoy at 2230. Again, a more definite central control seems to be needed. The control ship from which the Commodore unsuccessfully attempted to get his orders lay three cable lengths from the *Clara Barton*.

(j) Satisfactory.

RALPH M. ZINK, Ens. USNR
Armed Guard Commander

Thus began a series of shuttles involving the SS Clara Barton. *Of interest was the report that the now promoted Lt. (jg) Ralph Zink wrote on August 27, 1944 concerning the August 8 – 26 Cross Channel operation:*

(b) … Port of arrival, Omaha Beach, August 8th. Departed Omaha Beach August 26th, arrived Southampton August 26th.
(c) No enemy action
(d) Routine
(e) Unloading delays. Four days of rough weather delayed operations. Barge service was satisfactory. Unloading by U.S. Army stevedores was inept generally. Steve-

> dores went swimming, played cards and hid in corners of the ship to sleep. Cargo was broken and lost over the side through poor handling. A Pratt and Whitney aircraft engine was lost in this manner. When the engine went over the side, the ship's Bo' sun rigged a falls to retrieve it while the crate was still afloat. Use of the gear was refused by the stevedores who merely poked at the engine until it sank. It should be noted that the above-conditions did not exist during such times when E.J. Kensinger, 1st Lt., T.C. was aboard and in charge. This officer knew his job and the stevedores worked well during the periods when he was assigned to supervise them. [12]

The SS Clara Barton *which had been on duty since D-Day arrived back in New York on December 24, 1944.*

~~~

This story is a continuation of John Starkey's Archangel experience aboard the SS James Smith. *They sailed from Archangel alone for a day-and-a-half after missing their convoy. John wrote, "The Germans didn't bother us on our return trip and I still don't know why."*

How many guys can you fit under a mess table?

We arrived in Cardiff, Wales where we shuttled back and forth to England. I fell in love with a girl in Cardiff and wanted to marry her. My commanding officer said, no, which he had the authority to do. I am glad that he did because as he explained to me that after we got back to the States she would have wanted to come back and visit home and that could have been expensive. He was right as usual.

We left Cardiff one day and somehow we rammed another ship in one of the channels. We had to go to Antwerp, Belgium for repairs. Antwerp was a little scary because the Germans were sending V-1 "buzz-bombs" and V-2 rockets over the city. When you heard the motor shut off, you needed to go for cover. Have
~~~

you ever wondered how many guys could fit under a mess table at one time? Plenty, believe me.

We got our bow all fixed up nice and shiny and took off for France. We were at Omaha Beach one day and Utah Beach the next. Ducks came out and took our troops into the beach. It was scary again at night as German planes would fly over and drop bombs. They didn't know what they were doing but we did as shrapnel kept hitting the decks. It was something to see when we would get a German plane in the spotlight and the pilot couldn't get out of it until he was shot down. The Germans couldn't fly in close and strafe us as there were large balloons in the air anchored to the ground.

After the invasion was secured, our ship returned to the good old U.S.A. I was transferred to Pier 92 for further duty, which took me to Okinawa and finally, Port Directors, Sasebo, Japan. I was released from active duty, went home for five years and then back into the Navy for another four years. I was discharged at Little Creek, Virginia, just a short hop from where it all started at the Armed Guard Gunnery School.[13]

~~~

Robert Auer was a Navy Armed Guard Gunner S1/c from 1943 to 1946. He sailed in all three theaters of action; American, European and Asiatic. "Much has been told by our 'shipmates' about their experiences aboard various types of ships, mainly Libertys. But many of the Naval Armed Guard served on 'foreign ships'! The following is my experience aboard the M.S. (motor ship) Cavalcade, *from 1944-1945."*

Sailing Under Foreign Flags

On approximately December 6, 1944, the ship M.S. *Cavalcade* (Danish) sailing in convoy arrived at Antwerp, Belgium, carrying Army Quartermaster supplies. These consisted of cigarettes, food rations, medical and dental supplies. The deck cargo was made up of freight, Jeeps and laundry trailer units.

To reach Antwerp, via the English Channel, into the Scheldt River, which was extremely narrow, and mined with German
~~~

mines, we had a minesweeper ahead of the single line of ships. As the mines were cut and they broke to the surface passing the ships, we would shoot at them with rifles, hoping to explode them!

A Belgian pilot was put on board to navigate the river. It was his first "free" ship brought into port since the German occupation. An interesting moment occurred when we first saw a German airplane. The pilot said, "It was a German Jet." We asked, "What's a jet?" His answer was, "An airplane with no propellers."

After arriving in the port and docking, the unloading cranes (which moved on rails) had to be cleaned of dirt, grass, etc. by the German prisoners so that the cranes could move.

While the Battle of the Bulge was being fought, the weather conditions were very bad (snow, fog, etc.) so the troops could not be supplied by "air-drops." So supplies had to be delivered into Antwerp. Antwerp had endured a massive bombardment by German V-1 flying bombs and V-2 rockets. The port facilities and city had been a major target, and a number of ships and buildings had been hit. There was one occasion where a "buzz bomb" hit a movie theatre, and hundreds of people were killed. (A more accurate account was impossible). Some of us crew members worked at the site, rescuing the casualties and removing the dead.

> On the first day of the German Ardennes offensive, December 16, 1944, the worst disaster occurred. The "Rex" Cinema on Avenue De Keyserlei was packed full of people in the middle of the afternoon, nearly 1,200 seats were occupied, all watching the featured movie. At 15.20 hrs the audience suddenly glimpsed a split-second flash of light cutting through the theater, followed by the balcony and ceiling crashing down during a deafening boom. A V2 rocket had impacted directly on top of the cinema...
>
> The destruction was total. Afterwards many people were found still sitting in their seats – stone dead. For more than a week the Allied authorities worked to clear the rubble. Later, many of the bodies were laid out in the zoo for identification. The death toll was 567 casualties to soldiers and civilians, 291 injured and 11 buildings destroyed. 296 of the dead & 194 of the injured were US, British, & Canadian soldiers. This was the

single highest death total from one rocket attack during the war in Europe. [14]

It was calculated (by our radio operator) that over 454 bombs were "logged in" the vicinity. Many and constant air raid alarms were sounded. The Germans knew that the port would be used as an advance into Germany and were fighting back fiercely.

It was determined that the Navy personnel should stay within the ship as much as possible because the steel sides would give relative safety. It was "charted" (based on the number of V-bombs that fell) that morning was the safest time, and dawn, dusk and midnight the most dangerous! You could set your watch for what we called, the "Midnight Special." During our stay in Antwerp, one of our Armed Guard crewmembers (*William J. McQueeney S3/c 12/16/44*) was killed by a Flying Bomb.

On approximately December 22nd the ship left Antwerp bound for South England. On the return through the Scheldt River, we passed ships that had been hit through some kind of action. We came under attack (approx. 1700 hours) by German E-boats. The attack was repelled by the escorts and the Naval Armed Guard. Our ship lost her convoy and became a straggler but air coverage was supplied by the RAF to our destination.

The *Cavalcade* was the ex-*Gertrude Maersk*, a former Danish Flag vessel seized by the U.S. War Shipping Administration in early 1941. She was seized to prevent sabotage against Danish ships in American ports, but she never flew the U.S. Flag.

This ship was never built or reconditioned properly for Navy gun crews. The facilities were very bad, (i.e., no working showers), a Danish-speaking crew, at least six other nationalities, including non-English-speaking Chinese mess boys. The cooks were Danish, and cooked non-American food, but we did have lots of rice — no such thing as dessert (cake, ice cream, etc.). There were plenty of cockroaches in the food, especially in the bread.

The food was cooked aft, and carried in buckets through the ship and open areas to the Navy Mess. Located below decks, it consisted of one room with two tables and long wooden benches, no individual seats. Lacking portholes, there was never any daylight, and electric lights were used twenty-four hours a day.

News was non-existent, as there were no radios. The ship had a constant 15 degree-plus list; the decks in the Navy quarters were always wet. The cargo holds were made of mahogany since the ship carried raw silk from Japan in the 1930's.

Listed below are "excerpts" from the National Archives to the Port Authority from an Armed Guard Officer's Log on the *Cavalcade*:

1. No water for drinking or washing.
2. Drinking water has to be hand carried from galley to quarters in whatever containers are available.
3. Hot water (for washing) comes from boiling water from the steam pipes.
4. No steam tables to keep food warm.
5. Need further insulation against cold and dampness in crew quarters, mid-ship.

Miscellaneous comment from officer's log: "This ship is condemned for navy personnel!" Yet the Armed Guard Crews continued aboard.

Despite all this, the ship and her Armed Guard Crew did their jobs well — surviving a North Atlantic hurricane, Normandy, and the Battle of the Bulge (Antwerp, Belgium) action.

A final comment that may be of interest; When I inquired about joining the "Local" chapter of the Battle of the Bulge Veterans, they said, "I didn't qualify because I was not an Army combat veteran!" Where would they have been, if we had not gotten the "Ammo" and supplies to them?

The Armed Guard slogan has always been, "We Aim To Deliver, And We Did"![15]

~~~

Joe Toohill related his duties as the officer in charge of a gun crew:
~~~

I was an Armed Guard Commander and Gunnery officer in the U.S. Navy during WW II. I served on merchant ships, which were manned by Merchant Marine. I was the Armed Guard commander on the *Michael DeKovats* Liberty ship.

It was part of my duties as Armed Guard commander to keep a log or diary of the daily activities of my gunnery crew. When I reported in the U.S. I had to submit a copy of my log to the Port Director.

I kept a log in longhand and always managed to type the log before we docked in the U.S. We called the copies which we gave the Port Director a Smooth Log. The Smooth Log which I submitted was not a log of the ship per se but a history of activities of my gunnery crew aboard the ship and any enemy activities which were inflicted on the ship. The merchant crew kept their official log of the ship but I had nothing to do with it.

There were two types of German bombs which I became acquainted with. One type we called a Buzz Bomb that had a motor that sounded like a John Deere tractor. The other type was the German V-2 Bomb which was the type which hit the dock near our ship...[16]

From Smooth Log

2000, Docked port of Antwerp, Belgium. Pier 218.

1945

Jan.1.

0900, Muster. Inspected quarters and battery.

1007, General alarm sounded. Shore batteries on our starboard quarter were firing at three planes flying very low and at a high rate of speed. The planes changed course and flew towards our ship. Two of the planes altered course and flew back in direction from which they were first observed to be approaching. Remaining plane kept on course which would permit it to cross our ship amidships. Other ships docked near us opened fire on the plane which was now approaching at approximately a 30 degree angle. The plane was traveling at a rate of speed in excess of 275 knots per hour. Fire was opened by our Nos. 7, 5, 3 and 1, 20 mm guns in succession when the plane was approximately 1200 yards distant and at approximately 1000 feet altitude. The fire from our ship was well concentrated and leading the plane. The plane was observed to falter or stagger and a flash of fire followed by a puff of smoke came from the plane. Plane appeared to be on fire and altered course so as to cross our bow at a distance of about 800 yards. No. 4 20 mm gun was fired after plane had crossed our bow. Plane was observed to approach earth on a long glide and apparently landed or crashed three or four miles away from our ship. Landing was not visible owing to buildings and the City of Antwerp. A number of other ships docked near us also fired on plane. Plane is believed to be in an ME 109. At the time the plane was hit it was out of range of the shore batteries which had been firing at it and they ceased firing and there were no other planes of any kind near the plane which was shot down. It is believed by all on board ship who observed the action that several hits were registered by the gunfire from our ship. Gunnery Officer was on bridge during the action and directed the firing and all of the navy gun crew were in or near the 20 mm gun tubs as we had been advised not to use our large caliber guns while at the docks. 230 rounds of 20 mm ammunition was expended and no casualties were suffered by either personnel or equipment. All of the Armed Guard and Communication Liaison personnel were aboard during the action. The Naval Armed Guard unit were cool throughout the action and followed orders and directions in a calm manner. The Armed Guard Officer in charge recommends that the Navy Armed Guard Crew be commended for their action during this engagement. Sun was shining and visibility was very good.

1030, Secured from general quarters.

2355, General alarm sounded. New moon shining and sky clear. Plane observed to be approaching ship at high altitude and shore batteries were firing at it. Plane was crossing our stern and fire was opened by No. 8 20mm gun but altitude was too great and order was given to cease fire. 30 rounds of 20mm ammunition was expended and there was no casualties to personnel or equipment.

2400, Secured from general quarters.

Jan. 2.

0300, General alarm sounded. New moon shining and sky clear. Plane observed to be approaching ship but at very high altitude. Shore batteries were firing at plane but we did not open fire with our guns. Plane rapidly passed from view.

0315, Secured from general quarters.

Jan. 14.

0900. Muster. Inspected quarters and battery.

1717. A German Rocket bomb hit the dock on our starboard quarter at a distance of about twenty-five yards. Flying shrapnel put a hole in No. 3 20mm gun tub and two holes in 3"50 gun cover and considerable damage to the ship. The concussion tore all the doors off the hinges in the gun crew quarters aft. There were no injuries to any one in Naval Armed Guard Unit. The first Mate in the Merchant Crew received minor injuries. A soldier on the dock within a few yards of the ship was killed. There was damage to our No. 7 and No. 8 20mm splinter shields.[17]

Joe Toohill was in Antwerp retrieving the mail when the bomb hit. They had been unloading railroad irons when the bomb hit on the other side of them. The rails served as a shield against the shell shock. When Joe returned, he didn't recognize the dock area.

~~~

Clifford Davis joined the Navy on April 19, 1944 when he was seventeen. After boot camp held in Sampson, New York, he trained at Gunnery School in Shelton, Virginia.

A Comforting Letter

I shipped out on the SS *Wellesley*, a tanker. We made three trips to Liverpool, England. While we were in Birkenhead, I went to church and talked with the priest. I gave him my name and home address. Later I learned that he had written my mother, and let her know of my visit and that I was fine. I still have the letter.

Then I caught the SS *Morris Sigman*, Liberty ship and went to England and Antwerp, Belgium. There we docked and a ship named the SS *Elmira* was docked behind us. My hometown was Elmira, New York so this was a coincidence. There was not one
~~~

person aboard that ship from the state of New York, let alone Elmira. Their crew had a still set up under the 5-inch gun tub on the fantail, so we had a good time anyway!

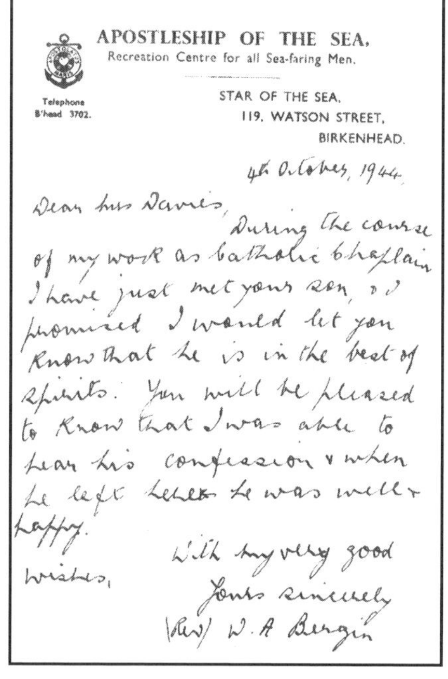

APOSTLESHIP OF THE SEA.
Recreation Centre for all Sea-faring Men.

Telephone
B'head 3702.

STAR OF THE SEA,
119, WATSON STREET,
BIRKENHEAD.

4th October, 1944.

Dear Mrs Davies,

During the course of my work as Catholic Chaplain I have just met your son, & I promised I would let you know that he is in the best of spirits. You will be pleased to know that I was able to hear his confession & when he left here he was well & happy.

With my very good wishes,

Yours sincerely
(Rev) W. A Bergin

Returning to the States I received further training and then was sent to the west coast where I served on two Victory ships; SS *Nicaragua Victory* and SS *Meredith Victory.* We were on our way to Tokyo, but as we passed by Pearl Harbor, the Japanese surrendered. After visiting several islands, we headed home with an Army escort. We were told that we were carrying an atomic bomb. We pulled into Port Chicago, California, which was an ammunition port. When I left the ship I had two sea bags with all my clothes and souvenirs. All my possessions were stolen while sitting at the dock. I had a heck of a time getting new clothes. I was discharged Sampson Navy Base on February 10, 1946.[18]

Below, Cliff Davis, left, the NAG crew of the Meredith Victory. Cliff Davis.

~~~

Howard Silverman has been a radio broadcaster most of his adult life and is still working as a part time newscaster for a radio station.

Antwerp Not Ghent

I was sworn into the Navy on April 19 (formerly Patriots Day in Massachusetts) in 1944. After Boot Camp at Sampson, New York and Signalman training at that facility, I received further training at the Great Lakes Training Station. After several leaves and delays, I was assigned to the Liberty ship S.S. *James Gunn*. We left in convoy from Staten Island, New York on January 28, 1945; destination Belgium.

All went well aboard the *James Gunn* in convoy and we arrived at an anchorage on February 12. We were told that our destination was Ghent, Belgium. But the strong current and the number of ships in the limited area caused problems. Our ship collided with another ship causing much damage to our bow area and severe listing. With a pilot on board it was determined that we would not be able to head for Ghent but were to seek anchorage in Antwerp for unloading and repair work. Hundreds of ships were also heading in that direction to what was called the second largest port in the world. We made it safely and docked comfortably at one of the canals. We were several miles out of the city and soon learned that playing ball on large fields near the ships could be dangerous.

At this time the Germans were sending V-1 and V-2 rockets from bases in Holland. Some had struck the city causing much damage and many deaths. Frequently, our ball playing was interrupted with a buzzing sound overhead. These were the V-1 "Buzz" bombs that proved to be more of a nuisance than a danger. When the fuel exhausted, the flying bomb just came down, with some landing in our area.

And so because of damage suffered by our ship in a collision our destination became Antwerp and not Ghent and our experience with German "Buzz" bombs and a lengthy stay in Belgium.
~~~

My other trips aboard the *James Gunn* were to Odessa, Russia and Italy.[19]

~~~

Dick Brown returned from the warm Pacific in January 1945 and spent a cold, but enjoyable fourteen days leave.

Buzz Bomb Alley

After leave it was time to report back to the old Armed Guard Center in Brooklyn. The center was a combination of wood and brick buildings that weren't too appealing. Nearly everyone's wish there was to be assigned to a new crew and move out quickly. I checked in on February 14th and had a ship (S.S. *Cornelius Ford*) the next day. After getting settled we found out that our destination was Antwerp, Belgium. By this time I had been away from the European scene for six months.

Our voyage was rather quiet except an escort vessel did tell us we were a menace to the convoy when a light was showing. On arrival we anchored near Dover, England and waited for clearance across the North Sea. At anchor or in port, we always had a gunner on a roving watch. I had just finished the midnight-to-4 AM shift and, being tired, fell into my bunk. I was not there long when the ship and my bunk started shaking. Something loud passed over and I ran out on deck but it was too dark to see anything. The putt-putt noise coming from it sounded like a model airplane engine multiplied many, many times. I later found out that this was a pulse-jet engine that took over when this flying bomb was airborne. The shore batteries fired at it but missed and it went far enough inland that no explosion was heard. These bombs were never accurate on target, but for setting your watch they were usually there at midnight and 4 AM. At this time these bombs only came over at night as they were easy targets to hit in the daylight hours.

It was not long before we were on our way single file across the English Channel. This area and the North Sea were loaded with regular and magnetic mines. Once in a while we would see
~~~

a mine float by and ships partially sunk with their masts sticking out of the water. All kinds of cargo would be floating by in water that was fifty to ninety feet deep. Still it was good to see the shoreline and the mouth of the Scheldt River. The run up the river was okay as both sides of the river were lined with barrage balloons. These balloons kept enemy planes away and at this stage of the war they were not out that often.

After the ship was secured part of our crew went on Liberty. The city had some ruins, but not as much as other places. We had seen where a theatre (*The Rex Cinema*) had been hit by a Buzz Bomb. Nothing was left of it except a pile of bricks.

While we were there the bombs came over nearly every night, but not in a number they had earlier. One night on our way back to the ship, two buzz bombs not too far apart passed over us. The army searchlights tracked them and you could see the shiny noses of the bombs. Both bombs exploded in the air. We were quite a distance away, but we still felt the concussion. There was a lot of power and death packed into a small package.

Another dangerous thing in the city was the trams (streetcars). The way they ran you wouldn't think they would stop if someone was lying on the tracks. The conductor would go faster and just pull harder on the bell. We left before anyone got killed that way and when we returned to Ghent, Belgium in May 1945, peace had arrived.[20]

The SS Cornelius Ford *went to the Reserve Fleet and then was scrapped in Kearney, New Jersey in January 1972.*[21]

~~~

This story is from W.G. (Will) Kitson who served as a Radioman 3/c in WW II.

The Tea Party

In the early morning hours of May 7, 1945, a U.S. convoy destined for the States was a few hours off the southern coast of England in the Atlantic Ocean when it met head-on with a British incoming convoy. I was in the convoy aboard the Liberty
~~~

ship S.S. *George W. Campbell* at the time. A total of five ships were heavily damaged, including the *Campbell.*

A few days earlier, the *Campbell* took on 500 German prisoners in Le Havre, France destined for internment in the States. We joined a small convoy in the English Channel and were assigned at that time as the commodore, or the lead, ship of the convoy.

Our convoy passed by the southern coast of England sometime before midnight on May 6. I had the 0400 watch in the radio shack the following morning. I was preparing to go on watch when I heard one blast on the ship's horn. I thought at the time that it was very unusual for the ship to signal a starboard passing, especially so when in convoy. It was a clear night with a full moon and the sea was calm, and visibility was unlimited. Again I heard one blast on the horn, followed soon after by two blasts (pass to port). Then three blasts on the horn (engines full astern), immediately followed by four blasts (general quarters), and then five (collision imminent). At the moment of impact, there was a sensation like coming to a slow stop at a traffic light, and the sound of paper being crumpled. I grabbed my life jacket and was on my way.

When I entered the radio shack, the merchant marine radio officer told me to warm up the transmitter that he would go on deck to check the condition of the ship and return immediately. The *Campbell* had three radiomen aboard; two merchant and me. The merchant marine officer was a few years my senior, and the other radioman was about my age. He entered the radio shack just before the officer left.

A few minutes had passed, and the officer had not returned as yet, so my "companion" said he would go on deck in search for the officer and return immediately. I was now alone in the radio shack and would be for the following thirty minutes.

During the thirty minutes I was alone in the radio shack, I had no idea about the condition of the ship, or whether it would stay afloat or go to the bottom. Men passed by the radio shack, but they were too busy to stop and talk with me. I remember looking at the porthole, but decided that it was too small to climb through. My best bet to escape was a long run through the passageway.

Thirty minutes had passed when the two radiomen finally returned, accompanied by the captain. The transmitter was warm and ready to go, and the captain had a distress message to send. I gave my chair to the radio officer; it was his responsibility to key the message.

When the radio officer put his hand on the key, it was obvious that he could not send the message. He was shaking so bad that he was unable to control his hand on the key. The captain then asked the other merchant radioman to send the message, but he shook his head, "No." I can understand why he said "No" to the captain. He was just as nervous as his mentor, and also, this was his first ship and first-time at sea as a radioman. The captain was now out of options.

After reading the captain's message, I told him that I could not send the message as written. I was aware of what I said, and that an immediate explanation was due. The captain understood my explanation; the message was corrected, and then was ready to send.

What the captain did was to include the "Secret War call" (SWC) of the ship along with the name of the ship in the heading of the message, which is a no-no. The SWC is known by the Allies only, designed to hide the identity of the ship from the enemy. By including the name of the ship along with the SWC in the heading of the message, the captain had defeated the purpose of the SWC. The name of the ship was then deleted from the heading of the message.

I was surprised that the radio officer was not aware, as I was, that the heading of the captain's message was not proper procedure. This was included on my final exam when I attended COMPOOL School in Noroton Heights, Connecticut to qualify as signalman. Or perhaps the officer was aware, but in his excitement he failed to recognize it.

Including both convoys, a total of five ships received extensive damage, all trying to get on 500 Kilocycles at the same time. There was no such thing as "take your turn." As soon as I heard "AR" (end of message), I hit the key. After several attempts, I finally got my message sent. The radio station at Lands End, England acknowledged my call at a speed so fast I was unable to copy by pencil. But I got the message; I was being told to "slow it down." I guess my nerves and reflexes were working double-time. I was sending over and above the recommended speed for a distress call.

I received and sent several messages during my four hours on watch. Lands End inquired about the condition of the ship, the prisoners, and the crew. We were advised at that time that tugboats and rescue ships were on the way to escort the damaged ships back to Portsmouth.

It was now 0800 and my watch was over. This would be my first opportunity to leave the radio shack since 0400 that morning. When I went on deck, the ocean was still calm, and there was an eerie silence. What remained of the two convoys had since departed and were out of sight, leaving behind five damaged ships. By now the ships had drifted apart and lay still in the water, waiting to be rescued.

It was about midday when the rescue ships arrived. Due to the prisoners aboard, a rescue ship stayed close by the *Campbell.* It was a motley-looking convoy of ships as it limped slowly back to port. The *Campbell* anchored off shore at Portsmouth just before sunset the same evening, May 7, 1945.

The sun had set, and several of the crew were standing at the rail looking toward shore, when suddenly, all the lights on shore came on, rockets were fired into the air, and we could hear the voices of people celebrating. The war in Europe was over. Germany had just announced its surrender to the Allies. The crew asked for shore leave to join the celebration but was denied. "For the security of the ship, all hands were to remain aboard." I think it was the rightful thing to do. After four years of war, it was the Brit's private-time to celebrate their victory. It was time for Yankee-go-home." Soon after, the captain and the Armed Guard officer went ashore on "Classified Business." Hm-m!

The following morning, the captain went ashore to attend a hearing. Upon his return, he had the answer as to why the British commodore ship did not acknowledge our ship's horn. As the captain explained; there was nobody on the wheel or on the bridge of the British ship. It was the turn of the watch, the wheel had been tied down, and the officer of the watch and all his men went below for their cup of tea! And the convoy sailed on.

The Armed Guard crew left the *Campbell* the following morning May 9, to be quartered at the Naval Base in Plymouth. As the launch passed by the bow of the ship, my heart skipped a beat. The deck at the bow was bent up slightly, and everything from just below the deck back toward the chain-locker bulkhead and down past the water line was completely sheared off. It looked like a Great White swimming on the surface of the water with its mouth wide open. If the British ship had continued forward just a few more feet, its bow would have gone through the chain-locker bulkhead and the *Campbell* would have eventually gone to the bottom taking the 500 German prisoners with it. These men would have had little or no chance of survival.

After five days in Plymouth, we caught a ride for home aboard the SS *Wendell Willkie*. The *Willkie* already had an Armed Guard crew aboard, so there wasn't much else for us to do but sit back and enjoy the ride.

I have never heard or read anything about the "Tea Party." If this was another "cover-up," it's understandable why it would be.[22]

~~~

D-Day

by George X. Hurley

The thunder was the 88s,
Machine guns were the falling rain.
God waited at his golden gate,
To take away our pain.

Some were spared to live 'till noon,
On that fateful day.
All the world was warm in June,
We were there to pay.
~~~

Angels gathered up the souls,
All worldly troubles over.
Death had taken such a toll,
Where are the cliffs of Dover?

What was the terrible reason,
That we traveled to our doom?
I guess this is the season
For cleaning out a room.

None of us ever asked why,
We had to reach that beach.
Sometimes at night I cry,
So far out of reach.[23]

10

Around the World With an Armed Guard Signalman

Walter Ream was a 3rd Class Navy Signalman in World War II.

I enlisted at the old post office in Pittsburgh, Pennsylvania. I was turned down by the doctor because of a hernia I had received while falling down the stairs when I was a toddler. However, the doctor said they would test me and, if I passed they would send me to school, after they operated on me. What a deal! I chose signal school. I became interested in Morse code and semaphore when I was a young Boy Scout. I was sworn in the day after my 19th birthday.

The Patch

I will tell you a little history about my particular signalman 3/c patch and some of the places it has been. I was awarded the rating for being in the upper third of my class in Signal School in

Newport, Rhode Island. We were trained for fleet duty, but after the course was completed, we were broken up into various groups: some signalmen going into the fleet, some into amphibious forces, and a very few volunteered for sub duty. The balance of us were sent to Stamford, Connecticut for more schooling for we were to be trained for signal-duty in convoys aboard merchant ships. This duty was called the Armed Guard duty.

The merchant ships were armed usually with a 3-inch gun on the bow for aircraft and surface attack, two twenty-millimeter guns directly behind the 3-inch, and four twenty-millimeter guns up on the bridge, one in each corner. The ship also had a 4-inch 50 caliber on the stern or fantail, and two twenty-millimeters directly behind the 4-inch. This was the way most of the Liberty ships were set up.

After school, I was sent to the Armed Guard Center in Brooklyn, New York. This was where all the gunners, signalmen, radio operators and boatswain's mates were stationed until assigned a ship. There was a lot of movement here as men were apt to be assigned to a ship at any hour of the day or night. I might add that the Armed Guard Center was a den of thieves. If a man was being shipped out in the wee hours of the morning and he needed some gear, he would steal the shoes off your feet if they weren't laced up, or you didn't have them under your pillow as you slept.

Walter Ream's 3rd class signalman's insignia for white and blue uniforms. Mary Ann Ream.

My first assignment was the SS *Christy Payne*, an oil tanker. The last thing in the world any of us wanted to go aboard was an oil tanker — especially me, the Navy's worst swimmer. How could I swim under a fiery ocean when I could just barely swim on top? Believe me, I gave this a lot of thought.

It was about one o'clock in the morning and we cleared the nets (most harbors had submarine nets) and the lights of New York City were beginning to disappear on the horizon. The parade was over and school was out. I was in the war!

While in convoy, most signal work dealt with course changes. The convoy seemed like it was forever changing course. The flagship told the other ships what course to steer and how many knots to travel. The signalman on watch kept his eye on the ship and the moment he saw (he used a long glass) a flag hoist start up; he tried to read the flags as they were coming out of the flag bag. The flags, two of each kind are hung down in this bag with snap and ring facing up. Numeral pennants were also done in this manner. The halyard also had a snap and a ring on it. The halyard snap was snapped onto a ring of a flag and the snap of the flag was snapped onto the other flag or numeral and the last flag or numerals were snapped onto the ring of the halyard. The exact flags and/or numerals that the flag ship is flying was hooked up and run half way up the yardarm (cross or tee). We had a book called, *Mersigs,* (merchantman signals). The hoist meaning would be looked up, and when deciphered, run the rest of the way up the yardarm. The hoist was two-blocked and run all the way up to the block or pulley. This meant the flagship hoist was fully understood. When the hoist or message was to be executed, the flag ship gave a blast on the whistle and the flags were smartly yanked down.

Signalmen took great pride in their work and each signalman tried to be the first up with his hoist and the first to smartly yank it down. We had to know what flag was what even if we could see only part of it. There were many days at sea when there was no movement of air at all and the flags became twisted around the halyards. This was another reason why we watched the flag ship so closely so that we could read the flags coming out of the bag.

It took us eleven days to reach our destination, which was Aransas Pass, Texas. The *Christy Payne* was a very old WW I German tanker and we were in a very slow convoy and always on a zigzag course. We made it to Texas without any incidents. Some depth charges had been dropped but this didn't always mean that a sub had been picked up by Navy escort sonar.

We loaded with oil, stopped off in Galveston, Texas and then headed back out into the Gulf of Mexico. It was July and it was very hot. The deck plates on the old *Payne* began to warp and this caused us some concern. We got back to New York and traveled through the Cape Cod Canal back out into the Atlantic and into Boston. We were in Boston perhaps a day or so and then formed up another convoy and delivered our cargo to the oil docks in Halifax, Nova Scotia. We came back via the same route and the entire crew was taken off the ship so that it could be repaired in Bethlehem Ship Yard, Staten Island, New York.

My second assignment was aboard the Liberty ship SS *John Cabot*. Everything about the *Cabot* was great. We always had a fine group of men, both Navy and Merchant. It was a happy ship, a lucky ship; a home away from home.

The first trip aboard the *Cabot* was a trip to Cuba where we loaded up with raw sugar. We were in a little village called Manzanillo just north of Guantanamo Bay. There were no docking facilities at Manzanillo so we had to anchor out in the bay. The sugar was ferried out to the *Cabot* by powerful men in a boat with one oar on the back, or stern in a sculling manner. When we went ashore we had to use the *Cabot*'s launch. The people in the village met us at the dock singing and playing guitars; not because we were good guys in the war, but because we represented "Yankee Dollars."

When the holds were full of sugar we returned to New York and picked up our deck cargo made up of trucks, staff cars, Sherman tanks, crates of airplane gliders and sundry other crated items secured to the *Cabot*'s deck. There was no room to walk. Carpenters had to build a catwalk for us to walk from the bow to the stern. The ship was so crammed with war material that I feared we would sink at dockside.

We were all loaded but there was some kind of delay. We were not leaving as planned because we were short food supplies, especially meat. It turned out that the steward had spirited the meat and other foodstuffs away under wraps of linen and had sold it on the black market. The FBI and the Coast Guard arrested him. We had to replenish our supplies and wait for another steward to come aboard.

We departed finally and were now out in the Atlantic heading north up the East Coast. The ships converged and formed up a convoy in their proper position in the columns. The first ship in the first column is No. 11 reading left to right. The first ship in the second column is No. 21 and so on across the spread. The first number is the column number and the second number is the position of a ship in that particular column. Number 36 would be the sixth ship in the third column. This number was very important because in a pea soup fog you couldn't see a man two feet in front of you. The engines would be turning dead slow and the only way one had of knowing where his position in the convoy was by sounding his convoy number. At least this way you knew if you were in the right column or not. You'd be surprised how far ships strayed off their course. This fog was the most eerie feeling I had in my entire experience of convoy duty. Can you imagine being loaded with ammunition and colliding with another ship, especially a tanker?

We were heading for England and the North Atlantic was as wild as I had seen it in some movies. I was communicating with a Canadian corvette, a small escort ship. It was almost impossible. We were using blinker lights and when the corvette was high up on the crest of a wave, he would send three letters of a word then disappear completely out of sight.

At night we couldn't sleep. The *Cabot* was rolling and we wondered if she would capsize. Now she was pitching and when this occurs, the ship's screw comes out of the water and entire ship vibrates. We now had great concern about the possibility of the *Cabot* breaking in half at midships. This happened to a number of Liberty ships. We were told to sleep in our clothes, for the water was very cold and chances of survival are slim even when fully clothed, if you are lucky enough to be plucked from the sea.

The icebox door had to be tied shut. We could only eat sandwiches. Soup was never on the menu.

The convoy continued plowing its way to the first port of call, Loch Ewe, Scotland. The sea eventually smoothed out and everything got back to normal. However, we were reminded to keep an extra sharp watch for aircraft attacks the closer we got to the British Isles.

I was awakened in the early morning sometime before daybreak to report to the bridge. We rammed the *Woodrow Wilson*! I was either dead to the world asleep or it was just a slight bump. I felt nothing. There was damage to the *Cabot* on the starboard bow and some damage to the *Woodrow Wilson*, but no crewmen on either ship were injured.

We were getting very close to Scotland. The ship ahead sent a blinker message that we would be passing a mine off to our starboard. I relayed the message to the ship astern and all down the line it was repeated. The mine was sighted and some of the gunners wanted to blow it up but the gunnery officer would not permit it. He told us that the British Navy would take care of it. Some of us thought we had a gun-shy officer. The convoy pulls into Loch Ewe, Scotland where we lie at anchor. There was no liberty and we remained there only for a day or two.

Some of the ships were beginning to move out of the lake. A ship passed close by our port side. I was on the bridge but the *Cabot* did not move out with this group of ships. The signalman on the ship to port was trying to get my attention. He had a semaphore message for me. We passed so close that we could both see each other's facial expressions. It was my good friend from the Newport Signal School, Ollie from Sharpsburg, Pennsylvania. His message said that perhaps his ship is to undertake its most dangerous trip, the Murmansk run to Russia. We wished each other luck. Months later I received a letter from him stating that he had a safe trip and that he was at a rest camp in Florida.

We sailed to England and then up the Thames River to our next port of call which was Tilbury, about thirty miles from London. The first night in port, the Germans flew up the Thames over Tilbury on their way to wreck havoc and destruction upon London. The British Air defense caught a plane in its spotlight but it was too high up to knock it down. The ships weren't allowed to fire at attacking aircraft because we would give away our dock area position. I did get into London for one day of liberty. Before we left Tilbury, the Germans hit a dance hall in London killing many patrons including U.S. Service men.

One night while "doing the town," I tried to drink the town dry. Amongst other problems that night was that I lost my I.D. card. The guards at the dock area wouldn't let me pass to board the *Cabot*. Luckily, the captain was directly behind me in the line and vouched for me. The next afternoon I was told that two British civilians wanted to talk to me in the officer's salon. I soon learned that they were from Scotland Yard. They were very nice but they did give me the third degree regarding my lost I.D. card. They asked about all the places I had been to the night before. Before the previous night had ended, I wasn't even sure that I was in England. Scotland Yard was concerned that my card would fall into the wrong hands.

We returned to the States without any problems and pulled into Caven's Point, New Jersey. Caven's Point was way out somewhere in the boondocks near a cemetery. The *Cabot* was at the end of a pier that extended quite a way out into the river. There were no other ships around and we were totally isolated. I hoisted the "B" (Baker) flag which must be flown when a ship is taking on fuel or explosives. There were to be no lights, smoking, or matches brought on or off the ship while loading. The Coast Guard came on board the *Cabot* and checked the ship out and the cargo loading which were munitions. It took us several days to load the munitions and we moved to Brooklyn, New York for deck cargo. Here we learned that we were to go to Calcutta, India. I was excited and anticipated an interesting trip. It was.

It was December 1943 when we left New York. We anchored in Chesapeake Bay and one night weighed anchor while Bing Crosby was singing "White Christmas." The crew was deeply saddened by the song as I'm sure each and every member was thinking of his family and home.

It was now Christmas Eve 1943 and a blinker message was relayed to all ships from the flag ship. "Lower the flag to half mast during the funeral service for the captain of the S.S.? (I cannot recall the ship's name). The captain had been sick while in the Chesapeake but did not want to leave for medical attention. I believe he died of pneumonia. We are now a day or two out.

All the time they were loading those explosives, we kept telling each other that they would probably put us in the middle of the convoy. They wouldn't put us in either one of the two outside columns — would they? Yes they would, and yes they did! We were not only placed in the portside outside column, but in the "Coffin Corner." (The two outside corners at the far rear of the box.)

We were well on our way towards North Africa. Most of our time off-duty was spent playing cards and drinking coffee in the mess room. I didn't play poker but the fellows tried to teach me the game one night. One or two guys would stand behind me and tell me what cards to play and we were playing for money. Each time I would come up with a good card hand and had a chance of winning, I would sit there with a big grin on my face or even laugh. I wasn't exactly a poker face. I did win a little money that night but gave the fellows a chance to win it back the next night. Of course I knew that I had won the money fairly the night before. In this game, I played on my own and they had me broke in a matter of minutes. "Sparks" the radio operator taught me how to play cribbage and I really enjoyed this game. We spent a lot of time challenging one another.

This night the off-duty gang was in the hangout (mess room) playing cards, drinking coffee, eating sandwiches and talking. It was dark outside and it was a nice ride on a relatively smooth sea. WHOOOOOMFFF! The *Cabot* was hit by an object with considerable force behind it. The ship rolled heavily to starboard and the alarm sounded. Our hearts were in our throats. We were always aware of what we were hauling. Was this the end of the *Cabot* and her crew? If whatever hit us didn't go off, would more be on the way? Would we even make it outside on deck? The mess room was cleared in seconds and we went to our stations. All eyes were straining to see something in the darkness. Everyone and everything was quiet. The *Cabot* was a floating bomb. If we got hit I wouldn't have to worry about my poor swimming ability. Our luck held as the alert was over. At day break I was ordered to ask the flagship if depth charges were dropped or if any subs had been reported. The reply was negative.

The next morning I was awakened by my lieutenant who called me "Dutch." He said, "We have an emergency aboard. The merchant seaman who had been at the wheel is sick." The third mate, who was a registered nurse, thought the seaman had appendicitis. There were no doctors aboard our ship and our ship was blessed with the third mate being a nurse. The off-duty members of the gun crew were told to clean up the mess room and scrub up the table because they might have to operate on him. I reported to the bridge and I was given a flashlight with a cone shaped shield over the lens. It was dark outside and flashing Morse code at this time was a bit risky, even with a shield.

The third mate had me send the following message - "B," "B," "B," (Baker, Baker, Baker, the flagship's code letter).

"K." (Go ahead. I am ready to receive). The flagship had caught my light.

"De," (from) *John Cabot*. Send doctor. Hot appendix. "Ar" (end of transmission).

"R" The message was received.

At daybreak a "DE" (destroyer escort) came close to starboard and signaled "slow to dead slow." The doctor and third mate were communicating via their respective signalmen. "What is pulse rate?" "What is temperature?" "Any pain during urination?" I stumbled over the word urination and it angers me for being so stupid for not anticipating this word. I relayed the third mate's answers.

The destroyer escort lowered a boat with the doctor aboard. The doctor confirmed the third mate's diagnosis. The patient was lowered into the boat and transferred to the DE and then to a Navy tanker. The day wore on and there was no word about our man from the *Cabot*. The captain ordered me to contact the flag ship and find out what happened to the merchant seaman. "Patient operated on aboard the USS *Pontchartrain*. Doing fine." We were now close to Africa and some of the ships were peeling off and heading to Oran. Our patient went to Oran. We never saw him again.

We anchored at Gibraltar where these "bum" boats approached the *Cabot*. We did a brisk business selling them cigarettes when the ship's command put us out of business. The people in the boats were told to move away from our ship but they were reluctant to leave the vicinity of the ship. The fire hoses were brought into play and the "bum" boats backed off. I felt sorry for them but not after I found out the reason for this action. The Germans had been up to sabotage and were placing explosive charges on ships screws. When the engine turned over, the explosive charge would be set off.

We sailed to Port Said, Egypt and waited our turn to go through the Suez Canal. I was surprised at how cold it got at night in this area. We had to wear jackets as it was quite chilly. I was a little disappointed in the scenery as the area was very barren and there really wasn't much to see. The grit made me feel like I was a goose eating gravel! At the end of the Canal were the Great Bitter and Little Bitter Lakes. We anchored in one of them and then it was into the Red Sea where we anchored in Aden, Arabia. From Aden we sailed the Indian Ocean to the Bay of Bengal and up the river to Calcutta, India. While unloading in Calcutta we saw the big ding on the port side of the No. 4 hold. We had been hit by something on our way to North Africa.

Calcutta was a very strange and fascinating city. People, people, and more people! Both native and servicemen were everywhere. The poverty was unbelievable. I walked around people whom I am sure were dying on the sidewalks from hunger. Others were there because they simply had no other home or place to sleep. People cooked on open fires along the wayside and most business was done out in the open. Both barber and patron would squat along the sidewalk. The Indian people did a lot of squatting rather than sitting down.

"Baksheesh, baksheesh, baksheesh" (give me a gift of money) was a very familiar cry from the kids tugging on our arms. Americans rich, Americans rich. Where servicemen were camped or stationed there usually was an empty oil drum outside and to the rear of the mess hall. This drum was used for the dispersal of uneaten food. It was common to see many young men reaching into this swill and placing whatever they came up with into an empty can each carried. Now, this was hunger!

The sacred cows roamed the streets just like cattle on the open range. If you complain about the neighbor's dog messing on your lawn, just be glad they don't have a cow like here in India. The cows were hide and bone. Even they looked hungry.

A bleached and bloated body was discovered floating amongst the dock pilings. We rushed to the ship's dockside and the body was there floating face down. It was a native and it must have been in the water for quite sometime. The authorities were called and the boatswain vomited over the side.

Many of the people lived on barges. We watched them pray, dip a can into the water and dump it on their heads as if it were a shower. They would then use their finger as a toothbrush. And, of course, the river was used as their sewage system. No place like home!

We left India and were homeward bound. The next stop was Ceylon (Sri Lanka now). Two stops were made in Ceylon; one in the capital city of Colombo and the other in Galle. We loaded up with sheets of baled rubber. This was a much safer cargo then we had carried over. I wondered whether we were unsinkable.

While in Colombo we saw many men in green army fatigues and we wondered why so many of them were hanging around the pier buildings waiting as we did for launches back to our respective ships. We learned that these men were survivors from sunken freighters that the Japanese had sunk while their ships were dashing to or from Aden, Arabia. This stretch of water was traveled unescorted and I never did find out the reason for this condition.

It was the *Cabot*'s turn to move out. The captain called us all out on deck for a pep talk. "We all know the situation. Keep an extra sharp watch and all hands are to sleep out on deck. We will make it!"

We left port and sailed back up through the Suez Canal into the Mediterranean. We were in convoy and the alert sounded one night. There was another scramble to our positions. It wasn't without duress as our eyes had been accustomed to the light inside the deck house. It took a few moments for the eyes to get adjusted to the darkness. We didn't see too well when we first got out on deck. I ran to my post on the bridge and immediately ran into a shroud (support cable) that runs from the stack to the deck. It caught me under the chin. I must have looked like an anteater as my tongue flew out of my mouth. It really hurt!

I looked toward the end of the convoy and there were a few lights drifting downward out of the black sky. In a moment or two the convoy was lit up like a stadium at night. Night became day by the use of parachute flares. This German pilot broke up a hot poker game and disturbed the peace and tranquility of the entire convoy. Fortunately, this was the last disturbance and excitement until we reached Baltimore, Maryland. We went to dry dock at Sparrows Point in Baltimore to repair the ding we had in our port side.

The lieutenant took a large group of us into a nice bar in Baltimore, which was the first leave we had ashore in weeks. Here we had a few farewell drinks. Some of the crew wanted to take their leave and go home and were detached from the *Cabot.* They were to be reassigned after their leave was over. The waitress questioned the lieutenant about our age. He said we were all over twenty-one. The manager looked us over and said he would take the lieutenant's word that we were of legal age. Rather than get the manager in any kind of trouble the lieutenant confessed that there were some minors amongst the group. However, we managed. The lieutenant's wife came down from New York for a day or two before the crew got liberty. We had to wait for physicals and then we went up to his hotel room and we had our farewell drinks with him and his wife.

Sometime before returning to the States, the lieutenant asked different members of the crew if they wanted to stay on board with him and go to Australia. Our ship was a West Coast ship and they wanted to get her back on the West Coast. The *Cabot* was going to the Pacific its next trip. I, and perhaps about half of the gun crew, chose to stay aboard. The *Cabot* was home and we loved this officer. So we decided to go to Australia with him.

Replacements came aboard and some of us were amazed because several of them were almost old enough to be our fathers. Some were married and had kids who were almost as old as I was. We knew the war was winding down but why disrupt a family man's life at this point in the war?

A new captain came aboard. We were not to become friends. He spoke in broken English (Dane he says, German we said), was bald, bowlegged, miserable and (we thought) a quart too low. He wasn't Mr. Nice!

Our holds were loaded and we were off to Norfolk, Virginia naval base to pick up our deck cargo. This turned out to be an LST and its crew. The craft was small and came in two or three sections. The crew was quartered in its own ship.

Whenever there was a course change I would tell the captain if he were on the bridge. We were now in the Caribbean and the captain was taking a sighting with his sextant. This captain told me that I didn't have to tell him there was a course change when he was on the bridge; he could see it. That was okay with me but now he had taken his reading and went below to the chartroom. He came back up and took another sighting. There was a blast on the whistle to execute the change and he almost jumped off the bridge. He was furious and had to do all his work over. He hopped all over me for not telling him of a course change. We got into a heated argument and I spoke to him in a foreign language called Western Pennsylvania Steel Town Talk. He understood it and told me I was to be taken off the ship in Panama.

I reported to my lieutenant and told him of the captain's intentions to "dump" me in Panama. Thankfully, the chief mate was on the bridge when the captain told me that I didn't have to keep him so well informed and he came to my defense. In no way was I going to leave the ship in Panama!

The Navy gunner on watch on the bridge told me he thought that the Navy tanker at the far end of the convoy had been hit. He said, "He saw the spray go up over the bow." We watched to see what happened. There was a blast on a whistle and "E I" was flown. Other ships were flying the same message: a sub was reported to starboard. We snapped the hoist together but the captain refused to let us two-block it. The *Cabot*'s signalmen were made to look like fools. An emergency hoist was flown and the two *Cabot* signalmen failed in this crucial moment. We were telling the other ships we did not understand the message. The captain said, "Don't put up the flags, we see nozzing!" To me, the captain was now two quarts low.

I kept my eye on the Navy ship for a while and I could read portions of his message to the flagship. His light wasn't trained on me so I could catch only bits and pieces of his message. What I was able to read was, "Minor damage. No casualties." I was again reported to the lieutenant for spreading false rumors. None of us were psychiatrists, but every man thought we had some kind of a "nut" for a captain.

When we reached Panama, half of the *Cabot* crew (Navy personnel that is) wasn't permitted to go into town for liberty because we were the "bad boys" while at the Norfolk navy base loading the LCT. Those of us that did get liberty were told to be back aboard the ship by midnight. Our gunner's mate was with us on this escapade and he was responsible for having us back on time.

The first thing we did was buy a bottle of wine which we intended to smuggle aboard when we returned. Rather than carry this bottle around, we hid it. We ended up in this Chief Petty Officer's Club just outside the base. We concocted a plan to get our "Sea Daddy" gunner's mate limbered up (drunk actually) so that we could stay out past midnight. In the process of limbering him up we all got limbered up! When the party broke up we tried to find where we hid the wine but forgot where we hid it.

The lieutenant was waiting at the gangplank for us. He was angry enough to shoot us. One of the guys passed out right at his feet and had to be carried to his bunk. The *Cabot* was only hours away from getting under way and the lieutenant had only half a gun crew. The crew that did get liberty in Panama was chased all the way back to the dock area by the police. Some guys had all the fun.

We proceeded through the Canal. The U.S. Marines came aboard ship and made the gunners cover all the guns with tarps. We thought this was strange. A merchant seaman's papers weren't in order and he wasn't permitted to sail through the Canal aboard the *Cabot*. He was taken off the ship and transported to the Pacific side where he re-boarded the ship.

We were now in the Pacific heading for New Guinea. Our first port of call was Milne Bay. Here we discharged the LST in sections out in the bay and said so long and good luck to its crew. From here we shuttled along the coast of New Guinea loading and unloading cargo at Finschhafen and Hollandia.

At Finschhafen truckloads of beer were brought to the dockside to be loaded aboard. Navy SP's (Shore Patrol) sat atop of the cases on the trucks to protect them from theft. Colored Army personnel ran the winches on the ship and occasionally would accidentally (on purpose) hit the side of the hatch spilling cans of beer all over the deck. Of course, we were most helpful in cleaning up the debris off the deck. The *Cabot* was a clean ship and we didn't want any dirty, old and full cans of beer cluttering up the deck. We gathered them up and hid them in our sleeping quarters.

A merchant seaman was caught by Captain "Mad" shoving beer under his bunk. The captain got into another one of his fits and wanted to hang the man right there for pilfering the cargo. This time the captain was right. He was responsible for everything aboard his ship and we all wondered if there was going to be a shakedown. Evidently, he thought this was the only man on the cleanup committee.

A trial was held in the officer's salon in Hollandia. The seaman was tried by Navy and Coast Guard lawyers. He was fined and his papers lifted. He was now subject to the draft upon his return to the United States. Our lieutenant sat in on the trial and the lawyers told him the punishment would have been more severe had it not been for the captain making such an "ass" of himself. They had to tell the captain to sit down and keep quiet more than once. I guess the captain wanted to do everything but hang the poor guy. Needless to say, we bought our own beer after that close call!

We moved south of New Guinea to Cairns, Australia where we discharged a staff car. Cairns was way back in the boondocks. It looked like a Wild West town even with its wooden sidewalks. I don't know why the town existed. As much as I hated the captain, we had a damn good navigator to find this port.

We were within a few feet of the dock and had our liberty uniforms on when the bad news came. The tide had gone out of the river and the *Cabot* was stuck in the mud. The seagoing tug, *Sonoma* tired to pull us off but to no avail. We were stuck in the mud and we were stuck on board. There was no liberty until the next day until the tide floated us free.

We became buddies with the guys on the *Sonoma.* One of their members was drunk and depressed. He felt that they'd never make it back home for they had been making all the invasions of the islands. I suppose after so much luck everyone had the thought of their luck running out somewhere along the line.

From Cairns we continued south to Brisbane. This was a really a nice city and just like the States. It was a good liberty town. One day at the dockside there was a lot of activity going on with some of the Australian military. Soldiers lined the dockside and several machine guns were in place as a ship tied up behind us. Its cargo was Japanese prisoners. This was as close as I ever got to see the enemy. They came in all shapes and sizes and they were such a bedraggled looking bunch. Some of their heads, arms and legs were bandaged. Some just hobbled using a stick for a cane or they had nothing. They were saluting everything and everybody in a uniform. The dog catcher would have rated a salute if he had been there. The last one to leave the ship left his miseries aboard. He was carried off wrapped in a sheet.

We picked up a man in Brisbane. He went back to Hollandia where he was to pick up another ship. The name of his ship was the *Sonoma*. This was quite a circumstance as we then told him of our acquaintance with the *Sonoma* and that he would like her crew. After reaching Hollandia our passenger came back to visit us one day and we asked him how he liked his new ship and shipmates. We were stunned and saddened to hear him say that he would never know. The *Sonoma* had been bombed and sunk.

(*Note: The ocean tug* Sonoma *(ATO-12) was sunk by a Japanese suicide plane in the Battle of Leyte Gulf on October 24, 1944, 10.57 N., 125.02 E.*)[1]

There was more bad news. While in Hollandia our Gunner's Mate found our officer lying on the floor in his quarters. He was ill but insisted he could walk on his own off the ship. The ambulance came but he was too weak to walk. After several days in the hospital it was determined he was suffering from malnutrition. We feared that he would be stuck in the hospital and we'd sail without him. Our officer was really upset and disturbed that he might miss the invasion of the Philippines. He wanted to be with his crew and we wanted to be with him. He was a father to us and we were his sons. Such was the bond between us.

The lieutenant recuperated and returned to the *Cabot*. It wasn't long after his hospital stay that he was hit by an Army truck. He wasn't badly hurt but we threatened to lock him in his quarters until we were safely back at sea.

We were still in Hollandia when one day I heard, "Hey! "Dutch," from Walker on the bridge. "See that destroyer over there? My brother is on it. Call them up and see if you can get a hold of him for me?" I called the destroyer and his brother was on the ship. The two ships were so close that the brothers could see each other. They carried on a reunion and communicated via the ships respective signalmen. However, neither ship granted permission to lower a boat so that the two could have met personally. We all thought this to be a stupid bit of regulation.

The *Cabot* didn't make the invasion of the Philippines. We returned to the United States and arrived back at Long Beach, California. The crew broke up with the exception of one man. He didn't want the hassle of being reassigned and sacrificed his leave. It was a sad day. The family broke up!

After a thirty-day leave I returned to the Armed Guard Center in Brooklyn, New York for a short stay and then I shipped right back across the country to Treasure Island, California. While being loaded, like so much beef on a truck, I heard a voice calling out, "Is Dutch Ream on this truck?" It was Lieutenant Morgan seeking me out. He had seen my name on the draft and we wished each other luck. It was our farewell handshake. He died of a heart attack some time after the war.

I was assigned to the *Stephen Hopkins II* and came aboard her in Alameda, California. I never got attached to this crew. I adjusted but there was an altogether different atmosphere aboard this ship. My service aboard this ship was dull and uneventful.

The *Hopkins* traveled alone most of the time and to keep busy I volunteered to spell off the watches. I was only needed to answer the occasional challenge from aircraft or when going into port.

We traveled to a dot on the map called Eniwetok, the island of Panay in the Philippines, Tacloban on the island of Leyte in the Philippines and to Manila. We also stopped in Noumea, New Caledonia. There were rumors that the war was coming to an end and for several days we had heard this rumor. Then one night I was in the washroom and I heard the fellows go wild. The war with Japan was over. Corregidor was just off our port side as we steamed into Manila Bay.

The *Hopkins II* returned to the States and I eventually was sent from "Frisco" to Sampson, New York where I was discharged. A bus was chartered for men traveling east. While in Pittsburgh waiting for a bus home I met another sailor. We had a few beers before catching the bus. We were two miles from home and neither of us could stand the agony of having a full bladder of beer on a bumpy bus ride. We both got off at a tavern to seek comfort. Two miles from home and we couldn't make it. We got off the bus and the first person I saw was my younger brother. After going to the restroom, my brother and his friend drove us both home to Midland.

The war was over. I served. I survived. I was home and I was hungry! This old crow had been around the world. I saw strange and exciting things. It was amazing and I never had to flap my wings. I was terribly missed by my family and often thought of by my friends. I wasn't a hero or a coward. Just a third class crow. Serial number 652-98-55, blood type A.[2]

The John Cabot *was scrapped in Portland, Maine in December 1959.*[3] *The* Stephen Hopkins II *was scrapped in New Orleans in June 1967.*[4] *This ship was named after the first* Stephen Hopkins *which was awarded the Gallant Ship Award by President Truman August 16, 1946. See Chapter 13 for details.*

11

Life at Sea and in Port

What was life like for the Navy Armed Guard? It was day after day of boredom occasionally interrupted by sheer terror — if they were lucky. One could understand why liberty was so highly anticipated and sought after, and why these men "let loose" whenever they had the chance.

Former Armed Guard member Lyle E. Dupra describes his experience aboard a merchant ship:

Aboard the merchant ships, our quarters, where we slept and relaxed, were approximately 8 feet long by 5½ feet wide and 7 feet high. There was no fan or air conditioner, no heat ducts, no sink, and no rug. We had one incandescent light bulb in the ceiling, one small porthole, and four men shared sleeping space on four bunks. For furniture, we had four lockers piled on top of each other, which measured about 1 foot by 15 inches by 5 feet tall. The rest of our gear was stored in seabags in storage lockers someplace else on the ship.

The "room" next to us had a stand-up shower, a toilet with no seat, and a sink — and because all these conveniences were operated with salt water, we had to use hard bar soap. Palatable [potable] water could be found only at the drinking fountain and in the cook's galley. We had no barber and no cigarette or candy machines. Neither did we have a laundry or a flat iron, so we washed our clothes by hand. Nor did we have a radio. These Liberty ships were designed to be constructed quickly, so there were few amenities. Interestingly, today there are complaints in some civilian prisons because the inmate cannot have his own room. Truthfully, I never heard one Armed Guardsman or Merchant Marine gripe about where we slept or how we had to "make do."

We shared a camaraderie and vowed to protect one another. We took an oath to never give up the ship until an order was given to do so. As a former member of the Armed Guard, I look back with pride to that unsung group that did so much with so little. As a self-contained and independent Navy unit, the Armed Guard was a natural for fostering esprit de corps.[1]

~~~

Despite not having radios or movies, life on board a merchant ship wasn't totally devoid of recreational activities. According to John Gorley Bunker:

> … so the Navy furnished an entertainment kit for every Armed Guard gun crew. That for the *Dan Beard* was typical: a punching bag, boxing gloves, and a medicine ball, and games — Chinese checkers, chess, cribbage, acey-ducey, checkers, and dominos — plus darts, playing cards, a phonograph, and records. All ships received books, usually from the American Merchant Marine Library Association, and the purser acted as librarian.[2]

The Brooklyn Armed Guard Center had a popular Ship's Library. At one time "10,000 books from the Victory Book Campaign headquarters was piled high to the ceiling… "[3] Later in the
~~~

war the Armed Services Edition became available to this library. These books consisted of good fiction, nonfiction, mysteries and westerns. Also included was "an atlas, a dictionary, World Almanac, *and a bible. A crew of twenty-five men gets fifty books and thirty magazines ... Bundles are ready-tied, because the men are always in a hurry."*[4]

And in the back of every Naval Armed Guard's mind was the following order:

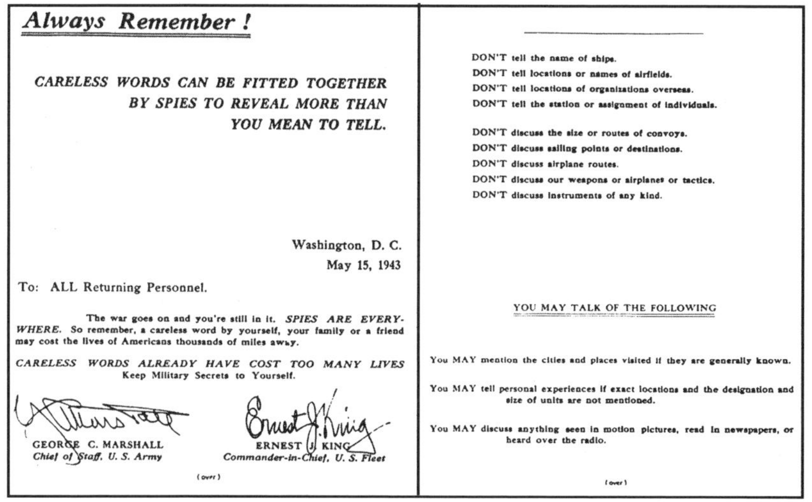

Always Remember !

CARELESS WORDS CAN BE FITTED TOGETHER BY SPIES TO REVEAL MORE THAN YOU MEAN TO TELL.

Washington, D. C.
May 15, 1943

To: ALL Returning Personnel.

The war goes on and you're still in it. *SPIES ARE EVERYWHERE.* So remember, a careless word by yourself, your family or a friend may cost the lives of Americans thousands of miles away.

CARELESS WORDS ALREADY HAVE COST TOO MANY LIVES
Keep Military Secrets to Yourself.

GEORGE C. MARSHALL
Chief of Staff, U. S. Army

ERNEST J. KING
Commander-in-Chief, U. S. Fleet

(over)

DON'T tell the name of ships.
DON'T tell locations or names of airfields.
DON'T tell locations of organizations overseas.
DON'T tell the station or assignment of individuals.

DON'T discuss the size or routes of convoys.
DON'T discuss sailing points or destinations.
DON'T discuss airplane routes.
DON'T discuss our weapons or airplanes or tactics.
DON'T discuss instruments of any kind.

YOU MAY TALK OF THE FOLLOWING

You MAY mention the cities and places visited if they are generally known.

You MAY tell personal experiences if exact locations and the designation and size of units are not mentioned.

You MAY discuss anything seen in motion pictures, read in newspapers, or heard over the radio.

(over)

Courtesy of Joseph McKenna.

~~~

This story was forwarded by Anthony E. Culik who served on board the S.S. Pan Gulf *in 1943.*

TNT

My last job before entering the Navy was at the Elwood Ordnance Plant in Illinois. Part of my work there consisted of breaking down chunks of TNT into dust in readiness of packing for shipment.

I enlisted in the Navy and received my basic training at the Great Lakes Naval Center. I then volunteered for Armed Guard duties and was moved to the Biloxi Gunnery School. From there I was assigned to the SS *Pan Gulf.*
~~~

Among the materials being loaded onto the ship was TNT, which was, you guessed it, produced at the Elwood facility. The loading of the *Pan Gulf* was completed in NOLA (New Orleans, Louisiana.) during which time we were billeted in the barracks there. In order to do some bartering overseas I bought gum, Hershey Bars, bar soap, and cigarettes and put same in a locker while liberty took place in the French Quarter. Returning to the barracks I found my locker inundated with ants drawn there by the chocolate.

To attack the ants would have been counter productive so I simply, and gingerly, picked up the box of chocolate and found my way to the nearest GI can and deposited same therein and then took the can outdoors. The ants began a slow methodical path to the can to continue their feast and there went part of my cache.

Boarding the ship the next morning we were surprised to find menus at each table from which we ordered breakfast. Menus were present for the next several days and served as a reference of the merchantmen's appreciation of our presence aboard to man the gun stations.

Heading for the gulf I became seasick and wanted to die right there and then. After several days I finally found my sealegs but never did overcome the stigma over the next three years.

Our convoy moved out of the St. John's area, and as far as I could tell we lost only one ship in mid-Atlantic as it could be seen aflame for what seemed like hours before it finally was no longer visible to the eye.

Approaching Ireland I will never forget the sight of the bright greensward rolling right down to the water's edge. Returning to New York and saluting the Statue of Liberty we were greeted at the dock with five-gallon cans of milk, fresh fruit and vegetables, fresh meat and papers allowing for fourteen days leave and a transfer to the USS *Nuthatch* AM60, but that's another story …

How ironic it would have been if we had been attacked by a U-boat and sunk due to exploding TNT which I had a hand in making. Fortunately, we weren't attacked and the materials were safely unloaded in Cardiff, Wales.[5]

~~~

James Farias sent this story of his experiences.

SS *Axtell J. Byles*

I was assigned to my first ship in October 1943 and boarded a launch from the Brooklyn Armed Guard Center to get out to my first ship. We weaved through the harbor in and out among ships large and small. There were some ships I would have been proud to be on. Eventually we pulled alongside a rusty, old, beat-up looking tanker, the SS *Axtell J. Byles.* "This couldn't be my ship," I thought, but it was!

I climbed aboard and the entire crew was on liberty except for two drunken merchant crewmen who were fighting; one guy had a bloodied chest. What kind of ship was I assigned to? I wondered. Remembering my training from boot camp, I saluted these two drunks and asked, "Permission to come aboard, sir?" They both looked puzzled. And when I asked where I could go with my seabag, the looks they gave me convinced me to keep out of their way. So, I waited in one of the gun tubs, and was very much relieved when the armed guard crew and Gunnery officer returned.

The *Byles* vibrated so much when she hit her top speed of 12 knots that we thought she'd shake apart. But the ship, built in 1927, was tough. She proved that when she was torpedoed by a U-boat off Cape Hatteras in April 1942, eighteen months before I went aboard. Her crew got her safely into Hampton Roads; she was repaired and went back into the war.

The SS Axtell J. Byles *was operated by the Tidewater Associated Oil Co., a subsidiary of Getty Oil.* Mariners Museum.
~~~

The General Quarters alarm bell aboard the *Byles* was so loud it sent vibrations throughout our sleeping quarters when it sounded. We had one gunner who could never hear it, and we had to shake him awake every time there was a G.Q.

We had a radioman who talked Morse code in his sleep — on and on with dit, dah, dit dah. He'd stop for a while, and then go at it again. Our signalman would sit beside the radioman's bunk, pencil and paper in hand, and copy his dream. We would ask what the radioman said in his sleep, but the signalman would never tell us. This signalman was a slow-moving somewhat fat southerner who would strip to his shorts and hit the sack before he had to go on duty, even if it was only for an hour. And then he'd have to dress all over again.

The *Byles* had an excellent Portuguese cook who sometimes would make a soup that reminded me of an old country soup my mother made. He also made a very tasty white bread. But after being at sea for a while, the flour became home to some kind of bug, (weevil), but that didn't stop him from turning out more loaves of bread.

One day I noticed little dark specks in the bread. We thought it was seasoning he used to flavor, but after eating the bread for a few days some of us got suspicious and started picking out the dark specks. We'd hold a slice toward the light making it easier to find them. When the cook found out what we were doing he added raisins to the bread. Some of us decided to eat the bread anyway, but maybe we should have left it around for the cockroaches, with which we had to share our mess hall. Till this day I won't eat raisin bread.

Another memory of the *Byles* was a wild liberty in Venezuela. It started at a bar. We went to where they sold only bottles of warm beer which tasted awful. After the third beer the taste improved and went down very smooth. The kick came later; it felt like I was kicked by a mule; that's how powerful it was.

Before the day was over, machete-armed police escorted us back to the ship. One of the crew had his fingers severed while fighting with them. As I recall, Lieutenant Fisher was told by the mayor of the town to keep us aboard while in his port "or else." We never did find out what "or else" meant. All liberty was canceled and we had to work our butts off until the lieutenant finally calmed down. But we didn't know what we did that day that was so bad. How could we? We were bombed out of our skulls. The lieutenant told us later that some of the sailors were molesting the respectable women of the town.

One port we hit while on the *Byles* was Palermo, Sicily. On liberty there one day with two other sailors we saw an elderly man riding on a cart being pulled by a small animal, probably a Sicilian donkey. We asked if he would take us for a ride and negotiated a price. He drove a hard bargain and wouldn't take fewer than six cigarettes. After all these years I still remember the price; six cigarettes. His going rate was two per passenger.

He drove us around the town through some narrow side streets. There were women, young and old, selling prostitution. Older women were sitting outside on chairs combing little children's hair and looking for lice. They would squeeze the lice between their thumbnails to kill the critters.

Young children following us would ask for candy and cigarettes. They wouldn't leave until we gave them cigarettes. They couldn't speak English except for a few choice words that they probably learned from sailors and soldiers who got to Sicily before us. "Cigarettes Americano," they would shout, also "F - my sister" or "F- my mother." These kids were actually pimping for their mothers and sisters; probably the only way they knew how to make money to support their family.

At one point along the way we stopped the cart and went into an old bombed-out church. Inside was a monk wearing a brown robe with a hood covering part of his face. He looked very sad so we offered him some cigarettes. He spoke very little English, took the cigarettes and asked us to follow him. We entered a narrow cave which at one time was probably the catacomb. On both sides were skeletons. At the end of the cave was a baby enclosed in an airtight glass coffin. The baby was perfectly preserved after hundreds of years, he said. Anyway, that's what he expected us to believe. We got back on our cart and went on our way.[6]

Palermo is the site of the famous Capuchin Catacombs.

~~~

The following are more stories from Signalman 3/c, Bob Norling aboard the SS Gold Heels *and* Abner Nash.

Crime and Punishment

It wasn't difficult to get into trouble in the Armed Guard. My first time was aboard the coastwise tanker *Gold Heels* when we put into Key West en route to Galveston in early 1943. The harbor water there was beautiful, just right for a swim. The merchant crew had already jumped in when word came down from the bridge that the Armed Guard crew couldn't join them.

Somehow, I wound up as the gun crew's spokesman to protest the order. Up I went to confront our gunnery officer and a pink-cheeked young ensign from the Port Director's office who said swimming was forbidden because of sharks. The only sharks around were hammerheads, and they weren't considered dangerous, I responded.

The argument got hot and I kept at it until our CO ordered me into the brig. Well, *Gold Heels* had no brig, as such, so I was restricted to a small area on the poopdeck. I slung a hammock under the after gun deck and immediately started getting more goodies from the galley than I could eat. I was the only signalman aboard, so the captain ordered my release two days later when *Gold Heels* sailed away from Key West. There was some discussion of an insubordination charge, but nothing came of it.

A frightening encounter with the authority happened when my next ship, the Liberty ship *Abner Nash,* was off-loading in Liverpool in October 1943. I went ashore one night and hooked up with a British WREN at a service club dance. She said I could walk her home, and when we got there we started groping around on her small porch.

But my hopes of being invited in were dashed when heavy footsteps came along the street and the WREN immediately cooled it. Right up onto the porch came a big English bobby, towering over me in that big hat he wore. "Don't stay out too long, daughter," he growled as he went inside. I said good night and fled.
~~~

My next encounter with a bobby was in May 1944 as the *Abner Nash* off-loaded at Swansea in South Wales. One of the gunners had a girlfriend in town and needed help getting a couple of whole bolognas to her. We stuck them up the sleeves of our peacoats, waited until dark — after 10 PM because of Britain's wartime double daylight savings time — and strolled through the dockyard gate.

"Hold on there," said a bobby on duty. He shook us down, found the bolognas, escorted us to a nearby police station and had us booked on suspicion of smuggling rationed goods ashore in wartime.

They released us after about five hours in a cell with a drunken Welshman. "And take the bologna with you," they said. "Oh hell," said the gunner, "Let's go back to the ship." And the two bolognas became surprise gifts thrust into the arms of a dockyard worker who just happened to be going out the gate as we went in.[7]

Some Characters

The *Readers Digest* magazine had a feature about "the most unforgettable character I ever met." Here are some characters from my Armed Guard days.

Our Liberty ship, the *Abner Nash*, was unloading at Murmansk in early 1944. Supervising the poor-wretched Russians doing all the hard work was a pompous Red Army officer, a captain or major. He came aboard every morning at eight bells.

On gangway watch was my "unforgettable character" in the gun crew. His favorite mess hall pastime was keeping a pea atop a column of air he'd blow upward for what seemed like minutes at a time. He was from Kentucky and we called him Mac.

Every morning when that Red Army officer came aboard Mac would throw him the sharpest high-ball salute you'd ever see, and then call him some of the dirtiest names you'd ever hear. The Russian would return the salute and jabber a response. Somehow, Mac had it figured out the guy didn't understand English, and every morning he came up with something nasty to call him. Of course, we'd try to be out on deck to near the gangway at eight bells to watch and listen to Mac's performance — until the day one of the ship's officers came by and didn't think it was funny. And Mac didn't have to stand gangway watch anymore.

On the *Abner Nash* and on the four other ships I sailed on the "F" word was everywhere in conversation. But I never heard it really used until I was assigned to the freighter *Admiral Halstead* in the Southwest Pacific and listened to the Australians in her crew.

The champion of "F" word usage, in my opinion, was a deckhand who even stuck it into two-syllable words. He couldn't say Tojo without using the word. It always came out "To f – ing Jo." Now that's unforgettable.

And so was Dan Coughlin, captain of the Liberty ship *Benjamin Ide Wheeler*, especially when an enemy bomber pilot decided to die for his emperor by crashing into our starboard side off Red Beach at Leyte in the Philippines. The plane is plowing right at us, the gunners are all blasting away at that SOB and I'm hugging the deck on the starboard side of the bridge topside. I looked up as the bomber came boring in and, standing right beside me, big as life, was Captain Dan, shaking his right fist high in the air at the bomber and shouting, "Keep away from my darling."

And that's how we learned Captain Dan's pet name for his ship: the "darling."[8]

"The Liberty ship SS Benjamin Ide Wheeler*, was bombed by Jap aircraft in three separate attacks starting at 0205 GCT on Oct. 26, 1944 while anchored between Palo and Tacloban, Leyte. She sailed from Hollandia on Oct. 18th carrying equipment for the U.S. Army Engineers and some 250 troops. Her crew numbered 42 and a Naval Armed Guard of 29. One AB and a Navy gunner were killed in the second attack. Most of the troops had been removed by the time of the first attack... At 1045 GCT another plane dropped its bombs and then crashed into No. 5 hold. The engine of the plane went through the port side of No. 5 hold making a hole about 9' in diameter... The ship was never abandoned during the attacks. The crew was removed from the ship on January 2, 1945 and repatriated to the U.S. The navy men were removed on Oct. 27, 1944.*[9]

Down the Hatch

Most of us weren't twenty-one years of age yet; many not over eighteen. But that didn't stand in the way of our becoming men when it came to consumption of alcoholic beverages.

My first beer was at age seventeen when some friends threw a farewell party for me before I went off to war. Boot camp at Newport, Rhode Island was a dry period. Signal school at Butler University in Indianapolis provided new found experiences. I don't know what Indiana's legal drinking age was in the fall of 1942, but all it took was a glib fib to be served at the Circle Tavern or at a liquor store next to the bus station.

Moving on to convoy signal school in Noroton Heights, Connecticut, we simply scooted across the state line to Port Chester, New York, to enjoy libations. Next assignment: the Armed Guard Center in Brooklyn. Again no sweat when it came to getting a drink.

Later, our thirst grew in greater proportion to time spent at sea. Norfolk was tough and practically dry for an eighteen-year-old. Texas oil tanker ports were wide open, as was Liverpool, Glasgow and Swansea in the U.K.

We could drink in Murmansk, but limited to two each at the main hotel and the International Seamen's Club — vodka served with warm tea in a glass.

Of course, there was some activity aboard ship, the basic ingredients for one concoction being raisins and leftover fruit cobbler dessert from the galley. Aboard the Liberty ship *Abner Nash* the 5-inch 38 gun motor room was the brewery until a gallon jug of the stuff exploded one night and gave away our secret.

Upon reaching New Guinea aboard the Liberty ship *Benjamin Ide Wheeler* we used coconuts instead of raisins and cobbler. Not really necessary though. There was plenty to drink on the *Wheeler* after the hatches were opened and we could get at the 45,000 cases of beer we had carried all the way from New York for the Navy PX at Hollandia.

At Leyte in the Philippines we learned to handle with care the native hooch called tooba. Australia was wide open, no matter your age. We had access to weekly rations of six liters of beer and two of spirits; and trading cigarettes for booze with the dock workers in Sydney and Melbourne was profitable for all parties involved. I was in Sydney on VE Day, but my memory of what happened remains lost in the alcoholic haze surrounding the night.

Back to the States in July 1945 with no questions asked in San Francisco. In Boston the next month at the Fargo Building Receiving Station on VJ Day — broke. But a sailor didn't have to buy his own drinks that night.

Not yet twenty-one, until November. Down the hatch, mates.[10]

~~~

This story from Bob first appeared in the January 1998 Drachen Foundation Newsletter. *This organization is devoted to preserving the history of kites and kite-flying.*

Battling Boredom

It was May 1944, in the harbor at Belfast Lough in Northern Ireland. I was signalman in the Armed Guard crew aboard the Liberty ship *Abner Nash*, at anchor off the town of Bangor waiting to join a convoy to New York.

Just sitting there on a Sunday afternoon, nothing to do, no chance of liberty ashore; boring, boring, boring.

I don't recall whose idea it was, but one of the gunners began constructing a kite on the stern 5-inch gun platform. The Wright Brothers never had it so good, what with the wind blowing fore to aft; perfect for kite flying.

The kite soared aloft in beautiful fashion. We were all so impressed we built a second kite and sent it up to join the first one.

What happened next and continued for several hours was a sky full of kites over Belfast Lough. They flew upward from the stern gundecks of at least a dozen ships at anchor, quite a sight.

We don't know what the Irish ashore thought of this. Through binoculars and log-glasses we could see people staring and pointing our way. Drivers brought vehicles to a halt and did the same. We hope it gave them some cheer because it sure did give us a big lift on that otherwise boring day.
~~~

On my next assignment aboard the Liberty ship *Benjamin Ide Wheeler* we spent fifty-one days in New Guinea unloading, supplying other ships and waiting to join the Philippine invasion at Leyte.

And guess what? It was kite time again. But the winds in the harbor at Hollandia were not very favorable. Our efforts, this time with box kites, fell flat in comparison to that Sunday afternoon four months earlier in Northern Ireland.

And we won the war, too.[11]

~~~

These liberty stories are from Dick Brown S1/c.

Glasgow: The Ideal Liberty Town

It was February 1944 and I was serving on board the S.S. *Joseph N. Nicollet*. During tours in the service one is always looking for the "Ideal" liberty town. For my choice in Europe, it would be Glasgow, Scotland. I was there three times during the war, twice for a one-day visit and once for thirty days. My stay there was as close to perfect as one could find during a war. The weather was mild in midwinter with plenty of Scotch beer and food (fish and chips).

Another find was a roller-skating rink where we would work off some excess energy. In the States this place would not be unusual, but in Europe it was the only one I ever saw. This place was a roughhouse to put it mildly. Skating fast was routine and then a whip would be formed. The first lesson in survival on falling was to get those fingers off the floor quick like. Whenever one had the misfortune to fall or get tripped, some roughnecks would push others into the pile.

The way they stopped on skates was something else. They would run into a railing or a wall. That changed after we arrived and they quickly learned to stop correctly. We had occasional fights between servicemen and civilians, but we never had the problem while we were there. While overseas, we always followed the good advice to never travel alone and be prepared!
~~~

Many people probably didn't care for the blacked out cities, but they were fine for the number one sport of meeting women. We usually stayed around the main drag which was Sauchiehall Street. You just picked a spot, lit a cigarette and waited for the girls that smoked. If a girl smoked she would always ask you for a light. If they passed you, you eased up on the conversation and they would move on. Then you'd wait for the next two to come by. However, there was always one drawback, which should have been worked out in advance. Just who would take the "dog" because, without fail, these girls traveled in pairs. One was always good looking and the other bad and you had to decide quickly who would take Miss you-know-what. I never could figure out why it was this way. Perhaps it was an early form of unionism for women so they all got an equal share of love.[12]

The Hot Dog Maru

In early June of 1944 I was home on leave during the big invasion in France. Then it was time to report back to the Armed Guard Center in Brooklyn, New York. We usually shipped out of there real fast, but this time I hung around doing vital work in the laundry. Finally, on a hot June 27th we departed the base and went aboard the SS *Winona*, a ship owned by the Weyerhauser Lumber Company. The ship soon loaded and we headed out to sea on June 30th. Our convoy formed and we had a quiet voyage to Birkenhead, England.

This gun crew was a lot different from my first one. We had one guy who drank too much and then became a fighter. His main dislike was anyone who was Italian. The captain gave him a break after one fight and didn't charge him with assault. One kid from New Jersey was a wise guy for his age and size. The twin gunner's mates, who had just earned their stripes, came on strong at times. Our gunnery officer had never been to sea and thought our crew was his high school gym class. And being an old ship, nothing was up to par and what might have been good soon turned bad. A case in point was the chow. Everything in the food line had bugs in it. Despite all these obstacles we managed to come through with flying colors.

Our cargo was for the Army commissaries and consisted of O'Henry candy bars, Lifesavers, and grapefruit juice. Somehow, a lot of these items came into our possession. By the time we got to Birkenhead, a suburb of Liverpool, we were sick of Lifesavers. Even though candy was scarce during the war, we tossed our supply to the kids as the ship tied up to the dock.

We enjoyed Liberty here and stayed in the area most of the time. We did spend some time in Liverpool and the girls there would ask us the name of our ship. Being patriotic and knowing the enemy had ears we had the right answer for them. Someone in our group came up with the name *Hot Dog Maru,* which we all agreed to. So during our stay there in July 1944 a lot of girls heard of the *Hot Dog Maru*. Now if they really believed it not, or just went along with the joke, we'll never know for sure.[13]

Bora Bora

In October of 1944 I was still on the SS *Winona*. We stopped at the French Island of Bora Bora out in the warm Pacific. This was a beautiful spot untouched by the war or pollution. This was the first stop on our South Pacific tour. The mountains seemed to disappear into the clouds and everything was a healthy green. It was hard to believe that halfway around the world in either direction a war was going on.

We couldn't get Liberty here and the CB's had it real rough because they would sail by in their LCI's with a brown-skinned girl in one arm while drinking a can of beer. We could understand why they wouldn't share their girls, but they wouldn't even offer us anything to drink.

Like most islands it wasn't long before the natives came out in their boats with souvenirs. Being poor sailors, our funds were low, and being out to sea, we didn't need money. The merchant seamen bought quite a few things, but what could we gunners do?

Suddenly, one of our gunners held up a pair of long johns saying they were nice and cool and that did it. Most of our gun crew began swapping winter underwear, which we didn't need, for trinkets. Everyone was happy and no one got beat. It wasn't even false advertising since it does get real cool in the islands at night. Years later I threw my aged trinkets away.[14]

~~~

Milan LaMarche's ship the SS Platano *sailed from San Francisco on January 19, 1944 for an extended island tour of the South Pacific. Milan writes, "As a radioman fresh out of training at an advanced communications school, I was eager to go to sea and join the Allied push towards Japan.*

Incident in New Zealand

The SS *Platano* was actively involved in supporting the troops with food supplies in the drive up the chain of islands north of Australia. Ports of call included the Solomon Islands, New Caledonia, and a number of other areas southwest of New Guinea. Usually sailing in convoy, the *Platano*'s principal cargo consisted of refrigerated meat: beef steaks for officers and mutton for the enlisted G.I.s. The return part of the shuttle run was to New Zealand, where the Armed Guard and merchant seamen could count on shore leave during reloading operations.

It is easy to understand that to sailors who spent weeks of endless duty under the tension of possible air or submarine attacks, shore liberty in New Zealand was the next-best recreation to a return to the States. The people were friendly, and the cost-of-living was reasonable. The citizenry was generally grateful for the protective umbrella of American forces since their own men were far away and heavily engaged against the Nazis in Europe. On the other hand, there were those "down under" who resented American servicemen for their brash confidence and aggressive attitude. Seemingly always provided with well-lined wallets, a boundless thirst for hard liquor, and inclined towards big-spending habits, they attracted girls long accustomed to a shortage of youthful male companionship.

My friend Regar and I were "liberty" buddies. Even though my duty as a radioman and Regar's as a gunner did not bring us together at duty stations, we had served together on the ship long enough to form a solid friendship. Regar was well liked, but
~~~

because of an unusual event that happened at sea he enjoyed a reputation of being a sound sleeper.

One day a Japanese plane was reported sighted on the horizon, and the general alarm sounded. The Armed Guard crew dashed to their guns. Lt. Wilson, the gunnery officer, checked to see whether all the men were at their duty stations. All were present and ready for action except Regar. Since nobody had seen him in the general rush, the lieutenant sent a man to the stern quarters to investigate. There in his bunk directly under the alarm which was still making a racket was Regar, sleeping as soundly as if he were in a sound-proof room. One could imagine what his shipmates had to say about that!

One day while Regar and I were in a bar in Wellington, New Zealand, we left our friends to go downstairs to a restroom. Apparently we had been quietly observed by some New Zealand sailors, who were no doubt jealous of us being Americans and our free-spending ways and success with the local girls. While we were indisposed, the New Zealanders bounced down the stairs and burst through the doors intending to provoke a fight. Making demeaning remarks about us that were absolutely fighting words, they closed in for an immediate confrontation.

Regar, left, and LaMarche on liberty in Auckland, New Zealand in 1944. Milan LaMarche.

We were hopelessly outnumbered, so we moved together quickly into one of the toilet stalls and locked the door. The frustrated attackers then removed their neckerchiefs that were filled with heavy links of lead. Swinging their deadly slings over the door, they attempted to whack the two of us and almost broke into the enclosure.

As luck would have it, a New Zealand Navy officer

suddenly came into the restroom. Sizing up the situation, he ordered the attacking sailors to come to attention, took their names and service numbers, and removed the lead from their neckerchiefs. Then he ordered the men to leave the bar and apologized profusely to us.

"What a relief," was my comment! The two of us also learned the value of carrying lead in our neckerchiefs for a tight situation. When we returned to the ship, I went down to the engine room to see a friend of mine. He made some shaped lead pieces to sew into our neckerchiefs. They did prove to helpful as our voyage continued. We were ready, but we were never confronted by the New Zealanders again.[15]

~~~

John H. Gross wrote of his Navy experiences.

My Navy Experiences

A few months prior to my eighteenth birthday, I decided to join the Navy rather than risk being drafted by the Army. I convinced my parents to sign permission papers allowing me to enlist. My enlistment date was June 17, 1943, the day before my 18th birthday.

I received my boot camp training at Newport, Rhode Island, Company 494 and completed boot camp in six weeks. I was assigned to base seaman guard for one month. I was then transferred to Brooklyn Armed Guard Center in September 1943. I was assigned to gun crews aboard the Liberty ships S.S. *Robert M. LaFollette* 9/43-6/44, and the S.S. *Pio Pico* 7/44-3/45…

I was detached from the S.S. *Pio Pico* in New York 3/45 and returned to the Brooklyn Armed Guard Center to await my next assignment. While at the Armed Guard Center, I was assigned to be a member of the Guard of Honor for deceased President Franklin Roosevelt 14 April 1945. Approximately ninety-five U.S. Navy Armed Guardsmen served as honor guards at Hyde Park, New York for the presidential funeral.
~~~

The Robert M. La Follette *under way in wartime with a full load. U.S. Coast Guard.*

I attended the Armed Guard School 5-inch 38 class; gun crew 4949 at Sheldon, Norfolk, Virginia 5/45-6/45. I was then transferred back to Brooklyn and from there to Shoemaker, California in the 11th Battalion in July 1945. We traveled via the Long Island Railroad day coaches. There were approximately 500 sailors aboard the train with no sleeping provisions. The cross country trip took five days.

I shipped out from Shoemaker, California to the Pacific late July 1945 aboard the transport U.S.S. *Warhawk.* We slept on bunks rigged up in the cargo holds of the ship. It was very hot down there. While aboard the *Warhawk*, we heard the news that President Truman had dropped the atomic bomb on Japan. We were all given a new lease on life! ...

P.S. I was able to recall many of the dates I've referenced in my write-up, thanks to my mother. She saved every letter and postcard I had written to her during my service time. She returned them to me some years ago.[16]

~~~

As of this writing, James W. Biscardi is ninety-one years old. Jim was a gun captain on three ships during the war. Jim said that he was a few years older than his crewmembers and that he was referred to as "Pops." [17]

Getting Sick

I had just returned from Egypt, Kenya and Capetown, where
~~~

it was quite warm. I returned to New York in one of the coldest years we had in years. An admiral had died and they took a bunch of us to march in a parade during a bitter snowstorm. I came down sick and went on sick call. My care consisted of having to go three times a day to the pharmacy window for a dose of medicine. The medicine did nothing to make me feel better.

About three days later I was called to report to the assignment officer and told to pack up for assignment to a ship. I told the officer I was being medicated and had not been examined. He sent me to sickbay to be examined by a doctor and to be determined whether I was well enough for sea duty. The doctor, whose name I still remember, asked me a few questions and handed me a chit stating, I was "well enough to return to duty." I demanded a physical examination. He replied, "If you repeat what you just asked again, I will have you thrown into the brig." I returned to the assignment officer and was told not to cry on his shoulder.

I then went to the chaplain who said, "He couldn't go against the doctor because he outranked him." I then went to the base commander's office and said I wished to speak with him because it was personal. It was granted.

I told the base commander my story and said if there is nothing wrong with me I would be ready to go immediately. I was given a chit to be thoroughly examined. I went back to the assignment officer and told him I was to go to sick bay and showed him the captain's chit. He blew his top for my going over his head. I told him that he had told me not to cry on his shoulder so I went to someone higher than him. This doctor still refused to examine me and made me wait for the next duty doctor.

The next doctor ended up calling an ambulance where I ended up in both the Brooklyn and Albans Naval Hospitals for a total of three months. I went from 154 to 120 pounds. I happened to overhear the doctors discussing my case one day. One doctor said, "Send him back to duty." Another said, "He should have a chance to gain back some of his weight loss." They offered me a seasickness discharge and I refused. I told them that was not what hospitalized me.

I was in my thirties, not like the kids they were taking advantage of. If I hadn't spoken up I would have gone to sea and died because of no medical assistance aboard a ship![18]

James Biscardi served on the following ships: MV Tarn *5/42-11/42, SS* Darien *4/43-2/44, SS* Esso Scranton *7/44-10/44, and SS* Paoli *10/44-6/45.*[19]

~~~

The Naval Armed Guards still party hardy as evidenced in George Hurley's 2002 Christmas party toast.

Our Toast
U.S. Navy Armed Guard
December 3, 2002

To Armed Guard sailors drink a toast
To Liberty ships we loved the most
To shiny guns we cleaned so well
And all the trips, that went to hell
To our shipmates, we loved so dear
Who stole our girls, and drank our beer
To all the sweet girls we left behind
Who really believed a sailor's line
Drink to living our glorious past
Things that happened at the mast
To ninety day wonders and gold Braid
Who tried to act like they weren't afraid
This elite Navy so brave and bold
Whose real story has never been told
It's vanishing now, like a good-bye kiss
This other Navy, that didn't exist
So raise your glasses, hand held high
To rusty old ships, and days gone by
To some shipmates, we just lost track
And all of our buddies, who didn't come back.[20]
~~~

12

Storms and Weather

Classic view of a Liberty ship in Winter North Atlantic. Imperial War Museum.

Even for experienced seafarers, nothing can match the feeling of terror and helplessness of being at sea in a raging storm. If you were an eighteen-year-old kid fresh off a farm or city street it was even worse. To be a "Real" sailor, a man had to go through the experience of surviving a big storm in order to join the naval fraternity.

~~~

H.D. "Stormy" Collins received a Bronze Star, sixty years after his participation in the North Africa Campaign.

Mountains of Water

I went to Gunnery School late in 1942 at Little Creek, Virginia and then went aboard the SS *Thomas Hooker* for sea duty. We went to Halifax to join a convoy for Europe. Our convoy split up with half the ships going to Murmansk and the other half (which I was in) thankfully went to North Africa. We unloaded in Oran, went back to Scotland for another load and then back to the Mediterranean.

We were docked in the Port of Anzio unloading cargo. We were sitting next to a British battleship when we were hit by dive bombers. This went on day and night and the area was a hot spot at that time. One of the bombs hit the dock next to our ship and damaged our superstructure. After the ship was examined, it was decided that we should try to get back to the States.

We first went back to Glasgow, Scotland to pick up a convoy. After picking up a convoy we encountered steering difficulties in a storm. We were able to make it back to port after almost beaching several times.

We left again and made it to the Gulf Stream when the weather turned really bad. Our ship was shaking all over especially when the bow of the ship was underwater. I had never before seen these mountains of water.

At dusk our ship was beginning to break up and we were just sitting ducks. Finally, the British Destroyer Escort HMS *Pimpernel* signaled and said they would stay with us. We tried to abandon ship but the swells were so great that they were hitting the lifeboats so we couldn't release the boat hooks.

We were in deep trouble and the temperature was around 40 degrees below zero.

The *Pimpernel* again signaled and told us to wait until morning (early morning is the calmest time of day) before we tried to abandon ship again. The water line was now nearly level with the deck. Our ship was ready to sink.
~~~

> On the night of March 5th, the storm increased to nearly hurricane winds causing the ship to crack across the main deck forward of No. 3 hatch port corner out to and down the side from the starboard after corner of No. 3 hatch out to and down to the storeroom deck. The ship did not actually break in two while the men were aboard but the crack across the main deck was opening and closing about two feet and considerable water was accumulating in the steward's storeroom...[1]

During the rescue, I was one of the oarsmen that shuttled our men to the *Pimpernel.* The destroyer escort would secure a mooring line to our boat and pull us back (on the lee side) close enough so we could use the oars the rest of the way. This went on for hours until everyone was aboard the *Pimpernel.* The weather was so bad we literally had to throw the men aboard that ship. We lost everything but pride!

They took us to St. John's, Newfoundland after going through icebergs at three knots. I have never seen anything like that storm. There were actually mountains of water coming at us. I had been across the Atlantic, but never encountered anything like this storm.

Our lifeboat crews did a wonderful job in not losing a man. Our U.S. Armed Guards and Merchant Marine crew all came through with flying colors. Prior to our losing the ship the Merchant Marine crew were a blessing to us gunners during air raids and sub-chasing. They were ammo loaders for our 20mm and helped bring up ammo from the magazine when we ran out of ammo.[2]

The drifting wreck of this ship was sunk 3/12/43 by U-653 *(Feiler). This sub was sunk ...on March 15, 1944 by HMS* Starling *and HMS* Wild Goose...[3]

~~~

This is Fred Huber's account of the Pacific Typhoon of 1943 and memories of the "Dog Days of August" which helped him get through the typhoon's fury.

Typhoon of 1943

When the Portuguese-born Spanish explorer, Ferdinand
~~~

Magellan, first saw that vast watery expanse in the 1500s, the calm, beautiful ocean must have given him a feeling of serenity. Expressing this inner feeling, he named it "The Pacific Ocean." On almost any day the hot sun shines brilliantly on the ocean, and the waves glisten with its reflection. But this is not always true. There are times when violent storms, with all their ferocity, disrupt this tranquility.

Such a time occurred in early April 1943, 6,000 miles out of Panama and 3,000 miles from Wellington, New Zealand. The 10,000-ton freighter, SS *Walter A. Luckenbach*, was being tossed about by a powerful typhoon with all its fury. The first threatening damage occurred when the steam pipe to the steering engine cracked, rendering the steering engine inoperable. Without the ability to steer into the storm, she lay powerless in the rolling trough of the unrelenting sea. With its mighty power the sea rolled the ship to starboard and the towering waves slammed against the deck, causing her to hesitate, seemingly to decide whether to continue the roll into the sea or to right herself. As suddenly as the vessel had been rolled to starboard she was righted, virtually being picked up and violently placed against the ocean's surface. Then the same procedure was repeated to the port side. With each roll, the ship listed 45 degrees which gave the appearance of being a watery wall high above the vessel. Having completed this cycle, the typhoon-induced sea raised the freighter's bow out of the water slamming her down with such force that the bow immersed itself into the ocean, and the sea angrily poured over the forward hatches and continued its violent journey to the bridge.

Then a more alarming incident occurred. The deck cargo, which consisted of army trucks, broke loose from their lashings, rolling from port to starboard with each roll of the ship. This caused gaping tears in the canvas that covered the hatches. Because the ship was still rendered helpless by being in the trough, the ocean poured over the bow and sides. The freighter started to take water in the holds. Something definitely needed to be done. Fortunately the vessel was equipped with twin screws (two propellers). By running one forward and the other astern it was possible to maneuver the ship out of the trough and into the storm.

Being a signalman in the US Navy Armed Guard, I was at my station on the flying bridge. My hands gripped the railing with all the strength I could muster; my feet were firmly placed against the deck. In this position it was my hope to keep from sliding into the sea with each roll of the ship. An "old salt" merchant mariner was standing beside me. He said nonchalantly that if the ship would roll again she would just continue into the ocean. It seemed as though he experienced none of the fear that had gripped me. He gave the impression of taking great pride in the fact that he was able to properly size up the situation. He then continued to explain the present circumstances drawing from his many years at sea. Whatever he was saying sounded as though it was from a distance; my thoughts were elsewhere. I had just turned eighteen years old and I began to wonder if I would see my nineteenth birthday. The tension started to ease and the fear seemed to ebb as my mind drifted back to those dog days of August 1940 in Patterson Park, Baltimore, Maryland.

August in Baltimore had always been considered the "dog days of August." Temperatures hover between 90 and 100 degrees. To make matters really worse there is always high humidity that sends the temperature index at least 10 degrees higher. To accentuate the misery further, there was no air-conditioning at that time. Even window fans were not to appear until the future. In order to find some relief from these conditions, at late night my two long-time friends, Warren Hays and Donald Pitcher, and I sought refuge in Patterson Park. A breeze seemed to emanate from the trees and nearby boat pond. I can still visualize the site of our haven. Patterson Park Avenue borders the park on the north. Approximately fifteen yards inward is a Chinese pagoda, and perhaps another fifteen yards in the same direction is (or was) a fish pond. Directly behind the pond is the site of our "conference table" — a long green bench. It was here that we discussed and made such great plans. Someday we would sail the South Seas to the Polynesian Islands. Of course important preparations were seriously discussed. Warren would be the captain, Donald the engineer, and I would be the navigator. No attention was paid to such trivial matters such as how we would obtain a ship, nor did it concern us as to how we would finance the trip —

including paying for our transportation. Our imaginations were filled with balmy weather, calm seas, Polynesian girls, and exotic food. It would be a carefree journey and time would be endless.

Ironically, some time later I would be the only one to make that trip, but it would certainly be under much different conditions than we visualized that August day.[4]

~~~

Part of John Lucarelli's story appeared in Chapter 9. What follows involves his experience before D-Day.

There was this large flash ...

I entered the service on August 27, 1943 and after boot camp left Baltimore, Maryland on the SS *Samuel Dexter*. Our holds were filled with 500 lb. bombs and our deck cargo consisted of trains, tenders, and aircraft.

We picked up a convoy off Newfoundland and some ships were hit by submarines. I believe one of the ships was a tanker. We arrived in Cardiff, South Wales, early in December 1943.

We left soon after for a return trip to the States. We were heading toward Greenland in a very bad storm when we lost control of our rudder. We had to drop out of the convoy and ships all around us were leaving their positions.

Several days later the storm got worse and everyone was pulling watch on the bridge. One of those nights I was pulling watch on the bridge when there was this large flash. Everyone thought we had been hit by a torpedo but it was the ship cracking. There were times when we thought the water was going down our stack. Being seventeen years old, I was so scared and I figured I'd never see my family again.

It got so the pumps couldn't keep up with all the water coming into the ship. The captain had the crew disconnect all cables to the forward mast. Some time later the bow of the ship broke off. We had to abandon ship several days later on January 21, 1944, and one of our crew members when going over the side grabbed the pulley line instead of the lifeline. He ended up with
~~~

burnt hands and a deep slice in his leg when he hit an oarlock in the lifeboat.

A British fishing trawler converted to a war vessel picked us up. They then fired several shots at the Liberty ship to make it sink faster. We were told that there was a surfaced sub on the horizon and more than likely wanted to board our ship for supplies.

We landed in Liverpool and all we had was our person. Our officer went to the Red Cross but couldn't get assistance without official orders from the Navy. The Salvation Army went all out and supplied us with sleeping quarters, clothes, cigarettes and meals.[5]

There were twenty-eight Armed Guard aboard and the survivors were picked up by the HMS Sapper, *an armed trawler. The* Samuel Dexter *didn't sink. She ended up beaching on Barra Island of the Outer Hebrides Group off Scotland.*[6]

~~~

Dick Brown tells of a terrible storm that occurred in early 1944.

I would have kissed the ship builders…

Not everyone would agree that a wartime year could be a vintage one. But for me, 1944 turned out to be such a year especially after one close call with death. It started quietly and sober for me in early January where I was aboard the SS *Joseph N. Nicollet.* We were anchored in Loch Ewe, Scotland waiting for a convoy to Russia.

Things were going good while we traveled in the convoy. But then a fog settled in upon us and the sea got rough. When the fog lifted, we had lost the convoy. Our storm soon grew to gale or hurricane. The catwalk and drums of gasoline and oil went over the side of the ship. Tragically, our youngest gunner was swept over the side by a freak wave coming directly over the stern.

We were told that the ship had cracked in seven places and we were someplace between Iceland and Norway. Questions were
~~~

running through everyone's mind, "Would the ship hold together; was this an act of God or nature; was there any difference between the two of them?"

But, "Praise the Lord," he did land us at Akureyri, Iceland with no other losses. I would have kissed the shipbuilders if they had been there that day. After a quick patch job we got underway for Glasgow, Scotland and drydock.[7]

~~~

William Oehlecker joined the Navy in March 1944 at the age of seventeen. He said that he "qualified for either Aviation or Motor Machinist Mate," but before he had made a decision, he encountered a fellow who was bragging about how great a deal you could have by joining the Armed Guard. The fellow said, "It wasn't regimented, that you were served the best food by the Merchant Marine mess department, and that you had only one or three other guys to share your fo'c'sle. Furthermore, that you were off-duty while your ship was in port until it sailed again and it was the greatest duty to pull in the Navy."

A Wave Floated Us High Off Our Feet

I really fell for that spiel and I signed up for the "Forgotten Navy." I then received four more weeks of gunnery training at Little Creek, Virginia.

I was assigned to the new Liberty ship SS *George Hawley* right out of a Kaiser Shipyard in Maine. (Cold, Cold, Cold). We had her outfitted with ammunition and wound up with a cargo of high explosives loaded to the gunnels. It was then out to sea where the weather was very rough and cold. The seas were running fifty to sixty feet high and you couldn't really see more than a few yards around you.

The weather was so bad and rough on this slow trip that I don't believe a gun could have been manned with any effect. You had all you could do to stand on your feet. Everyone had to stand General Quarters at dawn and dusk even if you had just gotten off of a four-hour watch. And frankly, the visibility was
~~~

so bad that you couldn't have spotted a periscope if you wanted to.

We reached England and wound up off Normandy on Omaha Beachhead four to six days after the invasion. It took the longest time to unload us with those Army ducks. We finally unloaded and headed back to the states. About two hundred miles from New York, we ran into a hurricane. I and one of my shipmates had to secure the forward gun tub and we were both washed down the deck to the forward housing where a wave floated us high off our feet. Talk about rough and being scared to death! We lost a lifeboat and one merchant seaman was crushed to death trying to secure it. That was really sad and quite an experience.

I could go on and on about the hardships we endured as kids. In some ways it was exciting and we had a job to do and completed it. Let's not forget to include our Merchant Marine shipmates who were real brave men and who are now are our fellow veterans.

I earned a four-day leave when we reached Brooklyn, New York. My dad, who worked on the docks, was on the dock waving to me. He was real proud of me. My ship turned around and I heard that she was torpedoed but most of the crew was saved.[8]

The Liberty ship, SS George Hawley, *was torpedoed by the German submarine* U-1199 *(Nollman) ...on January 21, 1945 about 3 miles off Wolf Trap Lighthouse ...while en route in Convoy TCB-43 (#23) from Cherbourg, France to Cardiff, Wales in ballast and carrying 77 bags of Fleet Post Office mail. Her compliment was forty-one merchant crew and twenty-seven Naval Armed Guard. Two men on watch in the engine room were killed by the explosion.*[9] *She was torpedoed and "beached (voyage Cherbourg/Mumbles). Later refloated and 14.6.46: Towed to Bremerhaven. Loaded with obsolete chemical ammunition and 10:46 Towed to sea and scuttled."*[10]

Compiler's note: The SS George Hawley, *along with five other ships, were loaded with toxic chemical ammunition found in Germany after the war. These ships were scuttled in the Skagerrak Sea, also known as the Norwegian trench. One of the chemicals, mustard gas, still burns fisherman today after they pull their fishing nets and come in contact with the toxic. [See* Nightmare in

Bari: The World War II Liberty Ship Poison Gas Disaster and Cover-up *by the same author.*]

~~~

F.H. Pearce describes his rough weather experiences.

"Sure glad that's over!"

I was on board the Panamanian tanker SS *New York*, a very tired rust pot. We ran coastwise to South America, Panama, etc. On this one trip back to the States, we ran into a hurricane, or I should say, it smashed into us. In those days, no ships had satellite information or warnings. We registered winds of 136 mph.

Needless to say, things got hazardous. I witnessed a Liberty ship close by with railway engines as deck cargo. One huge wave sent one over the side and another wave followed sending its partner into the deep six.

All communication from the bridge to the stern was lost. It must be remembered that the engine room was in the rear of a tanker. We therefore had a huge steering wheel on the outside. The men had to be lashed to it and it took four men to man it and keep the ship into the waves. The ship rolled so often you easily could have walked the walls.

One of the Armed Guard crew members said if he was going to die, that he was going to die clean. He took a shower, stepped out on deck, fell and slid on his butt all the way across the quarters. He banged into the locker and started to make the return trip part way when he grabbed on to one of the posts which held up a bunk. After that he went directly to his sack.

It finally calmed down nicely and I spoke to one of the merchant marine seaman. I said, like the complete rookie that I was, "Sure glad that's over!" He said, "Hang on Sonny, it's going to blow from the other direction just as hard real soon." So much for my knowledge of hurricanes!

We had cement gun tubs for all our 20mm guns. All of that and the ready boxes containing the ammunition were blown away.
~~~

We lost thirteen plates in the bow area and it was on to Baltimore for repairs. The first dockworker asked when he was looking at the ship, "Where in the hell have you been?"[11]

~~~

Irving M. Dickerman lives in a small New Hampshire town. The town newspaper, the Andover Beacon *published the following article that Irving wrote for their Guest Writer column.*

A Sea Experience

My experience begins in the fall of 1944 when I was seventeen years old. I had only been in the Navy for three months. At the time, I was part of a twenty-six-man gun crew with one officer, aboard a merchant ship. We were known as the U.S. Navy Armed Guard. The convoy of ships was taking war materials to Newcastle, England, bordering on the English Channel. I was very frightened as the entire cargo was bombs and ammunition. One of the ships was either hit by a mine or torpedoed by a submarine. Because it had the same cargo as our ship, it was a massive explosion.

Shortly we were attacked by German planes. At that time, I was firing a 20mm gun. Shrapnel hit both myself and the sailor loading my gun. Aboard merchant ships there were no doctors or medics. The Purser put sulfur powder on the wounds. We both prayed we would reach port before they became fatal.

After unloading in Newcastle, we formed another convoy and headed back to the States. We saw something en route that would boggle one's mind — B-17 Bombers were headed for Germany. I found out later there were one thousand planes that wiped out an entire German city.

Returning to the States, we ran into a hurricane with waves fifty to sixty feet high. It crossed my mind that I might be safer under enemy fire. Our quarters on the ship were in the stern so there was no way we could go across the deck to the mid-ship galley. However, there was a ladder that went to the bottom of the ship called the shaft alley. This went to the boiler room then up to the galley.
~~~

During the war there were all kinds of ships pressed into service. I saw a Great Lake freighter that turned broadside to the wind, then turned over and sunk. The ship I was on (SS *Bayou Chico*) was known as a Hog Island freighter built in 1917. Top speed was about eight knots. It was a riveted ship which was much stronger than one that was welded.

As the storm was receding, our ship came to a complete stop. If I remember correctly, I was told that the plugs in the boiler had blown out. The ship's carpenter mate turned some out of wood while we bailed sea water to put in the boilers. We did get underway, but the plugs didn't last long. Without power, all our perishable food had to be thrown overboard. On Thanksgiving Day we had pancakes and canned peaches. I remember seeing the cooks sifting flour to remove weevils.

A convoy passed, guarded by several navy ships. Conversing by microphone, they told us they could not break radio silence but when they arrived in England, our condition and position would be made known. I don't recall how many days we drifted before we saw a ship on the horizon.

A bucket brigade formed to gather sea water for the boilers. Irving Dickerman.

Our signalman signaled with his lights and we were manning our guns not knowing if the ship was friend or foe. We saw a flash from the ship and a shell exploded on our starboard side then one on our port side. We all knew they had the range and the next one would be us. The signalman sent another message. Thankfully, they ceased firing. Signal codes changed every few days and the captain had not given the signalman the code that time. Whew! The approaching ship was the *Aquitania,* a passenger ship with five thousand troops aboard. They came alongside and with their bullhorns, gave us hell as they might have sunk one of our own ships.

A few days later, we saw a small boat which was a sea-going tug that came more than a thousand miles from Newfoundland to tow us into the Azores. Parts were flown from the States and Portuguese workers completed repairs. When ashore, standing on the deck, it was plain to see the effects of the incredible power of the ocean as the bow of our ship had been dented from the force of the waves.[12]

The SS Bayou Chico *escaped an earlier encounter with a submarine. "En route Halifax to Archangel. Attacked by German* U-754 *on March 22, 1942. Reversed course and escaped arriving Halifax at 0502 on March 25th. Sub attacked on surface.*[13]

~~~

Edmund M. Fogarty sent this story of a potential catastrophe caused by the weather which will forever stand out in his mind.

Atlantic Fog

I was an Armed Guard radioman on the Liberty ship *Jonathan Trumbull* in 1945. We left Philadelphia on 9 April 1945, proceeded to New York and left in convoy for Antwerp on April 13 where we dropped off supplies for the battle of the Bulge which was going on thirty miles away.

After departing Antwerp we stopped at Le Havre, France and picked up 500 American G.I.'s who had just been liberated from German POW camps. We then crossed the channel to Southampton and a few days later joined a convoy of eighty-seven ships forming off the English coast.

Everything proceeded normally at the beginning of the voyage. I felt sorry for the G.I.s sacked out in our hold because it was cold, damp and dirty down there. But the soldiers were just happy to be on their way home.
~~~

On May 27 we were two days from New York. There was a heavy rain and thick fog and through the murk one of the ships in the first column spotted an iceberg. I was on radio watch at about 1545 when I copied a wireless-telegraph message from the commodore ordering a 90 degree turn for all ships. We waited for the signal to execute but when I went off watch at 1600 we had not received it.

I went to my quarters in a temporary shack built on the boat deck overlooking the main deck. I heard some yelling on the deck and looking out the porthole saw some of the merchant marine crew screaming and shaking their fists at a huge British tanker that was heading straight for the spot where we were positioned. As we froze on the spot, the British helmsman on the British ship acted fast and swung his ship to port. It scraped down the starboard side of our ship, ripping off the lifeboats. It then disappeared into the fog.

All over the convoy, ships were crashing into each other, some more than once. We were later rammed again in the rear quarter. Twenty-one ships were damaged before a signal was sent for all ships to stop dead in the water. When the fog lifted the next morning everyone was amazed to see the ships scattered around pointing in every direction. Our ship was not the only ship carrying troops so it was a miracle that none of the twenty-one ships were in danger of sinking.

The commodore ordered the convoy to re-form and proceed to their destinations. In his report on the incident the commodore said that he signaled the turn by radio and horn but due to the rain and fog the horn couldn't be heard. There was no explanation why the execute signal was not sent by radio.

When I recall this accident I am extremely grateful to the helmsman of the British tanker for his quick action in avoiding a major collision with our ship. I think it was an incident that the Merchant Marine and Navy would just as soon forget. There was supposed to be a hearing in New York but it never materialized.[14]

~~~
~~~

Against wartime regulations, Robert L. Somers kept a diary on board the SS Patrick Henry *and SS* Knute Nelson *during the years 1943 to 1946. His home base was the Brooklyn Armed Guard Center and this selection is from the* Knute Nelson *which he boarded November 29, 1944.*

S.S. *Knute Nelson*

November 29, 1944

Came aboard ship, Philadelphia, Pa.

Nov. 30, 1944

Inspected guns and equipment with officer.

1 - 3-inch 50 Dual purpose, 1 – 5-inch 50 Surface bag gun, 8 – 20mm Antiaircraft

Dec. 1, 1944

Port watch in order, everybody secure. Liberty started.

Dec. 2, 1944

Loading fast with crates of trucks & iron rails.

Dec. 7, 1944

Almost loaded.

Dec. 8, 1944

Had last liberty ashore tonight. Went to movies with Gilbert. Liberty expires at 12:00 midnight. Ship way down in water and almost loaded. Have 11 man gun crew & officer, Lt. (J.G.) P.H. Lanigan.

Dec. 9, 1944

Left dock at 2:30 P.M. headed down Delaware River. Lots of sights to see. Plenty cold. Just one man watch. Read a lot.

Dec. 10, 1944

Good clear, cold day. Carrier passed at chow. No. 69. (*CVE – 69 USS* Kasaan Bay, *commissioned in December 1943*) Cleaned & secured 3-inch & 1-2 20 mm. Entered Hampton Roads, Vir. at supper, and anchored in roadstead with rest of convoy.

Dec. 11, 1944

Pulled out at dawn heading east for Europe. Cold, cloudy day. Rough sea. Have 12-4 watch as P.O. Two man sea watch I'm 5-inch 50 plugman and No 5. 20 m/m gunner. Storm coming.

Dec. 12, 1943

I will remember this day as long as I live. Storm hit us hard from S.W. Many seasick. 30 to 50 ft. waves so big you had to look up to see the top of them. New men scared to death. Seas broke in storm doors & flooded amidships. Almost knee deep on 2nd deck. Officer's Quarters topside flooded. Water coming down ventilators. 3" deep in our forcastle. Everything wet. Sugar, flour, cookies most all destroyed by water. Christmas food gone. Two life-boats gone (1-3). Catwalk torn off part of deck. Davits gone & gangway. Cargo smashed. Had to bail water all night. Many ships turned back. Only men outside on bridge. Two men lost on 75 [sic], swept overboard. Wind very strong and some rain. Boys back aft sleeping forward. Ship is up on end most of time. No sleep of any kind. Are about 300 mi. out. Case of bombs got loose on one ship, so we were told to get far away from it. One Liberty ship split in half & is trying to make Bermuda. (Labels on canned goods were mostly washed off so cooks didn't know what was in can till it was opened).

Dec. 13, 1944

(Morning) Still rough, but wind has gone down some. Part of deck cargo shifted. Pumps working all the time. Cleaned up part of awful mess. Had water in magazine to drain out.

Not half bad tonight, but ship rolling a lot. Making good time near Bermuda. Split Liberty sent S.O.S. by radio.

Dec. 14, 1944

Convoy got together somewhat today. Still rough but at least you can sleep a little. All escort ships turned back but they came back today. It is warm but raining off and on. M.M. (*Merchant Marine*) repairing some of damage. Had steak and doughnuts tonight.

Dec. 15, 1944

Better weather today. Rain off and on. Water still coming over side. Cleaned guns. Food isn't so good. Set watch ahead 1 hr. tonight.

December 16, 1944

Very nice warm clear day, but sea not yet smooth. Cleaned guns most of day. Started on GM2/c (*Gunner's Mate*). Oh! Man what a thick book. Little over 1/3 of way across. New catwalk up.

(Gunner's Mate 1st, 2nd, and 3rd Class correspondence courses were sent to and administered by the gunnery officer.

They were sent back to the respective Armed Guard Center for grading. The highest score obtainable was 4.0. However, even if an Armed Guard passed with flying colors, his promotion recommendation was still up to his Gunnery Officer and was also based on attitude, work ethic and leadership qualities.)

Dec. 17, 1944

Wind blowing hard today. Rain squalls some. Washed clothes. ½ ships' stores damaged by water. Will have to pull into some port to repair damage done by storm. Bought candy – $1.40.

Dec. 18, 1944

Pretty good day. Sea calm with hot sun. Had gun practice on 5" gun. Am gun captain. Had fire & boat drills and worked some. Bought clothes and shoes in slop chest.

Dec. 19, 1944

One of my best days at sea. Beautiful clear, calm, warm day. Washed clothes and worked on guns. Had convoy maneuvers. ½ way across Atlantic. 37.12 N 38.48 S. Studying GM 2/c. Took first test (3.23).

Dec. 20, 1944

Test fired 5" & 20's. Shot over convoy. Recleaned all guns. Got message that ship was torpedoed this A.M. N.E. of us, and almost on our route. Position 42.06N. (sunk) (34.00W 37.14N). Good clear warm day. Had fire and boat drill.

(The ship torpedoed was most likely the LST-359. *"...*LST 359 *was sunk on 20 December 1944 by a torpedo in the eastern Atlantic.")*[15]

Dec. 21, 1944

Passed Azores at supper time. Good day. Will be at Gibraltar Tuesday. Learning signal flags some.

Dec. 22, 1944

Stiff wind but clear day. Covered about 2700 miles so far. Have eaten breakfast once aboard ship because of 12-4 watch. Guns in pretty good condition now.

Dec. 23, 1944

Wind choppy. Day quite cool. Got message from Comm. to stand strict watch and maintain radio silence. A U-boat is converging on our track from north. Believe it is the same one that sank ship the other day. Took test (4.0).

Dec. 24, 1944

Some ships broke off. Sea is quite rough again. Ship is bouncing around a lot. Spray coming over port side. Saw aircraft today. Night before Christmas and plenty of whiskey flowing topside.

Dec. 25, 1944

Christmas at sea. (12 Lon. 35 Lat.) Had turkey for dinner. Windy cool day. Captain sent Christmas greetings to crew.

Dec. 26, 1944

Had another rough night last night. Ship rolled as much as 30 degrees. Giant ground swells. Couldn't sleep. Many dishes and stuff broken. Have air cover now. Ships put torpedo nets down. Got cigarettes and gum. Took test (3.7).

Dec. 27, 1944

Went through Straits at dawn. (Slept all the way.) Had rainy night last night and sub alert. Convoy broke up after Gibraltar, so we are traveling alone now.

Dec. 28, 1944

Passed Oran in early morning. Still raining. Doing about 11 knots and almost 10 miles from shore. Lot of ships around. Storm coming. Took test (3.3).

Dec. 29, 1944

Storm hit us about midnight. (Painted new mess hall). Other two lifeboats (2-4) swept overboard. One took davits and all and had a motor in it. Taking heavy seas over the bow. Raining and blowing like hell. Have had no sleep now for 35 hours. Passed Algiers. What a miserable trip this is! Sure hope it ends soon. Had about six good days in a month.

Dec. 30, 1944

Cloudy, windy rough day. Ship pitching with bow going under a lot. About three miles from shore. Giant rollers tossing us around. Will pass Bizerte after supper. Water in 3" magazine.

Dec. 31, 1944

Good clear day and calm for a change. Passed Pantallera before breakfast and Malta in afternoon. Heading S.E. now. Have been sailing with lights on at night. Few aircraft seen. New Year's Eve. Blew the whistle at midnight.[16]

More of Bob's diary will appear in the South Atlantic – Indian Ocean Chapter.

13

The South Atlantic and Indian Oceans

These two theaters of action have been combined simply because they are connected. Both oceans saw a lot of action in World War II. Large amounts of armament, foodstuffs, and supplies traversed these waters in merchant ships protected by the U.S. Navy Armed Guard.

It was because of Germany's U-boat and commerce raiders that the American Navy established its Fourth Fleet in Brazil along with two naval air squadrons to assist in the air defense. Brazil's decision to support the Allies also put more ships in the South Atlantic on patrol. Defending this area known as the "Atlantic Narrows" was a large task — it stretched in a triangle from Trinidad to Cape Sao Rogue to the Cape Verdi Islands off Africa and back to Trinidad.

In addition to the U-boats, the Germans used disguised commerce ships in this theater with brutal efficiency. These ships were known as raiders. During World War I German raiders sank

108 ships of some 379,178 tons.[1] *They had even greater success in World War II sinking 132 ships of some 823,080 tons.*[2]

U-boat and raiders were also effective in the Indian Ocean. Here, the important shipping lanes ran from the Cape of Good Hope to Suez to India. Germany knew it was imperative to disrupt the Allied shipping of war material in this ocean and it had to be done with little help from her ally, Japan. The Rising Sun's military was spread too thinly to control these shipping lanes. Japan had enough to do supplying her own military and navy in her conquered possessions in the Far East.

Even Germany's fleet was spread too thin in this theater. She sent only six submarines and nine raiders to disrupt the flow of supplies in the South Atlantic and Indian oceans. Her military leaders should have paid more attention to raider successes. Despite having only nine active raiders, the damage they accounted for was 7 percent of the impressive U-boat total,[3] *of which there were about 1,100 submarines constructed.*

The U.S. Navy Armed Guard, merchant crews and ships paid a stiff price in these two oceans. The following table was generated from the American Merchant Marine at War website:

Theater	**Ships Sunk Or Damaged**	**Crew Deaths**	**Naval Armed Guard Deaths**
South Atlantic	69	476	147
Indian Ocean & Red Sea	49	386	148
	118	862	295[4]

~~~

On September 27, 1942 while en route from Capetown to Dutch Guiana, the brand new Liberty ship, SS Stephen Hopkins *observed two strange looking ships coming out of the morning mist approximately twenty miles off the coast of Africa. These ships were the German merchant raider* Stier *and her escort, blockade runner* Tannenfels. *Almost immediately the* Stier *opened fire. In doing so, Paul Buck, the* Hopkin's *Master, turned his ship stern first toward the other ships to present a smaller target. What*
~~~

ensued was one of the great sea-battles and survival stories of the modern era in which a smaller U.S. merchant vessel, SS Stephen Hopkins, *caused the destruction and sinking of a German naval vessel. This encounter, which took only twenty minutes, was the only time in World War II where a U.S. vessel fought a German naval vessel.*

The following is a transcription of U.S. Navy Armed Guard survivor S/2c Moses Barker's account of the battle. He received a commendation from the Secretary of the Navy.

Moses Barker's Talk to the SS *Stephen Hopkins* Chapter of the American Merchant Marine Veterans

(*Note: Unedited and, understandably, quite emotional*)

We left Capetown and I was on the 4-to-8 watch. I got off watch at 8 in the morning and went amidships for breakfast. Just as I finished I heard the damndest explosions going off. The ship was shaking all over.

I took off for the 4-inch 50 on the stern. I started out the passageway and man you wouldn't believe the machine gun bullets coming by. I mean it was something else. I was on my hands and knees running like a rabbit. Man was I moving. I got back and I can't say what was happening on the rest of the ship as I was occupied. I finally got on my 4-inch 50 and we had a pretty good time. Those Germans really knew what they were doing. Every time their guns would go off they would go off all at once and those shells would hit us every time.

Anyway, we fired all the shells I had in my ready box except five of them were on top. When we had the hurricane and the

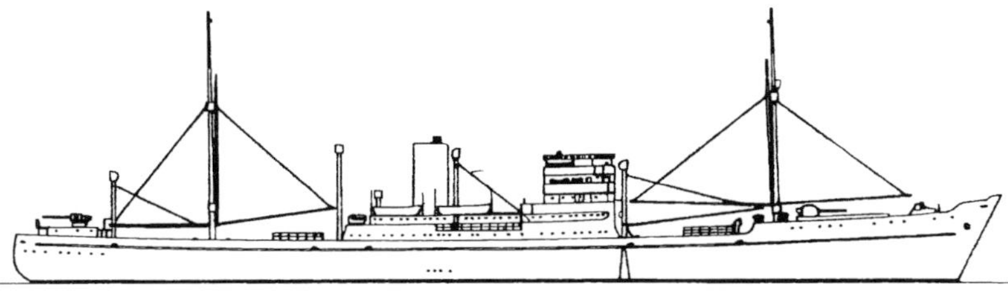

This drawing is of the Stier *as she appeared in 1942.* Conway Picture Library Collection.

water seeped into the box, they were all rusted. I tore the skin off my hands trying to get the shells out of there. I couldn't do it.

So, I think the last shell I put in there 'cause I was having to watch the machine gun bullets. [sic] I had to duck behind the gun and they would zoom by. One time they were coming so hard overhead I hollered, "fire." I had my face right against the breech. If he had pulled the trigger my head would have been a block down the street. But he was already dead. All of them was dead there except me. So I ran and pulled the trigger. I didn't even look to see what I was shooting or anything. I just pulled the trigger and got behind the gun again. I couldn't get any more shells out of the ready box.

We had .50 caliber machine guns; two on each side. I went over there to try to shoot one of them. I didn't know how to. The only thing I knew how to do was the 4-inch 50. I got up there looking at it but what the hell am I going to do? I got away from it.

About that time a shell hit underneath us. (I hate this).

(*At this point Moses is quite emotional and Bill Bentley, President of the SS* Stephen Hopkins *Chapter says, 'Moses hang in there, we're with you, we understand.'*

I got off the gun deck and went amidship. We picked up a passenger in Capetown. He was a soldier of fortune and he was standing there. I was trying to get by him in the passageway so I could get my lifejacket. He said, 'Son you don't want to go in there.' Steam was coming out of the engine room. He said, 'Everyone is dead.' He had a lifejacket on.

(*Pause. Bentley – Fine, Fine, it's OK)*

He put his lifejacket on me, tied it and said get into the life boat. He just stayed there on the ship and went down with it.

I got into the lifeboat. It was already down when I got to it. The captain then came to the lifeboat and he had a briefcase in his hand. He said, 'Barker, take this and hold onto it,' and he threw it to me. So I did for two weeks. (A metal case). I held onto it like it was a teddy bear. I wouldn't have turned that loose for nothing.

After about two weeks in the lifeboat — it was just monotonous just sitting there. We would once in a while talk about food.

We had one guy from California and he had a chicken ranch and for about a week he would talk about the different ways he was going to fix chicken. "You all coming to stay with me and I'm going to fix you the best chicken." We weren't as hungry as we were thirsty and you know we never had any bowel movement while we were on the boat. Everything in us was used by our bodies.

Let me get my head straight. May have been a couple hours and they shelled us in the lifeboat and machine gunned us both. A sailor sitting beside me and I don't know how it happened but he had his arm cut off right here. A shell hit right beside us. Meanwhile, we are bailing like hell because the waves and water are getting real strong — getting ready to have a storm. We were trying to bail the water out and I threw some water on his arm and oh that really tore me up because of the salt water. He screamed like a banshee. (That hurts). Anyway they quit shelling us and after a while the storm came up and solid clouds. We couldn't see them and they couldn't see us neither.

Quite a while we sailed like thirty-one days on that boat. I learned never to let my feet in the water — ocean. I wouldn't even do it on a lake out here. The boat rocking like this, the sun would burn and blister us and at night we would freeze. This was daytime and my feet were over the side and the boat would be rocking in the water and come back up. I was day dreaming and all of a sudden I saw the damndest barracuda you ever seen in your life. He came out of the water at I guess ten feet from the boat and that sucker went after my feet and I just made a flip over backwards and that thing hit the boat. I thought (the boat) would turn over. Boy he hit hard. I bet it knocked its brains out. Never again did I put my feet in the water.

We had canned pemmican on board. We'd take a can of pemmican and cut into it four squares and each of us would get a pie shape and then throw the can over the side. The water was clear. I wish it was like that nowadays and one day a shark grabbed a can. The sucker was really moving. Before this we would soak ourselves in the water. We'd get in and get out of the boat for half a minute, but no more.

I love the ocean but that was a long trip. We were just lucky we had a good crew. The Merchant Marine and Navy got along wonderful together. Usually you had a little conflict between the different branches, but with us there were no different branches. We were all the same.

(*At this point Moses Barker answered some questions pertaining to his experience in the lifeboat*)

We heard the explosions in the storm, we never saw it (*Stier*) sink.

We shelled them in the water before it (Stier) went down. The 4-inch 50 packs a wallop and we hit it (*Stier*) several times.

We went from Africa to South America in a lifeboat. We landed on a beach in South America. Twenty one started — fifteen landed, six died over thirty-one days. We laid right on the beach. It was a native village and the natives cooked a pig right on the beach in a pit. We couldn't eat it. Our stomachs were that size. A civilian airplane came down and there was an airfield nearby and a place where they could land. That is pretty country there. We went into the hospital nearby. We stayed in the hospital in Rio de Janeiro I think three days and they flew us back to the States. I could hardly walk as I was hit in the leg and once in the crotch and I worried about getting gangrene in my leg but they fixed that.

I gave the case to the merchant marine.

We had just left Cape Town, off the coast of South Africa the day before. We were twenty-four hours out. We never saw any ships at all in the lifeboat. We had a sail that we put up. We had an old time merchant seaman in the lifeboat with us. He told us the way we needed to go by looking at the stars when they came up and the sun and moon. He knew his business. We tacked the sail to get some rain water. If we saw it raining on the horizon we'd head that way – all of us rowing. We used the sail to catch water. It was salty as hell but not as salty as the ocean water.

We were lucky we never saw any bad weather except the first time when our ship went down. That saved us from doing us in quicker.[5]

The launch of S.S. Stephen Hopkins *in April 1942. Five months later she fought and sank a German raider.* Kaiser Shipyards.

Second Engineer George D. Cronk wrote the following statement. His report begins with observing the raider that had received the deadly burst from the Hopkins *and then continues with the action in which he was directly involved.*

After leaving the ship we drifted very near to the raiders, one a small ship about 4,000 tons had the most armament. She had at least four 4-inch guns firing together from a fire control system, but Ensign Willett had put between thirty-five and forty shells from our 4-inch into her along the water line. There was smoke pouring from her in several places. He concentrated on this ship handling the gun himself while badly wounded until our magazine was hit and exploded. Cadet O'Hara then fired the remaining five shells at the other ship which had held her fire except for machine guns. All the while our machine guns kept a steady fire on the decks of both ships. In the meantime the second mate who was in charge of two 37mm guns forward put shell after shell into the other raider until his shell handlers were killed and the gun platform wrecked. The *Stephen Hopkins* was hit repeatedly from stem to stern by four salvos at a time until she was a complete wreck and a fire all over. When the abandon ship signal was given the raider was using shrapnel and incendiary shells. I lowered the after fall of the only remaining lifeboat which was about five feet from a roaring inferno of flame. A shell burst along the boat on the way down killing two and wounding four men. The remaining crew was putting over rafts when I jumped overboard. I was later picked up by this boat and with all the able men we got out the oars and among the dying and wounded we got several men from the water and from rafts. Then the wind started rising and the sea running high, the visibility becoming very bad. All sighted the third mate in one of the smashed lifeboats that had been blown off the *Stephen Hopkins* by shell fire. He had bolstered it up at one end by a doughnut raft, but row as hard as we could we could not get to him on account of the wind and seas. A doughnut raft went by with at least five men on it, one of which I think was the captain. We rowed for two hours until our hands were blistered and still we could not pick up the men. The wind and seas were getting higher all the time and at last poor visibility blotted out everything. In the meantime we were very near the two raiders and before the mist got so bad I observed that both were motor ships of about 4,000 and 7,000 [tons] respectively. The smaller was the heaviest armed with guns in turrets or behind shields. She looked like a converted fruit boat which ran from the West Coast of the U.S.A. to Europe such as the Oregon and Washington Express streamlined with a clipper or aireform bow and cruiser stern. The other was a motor ship, larger, lighter armed and with a high stack like she might have been converted from steam. She had three masts and one set of Samson posts [kingposts] aft but with no booms. She also had an extreme clipper bow and cruiser stern and the upside down cross tree such as used on all Japanese built ships. She went alongside the other one which was aflame from stem to stern listing heavily to port and way down by the stern and apparently took off the crew, although the seas were running high. She went close alongside. After about ten minutes she backed away, turned around and left. She also appeared to be down by the bow but this may have been due to a boxlike structure built on the deckhouse on the fantail which made her seem high at the stern. The funnel or stack was set in the after part of the midship house like lots of motor ships but was high like a steamship built for natural draft. The ship was probably a mother ship for a float of armed fast raiders. We then heard a heavy explosion out of the mist which was probably the magazine or a time bomb left behind. I then put out the sea anchor and drifted until 12 noon next day looking for survivors, then set sail for the coast of South America.[6]

The following is the Lifeboat Log of thirty-one days kept by George Cronk.

ABANDON SHIP SIGNAL AT APPROXIMATELY 9.55 A.M. Sunday 27, 1942.

Log of No.1 Life Boat of SS STEPHEN HOPKINS

Course 313

Attacked by enemy raiders in South Atlantic, aprox. lat. 31, Long.16 at 9:38 a.m September 27th. Shelled by two armed merchant ships for about 20 minutes. All lifeboats destroyed except No. 1. All known survivors in this boat. Ship went down in flames at about 10.30. Two men killed and two wounded by shrapnel in life boat. Navy gun crewman Andrew Yanez and A.B. Seaman William Adrian killed. Buried them at sea. Eugene McDaniels, baker and 2nd cook, Athanasios Demetrades wiper, badly wounded by shell burst were given first aid by Chief Steward F. Stilson who was picked up from raft. 6 more men picked up from rafts and water. 2nd Engineer was picked up from water. 6 men were sighted on raft but could not get them due to high seas and poor visibility. Wiper Demetrades found to have broken arm. Arm was set and attended to by Chief Steward. Put out sea anchor and laid low till 12 noon next day looking for more survivors. One raider badly damaged and probably sunk by guns of Stephen Hopkins. Known killed by shell fire are gun crewmen Phil Smith and Andrew Yanez, A.B. Seaman William Adrian and Chas. Largergren, messman Herbert Lowe and wiper Pedro Valdez. Badly wounded and probably dead are Chief Mate Richard Moczkowski, Gunnery officer Kenneth Willett, carpenter Hugh Kuhl, Eng cadet Edwin O'Hara, deck cadet C. Chamberlain.

September 28th.

Found two abandoned rafts but no sign of men on them. Took stores and water beaker from two rafts and set sail for the coast of South America. Set course in a northwest direction steering by sun and compass and started food rationing. Making good time till sun down. Had to put out sea anchor and heave to on account of high seas.

September 29th

Took in sea anchor, rationed food and water and resumed a northwest course. No change in condition of wounded men. Sailed all night in a general westerly direction.

September 30th

Becalmed, very slight breeze enough for steerage way. Rationed food and water, put salt water drip on wounded men's arms and changed bandages. Steering due west by sun, compass deviation by course of sun 23 degrees. Good breeze at sundown. Changed course to northwest.

October 1st

Light breeze from northwest, steering southwest. Condition of men about the same. Rationed food and water. Cut water ration to 6 ounces per day per man, so as to give more to wounded men.

October 2nd

Strong winds from Southeast. Sailing due west. Have no idea of position of ocean currents or prevailing winds as there is no South Atlantic chart in boat. Condition of wounded men the same. Rationed food and water.

October 3rd

Making good time due west with a strong wind and following sea until about 2 a.m. Had to heave too and put out sea anchor till 6 a.m.. Set sail to the northwest wind S.S.W. Wiper Demetrades condition improved, others about the same. Rationed food and water, one water cask empty. Having trouble with whales, afraid of hitting one and capsizing. Raised water ration to 10 oz.

October 4th

Changed bandages on wounded men. Condition about the same. Strong easterly winds, making good time. Course due west by sun. Rationed food and water. Keeping sharp lookout for ships. Weather rather cool. Don't know the latitude.

October 5th

Becalmed from midnight to 6 a.m. Heavy rains, squalls, replenished water supply by catching rain in sail. Took sails repaired them. Strong wind sprang up 1 a.m. Hoisted sail making good time but sea pretty rough. McDaniels, 2nd cook condition getting worse. Think gangrene has set in. Wiper Demetrades improving. Messman Romero about the same. Men's spirits are high so far. Steering N.N.W. by compass. Changed course to due north 4 p.m. Replenished water supply to the extent of three gallons.

October 6th

Good southeast breeze all night, making good time. Demetrades still improves, Romero and McDaniels getting worse. Ration food and water. Trying to get farther north on account of cool nights. Men have very few clothes. Course N.W. Rain water caught has bad taste due to chemical in sail cloth.

October 7th

Very little breeze, making about 2 knots N.W. McDaniels becoming delirious, Demetrades better, Romero about the same. Ration food and water. Weather getting warmer, wind from S.S.E. McDaniels, 2nd cook died at 6:30 P.M. Stopped ship for 5 minutes and buried him at 10.30

October 8th

Good southwest wind, making good time from midnight until 8 a.m. Sailing west and northwest. Wiper Demetrades still improves. Messman Romero getting worse. Gun crewman Brock has infected shoulder from shrapnel splints. All of these shell burst wounds seem to fester and rot away. Shell must have been poisoned. Rationed food and water. Romero died at 2.30. Buried at sunset. Condition of Demetrades about the same. Arm was dressed by Chief Steward. Raised water ration to 14 oz due to extra rain water. Had good night's run, wind dies down in day time.

October 9th

Course northwest. Hope to sight something in a few days. Wiper Demetrades about the same. Got piece of shell out of Gun Crewman Brock's shoulder. Wound looks better. Rationed food and water. Not much wind sitrring [sic] N.N.W. Checked up on water and ship's stores. Romero had diamond ring, only possession, keeping it in brief case.

October 10th

Due to taking inventory, no water reduction contemplated in next ten days. Ample food for at least 25 days. Wiper Demetrades still holding on. Rationed food and water. Gun crewman's shoulder about the same. Messman Peter Enos has infection in right knee. Not much wind. Making very slow headway to N.N.W. Good breeze at sundown till midnight. Sailing due west.

October 11th

Good breeze until 9 a.m., ran into rain squall, caught 1 gallon water. Becalmed. Something sent up a green rocket right over our mast from a very short distance. Apparently from a submarine. We answered with 2 flares from Very pistol. All this at about 3.15 a.m. Rationed food and water. Wiper Demetrades still holding on, Gun crewman Brock and Messman Enos about the same.

October 12th

George Gelogotes, fireman, died this morning without apparent reason. Buried him at noon. Had $105.00 cash money in his possession and Seaman's papers. Will turn over to Consul first port of arrival. Wind from S.E. making good time north west. Rationed food and water. Wiper Demetrades still holding on. Gun crewman Brock and Messman Enos about the same.

October 13th
Very little breeze, hot. Rationed food and water. Wiper Demetrades still holding on. Brock and Enos about the same. Steering north west, little better breeze, at sundown.

October 14th
Fair wind, steering north west, days getting hot. No sight of land or ships or anything else. Everyone in fair spirits. Wiper Demetrades still holding on. Gun crewman Brock and Messman Enos about the same. Rationed food and water.

October 15th
Heavy rains, squalls, caught about 12 gal rain water, wind variable from S.E. Sailing N.W. Wiper Demetrades pretty low. Gun crewman Brock and Messman Enos about the same. Rationed food and water.

October 16th
Several squalls, not much wind. Wiper Demetrades died at 7 a.m. o'clock. Buried him at 9.a.m. Only possession Seaman's papers and bank book. Caught about 1 gal of rain water. Have about 40 gal of water altogether. No sign of land or ships. Still steering a northwest course. All water beakers about full. Rationed food and water. Still steering a northwest course. Seems as if we should have sighted land. Maybe currents are against us. Heavy squalls. Before midnight put out sea anchor, hove too.

October 17th
Took in sea anchor 6 a.m. Steering northwest. Fill all water casks and empty ration tins with water. Frequent squalls during day. Rationed food and water. Steering N.N.W.

October 18th
Heavy squalls all night, good wind in morning. Sailing due west.

Rationed food and water. Everybody about the same. Ordinary Seaman Piercy laid up with sore foot.

October 19th
High wind and seas, shipping lots of water, bailing all night, everybody wet from rain and spray. Most everyone has sores that won't heal. Violent squalls. Steering northwest. Hove to all night. High seas.

October 20th
Bright sun shiny day, good wind. Seas still rough. Steering a northwesterly course. Took inventory on food. Cut ration in half. All water casks full. Wind from southeast.

October 21st
Seas calm, plenty of sunshine, very little wind. Just steering way. Steering west northwest. Compass variation only 11 degrees by course of sun.

October 22nd
Good breeze all night, making good time due west. Condition of men about the same. Rationed out food and water.

October 23rd
Poor breeze, just steering way. Sun hot, everyone kind of weak. Cut ration in half 4 days ago. Now getting 1 oz of Pemmican, 1 oz of chocolate, ½ oz of malted milk tablets, 1 type C ration biscuit per man per day, water ration 20 oz per man per day due to rain water caught. No sight of land or ships. Everyone in fair spirits. Steering west, wind N.N.E.

October 24th
Been becalmed for 24 hours. Very hot, everyone very weak. Seen some kind of sediment floating in water. Saw a butterfly and two moths. All think we are near land. Very poor visibility. Repaired rudder and sail. Fair breeze at sunset. Steering west.

October 25th
Had fair breeze all night. Sea choppy, not making much time.

Seen a yellow moth. Makes us think we are near land. Steering northwest, very poor visibility.

October 26th
Very good breeze, water changing color. Very near land, so we believe.

October 27th
Hurrah, sighted land 4 a.m. Landed at small Brazilian village of Barra do Stabapoana [sic]. Police notified Consul at Rio de Janeiro. Trying to arrange transportation to Rio.[7]

U.S. Naval Armed Guard Survivors

Moses Nathanial Barker, Jr.,	Seaman 2nd
Ted Eugene Barnes	"
Virgil Orville Bullock	"
Paul Boyer Porter	"
Wallace Ellsworth Breck	"[8]

~~~

Al Ludlam contributed this story along with the menu from the Port Elizabeth Restaurant. It's always interesting to compare the food selection and prices to today's.

Port Elizabeth Tea

My first trip in the Armed Guard was aboard the SS *Horace Mann* in 1943. This was one of those speedy Liberty ships. The convoy was separated and we arrived in Cape Town, South Africa.

I don't remember how much time we had ashore, but one of the ports we hit was Port Elizabeth. I have a menu from the Astoria Restaurant and Tea Room. Main St. Port Elizabeth.

I don't remember what I ate, but I do remember the two waitresses that waited on us. They were twins and they took me and my buddy, a merchant seaman, back to their apartment for
~~~

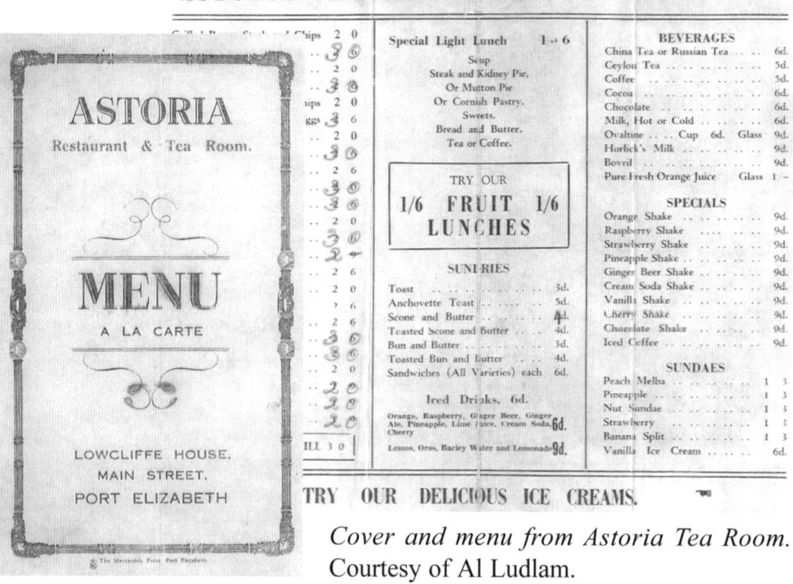

ASTORIA
Restaurant & Tea Room.

MENU
A LA CARTE

LOWCLIFFE HOUSE,
MAIN STREET,
PORT ELIZABETH

ASTORIA TEA ROOM AND SODA FOUNTAIN

Special Light Lunch 1 6
Soup
Steak and Kidney Pie,
Or Mutton Pie
Or Cornish Pastry.
Sweets.
Bread and Butter.
Tea or Coffee.

TRY OUR
1/6 FRUIT 1/6
LUNCHES

SUNDRIES

Toast	3d.
Anchovette Toast	5d.
Scone and Butter	4d.
Toasted Scone and Butter	4d.
Bun and Butter	3d.
Toasted Bun and Butter	4d.
Sandwiches (All Varieties) each	6d.

Iced Drinks. 6d.

Orange, Raspberry, Ginger Beer, Ginger Ale, Pineapple, Lime Juice, Cream Soda, Cherry 6d.

Lemos, Oros, Barley Water and Lemonade 9d.

BEVERAGES

China Tea or Russian Tea	6d.
Ceylon Tea	5d.
Coffee	5d.
Cocoa	6d.
Chocolate	6d.
Milk, Hot or Cold	6d.
Ovaltine .... Cup 6d. Glass	9d.
Horlick's Milk	9d.
Bovril	9d.
Pure Fresh Orange Juice Glass	1/-

SPECIALS

Orange Shake	9d.
Raspberry Shake	9d.
Strawberry Shake	9d.
Pineapple Shake	9d.
Ginger Beer Shake	9d.
Cream Soda Shake	9d.
Vanilla Shake	9d.
Cherry Shake	9d.
Chocolate Shake	9d.
Iced Coffee	9d.

SUNDAES

Peach Melba	1 3
Pineapple	1 3
Nut Sundae	1 3
Strawberry	1 3
Banana Split	1 3
Vanilla Ice Cream	6d.

TRY OUR DELICIOUS ICE CREAMS.

Cover and menu from Astoria Tea Room. Courtesy of Al Ludlam.

some homemade tea of a special variety. It turned out to be mostly White Horse Scotch. How could anyone forget such a wonderful after-lunch cordial?

Sailing further up the coast of Africa we landed in Portuguese East Africa, a neutral nation in WW II. Ships from all nations were in this port, including a German submarine that was trying to sink enemy ships, especially U.S. ships. Several ships tied up together and as you went ashore in your dungarees, you saluted their deck officer and their colors.

Very early every morning, the German sub would go out of the harbor and wait for us or some other enemy ship and try to sink it. This went on for about eleven days and finally two British corvettes showed up and we were told that they sank the sub. Meanwhile, the *Horace Mann* was the first ship out of the harbor and we were used as bait to draw out the sub.

It was during this exercise (that's what they called it) that one of the corvettes dropped a depth charge so close to us it almost lifted us out of the water. Anybody who was on the stern was bounced around. What an experience! What a gun crew we were at that moment trying to figure out which way was up. Boy would I have liked to have some of that Port Elizabeth Tea.

This is where I got my knee smashed, but they told me it was not serious and I believed the medic. I lived with it for fifty years and finally had to get a new knee at the V.A. Hospital in Northport, New York. This is what hurt Armed Guard Veterans as there were no records kept of these incidents.[9]

~~~

Here is another piece of Bob Somer's diary that he kept on his voyages.

Second Voyage on the SS *Patrick Henry*
Feb. 16, 1944 to Oct. 29, 1944

I made GM 3/c after passing exams at the Naval Headquarters in New York. Started loading at [sic] on January 28, 1944. This was the same day Mrs. Henry Wallace came aboard to see operations. She christened the ship. Captain presented her a plaque with a piece of shrapnel on it from Naples air raids.

Left New York Feb. 16, 1944 (very cold) as vice commodore. Cape Hatteras was very rough on way south. Passed east coast of Cuba Feb. 23. Entered Port of Spain, Trinidad, Feb. 29, 1944. Left March 1 down east coast of S. America to Brazil. Cut off from convoy March 15 and headed alone East S. East through South Atlantic alone and arrived Cape Town, S.A. Mar. 28, 1944. Discarded most of cargo. Supposed to leave April 1 but got ordered back to dock. Learned a ship was sunk just outside of harbor. (*This was the British ship* Dahomian)

Left April 5, 1944 around Cape of Good Hope and pulled into Dunbar, S.A. April 9, 1944. Unloaded rest of cargo and left Apr. 20, 1944 for Cape Town. Had a bad torpedo scare on Apr. 23. I was on watch on bow and saw white streak headed for bow port side. Went under overhang just missing and kept going toward coast. Watch on bridge saw it too. Into Cape Town Apr. 23, 1944 and left 24 to north.

Entered Takoradi, Gold Coast May 3, 1944. Started loading mahogany lumber and manganese ore. Got ashore a few times to native markets in jungle. (Very hot). Have R.A.F. picture of part
~~~

The Patrick Henry *on the launching ways.* Project Liberty Ship.

S.S. *Patrick Henry* – The First Liberty ship.

Making her first voyage in January 1942, the *Patrick Henry* gave valiant war service, including a voyage to Murmansk in a convoy carrying military supplies to North Russia and many transatlantic crossings. In March 1942 she was the first American ship — and thus the first Liberty ship — to transit the Suez Canal after America entered the war. The ship came through the war unscathed, but in July 1946 she struck a reef off the coast of Florida, in position Lat. 25º 08' N., Long. 80º 16' W. while on voyage from Sete to New Orleans.

Refloated, she limped home, but the incident ended her active career. Unrepaired, she was towed down the Mississippi and round to Mobile, to be laid up in the Reserve Fleet. After idleness lasting twelve years, some interest — tinged with a touch of irony — was generated when the ship (and thirty-four other Libertys) was bought by shipbreakers in a block deal. For the *Patrick Henry* was towed to Baltimore and, in October 1958, scrapped by the Patapsco Scrap Corporation — an associate company of her builders.[10]

of Armed Guard crew on deck cargo of mahogany timbers est. about (5,000 yds. board feet).

The SS Patrick Henry *then left for Freetown traveling to Dakar, Gibraltar, Augusta, Sicily, arriving in Naples July 7, 1944. There they laid at anchor for forty-two days (July 7 to August 18) during which their cargo of about five thousand tons of mahogany lumber and six hundred odd tons of Army equipment went untouched.*

Bob's diary continues:

Finally left August 18 to north of Piombino. On August 19 – unloaded mahogany lumber in a field. G.I.'s were building outhouses out of it and the Italians were using it for firewood…

… End of 8 months 13 days trip and about 24,000 miles and about fifteen months aboard SS *Patrick Henry* – one good ship![11]

~~~

This story is from Fred McLeod. As we have seen earlier, it's sometimes still a small world. Read on.

Calcutta with My Brother

I went aboard the SS *Harold D. Whitehead*, in Houston, Texas. She had just been christened in December 1944. I was on watch when the ship was being loaded with steel plates. After reading Calcutta printed on the plates, I knew that was going to be our destination.

We left Texas and sailed for Norfolk, Virginia where we picked up a convoy. We then sailed across the Atlantic, through the Mediterranean and Suez Canal. Sailing out we went through the Red Sea and Indian Ocean on our way to Colombo, Ceylon and finally Calcutta.

My brother Ross was in the Air Force serving in Calcutta. When we finally landed in Calcutta about four months later I went to the Red Cross to see if they could help me get in touch with him. I found out that he had been transferred to Burma. I thought that was the end of it.
~~~

The next day I was waiting to go on watch and in he walked. All the men in the crew stood my watches for me. My brother and I had about three days together and we spent a nice time seeing the sights and sounds of the city. We bought a lot of souvenirs. Our time together was the best thing that happened during the whole trip.[12]

~~~

John Neven tells of his world cruise aboard a tanker. He was assigned to the SS Front Royal *on November 21, 1944 along with twenty-seven enlisted personnel and one officer. The ship's cargo was high octane gasoline. His world cruise included San Pedro to Seattle and Tacoma to Honolulu, Eniwetok, Ulithi Atoll, Panama Canal, Curaçao, Netherlands West Indies, Texas, New York, Thames Haven –near London.*

World Cruise — SS *Front Royal*
November 21, 1944 to September 14, 1945

…Our destination was Port Said, Egypt the entrance to the Suez Canal. Ship traffic was heavy through the Suez Canal and at one point, midway through, we anchored for about one day. A number of the Navy Armed Guard crew, including myself, swam ashore onto Egyptian soil and were met by a Egyptian soldier sitting atop a camel. This prompted us to return to the ship. Finally the ship continued through the canal exiting near Suez City. Here she dropped anchor.

While the ship was anchored at Suez City, merchants in bumboats would come alongside to sell merchandise. This seemed harmless enough until one of the Armed Guard crew, who had the midnight watch, detected a spark, just above the water line, below the after deck. Close examination revealed that a bomb had been attached to the ship and that the wick had been ignited. The wick was severed from the bomb before any harm was done. After this experience merchants in bumboats were no longer allowed to come alongside. After investigation by United States Navy and British intelligence officers, the *Front Royal* continued
~~~

on its journey into the Red and Arabian Seas. She then proceeded into the Gulf of Oman and up through the Persian Gulf, finally docking at Abadan, Iran. This was early June 1945.

At Abadan, Iran the *Front Royal* once again took on a full load of aviation fuel. The heat at Abadan was intense at 130 degrees. This caused the paint on the deck to blister. The working day was from 4:00 AM until 10:00 AM. The crew did get to go ashore for a few hours with the warning to drink only bottled water or beer from Turkey.

After the ship was fully loaded, she was underway and steaming back through the Persian Gulf into the Indian Ocean. The ship was now headed for Ceylon (Sri Lanka). Before reaching Ceylon the *Front Royal* encountered a submarine, which was on the surface, approximately three miles off our starboard side. General Quarters was immediately sounded and all hands rushed to their gun stations. Being the signalman, I sent a coded blinker challenge that was initially answered incorrectly. I then sent a plain message advising the submarine commander that we would open fire if they did not answer correctly. This time the reply was correct and the submarine was identified to be British. After an exchange of communication the submarine skipper explained that they were out of food and that they needed to continue their assignment. Since we were about two days from Ceylon, the Merchant Marine skipper had me send a message that they should send a boat alongside and that we would transfer a supply of food. All this time the Armed Guard crew was ready in the event things were not as they seemed.

Before the ship reached Ceylon, the *Front Royal* received orders to proceed to Budge Budge, (*Baj Baj*) India, up the Ganges River. At Budge Budge the deck cargo of fifty-five gallon drums of oil was unloaded. Since we were within land travel distance from Calcutta, India liberty was extended to the Armed Guard crew who were not on duty.

Orders were to deliver the high-octane gasoline to Chittagong, India, which is now Bangladesh. Exiting the Ganges River, the *Front Royal* was on its way to the United States Air Force base at Chittagong. To arrive safely two obstacles had to be overcome. One was that the ship was running along the coast of Burma and the other was that the bay at Chittagong was only 30 feet deep and that the ship was drawing 32 feet. The latter caused the ship to anchor about one mile offshore. The gasoline had to be delivered through hoses that were strung out all the way to the *Front Royal.* This feat was achieved but we damaged two of the ship's screws. Again we could not replenish our food supply.

The ship was now in need of repair and was limping slowly toward Australia. It took about twenty days and the food supply consisted mainly of rice and flour. The food was barely edible since weevils and roaches got into the supply. Upon arrival at Sydney, Australia the ship went into dry-dock for repair of the ship's screws. The food supply was replenished and the crew had liberty in a great city.

Near the end of July 1945 the *Front Royal* departed Sydney with the destination Panama. On August 6, 1945, the atomic bomb was dropped on Hiroshima, Japan. I happened to be in the radio shack when the radio reports of the atomic bombing was received by Morse code. The crew thought I was nuts when I reported this fact to them… The Japanese formally surrendered on September 2, 1945. The ship continued to Panama and on September 14, 1945 most of the Armed Guard crew was transferred to a navy transport and returned to San Diego. Our world cruise was completed and a war ended.[13]

14

The Pacific

Harold E. Skinner, who contributed two earlier stories, was a Navy Armed Guard Radioman RM2C. His introduction to his experiences in the Pacific is a fitting introduction to this chapter. Harold writes:

The logistical problems confronting the U.S. Pacific fleet in World War II were of staggering proportions. When Admiral Nimitz's men began to plan the advance across thousands of miles of ocean towards their ultimate objective of Japan, they not only had to determine which Japanese-occupied islands might be conveniently by-passed and which must be captured, but they had to weigh the strategic value of the ones which might best serve as fleet supply bases. Providing such key rendezvous points as springboards for upcoming invasions was a new concept in naval history. While operations in hostile waters were tightening the ring on Japan, a stream of ships was expected to carry supplies to the forward bases being developed by the joint military efforts.

Hawaii was, by necessity, the initial starting point in this seaborne campaign, but by the spring of 1944 the atoll of Eniwetok in the Marshall Islands had become the principal fleet supply center in the northern Pacific. From that time onward fleet units would be able to operate indefinitely at unprecedented distances from their main landmass bases. Some warships would carry out missions for a year or more without returning to Pearl Harbor or the West Coast.

After the invasion of Guam, Tinian, and Saipan in the summer of 1944, American forces leapfrogged to the Caroline Islands and seized Ulithi in September. Bypassing Japanese-held bases, they managed to seize this palm-dotted atoll at little cost. It consisted of a series of flat coral islands strung out in a circular pattern, but what set it apart was its extensive 112-square-mile anchorage. This huge, peaceful lake was capable of holding nearly 1,000 ships of the U.S. fleet. Neither Guam, Eniwetok, nor Pearl Harbor could provide so much potential for the far-flung operations of the American navy. Within a short time the anchorage would become for U.S. sailors a home, a grocery store, a recreation center, and an arsenal. Soon concrete barges were turned into storehouses for innumerable items needed by a multitude of ships. Supply ships and tankers shuttled from the U.S. mainland to Ulithi bringing oil, food, tires and hardware to the warehouse barges that, in turn, unloaded their supplies onto carriers, battleships, cruisers, destroyers, and hundreds of amphibious vessels.

Ulithi atoll also became the funnel through which unescorted ships joined convoys that moved into the enlarging Philippines campaign and onto the invasion beaches of Iwo Jima and Okinawa in the final drive towards Japan.[1]

The U.S. Navy Armed Guard had to protect and fight against a ruthless enemy unlike anything they had previously encountered. Japanese submarine captains were cruel and sadistic. Immediately after Pearl Harbor this Naval Order to Submarines was issued by the Japanese:

> Do not stop with the sinking of enemy ships and cargoes; at the same time you will carry out the complete destruction of

the crews of the enemy's ships; if possible seize part of the crew and endeavor to secure information about the enemy.[2]

The U.S. Navy Armed Guard and U.S. Merchant Marine paid a very high price in the Pacific. These statistics are from the American Merchant Marine at War website:

Area of Action	Ships Sunk or Damaged	Merchant Marine Killed	Naval Armed Guard Killed	Army Personnel Killed
Alaska	48	62	17	7
U.S. West Coast	27	82	34	-
Pac. Ocean, Hong Kong Shanghai	148	211	29	143
Philippines	119	129	84	647 +
Okinawa	30	39	14	7
	372	523	178	804+[3]

~~~

This is a continuation of Milan LaMarche's story involving the SS Platano *appearing in Chapter 11.*

Duty in the South Pacific Aboard a Supply Ship

The men aboard *Platano* were of three special groups: the merchant marine crew, the Naval Armed Guard of gunners, radiomen and signalmen serving under a gunnery officer, and a supply contingent of an ensign, two chief petty officers and three rated men. The last group were known as storekeepers and supervised the cargo of provisions.

The mission of the ship became clear. The many Marine, Navy, and Army units scattered among the far-flung islands north of Australia were clearly placing a supply burden on strategic planners, and it would be *Platano*'s duty to carry out the shuttle-run between the resupply centers in New Zealand and military bases or fleet units in the New Hebrides, Friday Islands, Russell Islands, New Caledonia and similar areas near combat zones.
~~~

The service personnel at the many bases were pleased to receive fresh supplies, but they yearned for many things not really available on a supply ship. The Navy men were often approached by bored, homesick men asking if they had jewelry, liquor, toiletries, etc. for sale. Before long the idea of handling black-market supplies took root in the minds of some enterprising sailors. One day in Wellington shortly before the *Platano* sailed, a gunner approached me and asked, "Milan, do you want to make some money? I'll make a deal with you, fifty-fifty. Those men on Guadalcanal are crazy about wristwatches. I've got a deal offered by a jewelry man in town. Here's the setup."

The gunner went on to explain that the Marines and soldiers would pay good money for the high-quality watches which we sailors could buy in quantity for $10 apiece. The catch was that we would have to raise the cash for fifty watches. Fortunately we two benefited from a fat payday and eventually passed the word at Guadalcanal that we were selling excellent watches at $100 each. I could hardly believe it, but we sold all of them and shared a tidy profit. My gains were soon invested in war bonds.

By that time the profit motive was strong in me, but black-market profiteering was frowned on, and one had to be careful. Everyone knew that a tired soldier would pay a fortune for liquor, and some Armed Guard sailors managed to pocket easy gains from surreptitious dealings. I knew of such instances and decided to try my hand at it. It was fairly easy to smuggle a bottle of whiskey on board before leaving Wellington, but later my sense of humor undid my entrepreneurial instincts.

When the *Platano* made a port call at Green Beach in the Russell Islands a Marine came aboard on a trivial mission. Before leaving he asked if anyone had liquor to sell. I approached him quietly and let him know I had whiskey. At that moment, when all I had to do was quote a price and present a bottle, something of the practical joker took hold of me. I blurted out, "I've always wanted my own firepower; bring me a fieldpiece and the whiskey is yours."

The Marine looked startled, studied me for a moment and asked, "Are you serious?" I assured him I was and chuckled to myself at the joke. We shook hands and he left. I promptly brushed the incident from my thoughts and went about my business.

At three in the morning the gangway watch shook me awake, and as I rubbed the sleep from my eyes he said there was a Marine at the dock asking for LaMarche. I dashed to the rail and asked the obvious question: "I suppose you brought the fieldpiece?" The Marine replied, "As a matter of fact, I've just towed it to this pier with a Jeep. I'm thirsty. Where's the whiskey?"

Hardly believing this was happening to me, I went to my quarters, got the bottle and delivered it to the eager Marine. One thing was certain; I did not want to irritate a battle-hardened combat veteran. My gaze swept along the pier and sure enough, there was the fieldpiece. He had detached it from the Jeep, waved goodbye and was gone. I made my way unobtrusively to my quarters, wondering how in the world I would explain my purpose in acquiring a small cannon from the Marines. More to the point; how was I to get rid of it without having to answer embarrassing questions?

The questions did surface as to what was a fieldpiece was doing at the pier near the SS *Platano*. I said nothing to anybody about it, dreading that someone might have associated my name with the episode and would report it to the gunnery officer. In due time, it was with a profound sense of relief that I said a mental farewell to the gun still standing at the dock as our ship left the harbor. That sense of relief was worth the bottle of whiskey, and I often wondered what the Armed Guard gunners would have done with a wheeled cannon aboard ship!

The supply personnel aboard *Platano* normally had little association with other men since their duties seldom overlapped. In fact, the ensign was keenly disliked by the Armed Guard. His demeanor was aloof and self-centered, and his appearance was untidy and slipshod.

On one occasion the supply ship was waiting at anchor to enter a port, not certain of the first destination to off-load provisions. I was at the bridge relieving the signalman in visual communications. From across the water came a visual blinker-light signal notifying the ship that the Fleet Admiral in person would soon visit the ship to consider an order of supplies. Looking down from the bridge, I had an excellent view of the scene. The ensign, as the principal storekeeper-in-charge, was notified and rushed to the gangway. Wearing khaki shorts, an officer's cap and tennis shoes, he saluted smartly and greeted the admiral. The admiral paused and asked, "Who in heaven's name are you?"

"I am in charge of the ship's supplies," answered the ensign. The admiral's harsh gaze swept over the storekeeper and he said, "Get me someone responsible to handle this matter. I refuse to talk to you."

On the bridge I quickly took the initiative to call Lt. Wilson, our gunnery officer. He soon appeared at the gangway in regulation uniform, saluted properly and introduced himself. The admiral's response was, "Now you look like a Navy man who knows what he's doing." Wilson went into a conference with the admiral and reached an agreement on the disposition of the supplies.

Because of this event and other confrontations Lt. Wilson and the ensign (or "Insect", as we called him) were not on friendly terms. Shortly afterwards the signalman, Baker, and I were involved in an escapade that sorely tested the two officers' relations. For some reason Baker had just stolen a heavy carton of butter from the cargo hold below decks. I somehow happened to meet him on deck as he was rushing by, heading towards the bow of the ship. Gripping the carton and looking over his shoulder, Baker said, "Milan, protect my back side, will you?" Not understanding the situation, I followed him on the run. Little did I realize that the ensign had been following Baker from the hold and was in hot pursuit. Suddenly the carton of butter slipped from Baker's hands and hit the deck. Close on his heels, I tripped on the carton and fell flat. The ensign dashed up, saw Baker ahead and confronted me on the deck. He let out a string of oaths and instantly charged me and Baker with absconding with Navy property, threatening us with immediate court-martial.

Without waiting, I went directly to Lt. Wilson and explained what had happened. The gunnery officer listened closely and then said, "Don't worry about it. I'll see what I can do, but I don't think you will get a bad report out of this."

The ensign soon approached Lt. Wilson, breathing threats of court-martial against the two Armed Guard sailors who had been caught red-handed pilfering Navy supplies. The gunnery officer firmly held his ground and said, "You have no authority over my men. Leave it to me to discipline them. They will be punished."

When Baker and I were called together, the lieutenant gave us a sharp reprimand and then pronounced punishment; bread and water for two days in the small forward hold under the gun tub. The gunners were assigned to bring the bread and water to Baker and me. However, the gunnery officer in no way supervised the distribution of the food. The result was that the punishment was turned into a ludicrous comedy. Along with the "prison" food came milk, ice cream, chicken from the crew's mess, cookies, fruitcake, and extra quantities of snacks. In fact, the other sailors jokingly declared that the detainees were better fed than they were. Lt. Wilson only smiled and turned away when he heard the remarks.

In the end the ensign came to the lieutenant, asking to see the report that was to be submitted to create a black mark on the permanent records of us two sailors. The gunnery officer simply told him that he, Lt. Wilson, was taking care of the report and that it was strictly confidential. In truth, no report was ever filed about the incident. Case closed!

Lt. Wilson continued to endear himself to his men constantly looking after their welfare. After riding at anchor in Ulithi atoll for several days, the Navy crew were becoming restless, so the lieutenant announced, "I have business ashore, but I promise to send this ship enough beer for each of you to have a case." He was as good as his word, and a shipment of beer was soon brought aboard. The sad truth, though, was that it had never known refrigeration, and the sailors would not wait for it to be chilled. They drank the hot beer to their hearts' content and all were sick the next day. The merchant marine captain was not happy about the scene. Meanwhile the sailing orders came and the skipper gave the order to pull up the anchor. The embarrassed Lt. Wilson, still ashore, discovered his ship was gone and was compelled to arrange a flight by air to the ship's next port of call.

On October 13, 1944 the SS *Platano* sailed from the New Hebrides and arrived in San Francisco October 29. My first cruise to the South Pacific came to an end.[4]

~~~

Bob Norling contributed several more anecdotes concerning his experiences.

Counting the Days

That's what we did, count the days: fifty-four from New York to Hollandia in New Guinea, fifty-one unloading there and reloading for MacArthur's return to the Philippines; and seventy-five days at Leyte.

For the Armed Guard crew aboard the Liberty ship *Benjamin Ide Wheeler*, the first leg from New York to Milne Bay in the summer of 1944 was an easy cruise. But frustration had set in, considering that our cargo included 45,000 cases of beer plus other goodies for the Navy PX at Hollandia. (*See "A Thirst for Adventure," in this chapter*). We did get our share and the Hollandia brass extracted some revenge, but nothing very serious.

The shuttling between anchorage and dockside finally ended and we loaded for Leyte with the men and equipment of the 5201st Army Engineer Construction Brigade.

Our stay at Leyte started with a bang on October 24, D+4. Gone were the quiet days. The hook wasn't even down when enemy air attacks began. While we were in San Pedro Bay and at Tacloban from October 24, 1944 to January 7, 1945, we went to battle stations more than 300 times, 118 in first week. We were younger then. We could take it. How we did it I don't remember.

Our worst day was October 27. We cheered that morning when thirty Army P-38 fighter planes landed at Tacloban to beef up our air cover. Seven hours later, a Japanese Betty bomber veered away from its run at the airstrip, burst through some low-hanging clouds and crash-bombed the *Wheeler* at the waterline on the starboard side of No. 5 hold. In the lower hold were hundreds of
~~~

barrels of gasoline. That was one helluva fire, triggered by two bombs the plane was carrying.

The *Wheeler*'s stern hit bottom at 38 feet with her bow at a sharp up angle. We were lucky. Only two dead: one Navy gunner blown overboard and drowned and one deckhand in a fall from the main deck to the bottom of No. 4 hold. Later, two Army stevedores died in a fire in the same hold.

Navy salvage crews put on a temporary patch and for fifty-nine days we just sat there or helped unload the *Augustus Thomas*, another Liberty ship kamikaze victim. Our Christmas present was a final move to the inner harbor at Tacloban, where the Navy wrote off the *Wheeler* as a total loss and turned her into a floating warehouse. When we left Leyte January 7, 1945, the *Wheeler* gun crew had earned credit for five enemy planes shot down plus a dozen assists.

Back to Hollandia on the troop transport *Charles Lummis*; no survivor's leave. Sat around there for twenty-five days, assigned February 7 to the freighter *Admiral Halstead* and sailed two days later for — you guessed it — Leyte. February 18, we were right back at it in the Philippines.

Then more island hopping in the Southwest Pacific and back in the U.S. 106 days later. Lastly, another 153 days to discharge December 6, 1945.[5]

This story is a continuation of Bob's experiences in Tacloban.

Coincidences

Life can be a series of coincidences, in wartime and then years later. Something war-related will sneak up on you when you least expect it. Here's a couple of examples:

1. Good neighbors mind their own business. That was the case with Eric next door. Our conversations usually concerned just the weather, the lawn and during cribbage games, some challenging remarks.

We never told war stories, until one day some years after we became neighbors in Concord, New Hampshire. Somehow, the conversation got onto the invasion of Leyte in the Philippines fifty years earlier in October 1944. Eric told me he was there in

Lt. Eric Andrews at his 40-millimeter emplacement on the beach at Tacloban, Leyte, in October 1944. This was the gun that fired the three-shot warning to Armed Guard crews aboard ships there of imminent enemy air attacks. Courtesy of Mrs. Andrews.

an artillery outfit that came up from New Guinea. I told Eric I also had come up from New Guinea, on the Liberty ship *Benjamin Ide Wheeler*.

I also mentioned to Eric that our warning for incoming enemy air attacks was when we heard three shots from a 40-millimeter on the beach near the Tacloban air strip. We heard that ka-boom, ka-boom, ka-boom signal more than 100 times in our first week there, October 24-31, including one late in the day October 27 when we got clobbered off Red Beach by a suicide Betty bomber.

And then came the coincidence: "That was my 40 millimeter," said Eric, my neighbor.

2. It's late afternoon on a warm autumn day in 1955. The front door is open to catch what's left of that day's breeze. The house in Portsmouth, New Hampshire, is quiet. And then it happens.

A nasal-twang voice comes into the house through that front doorway. What you hear is the shout, "Egg man. Egg man." The voice is familiar, but not until you go to the door is the connection made.

Standing there holding a couple of cartons of eggs was Dave Noyes. We went through boot camp together at Newport, Rhode Island, to signal school at Butler University in Indianapolis, to a special convoy-procedure signal school at Noroton Heights, Connecticut, and then to the Armed Guard Center in Brooklyn.

There, in January 1943, we went our separate ways, Dave aboard the new Liberty ship *John Fitch*, me on the old tanker *Gold Heels*. Our paths never crossed during the war and for years afterward — until I heard "egg man" and became one of his regular customers.[6]

~~~

John Neven continues his experiences aboard another Liberty Ship.

S.S. *Wallace R. Farrington*
August 2, 1944 – October 26, 1944

On August 2, 1944 I was ordered to the *Wallace R. Farrington*, a Liberty ship, at Port Hueneme, California. She had a complement of twenty-seven enlisted men and one gunnery officer. I was replacing a signalman who was transferred ashore. The other twenty-six men had been aboard the ship on a previous cruise.

The *Farrington* left Port Hueneme, California almost immediately after I went aboard and headed to Pearl Harbor, Hawaii and to its final destination of Guam. The Marines were still fighting the Japanese when we arrived at a port in Guam. Pontoon docks were laid out so the ship's cargo could be unloaded.

The Navy coxswain and I were given the assignment to deliver mail to the nearest Marine base. This proved to be most exciting. We needed to hitch a ride to and from the Marine base since it was some distance away. This is where I saw my first Japanese prisoners. On the return trip our Marine driver let us off explaining that our ship was in the harbor just over the hill. The driver drove away leaving the two of us. The ship turned out to be a damaged Japanese freighter. We started to walk and ended up in a small battle-scarred village. A few native Guamanians, who met us, welcomed us like heroes. They then roasted a pig in our honor. They also informed us that we were not safe since Japanese troops were in the area and that we should remain out of sight until they could escort us back to Marine lines. When we arrived at the Marine outpost, Marine officers interrogated us about Japanese sightings. We didn't see a thing and did not realize that we were
~~~

in danger. Meanwhile, back at the *Farrington*, the crew was exposed to rifle fire from Japanese soldiers located in the hills.[7]

~~~

Julius W. Bellin forwarded this incredible story. It tells of the ruthlessness displayed by a Japanese submarine (I-12 –*Kudo*). *In a letter to this author, Julius wrote the following. "This is the first time the story was ever told by me to my family and friends because the words would not come out. I felt like there was never the right time to tell a story of this magnitude. I feel good to get this out. Thank you for the opportunity to bare my soul."*[8]

The names Christensen, Boling and Bunch have stayed in my memory for all my years.

At the age of twenty-three I began to see a lot of my friends enlist in various branches of the service. I heard that there was a place in St. Louis, Missouri that would explain the various branches of the service, where I could make the right choice in a career in the military. After thinking about it long and hard I made the choice to join the Naval Reserve. I went home and told my family that I was joining the Naval Reserve. I hated to say farewell to my mother and father, relatives and friends but this was something that I really wanted to do in serving my country.

So on October 7, 1941 I proudly took the oath and was inducted into the Naval Reserve. After a few days in St. Louis, I joined a group of recruits boarding a train for the Great Lakes Naval Base. There I received a medical exam, was issued gear, got my military crew cut (we all heard about that).

My paycheck was twenty-one dollars a month. Out of my check came insurance — six dollars a month. All day long we drilled, took target practice, and did gas mask practice. This kept us busy until sack time, which was around 10-11 PM. Chow time was a great time for me. The food was really good after all the drilling we had to do. I was always hungry. Twice a week for breakfast we had pork n' beans. That was it! There were never any leftovers. The sign in the mess hall read – "TAKE ALL YOU
~~~

WANT. EAT ALL YOU TAKE." I finished my boot camp training November 30, 1941.

I received a seven-day leave and went home to see my family and friends. As I was preparing to return to Great Lakes on December 7, 1941, my neighbor came running over to tell us that Pearl Harbor had been bombed.

The next three days all we did was drill. All passes were cancelled. On December 15, 1941 we boarded a train for San Diego, California Destroyer Base. We were there only one day when we were awakened the next morning at 3 AM only to have thirty minutes to get ready and then we were shipping out on the destroyer U.S.S. *Crosby*, a four stacker. I was assigned the aft .30 caliber machine gun. We picked up a convoy to Seattle, Washington and then headed back home to San Diego. On the way back somewhere about 300 hundred miles off the coast of San Diego the destroyer got a distress call that a ship was torpedoed. The U.S.S. *Crosby* was the closest destroyer so we headed full speed ahead to the area. Before we got there they had sent planes to that area and sank a Jap sub. When we got there we finished the sub off by dropping depth charges and bringing up a lot of oil and we knew the sub was finished off. We continued on to San Diego. On January 13, 1942 I went on board the U.S. destroyer *Kilty* (four stacker) for aircraft target practice. The next day I went aboard the U.S. *Cane* (also a four stacker) for surface target practice. The gun was a 3-inch 23 tripod gun. When the gun was shot it made a crackin' sound that was very hard on the ears.

On January 15, 1942, I was transferred to Treasure Island, which was in San Francisco Bay. On January 23, 1942 I reported for duty on the S.S. *Mahi Mahi*. We went in convoy to the Hawaiian Islands and back to San Francisco where we loaded up and sailed for Australia without a convoy. Thirty days later we arrived in Auckland, New Zealand, took on fresh water and headed for Brisbane, Australia. We unloaded some cargo and then it was on to Chile where we picked up a full load of nitrate which is used for explosives or fertilizer. We unloaded part of this in Hawaii and then it was back to San Francisco with the remainder of this cargo. This trip took six months.

I took a test for gunner's mate third class and passed. I then got a fourteen-day pass to go home and when I returned to Treasure Island I was transferred to Seattle, Washington for duty on the S.S. *Alencon* on January 1, 1943.

During 1943, Julius made many Alaskan voyages to Anchorage, Cold Bay, Dutch Harbor, Hanes, Ketchan, Skagway and to Prince Ruppert, Canada, carrying such supplies as canned salmon and paper. In September he transferred from Seattle back to Treasure Island. Then it was off to New Guinea, finally arriving back in San Francisco where he took the test for 2nd class gunners mate and passed. The time was now October 20, 1944 when Julius was transferred to the S.S. John A. Johnson.

They say "a sailor has a girl in every port." I won't dispute that. I didn't want to be an oddball so I did have a "girl in every port." One day I went to visit a lady I knew and on the way back I had to walk about five blocks before I got the streetcar. About a block away a lady came out of a building and held my arm and begged me to come back and have my fortune told. I told her no! I walked another block and she kept pleading with me. She actually cried and begged me to come back. Finally, I asked her how much she charged for her fortune telling. She said "Five dollars and no more." I thought maybe she might need money so I gave her five dollars and wanted to leave, but she insisted that I come back with her because she had lots to tell me. So I did.

The first thing she told me was that I was going to sea and that it would be the shortest trip I would ever make. That something was going to happen at sea but I would be all right, and, that some of my friends wouldn't return. I didn't believe in fortune tellers so I didn't believe her. What amazed me was how this lady pleaded with me and cried to have my fortune told. (I still don't believe in fortune tellers). I returned to my ship and went to sea.

As a gunner's mate second class my duties were to be in charge of the gun crew and to see that all guns were cleaned and in working condition at all times, and to inspect the living quarters every week. I made the report to our lieutenant in charge on the S.S. *John A. Johnson*, Wynn Del Yates.

On October 29, 1944 we were about halfway from San Francisco going to the Hawaiian Islands. The sea was a little rough that day. A wave hit the starboard side of the ship tearing the life raft off the side of the ship.

On the evening of October 30, 1944 sometime after 9:30 PM a Japanese submarine fired two torpedoes at us. One of the torpedoes hit amidships. The other missed the aft part of the ship by fifty feet. When the torpedo hit, I was in my room and it knocked me down. When I got up I ran topside to the guns. Our phones went dead at that moment. The gun crew on watch said that a torpedo had hit the ship. The ship started to twist apart. The aft part of the ship started twisting toward the port side. I could hear someone from amidships say that we were abandoning ship. I went to the life raft at the port side and tripped the catch which released the life raft. But it was hung up because of the listing of the ship. I took my knife and cut the rope that held the life raft. It then fell to the water. I went back to our quarters to see if anyone still remained, especially Brownlee because he was very seasick. But he was already gone. I saw someone sitting on the rail so I pushed him off. Then I didn't see anyone left on the ship so I jumped overboard. When the ship was breaking in two, the twisting sound made a terrible noise. The forward part the ship was coming together with the aft part of the ship. We were almost crushed between the two parts of the ship as they missed us by about ten feet. We were all covered with fuel oil. I was afraid that the oil would catch fire. I was deathly afraid of fire.

About twenty of the seamen made it to the floating raft. I heard Bunch and Boling calling, "Guns, help me!" The gunner's mate had the nickname of "guns." I swam out to where they were which was about fifty feet away. I then told them, "Hold on to one of my legs and paddle with the other hand. And for the other mates to do the same." We made it back to the life raft that I was on.

Shortly afterwards, the Jap sub fired and hit the 3-inch 50. The gun was ripped right off the ship. Then they fired on the aft part of the ship again and after ten minutes it sank. We were only about 500 ft. away when the aft part of the ship went under the water. The Jap sub fired again on the forward part of the ship which then caught fire. The part of the ship started to drift away which was a good thing because that part of the ship carried a large amount of dynamite in the forward cargo holds. We then spotted a Jap sub heading right toward us. We then jumped off the life raft and the Jap sub rammed our life raft and damaged one corner. The life raft stayed afloat as the sub passed us and continued to fire its machine guns at us hitting some of the mates. I don't know how many were hit on our raft, but I do know some were killed.

During my training at Great Lakes Illinois Naval Base I was trained that if ever fired upon in the water, stay under the water for as long as possible because it could save your life. I tried to stay underwater for as long as possible. When I came up to the surface I realized that I was next to the life raft. I climbed aboard the life raft and I then tried to grab onto Christensen but my hands were very slippery from the oil from the ship. The sub propeller pulled him under. (You know what happens with the suction of the propeller). The Jap sub stayed at a distance for a while. I could hear Bunch and Boling calling "Guns, help, Guns, help," which made me believe it was them again. I could not figure out which way the calls were coming from. If I knew I would have taken the chance to save them.

The names Christensen, Boling and Bunch have stayed in my memories for all my years. They will continue to stay in my memories. I have often wondered how Boling and Bunch died. Did they drown or were they captured by the Japs?

The forward part of the ship that was still burning at a far distance suddenly blew up with a "whump" sound. As the flames shot up in the air the forward part of the ship sank.

About fifteen minutes later a plane flew over. I guess it was on its way to the Hawaiian Islands. They somehow spotted the flames from the explosion. We sent up flashlight signals to the plane and they responded by dropping a flare. The plane sent out a distress signal for us because we couldn't send a message ourselves because the transmitter was swamped with water and was useless. I believe if it wasn't for the ship blowing up and the explosion, the plane would never have spotted us in the water.

The crew of the John A. Johnson *in the process of being rescued by the* Argus. *Note the line extending from the lifeboat to the rescue ship (out of picture on left).* National Archives.

The Jap sub would have stayed in the area and shot us all by daybreak if it hadn't been for the plane. The life rafts and boats stayed close together in the area and we knew that help was on the way.

Early the next morning planes flew over and dropped medical supplies and a package. In the package was a large balloon filled with helium which was to be cabled to the boat so the rescue vessel could spot us. Every hour or so planes would fly over us. During the day a case of tomato juice floated by our raft which we drank.

That afternoon of October 31, 1944 somewhere between 3 – 4 PM the sub-chaser *Argus* picked us up. On board we took showers, were given clean clothes and chow. We then headed toward Treasure Island to give our accounts of the torpedoing to the Navy Department.

Mrs. Johnson, the wife of the Governor of Minnesota christened the S.S. *John A. Johnson* at the Oregon Shipbuilding Company. The governor's wife wrote me a letter a letter wanting to know all about torpedoing. I also received a letter from Mrs. Christensen wanting to know how her husband died, but at the time I didn't have the heart to tell her the circumstances. All I told her was that he died.

The captain sounded abandon ship on the ship's whistle. All hands left without injury, getting away in No. 2 and No. 4 boats. Lifeboat No. 1 was damaged in the explosion and No. 3 boat swamped when it hit the water. Those in the water climbed aboard No. 2 and No. 4 boats. A raft got away safely. The sub (I-12 - *Kudo*) *surfaced and rammed No. 2 boat with twenty-eight survivors in it, firing pistols and machine guns at the men swimming in the water. After the sub left, the men reboarded the boat but when the sub returned, those who were able jumped overboard again. No guns were fired this time, but the sub tried to catch the men in its screws. Five from this group were killed by gunfire. The sub then headed for the raft which held seventeen men. When about 150' away, machine gunfire was directed at the occupants of the raft. The men jumped into the water and kept the raft between them and the sub until it passed. The sub circled and again attempted to ram the raft, but a wave threw the raft clear. When the sub returned a third time, it sank the raft and directed its machine guns at the men in the water. Five more men were killed by this strafing.*

At 1012 GCT, a Pan American Airways plane sighted the boats. At 2135 GCT October 30, the survivors were picked up by USS Argus *(PY-14) and landed at San Francisco on November 3, 1944.*

The I-12 *(Kudo) was not heard from again after January 5, 1945. She was a probable marine casualty in Pacific waters.*

Four merchant crew, five Navy Gunners and the Army Security Officer were lost when the Japanese submarine rammed the lifeboats and rafts and then machine gunned survivors in the water."[9]

Julius Bellin continues:

The Armed Guard personnel who lost their lives were:
Frank E. Boling, S1/c – Drowned or picked up by Jap sub.
William H. Bunch, S1/c – Drowned or picked up by Jap sub.

William E. Burman, S1/c – Presumed shot by Japs.
Donald R. Christensen, S1/c – Killed as a result of entanglement with propeller of Jap sub.
Cloyd L/ Thurman, S1/c – Presumed drowned.[10]

I-12 *on 20-31 December 1944 reported that it sank a transport and a tanker in mid-Pacific and on 15 January 1945: Cdr. Kudo sends a message that he has been spotted by the enemy N. of the Marshals. This is the last signal received from* I-12**.** *31 January 1945: Presumed lost with all 114 hands in the mid-Pacific. The cause of the* I-12*'s loss remains unknown. Some sources credit the USCG cutter* Rockford *(PF-48) and the minelayer USS* Ardent *(AM-340) with sinking* I-12 *in the Central pacific on 13 November 1944, but Cdr Kudo's last message belies that claim."*[11]

~~~

J.W. (Bill) Janes continues his World War II experiences.

Pacific Experiences

Leaving the *Ezra Meeker* in November 1943, we reported in at the Brooklyn Armed Guard Center. Soon we were on a two-week leave with delayed orders to report in at Treasure Island. From there I was assigned to a temporary station on Market Street in San Francisco as a mess cook. This was great while it lasted; first at every meal and liberty every evening. I could walk out the front door and within walking distance were many movie theaters to go to. Often, I would take a one-hour bus ride to Palo Alto to see several cousins that lived in the area.

On 8 Apr 1944, I was assigned to Landing Craft School at Oceanside, California with living quarters at Port Hueneme and later at Coronado Island. Two of the schools were at Ventura and Oxnard. One afternoon at Coronado Island I could see the USS *Villa Gulf* (carrier) as it pulled into port. Knowing Johnny (my brother) was aboard; I got liberty, went aboard, and located him. We went over on the beach, had a big dinner, took some pictures, and went to a movie. That is the last time we ever saw each other.
~~~

(*See end of this story)* Also, while at Coronado, another fellow and I were strolling around the grounds and we had a ringside view of a Navy pilot training that had run out of gas and had to make a belly landing on the grounds next to our barracks. The Pilot got out and walked away.

While at Port Hueneme, the Army and Navy held joint landing-craft training exercises. A large transport anchored offshore and unloaded troops and cargo onto landing craft and Army ducks. At noon, the main cook at our base had made up five gallon containers of salads and drinks for our E8-305 unit of fifty some men. They brought them to the beach where we were and I was assigned the job of making tuna salad sandwiches for our unit. The cook told me to give them to no one else. Out of the clear blue sky, as I was about to hand one to our crew, some high-ranking Army officer stepped up behind me and asked if he could have one of these sandwiches, and, he got one. A few moments later, the head cook came by and asked me if I knew the Army officer that I gave the sandwich to. As I had no idea who he might be, the cook said he was the son of F.D. Roosevelt. That was the largest group of high-ranking officers I had ever seen in one place. A few days later we moved to a shipping base near San Francisco.

In August 1944 I had twelve days leave. Returning from leave our unit was loaded aboard the S.S. *Zoella Lykes* in September 1944 and we left for Pearl Harbor. Our unit was unloaded and taken to the Navy base for several days. While on base, a USO show headed by Hilo Hattie put on one of the best shows I have ever seen. As Hilo Hattie was ready to sing the last song, she had everyone in the crowd turn their colored flashlights and direct them toward the stage while the stage lights were being turned down. Until I sat through that show I had no idea of the meaning of homesickness. While at Pearl Harbor, we received one batch of mail. One letter told about my mother having a stroke. We had no more mail until the first of February 1945.

Leaving Pearl Harbor in a convoy, we headed southwest, crossing the International Dateline on 17 Oct. 1944, and stopped at Kwajalein in the Marshall Islands. This where we were for Christmas 1944. It was the last of January 1945 when our unit unloaded at Leyte Island. Across the bay from our base, you could see the village of Tacloban. The one thing so memorable about the islands was the monsoon season. During that time it rained so hard as though it was coming out of a bucket.

Our first living quarters were five guys to an army tent. The kitchen and mess hall were the first permanent buildings built. Next on the list were four large and three small Quonset buildings for workshops and offices. The last buildings to be built were the two-story open-sided sleeping barracks. Each of the bunk beds had a mosquito net on them. One night, I had just fallen asleep, when I felt something move against my arm. My first thought was a snake, so I swung my arm hard enough to get whatever it was out from under the net. In doing so it stung me on the wrist. By then, I could see it was about the size of a large mouse. When I got my flashlight on, my wrist was swelling and burning. I got my shoes on and took off for sick bay. They said it was a centipede and painted my arm was some bright colored liquid.

Most landing craft boats were equipped with Gray Marine diesel motors, and whenever a ship came in with a boat needing repair, our unit had the equipment to take the motor to the shop and completely rebuild it. We even had a boat-sized dry-dock. After the buildings were completed and we got organized, it was just like public work, muster for work each morning at eight o'clock, one hour off for dinner, workday ended at four o'clock. If it was not raining, there would be a movie on the hillside in our base.

Some of the guys would spend the weekend in the shop making different handicrafts. One of the carpenters made me a footlocker with my name engraved on it in fancy English printing. As I was in charge of the sail loft, I made a heavy canvas sack that it would fit in and shipped it home.

When Christmas 1945 arrived, some of the guys heard about American liquor being bootlegged a few miles up the river from where we were, so a couple of guys went and got some Christmas drinks. As I recall, it was $20.00 a fifth. That was the last bottle of hard liquor I ever bought.

On 27 February 1946 our unit returned to the States. The first night we had liberty and several of us went to a big restaurant just off Market St. in San Francisco. A few days later we were on a thirty day leave. I got home in time to help sow the oats and drive the new tractor.

Concerning Bill's brother:

Dad had just started shucking corn when I arrived home, so I had a job waiting. On 8 October 1946 I was in the field when Dad came by with a telegram as follows:

> Have body of man five foot eleven inches 165 pounds brown eyes and hair identified by papers in pocket as Johnny Calvin Janes your son wire instructions. B.D. Bungarz, Deputy Chief Coroner.

My brother had been killed by a drinking hit-and-run driver just as he stepped off a streetcar in Oakland, California. He had just started his Navy terminal leave and had started working at the Caterpillar factory. The Navy sent an escort, Chief Petty Officer Fred McAdams of Little Rock, Arkansas when Johnny was returned for burial.[12]

~~~

This story from Don Kloenne is a continuation of his story that appeared in Chapter 2.

Some of the Armed Guard crew on the John P. Altgeld. Courtesy of U.S. Navy Armed Guard WWII Veterans.
~~~

Pacific Travels

Although not mentioned in the story, the John P. Altgeld *once carried a mascot, Spinny, shown in full uniform.* Courtesy of U.S. Navy Armed Guard WWII Veterans.

The *Altgeld* was dedicated to the civilian trade, filling up at Long Beach or San Pedro and making deliveries to oil terminals serving San Francisco, Portland, Seattle and Honolulu. It's a good thing the *Altgeld* never ventured farther west than Hawaii, for it was practically unarmed. Its only weapons of any consequence were an obsolete 4-inch gun at the stern, while so-called antiaircraft defense consisted of a .50 caliber machine gun mounted in each of the bridge wings. Running mostly coastwise had its advantages and disadvantages. The big advantage was that with short duration port-to-port-trips there was always plenty of fresh food. The principal disadvantage was that it never took more than twenty-four hours to pump out, rather limiting shore liberty opportunities. As a radioman, I had one special advantage over the gunners while standing watch: at scheduled times I had to copy the scheduled Morse code BAMS traffic list transmissions to see if there was anything pertaining either generally or specifically to us and if there wasn't, go back to my splitting earphones, listening with one ear to various coastal radio broadcast stations while with the other ear I monitored 500 Kilocycles, the Emergency/Distress frequency. Once in a while, both civilian operators and I would get annoyed when instead of first giving a traffic list, a sadistic transmitting operator would simply launch into messages, so that you had to listen to each and every one to make sure there was nothing for you.

After leaving the *Altgeld*, I reported for the first time to my official home base, the Armed Guard Center (Pacific) located on the former 1939 Treasure Island World's Fair site in the shadow of the San Francisco-Oakland Bay Bridge. Here I saw my first and only POW's: German prisoners captured in North Africa on permanent KP duty so that U.S. sailors didn't have to do it. The Germans didn't mind. While other members of the Wehrmacht, captured in Stalingrad, were starving to death in Russian prison camps, they were "living high on the hog" by comparison. Since my arrival was sudden and unscheduled, it was several weeks before a new assignment was found for me and I used that time to become acquainted with San Francisco, finding out for myself how it came by its reputation as one of America's favorite cities. Finally, a new radioman slot opened up, and I was soon on my way to Australia aboard the MV *Cape San Antonio.*

The *Cape San Antonio* was a Maritime commission C1 type and carried a decent armament: a 5-inch on the stern, a 3-inch at the bow and eight single 20mm antiaircraft guns. It was also faster by several knots than a Liberty, being capable of fifteen knots with no strain. In the Pacific we were almost always independently routed and the radio shack was given an updated position at each change of watch, so that I always knew where we were and how fast we were traveling. A second advantage was that with no convoy commodore looking us over, the "uniform of the day" was anything that covered the genitals. One exception: at the mess tables, a shirt was a "must." As indicated by the "MV,"

Part of the gun crew on the Cape San Antonio. *Left to right, Pianin, Dempsey, Bryson and Campobasso.* Courtesy of U.S. Navy Armed Guard WWII Veterans.

the *Cape San Antonio* was diesel-engined and unfortunately vibrated like the proverbial Ford "Tin Lizzie" while underway. I never did get used to it. In addition to the usual war material in the holds, we carried as deck cargo a fully assembled OS2U Kingfisher scout floatplane perched on each of the five hatches. In due time we crossed the equator for my first time and became a genuine "shellback." At about this time, some of the merchant crew managed to break into Army PX supplies in one of the holds, and for the rest of the way to Australia the ship was awash with candy bars, Coca-Cola and cigarettes.

In due course we entered the Brisbane River where a Navy crane barge came alongside and unloaded the floatplanes, after which we moved further up the river to Brisbane proper and unloaded the rest of what was consigned to that port. One thing that particularly struck me was the power of Australian labor unions. Even with the Japanese almost breathing down their necks and with manpower shortages, they still insisted on two men to a winch while unloading, one to lift the material out of the hold to above deck level, and one to swing it out over the side and lower it to the dock. Everywhere else but in Australia this was a one-man job.

From Brisbane it was on to Sydney, where we tied up near the Circular Quay, close by the Sydney Harbour Bridge. Considering the number of military personnel there, I had found the people of Brisbane to be most friendly, but compared to Sydney they were positively hostile. Americans in general and U.S. sailors in particularly were welcome everywhere and there was unanimous agreement among the Armed Guard that if we couldn't live in the U.S., then Australia would be our alternate choice.

As the saying goes, "all good things must come to an end," unloading was completed, and it was back to San Francisco where I was granted two weeks leave. Two weeks? Unfortunately, I lived on the East Coast, and four days heading east and four days heading west left only six days at home. At Oakland, I boarded the Union Pacific's "Furlough-ee Challenger" headed for Chicago. The train was restricted to military personnel only, so the only civilians were the train crew, and dungarees or fatigues served as uniforms. The one break on a dull, boring all-coach trip was provided by the good citizens of North Platte, Nebraska, who met the Challenger from each direction with homemade goodies. How they did it in those days when everything was rationed, I've never been able to figure out. From Chicago via the New York Central, undress blues were required rather than dungarees, switching to dress blues at Harmon, where the steam locomotive was replaced by an electric engine for the remainder of the way into Grand Central Terminal. My first order of business after getting home was to obtain temporary ration points so as not to be too much of a burden on my widowed mother. Although I would only be in New York for those six days, my leave papers said fourteen days, so I was actually able to get ration points for the whole two weeks, giving my mother a little bit 'extra' to work with.[13]

~~~

This is the final piece of James Gailey's story that was printed in the March/April 1993 Pointer. *It tells of some very interesting and often hilarious adventures the Navy Armed Guard was asked to do, all in the line of duty.*

Other duties…

They transferred thirty of us coxswains to the Naval Landing Force Base in Norfolk, Virginia, which was a landing craft repair shop. We stayed there a month and they didn't know what to do with us so they sent us to Camp Allen which was also in Norfolk. Here they put us back in training again. We would march and drill all day, get more shots, and we received a rifle and helmet. They were trying to make soldiers out of us. We trained at this for several months and they finally moved us to Portsmouth, Virginia Naval Yard. We were bused each day to the shipyard with a packed lunch, where we worked all day with civilians. We did this for about three months. This outfit was a ship repair outfit with about a thousand men in it with all rates, carpenters, welders, etc. We had everything in which to set up a base to work on ships.
~~~

They finally put us on a troop train for San Francisco. It took about six days to get there and we had a great time on the train. Upon arriving, they took us to a camp at San Bruno. Then they took us to a "San Fran Racetrack" which was for horse racing and they made us sleep in the horse stables. They didn't have a place to put us up but finally after about three weeks they transferred us to Tiburon, a base across the Golden Gate Bridge, thirty miles North of Frisco. It was a base on the bay on the side of a mountain. We were also eaten up by bedbugs there. I don't know if we caught them at the racetrack or at this base. They sprayed everything to get rid of them.

We would ride a boat to San Francisco on liberty and it would pick us up at 11 PM to take the one hour trip back. There were two little towns between 'Frisco' and the base and I started going out with a welder (girl) in the shipyard. She was from Wisconsin and she had a brother in the Armed Guard in the Pacific Theater. She was a lovely, pretty Polish girl and she fixed me supper many a time.

We stayed at this base for a couple of months and finally after not seeming to know what to do with us, they put us on a troopship headed for Guam. About eight days later, we pulled into Pearl Harbor where we were taken off the ship. We were sent to a Naval Base called "Aica" which was on a mountain overlooking the bay with sugar fields all around us. I don't know why they took us off the ship but I was glad because I got to see Hawaii. We could go into town every day but we couldn't be there at night. We had a curfew imposed on us and we had to stay in groups as some Japanese would jump you if you were by yourself in certain areas.

They had these photo shops all around where you could take your photograph with a Hula girl, grass skirt and all, for fifty cents. I had one made with her sitting on my lap but she was so dark, I tore it up. I thought at the time that I had better not sent that home, but now I wish I had kept it. I spent Christmas 1944 in Hawaii. We would go into town as the beach was right there. The Royal Hawaiian Hotel was on the beach and the Navy had pretty much taken the place over and you could go there to hang out. The chow was good and we could catch a ride to anywhere on the island in these Army trucks. We also worked in the Fleet Post Office.

After a couple of months, we went back on board the same troop ship. I'll never know why we were taken off in the first place. The ship was real crowded and hot down below and of course there was some seasickness. I never got sick again after being sick on my first ship. After traveling several weeks in this hot condition, we pulled into Eniwetok, a small military occupied island in the Marshall Islands. We were there only a couple of days, enough to stretch our legs and go swimming.

Then we boarded the ship again and sailed on across the International Dateline and we had two Sundays in a row. On the way back, we skipped a day. A few weeks later, we were in Guam. There was nothing there! We had to sleep in tents near the water with four to a tent and it rained every hour or so. Each time a cloud would pass over it would rain and there was mud everywhere; inside tents, in the chow hall, etc. As long as it was a dirt and water mixture, there was mud!! You had to sleep under mosquito nets and they would still get through at night. They fed us Spam three times a day. We had powdered eggs and Spam for breakfast. The toilets were "Outdoor Johns" and our shower was a big tank up in the air. You got in, pulled the chain, cold was wide open, hot was closed. You drank water from a lister bag hanging up in the sun and it was hot with chlorine added. It wasn't good. The tank truck came by every day to fill them.

We had a movie each night in a field with no seats or roof. If you had a seat, it was the bucket that you washed your clothes in and you carried your poncho to cover yourself when it rained, which it always did. They were building barracks but we had to live like this until they were ready.

They soon dropped the Atom Bomb and we were sent home. I've always wondered what happened to the "men and women" I had met during my service days. I am proud to have served my country in a Special Service called the U.S. Navy Armed Guard and it is great to be a member of the U.S.N. Armed Guard WW II Veterans. Now you know of the other duties that our crew was required to do to end the conflict started by the Japanese and German people.[14]

~~~

Here are two more of Bob Norling's stories concerning friendly fire and being thirsty.

Friendly Fire

We called it friendly fire — and it really was. It did the job without hurting anyone, that is, if you aimed very carefully to miss the target accidentally on purpose.

It was the Very pistol, used for signaling with flares. We always kept one on the bridge, but we never thought we'd see the day when it became a weapon.

It happened at Leyte in the Philippines. Natives came out in bumboats to sell trade with the sailors aboard the ships in the harbor. It was free-wheeling commerce until the enemy caused the market to crash.

Japanese soldiers in native dress went out one day in a bumboat and tossed hand grenades into a couple of PT boats. So the order was issued: no more trading with the bumboats.

That didn't deter many Filipinos who still had things to sell. But orders were orders. No bumboats allowed alongside.

On the bridge, our shouted warnings to keep away were more or less ignored, and we had to do something. The weapon of choice was the Very pistol.

Aim carefully at the surface on either side of the bumboat. The flare — red, green or white — would arch out and bounce by the bumboat, sometimes with near misses. We never scored a direct hit, thank goodness. It gave the Filipinos a good scare and bridge watch became fun duty.

The enemy, meanwhile, also had a Mickey-Mouse method of attack that came close to matching our non-lethal friendly fire at Leyte. We were bombed twice by planes whose pilots dropped small, antipersonnel bombs known as daisy-cutters. They couldn't have seriously believed they could sink us that way.

We saw one pilot dump what looked like a bushel basketful on our ship. Our defense was to get flat on the deck and when the
~~~

bomb hit, its contents (usually small, sharp pieces of metal) would spew outward and upward well over us.

No one ever got hurt, and the damage was minor: some small holes in the deck and any nearby rigging shredded, especially lifeboat falls, signal halyards and tarps.

Our gunners tried to shoot them down, but failed. Maybe we should have fired instead with our Very pistol to scare them away.[15]

A Thirst For Adventure

For fifty-four days we thirsted, as we sailed nearly halfway around the world on the Liberty ship *Benjamin Ide Wheeler.*

After we left New York, Armed Guard Commander Lieutenant Douglas Woodring issued strict orders to stay away from our precious cargo. Woe to anyone who got into the 45,000 cases of beer destined for the Navy PX at Hollandia in New Guinea, as well as a good supply of 180 proof medical alcohol.

New York to Guantanamo Bay, to Panama, to Milne Bay and Finschhafen and, at long last, Hollandia. So far, we had followed orders and the Armed Guard log even noted that the captain of the *Wheeler,* Dan Coughlin, "commended our performance to date." Ha!

We moved to a dock, Seabee stevedores came aboard and the fun began. They were experienced cargo handlers and made straight for the alcohol. They offered to share some with us if we provided the canned grapefruit juice needed to help it down. Someone did, and it was a grand scene.

For weeks we had staked out places to hide any ill-gotten loot. That wasn't much of a problem on a Liberty ship. The bottom of my flag-bag on the port side of the bridge even held four cases without noticeably scrunching up the flags.

Gunners had their special places and some loot even got into the lectern used for Sunday services on the fantail under the gun platform. An astounding supply of beer – about fifty cases – was stashed in a bulkhead cofferdam near the laundry on the starboard side lower deck.

In the meantime, trucks were being hijacked on their way to the PX warehouse. And many slings of beer went over the dark side of the ship into boats that crept alongside during the night unloading.

And when we had to move out to anchorage to make dock space available for ships with cargoes deemed more vital to the war effort, we were ordered to "watch over the holds and escape hatches." Talk about foxes guarding the henhouse!

Finally, the Navy struck back. Gun-toting guards rode the trucks, lights were ordered on all night all around the ship and a surprise search party came aboard.

That was the beginning of the end, for my supply and especially for proprietors of that cache in the bulkhead. A sharp-eyed PX officer noticed the freshly painted lugs over the cofferdam cover. "Open it up," he ordered, and a great sadness descended on the ship.

No one got into serious trouble over what happened to all that beer. We didn't get a helluva lot of it, anyway. It was only 3.2 beer. But oh my, it tasted good.[16]

~~~

This is the continuation of Harold Skinner's excerpt found in the introduction of this chapter.

Ulithi, the Mighty Atoll

I was a RM2C when I first became acquainted with Ulithi in late May of 1945. I and my shipmates had experienced an uneventful five-day voyage from Eniwetok on the S. S. *Francisco Coronado*, a travel-worn Liberty ship that had sailed unescorted from Pearl Harbor and averaged 10 knots, the normal speed of those mass-produced cargo ships. In the radio shack the only cause for concern had been a submarine-alert signal transmitted about ninety miles from the *Coronado*'s position. I recorded a memo that the weather was perfect and there was nothing but a calm surface of the ocean in every direction to the distant horizon. The brilliant sunshine was idyllic, and the bright moonlight would have made young sailors dream about lighter moments if it had not been for the constant awareness that the ship was silhouetted
~~~

for miles, exposing her image to the searching gaze of any alert enemy submarine commander.

I had 12-to-4 watch at the moment, a duty time that I enjoyed. Observing the clock on the wall, I duly noted the occasional on-the-hour schedule of "BAMS" (British and American merchant ships messages) in international Morse. I knew I must not fail to copy these coded messages coming from the Navy station in Hawaii. Usually they were not intended for my ship, but sometimes the secret call sign on this vessel would appear among the number of call signs in the heading of the message. When that happened, I would alert the chief radioman and the ship's captain, both civilian merchant marine officers. Using a top-secret codebook, they would decipher the contents. Often the ship would be notified of an en route change of destination. On this voyage, however nothing of the sort disturbed the duty-watch routine in the radio shack. I dutifully kept the receiver tuned to the distress frequency of 500 kilocycles, just below the AM broadcast band, aware that any enemy action against merchant shipping would come crackling over the speaker in the form of "SSS" (submarine alert), "RRR" (armed raider alert), or "AAA" (aircraft attack). The ship was by that time far in the western Pacific as evidenced by the fact that it was seven hours behind Pacific Coast time.

Two days later, May 25th, the S. S. *Francisco Coronado* proceeded slowly through the submarine-net protected opening into the placid anchorage of Ulithi. My first impression of the setting was that it resembled Eniwetok, since distant cargo ships and tankers could be seen neatly aligned at anchor, and the silhouettes of destroyers and escorted vessels were visible as well. Once at anchorage the ship made contact with harbor officials, and an occasional boat came alongside to take the ship's officers and the Navy gunnery officer to a conference involving further sailing instructions.

Rumors somehow spread from ship to ship and I heard that all radiomen and signalmen in the Armed Guard would henceforth undergo required gunnery training before shipping out from the West Coast Armed Guard Center at Treasure Island in San Francisco Bay. This was welcome news to my ears, since I long wanted to train on the twin-mount 20mm rapid-fire gun that was the principal antiaircraft weapon used by the gun crew. Eight of these weapons on the ship constituted a formidable opposition to enemy aircraft.

The bright, clear weather of the open sea gave way to frequent showers that materialized suddenly from a low cloud on the horizon. After providing a sudden downpour for ten minutes, the cloud moved away and the sun shone again on the hot, steaming deck. Although the continuous monitoring of the radio distress frequency ceased while the ship was in port, the radiomen maintained watch on a port-security frequency. They were also expected to alternate daylight watches on the bridge with the signalmen. This might involve "arm waving" semaphore messages from ship to ship, but usually their duty required "Sparks" (the radioman) to come running to the bridge to read a blinker-light message (Morse Code) from another ship, then send back the answer by the light.

Also, while in port, the Armed Guard gunnery officer would from time to time request that the Navy radioman type formal reports for him, or possibly a crew member made a similar request. Another responsibility that fell to the lot of the Navy radioman while in sea was to produce a ship's newspaper. Since only they had regular access to the radio, they were aware of Navy shore stations that broadcast in plain-language Morse the news of the day. Now, at anchor in Ulithi, they were relieved of this duty. Such work required me to sit at the typewriter, earphones on my head, and painstakingly type for forty-five minutes all the reports from the world's battlefronts. The other radioman would then edit omissions due to static, or correct errors and produce a neat copy in duplicate, add a few shipboard jokes, and the next morning one copy of the news would be on the merchant marine mess table and another on the Armed Guard mess table. Now, in port, however, the Navy radioman used the radio to monitor port security on a regular watch.

One day the men enjoyed watching a battleship anchored at a short distance. Attention was focused on a Navy fighter plane flying past the ship and towing a target sleeve to provide gunnery practice for the sailors. As the guns of the big ship opened fire, antiaircraft bursts could be seen all around the moving target. Suddenly one of the bursts cut the towline, and the Armed Guard crew laughed as the target sleeve slowly floated down.

Now that the ship was in port, the young sailors began to wonder anxiously how soon mail would be brought aboard. Everybody knew almost instantly when the boat was authorized to go ashore for that purpose. At last, when the names were called out and the letters eagerly clutched by impatient hands, each turned aside quietly to share a piece of private news from the home front. Some would stand aside, silently engrossed, their faces suddenly brightened by positive news, then share it with their closest shipmates. Others would brood silently, meditating on the report of death in the family or other unfavorable news. Occasionally a sailor would receive unpleasant news stoically and then turn it into a joke to deflect the depressing impact. Such was the case of one who received word that his girlfriend had married someone else. Being teased as the victim of a "Dear John" letter, he pleaded mock bereavement by wearing a black armband for thirty days.

Most Navy veterans of the Pacific war will recall the recreation island in Ulithi atoll. Mog-Mog, as it was called, was a long narrow, sandy strip of land, one that harshly typified in microcosmic dimensions the discrimination of the Navy class system. Thousands of sea-wobbly enlisted men were at some time granted the only form of shore leave available in that corner of the Pacific. As they thronged onto the hot sand, they discovered that the only relief from the glaring sun was the thin shadow cast by an occasional palm tree. The beach offered the appeal of unrestricted swimming, provided one ignored the danger of serious sunburn. Going ashore for the first time in weeks or months, a sailor could also play basketball or softball, curse the hot sand and everything about the tropics, and drink his two cans of warm beer. His relief at feeling something other than a steel deck underfoot was soon tempered at the sight of a shady, green paradise just beyond the fence that divided the island in half. Nestled in the lush bower-like shrubbery just out of the enlisted man's reach was the neon-lighted, thatched officer's club outfitted with a 100-

foot bar for junior officers and a 50-foot bar for lieutenant commanders and above. There was a third and better lounge with chairs for admirals, and someone reported that as many as twenty at a time could be found there. The officers could sip their cocktails and blended whiskey, totally oblivious to the hundreds of young men who were only a few hundred feet away, pretending they were having the time of their lives under the blazing sunshine but grateful for even this short respite from the endless grind of standing alert at battle stations.

The Armed Guard crew of the *Coronado* heard the rumor on Saturday, June 2, that a boat would come to pick them up and take them ashore for a "beer party." By 0830 they were scrambling into the boat, and an hour later they were playfully throwing Mog-Mog sand at one another on the beach. I received my can of warm beer with mixed feelings, deciding I much preferred draft beer that was chilled, then wolfed down with some sandwiches. While some of the crew brought out softball equipment, the Navy men challenged a combined merchant marine-Army team, and the contest began. It was a hard-fought game. I played second base and managed to run in two of the Navy's five scores. In spite of the fine showing, the Navy crew lost, eight to five.

After the exertion and perspiration, a plunge in the warm waters of the lagoon was a welcome relief. I practiced my underwater swimming, and floated and splashed about with my shipmates. For most of the Navy crew this was the first release from shipboard tension and the first opportunity to get acquainted in relaxed conditions since leaving Pearl Harbor. What pleased me the most as an ardent swimmer was that, in spite of a swift, dangerous undercurrent, the water was cleaner than at Waikiki Beach, and there was no coral on the bottom to cut one's feet, as at Waikiki.

With sunburned faces and slightly swollen eyes, we were relieved when our ship's boat came ashore for us. We had hardly covered half the distance to the *Coronado* when we were caught in a drenching downpour. Soaked to the skin but satisfied with our Sunday on Mog-Mog, we nursed our sunburns and sore muscles and resumed our duties. I went on watch at midnight, managing with difficulty to stay awake.

At 0800 on June 10th all hands dashed to their battle stations as an air-raid warning was heard. The all-clear signal was sounded at 0830 without any sign of the enemy. The monotony of shipboard routine continued. I used some of my off-duty time to study radio theory and electricity, looking towards the next tests for promotion, and exchanged "scuttlebutt" with the Armed Guard bunch and formed casual friendships among merchant marine crew.

Although the ship had been at sea for some time, the food was good. Fresh milk, eggs, and ice cream had naturally long since been consumed. What was obvious to everybody, however, was that the mild physical exercise derived from ascending and descending the steel ladders was insufficient to produce a keen appetite. The ship's baker was a friendly type and I easily warmed to his jovial, good humor. The relationship paid dividends, too, for occasionally after coming off the new watch schedule in the early morning following the 0300-0600 watch I would find a piece of cake or pie in the corner of the galley.

By June 12th a new form of recreation was permitted to the off-duty Navy men. Coming off signal watch on the bridge at noon, I noticed some of the gunners diving amidships from about thirty feet. Not caring to join them because of flotsam visible in the water, I watched them build a springboard, using a large plank placed far out over the water with the base held solidly. After much careful adjustment, the board was pronounced ready for use. The diver bounced lightly two or three times before making a final heavy spring. C-r-a-s-h! The plank snapped at the ship's edge and the surprised diver, plunging feet first, yelled all the way to the water. What an outburst of shouts and laughter from the onlookers!

Being frequently on duty at the signal light to relieve the signalman, and having access to the lists of incoming and outbound ships, I discovered that a certain tanker was due to arrive soon in Ulithi. It was the ship of my radio school buddy from near my hometown in Idaho. The question then came to mind whether it might be possible for the two of us to establish contact. On June 15th the S.S. *Lundy's Lane* did take its place in the anchorage lineup. I studied the "restricted" anchorage map and estimated the direction of the tanker from the *Coronado*. Pointing the light in that direction I blinked out a call to the ship across more than a mile of placid water and asked for my friend by name. There was a long pause and then an answering signal. Sure enough it was my friend. We chatted by flashing light for a while, asking about our respective girlfriends, and then the tanker radioman invited me to come over to his ship. Suddenly, in the middle of a statement the light ceased. I waited, then blinked a question mark, but nothing more came back. For a long time I wondered why my friend had so abruptly ended contact, and in a few days both ships had left Ulithi. Many years later we recalled our venture at sea when I asked him point-blank: "Why did you break contact with me on the light in the Ulithi?"

My friend thought for a moment and said, "The signalman came rushing to the bridge and shouted to me that the gunnery officer wanted to know if I realized we were in a war zone, and that I'd better get the h... off that blinker if I didn't want some extra duty."

The S.S. *Francisco Coronado* left Ulithi on June 20th in an eleven-ship convoy bound for Okinawa. She returned to the atoll at 1215 on July 18th in convoy, stayed only six hours and departed, sailing independently on a 20-day voyage to San Francisco. Another chapter in the many adventures at Ulithi atoll had ended, and the war would end in less than a month.

What is puzzling about the Ulithi anchorage is why the Japanese paid such little attention to it. It is true, of course, that nearby enemy bases such as Yap and Truk had been severely pounded by U.S. forces, but the major fleet activities at Ulithi offered an alluring target for Japanese planes and submarines. With only a few exceptions, nonetheless, the base remained relatively secure to the end of the war.[17]

~~~

George Pavlovic wrote, "This story is unusual, but true. The names are fictitious; the rest of the story is true. The dates were taken from the Gunnery Officer's daily log."
~~~

The Antigua *entering Havana harbor on her maiden voyage. Launched in 1932 by Bethlehem Steel in Quincy, Massachusetts, she operated for the United Fruit Company.* Publisher's collection.

The Stowaway

In February 1945 I was assigned to the S.S. *Antigua*, one of six sister ships that belonged to the United Fruit Company. She was a combination transport and reefer. These ships were taken over by the navy with the exception of the *Antigua*, which was manned by the merchant marine during the war. We had a large gun crew, forty-eight men, including some storekeepers whose responsibility it was to keep track of the cargo. Our ordinance consisted of eight 20mms, four 3-inch 50s and a 5-inch 51 on the stern.

The ship was moored at a pier in Guam on August 6th, when the first A-bomb was dropped on Japan. On August 7th we left port, destination unknown. On August 10th we crossed the Equator and arrived at Manus, Admiralty Islands later that day. Two days later we sailed from Manus and arrived in Auckland, New Zealand on August 19th. The ship was then loaded with a cargo of frozen meat. Just before we left on August 26th, a straggler (John Smith B/M 2/c) was brought aboard and put into the custody of our gunnery officer. He was to be transported to a Receiving Station and turned over to the Provost Marshall. I guess he must have jumped ship because at the time there were no Americans stationed in Auckland. Anyway, he was quartered with the gun crew and given the run of the ship as a prisoner-at-large.

This guy had a very nice personality and became friends with just about everyone in the gun crew.

We arrived at Manus on September 3rd and left the next day. Subsequently we discharged some of our cargo in Tinian, the balance in Guam. At Guam our gunnery officer turned the bos'n over to the Receiving Station.

I figured that was the last we would see of him. They had working parties unloading cargo with men from the Guam brig. On August 29th we left for the States and were one happy crew. After all, the war was over. In a short time we would become civilians again

Later that day, my buddy Bill asked me if I would help him. I told him certainly, that's what buddies are for, right? Well it seems that (John Smith) was aboard that morning, as a member of a working party, and when the work party was returned to the brig, he hid aboard ship. Later he saw Bill and asked if he would help him. Bill then hid John in a storage locker that was down the passageway from our cabin. Later Bill approached me and asked for my assistance. The best plan we could think of was to conceal him in our cabin, which had bunks for four men. We got a mattress out of storage and laid it on deck below my bunk. When I made my bunk, I draped the bedspread so it reached down to the deck. We figured that way when he lay on the mattress he would not be seen. This is where he spent the day on our return to the states. At night he had the run of the ship.

The food aboard *Antigua* was excellent and they put out a very good night lunch. Bill and I would go down to the mess hall

The lounge of the Antigua *as it appeared in peacetime. It was paneled in English bog oak.* Publisher's collection.

after it was set out and get coffee and a couple of sandwiches and bring them to John. I remember one day while on deck, an AB (Able-bodied Seaman) said to me, that he had heard that there was a stowaway aboard. I looked at him with a straight face and said, "You have got to be kidding." But that kind of shook us up as we thought the gunnery officer might pull a shake down. The *Antigua* had two gunnery officers aboard, and we didn't have much respect for either one. The rest of the trip was uneventful until we arrived in San Francisco on October 10th.

At this point we thought of a scheme, with some help from other members of the crew. (John) told us his home was a small town just west of Chicago. The storekeepers had a typewriter they used to print their reports. One of them typed fictitious leave papers in the event that (John) met the Shore Patrol on his way to Chicago. He told us he planned to go home and after thirty days turn himself in at Great Lakes. Some of us pitched in so he could pay for his transportation home. I had duty the first day in port but some of the men said they saw him in town that night, drunker than a skunk. This really scared me as I had visions of winding up in Leavenworth if he was picked up by the Short Patrol and all the details came out. However, that was the last I saw or heard of him.

A few days later I was detached from the *Antigua* to Armed Guard Center, Treasure Island, and a couple days later sent to Shoemaker, California. On November 1st the Navy cut the points required for discharge to forty-one. There it was decided I had forty-one-and-a-half points, enough for my discharge. I was put in a 500-man draft to Great Lakes Naval Training Center. It took our troop train five days to get there, but apparently we were low priority because we sat on a siding in Iowa all night. We spent Thanksgiving on the train and our Thanksgiving dinner consisted of a Spam sandwich and a cup of coffee at 10 AM. At that point they ran out of food in the kitchen car. We arrived about 2 AM Friday the following day.

The separation center was operating twenty-four hours a day. Processing began immediately after we had something to eat. Most of the men received "Convenience of the Government" discharges. Mine read "Expiration of Enlistment." This really surprised me because I had thought I had been drafted. Then about five years ago I requested my service records from St. Louis. They stated that I was drafted and then enlisted the same day. It seems that while at the Naval Recruiting Station, we were told to sign a stack of papers and one of them included an enlistment for two years. I never realized it until I saw my records. Although I lived just two miles from Great Lakes, the Navy didn't even pay me enough transportation money to get home; right on my discharge it shows a travel allowance of five cents. Even the trolley ride cost seven cents. I then took a cab the rest of the way home. It was wonderful being a civilian again.[18]

~~~

Tom's Parade
by George X. Hurley

As the veterans start to fade
Who will march in Tom's parade?
Down the street in Ludlow town
One more time before we are down.

Bugles playing, the cannons blast
Memorial Day is here at last
Heads held high, flags are flying
Gold Star mothers all are crying.

What a sight to behold
Grey haired veterans in the fold.
Out of step, out of breath
Yet they march, do not fret.

Armed Guard sailors, only nine
Every year right on time.
Honoring shipmates in the deep
All their memories we do keep.
~~~

World War II has come and gone
Like an old familiar song.
Watch these men who soon will fade
Who will march in Tom's parade?[19]

15

Epilogue

This chapter serves as a final tribute to what these magnificent veterans contributed in World War II. Without the logistic support of armament, equipment, food, fuel, machinery, planes, soldiers, and supplies, the war would have been lost. The U.S. Merchant Marine provided the logistical transportation and the U.S. Navy Armed Guard provided the protection. It was a unique symbiotic relationship and nowhere else in military history has this been duplicated and on such a grand scale. Two mottoes come to mind whenever the Armed Guard is mentioned: "We Aim to Deliver," and "Don't Give Up the Ship!" They did deliver and they never surrendered.

The following pieces are reminders of what these heroes felt and experienced then and now. Behind much of what these veterans say and feel is the ever-nagging feeling of being "stepchildren" of the Navy and not getting the thanks or recognition they deserve. Hopefully, this history will shed much light on a too-often forgotten service.

~~~

Many Armed Guard veterans speak to various groups including schools about their World War II experiences. James E. Sheridan of Rhode Island volunteered his service in such a manner, along with three other World War II veterans. They spoke before the 5th and 6th grade classes in the local elementary school. Jim writes,

> I was the last of four men to speak and I was doing fine until we started taking questions. The first question was from a little girl who stood up and asked me, 'Did you ever kill anybody?' That was all I had to hear and I couldn't say another word. They stopped the program and we left. The one teacher wrote to us and advised us if we ever talk to another group, tell them about the blood, guts and gore as that's what they want to hear. We were very upset as that is the one subject we did not want to talk about. We never went to another school to talk.[1]

Fortunately for other school children and adults, Jim turned his voluntary teaching into letter writing to explain his World War II experience. The following is a portion of a five-page letter written to Mrs. Cournoyers 5th grade class at the Oakland Beach School in Warwick, Rhode Island.

Dear Mrs. Cournoyers: 6/4/98

First I would like to thank you and your wonderful students for your very nice letters. I would like to answer each and every one but it is impossible due to bad arthritis in my hands and I couldn't write that much but I will try to answer all the questions if I can.

I went into the Navy when I was seventeen years old in early 1943. I had seven weeks of boot camp at Sampson, New York. Then home for one week. I was then put into the Armed
~~~

Guard and I had no idea what it was. I was sent to a gunnery school to learn all about the guns we would use on various ships. It lasted four weeks as it was like a crash course as they needed replacements for all the new ships and also for the men that were being killed.

After gunnery school we were sent to the Navy base in Brooklyn, New York for ship assignment. We were put on a large balcony with a guard on each end and slowly we were assigned to ship gun crews. A full crew consisted of one officer, one radioman, two signalmen, one coxswain, two gunner's mates and twenty-one gunners.

Most of us had never been on a ship in our lives or had ever seen an ocean. After we were assigned to a ship we were guarded until we got our supplies which were all kinds of foul weather gear. When we got Eskimo hoods, boots (fur-lined), gloves, and facemasks we knew we would not go south.

Then we were taken to our ship. Everybody got a bunk and then we had to load the ammunition aboard to the magazines. We assigned to guns. Then we were taken to the chow hall where we would always eat. We had gun drills and boat drills so we would know what to do if we had to abandon ship as everybody went to a certain lifeboat.

After our ship was loaded with cargo we pulled away from the dock and we slowly left the harbor and took our position in the convoy where we stayed until we reached our destination. We had eight men on each watch period. We stood two men on the bow gun, two men on the stern gun, two men on the bridge guns and two men to go from gun to gun to relieve the men to get a hot coffee and go to the bathroom. The watch periods were ... This schedule was just repeated day after day until we reached port.

Anything done at night was done in complete dark as no lights were allowed. We had to be very careful as it was possible to stumble overboard. To be an Armed Guard we all had to have perfect eyesight. It was the best teamwork I ever saw and everyone had his job and he did it.

You never knew where the subs were and when the escorts made contact with a sub through sonar they would drop depth charges and you could feel it as it echoed off the ship. If

James E. Sheridan, Jr. as he appeared in 1944. Courtesy of James E. Sheridan, Jr.

a couple of ships got hit no one was allowed to stop as each convoy had a couple of rescue ships who would pick up survivors if there were any. We were told that if we had to go in the water we had only fifteen minutes to live in the ice-cold water of the north Atlantic.

Ships in a convoy used to remind me of a flock of ships being herded across the ocean with the escort ships like sheepdogs guarding the flock and the subs trying to make the flock scatter so they could pick off a stray. The subs used to form what they called Wolf Packs, subs strung out in the path of a convoy. But they would be spread out to cover a large area. As the convoys got close to land, planes would try to attack the convoy but with eighty ships with eight or ten guns on each and the escorts with many guns, they would have a good fight on their hands.

I became a marksman right away as I had very good eye-sight and nerves of steel and I would hold my fire until the plane was in range even though it was shooting at me. I never was scared. I knew my job and I did as I was taught.

I was on four different Liberty ships in two-and-a-half years. I was in the invasion of Anzio which was in Italy just south of Rome. It was a very risky invasion as the Germans were ready for it and made things hot for us. But we delivered the troops and supplies and were able to leave without getting hit. Our only job was to deliver the goods and get out quick. On the way back through the Mediterranean Sea, we were attacked by German planes and had no hits. Then as we passed North Africa a ship in front of us and one behind us were both sunk at the same time and we were never touched.

We went back to New York and loaded up with all kinds of war goods and joined another convoy and crossed the Atlantic without much action. We unloaded and were converted to carry troops. Then we were sent to Oban, Scotland with a lot of other ships. Nobody had an idea of what was going on. We had very hard gun drills all day long. Then after three weeks of drills we sailed to Cardiff, Wales where we had more drills with friendly planes diving on us.

Then on June 4, 1944 we loaded troops and battle gear of all types. It was then I knew that the D-day invasion was on. On the docks all we could see for miles was troops, tanks, trucks and Jeeps. What a sight that was. After we loaded we were taken out into the channel and we dropped anchor. Next morning we started to go but the rain and wind was so bad that we had to stop and wait until next morning which was June 6 (D-Day). As daylight came we were at the beach of Normandy facing the most fortified army in the world. The sky was full of Allied planes from horizon to horizon and the water was full of ships as far as you could see.

As we got closer to the beach, the water was full of dead soldiers and sailors who died in the open assault. It was a horrible sight as they were mostly men as old as I was which was eighteen years old. They were dead and their family didn't even know yet. They gave their lives so we could be free.

The first night as soon as it got dark the German planes attacked. I was strapped in a 20 mm cannon on the bridge and I saw a bomber heading for us. My gunnery officer was right next to me and he shouted, "Commence firing!" Then I did what I was trained to do. I blew the plane right out of the sky. The plane had a crew of three. The troops we had on board saw the action and treated me like a hero and I've never forgotten that moment.

We were bombed every night until we were unloaded. Then we loaded with hundreds of German prisoners. We took them to Plymouth, England and as we approached the harbor, the shore was lined with thousands of people as we were the first ship to bring prisoners from Normandy. We made seven round trips over to the beach with troops and arms of all kinds and we brought back prisoners or survivors from sunken ships and wounded men.

During those trips we were bombed every night and hit with gunfire from shore. Many other ships were hit. My ears were damaged from all the concussions as were many other Armed Guards. After the war I was in the Veteran's hospital and they removed part of my skull on the right side and my eardrum.

After seven trips to the beaches and a collision with another ship we were sent home to New York and we all got thirty days leave. My next ship was in Antwerp, Belgium during the battle of the Bulge.

During my time in the Armed Guard I saw so much action I could probably write a book. We are all in the twilight of our lives and we forget a lot but we are so glad to get to talk to children like you and let you know why we feel so strongly about our country and our great flag. We hope you will always appreciate what democracy really means and how it was saved by people who did so much in our young lives so children like you won't have to go through what we did. Please always fly and respect your flag and each other.

Jim Sheridan
USN Armed Guard WW II Veteran[2]

~~~

July 4th is one of America's most important holidays. This one was special for Dick Brown.

July 4, 1945

We sailed into Bremerhaven, Germany aboard the S.S. *Cornelius Ford* on July 4, 1945. Amongst all the fireworks, flares and whatnot noisemakers, we were delivering the U.S. Army 17th Port Company from Ghent, Belgium. The war had been declared over for a short time now and peace was great! It was also a somber time as we knew our old Armed Guard outfit would be finished. As a wartime only outfit, the small group camaraderie that had been developed would be sorely missed.
~~~

Bremerhaven hadn't suffered the major damage like most German cities and while there we did have a bona fide liberty pass, but we seldom had to use it. We didn't even go ashore in our dress uniform. We just wore our blue dungaree work clothes.

There was an Army guard post near our ship and a hole in the fence as well. Sometimes there would be a guard posted, but most of the time there wasn't. If we were coming back off free liberty we would sing out just so they wouldn't get trigger happy. We didn't want to get killed in an accident now that the war was over.

We would trade and deal with the troops who lived in the requisitioned apartments nearby. All the apartments were furnished by the people who had vacated them. They were very nice indeed. We were fortunate to find souvenirs left in an old warehouse and I managed to get some metal and cloth Swastikas.

It was great to be alive and celebrating the Fourth of July and the war's end. The best part was that we would soon be sailing back to the old U.S.A. This was to be my last trip as it was the end of the line.[3]

~~~

This story is from our prolific Signalman, Bob Norling.

And Grown Men Cried

Who says grown men don't cry? I know they do because I've done it myself and I've seen others do it, too.

Sailors cried when painfully injured in action or when they broke down under the strain of battle; and also when they were far, far away and got word that a loved one had died back home.

I almost cried when my pet dog was killed on a Murmansk Street by a hit-and-run Russian soldier. When a nearby tanker in a convoy with us was torpedoed by a U-boat, I cried in anger knowing full well that men were dying in that roaring inferno.

I shed some tears during a memorial service we held for a shipmate blown overboard and drowned when our Liberty ship was suicide-crashed by an enemy plane at Leyte.
~~~

On a lighter side, I saw a sailor practically cry when he dropped the bag containing his weekly ration of Australian beer and spirits on a street in Sydney. And I'm sure a shipmate cried when he was struck down in Australia by that most serious of social diseases, syphilis, just before he was to ship home after two years in the Southwest Pacific.

Many years later, I saw grown men cry at a memorial service for the 129 men lost when the nuclear-powered sub USS *Thresher* went down off Portsmouth, New Hampshire, in 1963.

My last Navy-related cry was on June 19, 2000. I choked up and let it all out during the funeral service for Dave Noyes, a fellow Armed Guard signalman. We went through boot camp and signal schools together in 1942 and kept in touch over the years.

I visited Dave at his home in Stratham, New Hampshire, two months before he died. We played what turned out to be our final cribbage match. Much to his delight, he beat me two out of three games while using my board and my own cards.

What did me in at Dave's funeral was singing the Navy Hymn at the conclusion of the service. "… O hear us when we cry to thee, for those in peril on the sea."

I had to step outside the church and regain my composure. It was a good cry, for a shipmate from the old days.

Do grown men cry? Just ask me.[4]

~~~

Joe McKenna wrote this interesting passage concerning recognition.

Our Day

I'm a U.S. Navy Armed Guard veteran of WW II. The reason why people never heard of us is that we had no distinguishing patch or insignia. In short, we were not as glamorous as aircraft sailors, submariners, destroyer men or sailors from other fighting ships of the fleet. But the thing to remember is that for every man and ship afloat, for every invasion, air strike, submarine
~~~

attack, etc., there was food, fuel, ammunition, medical supplies needed and these were transported by merchant ships manned by merchant seaman and Naval Armed Guard gunners.

The Armed Guard and merchant seaman were not only in danger of submarine attacks, but they also had to deal with mines, aircraft attacks, surface warships and armed raiders and storms at sea. We slept fully-clothed with a life jacket nearby. (I know – my first ship was torpedoed!)

The nights were not a happy time, for it was then that danger was most likely to strike. The Armed Guard gunners and merchant seaman showed exemplary courage while doing convoy duty.

Throughout the war we never received the recognition we deserved. However, we still manned the guns. To this day the Navy Department has not given us "Our Day." If it wasn't for the merchant seaman manning the ships and the Navy Armed Guard maintaining the guns, World War II would have been lost![5]

~~~

Jim Biscardi, who contributed "Getting Sick" in Chapter 11, is now ninety-one years old. He was a gun captain aboard three ships in World War II. He has always been a strong advocate for recognizing the contribution of the Naval Armed Guard. In 1994, his "Letter to the Editor" entitled, "Armed Guard gets no respect," was published in the Intelligencer *of Doylestown, Pennsylvania. His letter also paid tribute to the Merchant Marine and pointed out the unique and special relationship between the Armed Guard and merchant seaman.*

Armed Guard Gets No Respect

To the Editor:

Memorial Day and the Fourth of July are times of the year when the public remembers those who gave their lives so that we could remain free. Many of those living today are unaware of different happenings during World War II, especially the work
~~~

of the merchant seamen who were called bums and said to be overpaid.

We, the veterans of the United States Navy Armed Guard, who served aboard ship with these merchant seamen, are proud to have been their shipmates. These men chose to serve their country even though many were declared unfit for military duty. Many were between the ages of 40 and 70 and could have stayed out of harm's way. Believe me, these men were considered second-class citizens.

Now we Navy Armed Guard veterans are in the same position as they were. We are the only branch of all our services that has never been honored by a congressional resolution for our sacrifices. Ironically, Great Britain, France, Russia and the Philippines have accorded us this honor.

I wrote to President Clinton twice this year asking if he would attend the national reunion of the Armed Guard and merchant seamen at a ceremony at the U.S. Navy Memorial Building in Washington, D.C., on May 4. I received a letter March 17 from Bernard V. Shinnal, Director of the White House Liaison Office, stating it was not possible.

My question is, why was it possible for the president to honor groups and single persons many miles from Washington, but he could not attend a ceremony of a half-hour duration, when all he had to travel was about three blocks? This should be conclusive proof that we are second-class citizens.

This is not to be construed as an instrument of confrontation. Our group comprises many creeds, nationalities and political parties. We are motivated only by our desire to receive justice and our place in history before we all pass away.

James W. Biscardi
Milford Township[6]

Jim was not to be denied in his quest. He was able to get Pennsylvania Congressman James C. Greenwood, to sponsor a resolution which was passed in 1998 and signed by the President.

And finally on October 17, 1998, Public Law 101-261 contained the following:

This Law was some satisfaction for Jim Biscardi, but in a letter to this compiler, Jim stated, "It might as well have never passed as it was a nonevent as far as the National news media goes because today, the Navy brass, does not know we were a

United States of America

Congressional Record

PROCEEDINGS AND DEBATES OF THE 105th CONGRESS, SECOND SESSION

Vol. 144 WASHINGTON, THURSDAY, MAY 21, 1998 No. 66

House of Representatives

Mr. GREENWOOD. Mr. Chairman, I rise today in support of the FY 1999 Defense Authorization Act and in appreciation of the inclusion of a provision, brought to my attention by my constituent, Mr. James Biscardi of Quakertown, Pennsylvania. Without his continued dedication, the men of the Navy Armed Guard, who served with honor, dignity, and courage, would still be awaiting their deserved congressional recognition.

In the beginning of the 104th Congress, Mr. Biscardi, a true American Patriot, contacted my office seeking recognition for those who served in the Navy Armed Guard. By working with him, I drafted legislation, now part of the FY 1999 Defense Authorization Act, that recognizes the outstanding service of the members of the Armed Guard during World Wars I and II and thanks the surviving crewmen of the Armed Guard for their service.

The Armed Guard was created as a branch of the United States Navy during World War I to protect the merchant ships of the United States by maintaining weapons on 384 merchant ships. During World War II, the Armed Guard was reactivated as a response to the German strategy of attacking and sinking merchant ships, even those of neutral countries, which appeared to be bringing goods to the Allied Nations in Europe. Over 144,900 men served in the Armed Guard on 6,236 merchant ships during World War II. Nearly 2,000 of these men made the supreme sacrifice, and gave their lives in defense of their country.

The dedication of, and sacrifices made, by the men of the Armed Guard deserve the recognition and gratitude of the United States. Through the passage of the Defense Authorization bill, the United States Congress will be acknowledging the outstanding service of the 144,970 men who served in the Armed Guard during World War II, and the men who served in World War I. These men have earned a heartfelt thanks from the country that they so gallantly fought to protect.

Jim, Thanks for making this happen and for your service to your country. Jim

Courtesy of Jim Biscardi.

This is to certify that the U.S. House of Representatives and the United States Senate passed, and on October 17, 1998, the President of the United States of America enacted,

Public Law 105-261

The Strom Thurmond National Defense Authorization Act for Fiscal Year 1999 and that this law contains the following:

SEC. 534. APPRECIATION FOR SERVICE DURING WORLD WAR I AND WORLD WAR II BY MEMBERS OF THE NAVY ASSIGNED ON BOARD MERCHANT SHIPS AS THE NAVAL ARMED GUARD SERVICE.

(a) FINDINGS- Congress makes the following findings:

(1) The Navy established a special force during both World War I and World War II, known as the Naval Armed Guard Service, to protect merchant ships of the United States from enemy attack by stationing members of the Navy and weapons on board those ships.

(2) Members of the Naval Armed Guard Service served on 6,236 merchant ships during World War II, of which 710 were sunk by enemy action.

(3) Over 144,900 members of the Navy served in the Naval Armed Guard Service during World War II as officers, gun crewmen, signalmen, and radiomen, of whom 1,810 were killed in action.

(4) The efforts of the members of the Naval Armed Guard Service played a significant role in the safe passage of United States merchant ships to their destinations in the Soviet Union and various locations in western Europe and the Pacific Theater.

(5) The efforts of the members of the Navy who served in the Naval Armed Guard Service have been largely overlooked due to the rapid disbanding of the service after World War II and lack of adequate records.

(6) Recognition of the service of the naval personnel who served in the Naval Armed Guard Service is highly warranted and long overdue.

(b) SENSE OF CONGRESS- Congress expresses its appreciation, and the appreciation of the American people, for the dedicated service performed during World War I and World War II by members of the Navy assigned as gun crews on board merchant ships as part of the Naval Armed Guard Service.

Courtesy of Jim Biscardi.

Unit. We are like our shipmates the Merchant Mariners, both classed as second citizens."[7]

~~~

Other Armed Guard veterans have rallied to the cause, notably Lyle Dupra. He is the author of We Delivered! *Lyle has remained an ardent advocate for the Armed Guard through his writings and speeches. The following excerpt was from one of his speeches given August 16, 1994, to the New England Armed Guard Veterans' meeting aboard the battleship* Massachusetts, *in Fall River, Massachusetts.*

New England Armed Guard Speech August 16, 1994

...Undoubtedly, some of you here today have been participants in the Atlantic Ocean off and near to our Eastern seaboard coast, and sometimes within sight of the mainland. Few people realize that a real holocaust existed so near our homeland during WW II. It is a proven fact that more lives, ships, and cargoes were lost in this area than those sustained at the Pearl Harbor. In fact, it pales that place and yet, nearly everyone remembers Pearl Harbor!

The din and noises of battles large and small at sea are only heard and lived only by those in attendance. We had no Ernie Pyle, nor a Walter Cronkite, or any others who captured those moments of confrontation. There were no TV cameras or radio amplifications to send on and out to the rest of the world. It is up to those of us remaining, to erect these permanent historical markers. They will remain our legacy of "silent witnesses," so that each generation that follows us may be apprised by these conveyances. By these modes, they will be alerted to the facts that we were there and made the necessary sacrifices to help preserve and save for them, that which they now so freely enjoy.

It has taken me years to comprise a fitting name for my book which I hope to bring to fruition by year's end. It was not any one group that delivered the "goods." It was the two of us, the Armed Guards and the merchant seamen. Each group was interdependent upon the other in all related instances. When it became time to defend those ships against the enemy, each and every man helped in his assigned place. The name for my book is, We Delivered! I thank you, and salute you – one and all.[8]
~~~

Lyle wrote and delivered the following address in Albany, New York.

Plaque Dedication and Installation Honoring the United States Naval Armed Guard of World War II Albany, New York, June 9, 1998.

We who are gathered here, on this day, in the year of our Lord, 1998 by witnessing the erection of a permanent plaque attesting to, and proclaiming the formation of a little known special force of the United States Navy, named the United States Naval Armed Guard.

This great State of New York recognizes the untold accomplishments and sacrifices of this great force, resulting in what is transpiring here today. By the caring and graciousness of our elected officials in declaring the recognition of those who have honorably served this nation in a time of great peril, this permanent plaque, is being erected in this place of honor by causing all of us to come together to pay homage and gratitude.

The essence of the plaque displayed at this place is to bear witness to historical facts and to remind those who enjoy freedom, that the men of the Armed Guard laid their lives on the line. Over 1800 of this small group of men gave their full measure. Everyone who reads the silent sentinel's words shall be apprised of the Armed Guard's presence before and during World War II. Deeds not forgotten shall be preserved for all time. This place which may be viewed and visited by all who care, and for those who will come after us, will be keeping the memories of alive of those who have gone before us.

Who were these heroes and why were they formed? World War I records indicate that they served on 384 ships. World War II records indicate that they served on 6,236 merchant vessels. Of these, 710 were sunk beneath them. These unsung heroes never left their guns until it was determined that the ship was either going to explode, burn up, or were definitely going under. Heroes, all!

They were officially formed as a force on April 15, 1941, before the start of World War II. Deactivation of the Armed Guard did commence sometime in 1945, and nearly all were melded back into the fleet and/or discharged by war's end.

Their duties were to arm and protect the merchant vessels, and the merchant seamen of said ships, grandly assisted at the guns in times of enemy action. These men being in such close proximity with each other, and as shipmates all, were in close association. They became close-knit, which fostered camaraderie, and Esprit de corps. Together, they all performed their duties with outstanding valor and attention on their many dangerous voyages in areas of hell and fire!

Among this audience, there are some of us here today, who recall vividly, certain scenes. There are those also, who no doubt experienced many agonizingly reoccurring nightmares of that dreadful unwanted era which resurfaced involuntarily. We can now take comfort in knowing that our place in history will be remembered, preserved, and enriched.[9]

~~~

The Navy Armed Guard Poet, George Hurley has also been busy writing poems and giving invocations at various monument dedications.

Hillcrest

All their earthly tasks now over
Buried beneath the sod's lovely clover
Father bless their families weeping
These so faithful who lie sleeping.

Jesus guard our shipmates well
Let nothing disturb their peace
Bring their tired souls to heaven
All their troubles will now cease.

Armed guard sailors are so special
Denied their glory on your earth
Now they're in your care and keeping,
You alone who knows their worth.
~~~

All the medals long denied them
Forge for them a halo of steel,
Let your angels in the heaven
Know these sailors were for real.[10]

This poem was written for the Monument Dedication Ceremony at the Massachusetts National Cemetery in Bourne, Massachusetts on May 28, 1995.

Monument Poem

Today we tell in praising voice
Honoring our dead, God made the choice
On this hallowed soil in Bourne
American People come to mourn

Dedicating this monument of stone
To those men who never came home
Their glory was not sleek Navy ships
On rusty tubs, they made their trips

They went wherever they were sent
All over the world, to ports they went
Planes knew better than to attack
Armed Guard Gunners gave them flak

God give them now eternal rest
To us they were the very best
Pride in life, glory in death
Best of men we ever met.[11]

And finally this is the program concerning the Monument Dedication for the Massachusetts Veterans' Memorial Cemetery, Agawam.

The Plaque

Today, we place this Plaque and Stone
Honoring those, who God called Home
May it last after we are gone
Sleeping under this soft green lawn

Teach the children to remember well
These brave men, who fought and fell
Read this Plaque, and share our pain
Then this stone, was not in vain
Freedom was fought for every race
To make this World a better place
They gave their life, so we may live
No greater gift, was theirs to give
In His mercy, and His giving
He let us return with the living
This small token on His lawn
May it last, when we are gone.[12]

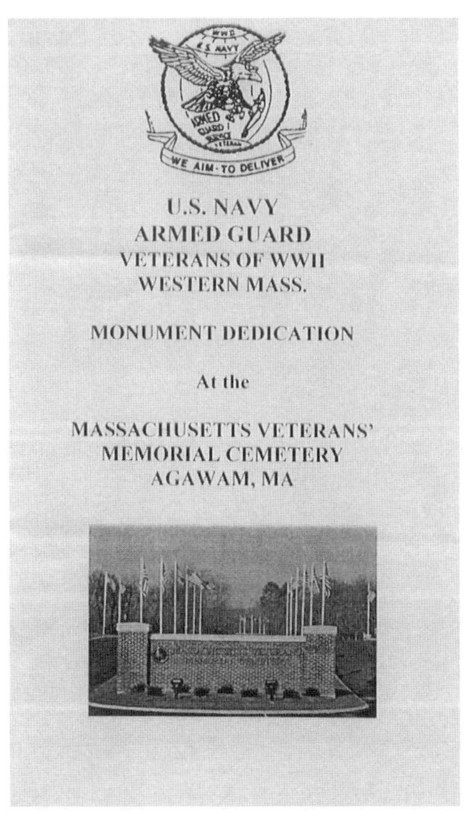
WE AIM-TO DELIVER

U.S. NAVY
ARMED GUARD
VETERANS OF WWII
WESTERN MASS.

MONUMENT DEDICATION

At the

MASSACHUSETTS VETERANS'
MEMORIAL CEMETERY
AGAWAM, MA

AFTERWORD

Due to the tireless efforts of Charles April Lloyd (better known as "C.A.") a two-volume history of the Armed Guard titled, United States Navy Armed Guard Veterans Of World War II: A History of the Armed Guard Veterans of World War II *was written. These treasures of Armed Guard History exist because of C.A.*

C.A.'s devotion to preserving the history of that forgotten branch of the Navy is explained in the following dedication, "This book is dedicated to the 1,810 [now 2,085] Armed Guard who died in the line of duty and all men from all the branches of service who served and those who died." The following are more excerpts from Charles Lloyd's biographical sketch in this Navy Armed Guard history.

C.A. was the organizer of the USN Armed Guard Veterans Association and its Chairman. Starting from scratch, this organization grew to more than 6,900 members out of the 144,970

Armed Guards who served in WW II. It was "an endless task of locating other shipmates. He recorded names and ships into a computer in order to 'match-up' shipmates, put together the Pointer *[The U.S. Navy Armed Guard quarterly newsletter] and mailed out information to over 6,900 of the original 144,970 who served in the Armed Guard."*

C.A. was born near Raleigh, North Carolina in 1926. He joined the Navy as an eighteen-year old in 1944. He "was sent to Bainbridge, Maryland for 14 weeks of 'boots.' After a twelve day leave, he volunteered for the USN Armed Guard Unit upon the advice of his brother, Whitson, who served as an Armed Guard from January of 1942 until May 5, 1945, when he was killed in the torpedoing and sinking of the SS Black Point *three miles off Port Judith, Rhode Island."*

There were five Lloyd brothers who served in the service in WW II; Charles, Lonnie and Whitson were in the Naval Armed Guard, Jack was in the Merchant Marine and Codee in the U.S. Marines.

Charles attended Camp Shelton, Virginia Gunnery school and was sent to the Brooklyn, New York Armed Guard Center, 1st Avenue and 52nd Street. He went aboard the SS *Miaoulis* to England in convoy with food provisions and over to Antwerp, Belgium in time for VE Day. He returned to the States in June to learn of his brother Whitson's death, and after a 12-day emergency leave, he was sent to Baltimore, Maryland, and joined the crew of the USAT *J.W. McAndrews*. The *McAndrews* was in dry dock for a bow replacement for damage caused by ramming the French Carrier *Berne* off the Azores. After repairs were complete, he sailed to Newport News, Virginia, to pick up provisions and 2,800 troops waiting in Naples, Italy for the Japan invasion. Thanks to President Truman's orders, the Atomic Bombs were dropped saving millions of American and Allied lives, plus the enemy. The *McAndrews* was loaded with troops and ready to sail when the news arrived. Orders for the troops on board were changed and they returned to Newport News. C.A. stayed aboard, and helped bring back two more loads of troops before being removed and assigned to the SS *Phillip Barbour* until guns were removed from the ship.

"C.A. returned to the States and married Hilda Juanita Perry, who had written him every day while he was in the service." They have two daughters ... and three grandsons .... "C.A. served as captain of the Raleigh Fire Department for the last twenty-three years ..."

According to C.A., his greatest achievements in life were to serve his country in time of need, marry a wonderful person, and rear two wonderful daughters who gave life to three grandsons. He also said it was an honor to serve the City of Raleigh and its people for twenty-three years and to serve the USN Armed Guard WW II Veterans Association as chairman in an endless task of locating other shipmates ...[1]

Appendix A

Saga of the Murmansk Run
(Originally written on paper bags in 1943)
by George X. Hurley

Liberty ships are rusty and slow
But where they sail, I must go
Scarred old derelicts, sweet piles of junk
I walked your deck, slept in your bunk

I felt like a bird in a steel nest
To me you were a home, I loved you best
Things I learned while still on shore
Was Liberty Ships were winning the war

No finer ship ever sailed the blue
Than a Liberty Ship with it's Armed Guard crew
There is no glory delivering by the ton
So just enjoy it, have your fun

England was tough, we all agree
Tanks in a storm, they all broke free
Then a collision, we all should be dead
Ammunition stored safe in its bed.

I am a sailor, a Liberty Man
I do my best, the best I can
I will protect you from all in the air
You're all we have, we really care

But now it's different, I don't feel well
We're going to Russia, "the Gateway to Hell"
I know we can make it, I will return
Minus the bow, probably the stern

Scotland was great, kilts are my style
Forming our convoy takes quite awhile
Escorts are ready, prancing ahead
Don't leave us behind, we all will be dead

First day out, I'm chilled to the bone
Even in convoy you just feel alone
Cooks are like witches making your brew
Gallons of coffee just for the crew

Coffee, oh coffee, drink all you take
Black and steaming to keep you awake
Depth charges dropping most every night
Keeping the submarines deep out of sight

Every few hours alarms seem to screech
Run to your guns, close up the breech
Twenty millimeters ready for hell
"Come on you bastards!" That is your yell

One ship explodes just down the line
Up goes a tanker two ships behind

Sea's all afire, kissing some ships
I heard a scream, was it my lips?

German planes came making their run
Earning their cross in the arctic sun
God be my judge I'll never tell
How often I softened on the "Gateway to Hell"

J.U. 88 you won't hear us beg
Be careful of us, we want your egg
Shrapnel, like rain, falls on our deck
I've had this trip up to my neck

Where is my jacket, my rubber suit?
No one will answer, they're all scared mute
"Wake up you dummies, I will survive"
I'll leave this ship free and alive

Powder and smoke, low flying planes
This was a day just made for dying
Heroes so many they can't be counted
Here they come! Another attack mounted

Death you seem so friendly a hand
Torturing the souls of this tired band
No one can ever describe this story
Of these fighting men, men without glory

Ice and the cold, you too are our foe
Taking your toll, laying us low
Someday with pride say to your son
"Your father survived the Murmansk run"

A separate war fought by a few
Merchant seamen, an Armed Guard Crew
British Navy fighting with pride
Out in the Arctic, no place to hide

Ducks in a pond, I know how you feel
Waiting for death, this is for real
No movie, no newsreel, no happy end
Death sits and waits just down the bend

I'm saying my prayers, my gun is so hot
Don't say I'm scared, I know that I'm not
All of my fear is now just a rage
I'll make some history, if only one page

Stand by your gun, there's no place to hide
Fight like a tiger, where is your pride?
Let them all know we must be free
England can crow but we rule the sea

My officers babbling "Change the barrel, son"
Why am I smiling? This isn't fun
"Sorry, Sir, I respect all your freight
The barrel's in the tube, froze very tight"

Old Joe, the boatswain, picking up the shells
Mike the Messman hit and he yells
All brave men fighting as one
Giving their all 'til the battle is won

Look to our Captain, he never broke
Giving his orders in all of the smoke
Chain of sailors, some on the bridge
Passing the shells in this cold fridge

Planes like bees searching for honey
It is so bright but it's not sunny
If we had fog we'd prolong our doom
Don't get downhearted, we don't need gloom

Life or death is only a thread
Speak to a shipmate, then he's dead

Ocean's just a graveyard of sorrow
The tonic is hope, a wish for tomorrow

Rosary beads are my frozen tears
Will they thaw in future years?
Valor so common not recorded in history
Ships just vanish, a Russian mystery

Ships keep moving, Pied Piper calling
Bringing aid to dictator Stalin
Young blood and some so old
Will their story ever be told?

Who were these men? Someone's son
There is no glory on the Murmansk Run
Men so brave slaughtered like cattle
Don't ever mention this Russian battle

Bodies like chocolates dipped in black oil
Your journey is over, free from toil
Blinking red lights, not summer fireflies
Everything's quiet now, no more cries

Give no quarter, fight till the end
No surrender, iron men don't bend
If I survive and again reach shore
I'll never knock at this Russian door

My feet are so cold but this gun is manned
Body is aching, I can't feel my hand
But my twenty millimeter is working fine
We'll keep firing till the end of time

No life boat for me, I die where I stand
Like an icicle, shiny and grand
The Arctic is neutral, it takes no side
All dressed in white, waiting for its bride

We are so cold but we will deliver
Even polar bears are cold and they shiver
Why God made this place I'll never know
Keep all your ice, send it below

Temperatures so cold it cast a spell
No one can live in the devil's well
Slowly more bodies in clusters float by
Eyes frozen in sockets turned to the sky

Twelve submarines circling the foe
Where is the heaven sailors go?
Another destroyer torpedoed twice
Luck just ran out like the roll of the dice

Now comes the fog, can we hide?
Keep your position on this suicide ride
Coffee please, till the battle is done
How will we tell who lost or who won?

But the planes see our mast
Dropping bombs in another pass
More ships hit, more men die
I only looked, too cold to cry

Dear friend, Jesus, to You I call
Help your lambs before we fall
I can't promise I'll be good tomorrow
But the Bible says you watch the sparrow

If I should die in some ship's wake
Don't tell St. Peter, give me a break
Just try and judge good intentions
My black deeds, don't even mention

Churchill said "We have no ships"
Roosevelt said "Ours are on the Pacific trips"

Stalin boasted "I fight all alone
Deliver the goods and go back home

The Kola Inlet is bleak
German planes have access to the air
Air raid shelter is hit, where are you God?
Hundreds buried under Russian sod

No place a haven, only a death trap
They try to bomb it right off the map
No buildings are standing, everything's down
Pocked by craters, there is no town

No water, no lights, no scraps of food
All is depression, death is the mood
Bodies all over killed by some hand
No one gets buried in this frozen land

A pretty asked me, "Do you have some bread?"
She told me her mother and sister were dead
I gave her my sandwich and an old candy bar
I looked to the sky, God was so far

Everyone runs at Stalin's call
But this is a war hurting us all
Who is this man, butcher of men?
Hitler or Stalin, who is our friend?

I won't forget till I'm peaceful and dead
I carry these scars deep in my head
Life will go on but I'll never lose sight
Of freezing peasants, starving but right

They're forming a convoy, we're going back
No one can sleep, not time for the sack
Submarines lurk to kiss us good-bye
Drop all your depth charges, let them fly

Alarms, alarms, you're always ringing
Sounds like a devil chorus singing
But I could care less, gone is all fear
Stumbling to my gun with all this gear

Ghost of ships carrying young men
They'll never be seen in this world again
If weather and ice don't sink your ship
Submarines and planes will finish your trip

Nothing more cruel was ever done to man
Send you to hell on a rusty tin can
God will forgive, that's a sure bet
I may forgive, but I won't forget

Frozen toes, fingers that pain
Cheeks that you rub, seems all in vain
Wind like a knife cuts through your clothes
It's part of learning, I suppose

Where is everyone? Have they left too?
Am I alone in this cold stew?
Cool off your barrel, hey, wait a minute
Here comes a plane, we're right back in it

Down goes the plane, whining in flames
Cursing us all, who is the blame?
No iron cross, pilot so brave
Only reward is a watery grave

Step out on deck, breathe that cold air
Lift up your heart, who's left to care?
Submarines below, planes up on high
All I can say "It's a good day to die"

We're the warriors, like Roman Legionnaires
Like great Sioux Chiefs, men without fear

Armed Guard sailors such as I
Showed all the world just how to die

What would life be under Germany's heel?
Concentration camps, bars of steel
So no surrender, fire to the sky
We'll leave as free men if we say good-bye

No one is talking, I hear no voices
Am I spared? Has God made his choices?
Why did he leave me, I'll never know
But it looks to me like the end of the show

No one relieves me, I stand by my gun
Looks like it's over, who really won
I'll never go back, just hear me tell
Close to the door to the gateway to hell

Sailors are dead, frozen and stiff
Lifeboats with bodies floating adrift
Smoke in your eyes, can't hardly see
But I made my payment to keep us free

Please more coffee, I can't go below
Not for a moment, they won't stop the show
Each day we're closer, Scotland is home
Where are the escorts? Are we alone?

"Silence is golden" my mother once said
It's really quiet, is everyone dead?
But we're still moving, still afloat
Our only damage, a shattered lifeboat

Peel off your clothes, they stick to your skin
We get a shower, I guess we win
Shave off your beard, put on something nice
Clothes thrown overboard, covered with Lice

Dear old Scotland, open your gate
For many sailors it opened too late
I feel this surge, I made it back
Frozen and tired, my brain's out of whack

A drink with a lass with skin so fair
No war stories, she doesn't care
We never existed, the Navy won't tell
All those ships on the bottom, in hell

Drink a toast to the bastardly sons
Don't mention the battle we surely won
God took a vacation, left us alone
Out in the ocean, so white with foam

Pretend we're not there, we'll go away
Carrying a suitcase, holding our pay
Marines guard the street, singing their hymn
But we guard the gates, we let you in

Oh we cursed you, old ship, you were so slow
But you took us there, where no one would go
Brought us back to the American shore
No one could ask for anything more

Today I'm a man, I'll curse and I'll drink
No longer afraid of torpedoes that sink
I have survived, I'm a better man
My gun is my arm, we made our stand

So much suffering, so many dying
So many shipmates died just for trying
All of their labor, all of the toil
All of the bodies covered with oil

I only lived with memories of home
As I watched the sky, frozen alone

With this door to my mind I could escape
Back to my childhood, away from this place

My mother at the table looking so fair
Serving the meal with face, oh so fair
My brothers and sisters, all in a dream
But then there's a noise off the port beam

When men go to sea and the stories are told
I'll only say that I was cold
Nights in the summer, heart all aquiver
Every so often I still will shiver

When there's a homer and people cheer
One thing haunts me forever, I fear
It sounds like the noise when people are dying
I still remember, but I stopped crying

So I'll go to my grave, at least on land
Don't ever tell me war was so grand
My mother, dear mother, didn't raise a son
To live or die on the Murmansk Run

The gateway to hell will never fade
There's not enough money could ever be paid
So old Joe Stalin, when you rot in the ground
Where was your help? Never around

Arctic winds blow, sea moves at night
This watery grave is still quite a sight
All the young men, so brave and so bold
Now, at least, they're warm from the cold

No man in his right mind should make this trip
For sure he'll come back, not with the ship
Mother, oh mother, don't raise your son
To have to die on the Murmansk Run.[1]

Endnotes

Foreword

1. Lyle E. Dupra, "Armed Guard Speech at the 2000 Convention," May 2000.

Chapter 1 – Before World War II

1. Clay Blair, *Hitler's U-Boat War: The Hunters 1939-1942* (New York: Modern Library, 1996), 13.

2. "Declaration concerning the Laws of Naval War, 208 Consol. T.S. 338 (1909)," 19 Nov. 2002 <http: //www1.umn.edu/humanrts/instree/1909b.htm>

3. Justin F. Gleichauf, *Unsung Heroes: The Naval Armed Guard in World War II* (Annapolis, MD: Naval Institute Press, 1990), 5.

4. "Sell Wartime Ships," *Business Week*, 17 July 1937, 42.

5. Agnes Bridger and Tom Bowerman, eds., United States Navy Armed Guard World War I And II," *U.S. Navy Armed Guard Veterans – Volume I* 31 October 2002 http://armed-guard.com/agv1a.html.

6. Gleichauf, 10.

7. U.S. Department of Commerce Maritime Administration, *The United States Merchant Marine: A Brief History* (Washington, D.C., 1972), 3.

8. Ibid.

9. Department Of The Navy – Naval Historical Center, "Naval Armed Guard Service in World War II," 18 January 2002 http://www.history.navy.mil/faqs/faq104-1.htm.

Chapter 2 – Training

1. Agnes Bridger and Tom Bowerman, eds., "United States Navy Armed Guard World War I And II," *U.S. Navy Armed Guard Veterans – Vol-*

ume I 31 October 2002 http://armed-guard.com/agv1a.html.:8.

2. Bernard Wolfe, "Getting the Convoys Through," *Popular Science*, May 1943, 112.

3. Samuel Eliot Morison, *History Of The United States Naval Operations In World War II. Vol. 1:* (Boston: Little, Brown And Company, 1966), 392.

4. Bridger and Bowerman, Ibid.

5 Ibid.

6. Ibid, 9.

7. Ibid.

8. Van C. Mills, "Remembering Pearl Harbor," 1 December 2001.

9. James J. Gailey, "U.S. Navy Armed Guard WW II: Training," *The Pointer*, March/April 1993, 9-10.

10. Donald G. Kloenne, "Training," March 2001.

11. Harold E. Skinner, "Survival In A Navy Service School," November 2002.

12. George X. Hurley, "Armed Guard Song," 1946.

Chapter 3 – Not Without Problems

1. Robert C. Ruark, "They Called "Em Fish Food," *Saturday Evening Post*, 6 May 1944, 24.

2. Felix Riesenberg, "Communists at Sea," *Nation*, 23 October 1937, 432.

3. Felice Swados, "Seamen and the Law," *The New Republic*, 9 March 1938, 124.

4. Ruark, 25.

5. Beverly Britton, "Navy Stepchildren; The Armed Guard," *Proceedings of the United States Naval Institute*, 73 (1947): 1496.

6. Frank R. Briggs, Jr., "Detached Command – Multiple Duties of the Armed Guard Officers," *Proceedings of the United States Naval Institute*, 69 (1943): 1469.

7. Ibid, 1470.

8. Dan and Toni Horodysky, eds., "Salary Comparison U.S. Navy vs. American Merchant Marine During World War II," *American Merchant Marine at War*, 1 November 2002 http://www.usmm.org/salary.html

9. Telfair Knight, Letter to Mr. Arren H. Atherton - The Answer to the Supposed Inequity in Pay Between Merchant Seamen and Members of the Armed Forces in World War II. 1943.

10. Gun Crew 651 – S.S. *Ralph Izard*, "A Farewell Letter - 24 August 1943," *Tales of Hoffman: Hoffman Island Radio Association Newsletter*, June 2002, 18.

11. L.A. Sawyer and W.H. Mitchell, *The Liberty Ships* 2nd ed. (London: Lloyds of London Press Ltd, 1985), 41.

12. Wendell Hoffman, "A Tribute to a Shipmate, Channing Reeves," (Letter) 20 February 1994.

13. Sawyer, 105.

Chapter 4 – First Voyage

1. Agnes Bridger and Tom Bowerman, eds., "United States Navy Armed Guard World War I And II," *U.S. Navy Armed Guard Veterans – Volume I 31* October 2002 http://armed-guard.com/agv1a.html.

2. Edward T. Woods, "A Teenager Goes to War," *Patriots and Heroes: True Stories of the U.S. Merchant Marine in World War II* (Palo Alto, CA: The Glencannon Press, 2000), 88-89.

3. James J. Gailey, "U.S. Navy Armed Guard WW II: First Voyage," *The Pointer*, Mar/Apr 1993, 10-11.

4. Gaylord T. M. Kelshall, *The U-Boat War In The Caribbean* (Annapolis, MD: Naval Institute Press, 1994), 109.

5. Albert Lowe, "My Voyage on the S.S. *Steel Engineer* –September 24, 1942 – August 9, 1943," April 2001.

6. Joe Webb, "America the Beautiful," 2001.

7. L.A. Sawyer and W.H. Mitchell, *The Liberty Ships* 2nd ed. (London: Lloyds of London Press Ltd., 1985), 169.

8. Robert Norling, "Shooting Back," Copyrighted 1991.

9. Harold E. Skinner, "The Banana Cruise," 2001.

Chapter 5 – The Gulf of Mexico

1. Dan & Toni Horodysky, U.S. Ships Sunk or Damaged on East Coast and Gulf of Mexico During World War II," *American Merchant Marine at War*, 21 December 2002 http://www.usmm.org/eastgulf.

2. Ibid, "U.S. Ships Sunk or Damaged in Caribbean Sea During World War II," 21 December 2002 http://www.usmm.org/carib.html

3. Gaylord T.M. Kelshall, *The U-Boat War In The Caribbean* (Annapolis, MD: Naval Institute Press, 1994), 128.

4. Ibid, 175.

5. Willem Cool, "History of the artillery-training ship Van Kinsbergen," *Royal Netherlands Navy Warships of World War II*, 30 December 2002 http://leden.tref.nl/~jviss000/Vankin_his.htm.

6. Arthur R. Moore, *A Careless Word ...A Needless Sinking* 7th ed. (New Jersey: Dennis A. Roland Chapter of the American Merchant Marine Veterans, 1998), 192 & 508.

7. J.W. Janes, "S.S. *Meton*," April 2002.

8. Van C. Mills, "Key West, Florida – Hell Hole of the Navy," 23 August 2003.

Chapter 6 – The Atlantic Ocean

1. Terry Hughes and John Costello, *The Battle of the Atlantic* (New York: Dial Press/James Wade, 1977), 42.

2. Dan and Toni Horodysky, eds. "U.S. Ships Sunk or Damaged…," *American Merchant Marine at War*, 2 January 2003 http://www.usmm.org/shipsunkdamaged.html>

3. Leonard E. Amborski, Letter to compiler, 16 August 2001.

4. Ibid, *The Last Voyage: Maritime Heroes of World War II* (Orlando, Fl: First Publish, 2001), 75.

5. Ibid, 67-71.

6. Gudmundur Helgason, ed. "U-594," *The U-boat War 1939-1945,* 3 January 2003 http://www.uboat.net/boats/u594.htm

7. James Montesarchio, "I never told my C.O. that …," 15 March 2001.

8. Louis V. Ritter, "The First of Four Trips Across the Atlantic," 13 March 2001.

9. L.A. Sawyer and W.H. Mitchell, *The Liberty Ships* 2nd. ed. (London: Lloyds of London Press, Ltd, 1985), 120.

10. Arthur R. Moore, *A Careless Word ...A Needless Sinking* 7th ed. (New Jersey: Dennis A. Roland Chapter of the American Merchant Marine Veterans, 1998), 90.

11. Franklin H. Pearce, "Then Everything Broke Loose," 27 June 2001.

12. Moore, Ibid.

13. Ibid, 702.

14. James J. Gailey, "U.S. Navy Armed Guard W.W. II: Ice Fields and Fog," *The Pointer*, Mar/April 1993, 12.

15. Alvin J. Kemble, Jr., "34 Days," 2000.

16. Moore, 145.

17. Helgason, "U-177," Ibid. 9 January 2004 http://www.uboats.net/boats/ul177.htm

18.Ibid, "U-195," Ibid.

19. Moore, 650

20. Joseph McKenna, Jr., "Thank God for Joe McKenna ," January 2002.

21. William H. Hicks, Letter to compiler, 12 June 2002.

22. Robert Norling, "The Captain's Dead," Copyrighted 2000.

23. Ibid, "Action in the North Atlantic," Copyrighted 2000.

24. Joseph V. Wagner and his Naval Armed Guard shipmates of the S.S. *Abraham Baldwin*, "The Curse of the *Abraham Baldwin* or Twenty Ways Not To Cross The Atlantic," (Poem), 1943.

25. Sawyer, 77/227.

Chapter 7 – Northern Russia

1. John Creswell, *Sea Warfare 1939-1945* (Berkeley: University of California Pr., 1967) 197.

2. Bernard Wolfe, "Getting the Convoys Through," *Popular Science*, May 1943, 108.

3. Department of the Navy – Historical Center, "Naval Armed Guard Service: Convoys to Northern Russia – an Overview and Bibliography," 18 January 2002 http://www.history.navy.mil/fags/faq104-2.htm

4. John Gorley Bunker, *Liberty Ships: The Ugly Ducklings Of World War II*. (Salem, N.H.: Ayer Company Publishers, Inc., 1990), 62.

5. Dan and Toni Horodysky eds., "U.S. Ships Sunk or Damaged in Murmansk Run…," *American Merchant Marine at War*," 7 January 2003 http://www.usmm.org/europe.html

6. Arthur R. Moore, *A Careless Word...A Needless Sinking* 7th ed. (New Jersey: Dennis A. Roland Chapter of the American Merchant Marine Veterans, 1998), 274.

7. Ibid, 186.

8. Charles J. Hayes, "Murmansk Experiences," *The Pointer,* March-April 1996.

9. Louis Paessun, "The Secret Navy of WW II," 2003.

10. Moore, 96.

11. Ibid, 233-34.

12. Joseph Benedetto, "Murmansk," August 2001.

13. George X. Hurley, "I vowed if I ever came back, I'd never go near Murmansk again," 1943.

14. Robert Norling, "Stuka," Copyrighted 2001.

15. John M. Sheridan, "S.S. *Owen Wister*," *Linda and the Gunner's Mate*, 1985.

16. John A. Starkey, "My Trip to Russia," March 2001.

17. John York, "Action On The Murmansk Run: Diary September 1944 – May 1945," In *Patriots and Heroes: Vol. II* (Palo Alto, California: The Glencannon Press, 2003).

18. Hurley, "My Snowstorm," (Poem) Copyrighted 2003.

Chapter 8 – The Mediterranean

1. John Slader, *The Fourth Service: Merchantmen at War 1939-1945* (London: Robert Hale, Limited, 1994), 246.

2. Dan and Toni Horodysky, eds., "U.S. Ships Sunk or Damaged in Approaches to Mediterranean Sea, and Black Sea," *American Merchant Marine at War*, 23 January 2003 http://www.usmm.org/medit.html.

3. Samuel J. Pitittieri, "How My Trip To Bari, Italy Started," In *Nightmare In Bari*: by Gerald Reminick (Palo Alto, CA.: The Glencannon Press, 2001), 36.

4. George A. Peak, "What A Small World," March 2001.

5. Arthur R. Moore, *A Careless Word ...A Needless Sinking* 7th ed. (New Jersey: Dennis A. Roland Chapter of the American Merchant Marine Veterans, 1998), 382.

6. L.A. Sawyer and W.H. Mitchell, *The Liberty Ships* 2nd ed. (London: Lloyds of London Press, Ltd., 1985), 169.

7. J.W. Janes, "S.S. *Ezra Meeker*," April 2002.

8. Dante Nieri, "S.S. *John M. Clayton*," September 2002.

9. "A Ships Log: The S.S. *William Patterson* Liberty Ship." August 18, 1943 – March 5, 1944." Courtesy of Albert Lowe.

10. Gerald Reminick, *Nightmare In Bari:* (Palo Alto, CA.: The Glencannon Press, 2001), 2.

11. Bernard L. Anderson, *Diary*, 22 November 1943, In *Nightmare In Bari*: (Ibid), 59-60.

12. Reminick, 2-4.

13. Anderson, Ibid, 2 December 1943, 94.

14. Ibid, 3 December, 158.

15. Ibid, 4 December, 107.

16. Ibid, 6 December, Ibid.

17. Ibid, 7 December, 156.

18. Ibid, 10 December, 157.

19. Ibid, 11 December, 155.

20. Ibid, 12 December, 157.

21. Joseph Benedetto, "Well done, Guisseppe," 2001.

22. Ibid, "Reunion," 2001.

23. Sawyer, 98.

24. Louis V. Ritter, "Three Dynamite Sticks," March 2001.

25. Robert Hassard, "A Message to a Friend," July 2002.

26. Sawyer, 169.

Chapter 9 – D-Day and Europe

1. Tony Hall, ed., *D-Day: Operation Overlord: From landing at Normandy to the liberation of Paris* (New York: Smithmark Publishers, Inc., 1993), 22.

2. Emory S. Land, *The United States Merchant Marine At War: Report of the War Shipping Administrator to the President* (Washington, D.C.: 1946), 22.

3. Department Of The Navy – Naval Historical Center, *Naval Armed Guard Service: Merchant Ships at Normandy during the D-Day Invasion (Operation Neptune), June-July 1944,* (Washington, D.C.), 8 February 2003 http://www.history.navy.mil/faqs/faq104-7.htm 1-2.

4. Ibid, 3.

5. Dan and Toni Horodysky, eds. "U.S. Ships Sunk or Damaged in Murmansk Run, Normandy…," *American Merchant Marine at War*, 8 February 2003 http://www.usmm.org/europe.html

6. Harlan P. Ross, "The Tug of War," (Abridged version) Published in *Sea Classics* May-June 2002.

7. James Montesarchio, "D-Day," March 2001.

8. L.A. Sawyer and W.H. Mitchell, *The Liberty Ships* 2nd ed. (London: Lloyds of London Press, Ltd., 1985), 44.

9. Department of the Navy, Ibid.

10. John A. Lucarelli, "The Next Morning the Harbor Was Full of Ships," 24 January 2002.

11. Arthur R. Moore, *A Careless Word...A Needless Sinking* 7th ed. (New Jersey: Dennis A. Roland Chapter of the American Merchant Marine Veterans, 1998), 48 and 425.

12. Ralph M. Zink, *Voyage Reports, S.S.* Clara Barton, *11 June and 27 August 1944.* (Courtesy of Albert Lowe).

13. John A. Starkey, "How many guys can you fit under a mess table?" March 2001.

14. Tracy Dungan, "Antwerp 'City of Sudden Death,'" *V2 Rocket. Com – A4/V2 Resource Site,* 18 February 2003 http://www.v2rocket.com/start/chapters/antwerp.html 4/5.

15. Robert Auer, "Sailing Under Foreign Flags," May 2001.

16. Joseph V. Toohill, Letter to compiler, 7 March 2001.

17. Ibid, "From Smooth Log," 31 December 1944 (Excerpts to) 14 January 1945.

18. Clifford N. Davis, "A Comforting Letter," 21 June 2003.

19. Howard L. Silverman, "Antwerp Not Ghent," 12 December 2001.

20. Richard M. Brown, "Buzz Bomb Alley," April 2001.

21. Sawyer, 180.

22. W.G. Kitson, "The Tea Party," November 2002.

23. George X. Hurley, "D-Day," (Poem) Copyrighted 1998.

Chapter 10 - Around the World With an Armed Guard Signalman

1. "October, 1944," *Ibiblio.org*, 2 March 2003 http://www.ibiblio.org/pha/chr/chr44-10.html

2. Walter E. Ream, "The Patch," 1978.

3. L.A. Sawyer and W.H. Mitchell, *The Liberty Ships* 2nd ed. (London: Lloyds of London Press, Ltd., 1985), 94.

4. Ibid, 153.

Chapter 11 – Life at Sea and In Port

1. Lyle E. Dupra, *We Delivered!: The U.S. Navy Armed Guard in World War II* (Manhattan, KS: Sunflower University Press, 1997) 5.

2. John Gorley Bunker, *Liberty Ships: The Ugly Ducklings* (Annapolis, MD: Naval Institute Pr., 1972), 30.

3. Marjorie H. Martin, "Growth of an Armed Guard Library," *Library Journal* 1 November 1944, 921.

4. Ibid, 923.

5. Anthony E. Culik, "TNT," February 2001.

6. James Farias, "*Axtell J. Byles,*" March 2002.

7. Robert Norling, "Crime and Punishment," Copyrighted 2001.

8. Ibid, "Some Characters," Copyrighted 2001.

9. Arthur R. Moore, *A Careless Word...A Needless Sinking* 7th ed. (New Jersey: Dennis A. Roland Chapter of the American Merchant Marine Veterans, 1998), 561.

10. Norling, "Down the Hatch," Copyrighted 2001.

11. Ibid, "Battling Boredom," *The Drachen Foundation Newsletter: Kite Archives, Science & Culture* (4) January 1988: 13.

12. Richard M.Brown, "Glasgow: The Ideal Liberty Town," 2001.

13. Ibid, "The Hot Dog Maru," 2001.

14. Ibid, "Bora Bora," 2001.

15. Milan LaMarche, "Incident in New Zealand," 2003.

16. John H. Gross, "My Navy Experiences," 2001.

17. James W. Biscardi, Letter to author, 11 October 2002.

18. Ibid, "Getting Sick," October 2002.

19. Agnes Bridger and Tom Bowerman, eds., "B Member List," *WW II US Navy Armed Guard and WWII Merchant Marine,* 13 March 2003 http://www.armed-guard.com/bbbb.html

20.George X. Hurley, "Our Toast – U.S. Armed Guard," 3 December 2002.

Chapter 12 – Storms and Weather

1. Arthur R. Moore, *A Careless Word...A Needless Sinking* 7th ed. (New Jersey: Dennis A. Roland Chapter of the American Merchant Marine Veterans, 1998), 419-20.

2. Hansel D. "Stormy" Collins, "Mountains of Water," March 2001.

3. Moore, 581.

4. Frederick C. Huber, "Typhoon of April 1943," February 2002.

5. John Lucarelli, "There was this large flash," January 2002.

6. Moore, 418/581.

7. Richard M. Brown, "I would have kissed the ship builders," April 2001.

8. William Oehlecker, "A Wave Floated Us High Off Our Feet," February 2001.

9. Moore, 109.

10. L.A. Sawyer and W.H. Mitchell, *The Liberty Ships* 2nd ed. (London: Lloyds of London Press, Ltd., 1985), 100.

11. Franklin H. Pearce, "Sure glad that's over," July 2001.

12. Irving M. Dickerman, "A Sea Experience," *The Andover Beacon, Inc.,* April 2001. [Reprinted with permission of the *Andover Beacon, Inc.*]

13. Moore, 550.

14. Edmund M. Fogarty, "Atlantic Fog," June 2003.

15. MultiEducator, Inc., "LST of the United States," *Navy History.com,* 22 February 2003 http://www.multied.com/navy/patrol/19.html

16. Robert L. Somers, "Diary Aboard S.S. *Knute Nelson* 29 November - 31 December 1944.

Chapter 13 – The South Atlantic and Indian Oceans

1. Paul Schmalenbach, *German Raiders: A History of auxiliary cruisers of the German Navy 1895-1945* (Cambridge, Great Britain: Patrick Stephens, 1979), 141.

2. Ibid.

3. August Karl Muggenthaler, *German Raiders of World War II* (Englewood Cliffs, N.J.: Prentice-Hall, Inc., 1977), Vii.

4. Dan and Toni Horodysky, eds. "U.S. Ships Sunk or Damaged in South Atlantic, Indian Ocean and Red Sea," *American Merchant Marine at War*, 25 March 2003 http://www.usmm.org/satlantic.html

5. Moses Barker, "Moses Barker's talk to the SS *Stephen Hopkins* Chapter of the American Merchant Marine Veterans, (Audio-tape) March 2001. [Courtesy William Bentley and the SS *Stephen Hopkins* Chapter of the American Merchant Marine Veterans.

6. S.S. *Stephen Hopkins* File, Timothy J. Mahoney, "Memorandum re: trip to Barra Itapoana … 24 November 1942.

7. Ibid.

8. Ibid.

9. Albert S. Ludlam, "Port Elizabeth Tea," March 2001.

10. L.A. Sawyer and W.H. Mitchell, *The Liberty Ships* 2nd ed. (London: Lloyds of London Press, Ltd., 1985), 36.

11. Robert S. Somers, "My Diary of Second Voyage on the SS *Patrick Henry* – February 16, 1944 to October 29, 1944."

12. Fred McLeod, "Calcutta with My Brother," April 2001.

13. John Neven, "World Cruise – SS *Front Royal* November 21, 1944 to September 14, 1945," December 2001.

Chapter 14 – The Pacific

1. Harold E. Skinner, "Ulithi, the Mighty Atoll," 2002.

2. Robert Carse, *The Long Haul: The United States Merchant Marine Service in World War II* (New York: Norton, 1965), 38.

3. Dan and Toni Horodysky, eds., "U. S. Ships Sunk or Damaged in Pacific Area During World War II," *American Merchant Marine at War* 4 April 2003 http://www.usmm.org/pacific.html

4. Milan LaMarche, "Duty in the South Pacific on a Supply Ship," 2003.

5. Robert Norling, "Counting the Days," Copyrighted 2001.

6. Ibid, "Coincidences," Copyrighted 2001.

7. Neven, "S.S. *Wallace R. Farrington* August 2, 1944 – October 26, 1944," 2001.

8. Julius W. Bellin, Letter to compiler, 12 March 2001.

9. Arthur R. Moore, *A Careless Word ...A Needless Sinking* 7th ed. (New Jersey: Dennis A. Roland Chapter of the American Merchant Marine Veterans, 1998), 148.

10. Bellin, "The names Christensen, Boling and Bunch have stayed in my memory for all my years. They will continue to do so," March 2001.

11. Robert D. Hackett and Sander Kingsepp, eds., "HIJMS Submarine I -12: Tabular Record of Movement," *Sensuikan: Stories and Battle Histories of the IJN's Submarines* 11 April 2003 http://www.combinedfleet.com/I-12.htm

12. J.W. Janes, "Pacific Experiences," April 2002.

13. Donald G. Kloenne, "Pacific Travels," March 2001.

14. James J. Gailey, U.S. Navy Armed Guard WW II: Other duties our crew was required to do…," *The Pointer* March/April 1993, 13.

15. Norling, "Friendly Fire," Copyrighted 2001.

16. Ibid, "A Thirst For Adventure," Copyrighted 2001.

17. Skinner, Ibid.

18. George J. Pavlovic, "Stowaway," 24 February 2001.

19. George X. Hurley, "Tom's Parade," (Poem) Copyrighted 2002.

Chapter 15 – Epilogue

1. James E. Sheridan, Sr., Letter to compiler, 12 June 2003.

2. Ibid, Letter to Mrs. Cournoyer's 5th Grade Class, 4 June 1998.

3. Richard M. Brown, "July 4th," 2001.

4. Robert Norling, "And Grown Men Cried," Copyrighted 2001.

5. Joseph McKenna Jr., "Our Day," 2002.

6. James W. Biscardi, "Letter to the Editor – Armed Guard gets no respect," *Intelligencer* 16 May 1996.

7. Biscardi, Letter to compiler, 11 October 2002.

8. Lyle E. Dupra, "The New England Armed Guard Meeting Speech," 16 August 1994.

9. Ibid, "Plaque Dedication and Installation Honoring the United States Naval Armed Guard of World War II, at Albany, New York – Speech," 9 June 1998.

10. George X. Hurley, "Hillcrest," (Poem) Copyrighted 1995.

11. Ibid, "Monument Poem," Copyrighted 1995.

12. Ibid, "The Plaque," (Poem) Copyrighted 2002.

Afterword

1. *United States Navy Armed Guard Veterans Of World War II: Volume II (*Dallas, Texas: Taylor Publishing Company, 1990), 148-49.

Appendix

1. George X. Hurley, "Saga of the Murmansk Run," (Poem) Copyrighted 1944.

About the Author

Gerald Reminick is a Professor of Library Services at the Grant Campus Library, Suffolk County Community College, Brentwood, New York. He received his Bachelor of Science degree from Adelphi University in 1967, a Master of Arts from State University of New York (SUNY) at Stonybrook in 1975 and a Master of Science in Library and Information Science at Long Island University in 1979. When not researching or writing about maritime history, he can be found on his tiny sailboat.

His published works include *Patriots and Heroes, True Stories of the U.S. Merchant Marine in World War II; Nightmare in Bari, the World War II Liberty Ship Poison Gas Disaster and Cover-up; Death's Railway, A Merchant Mariner POW on the River Kwai; Patriots and Heroes, True Stories of the U.S. Merchant Marine in World War II, Vol. 2* as well as a number of poems. He is an associate member of the North Atlantic, Edwin J. O'Hara and Kings Point chapters of the American Merchant Marine Veterans and the U.S. Merchant Marine Veterans of World War II..

He and his wife, Gail, have two children, Danielle and Bradley.

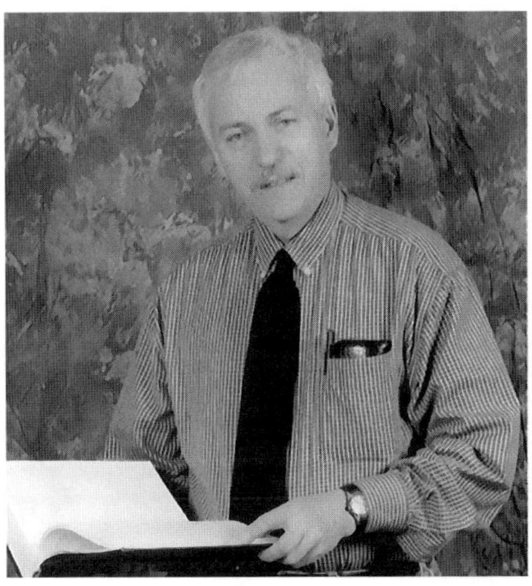

Bibliography

Albright, Suzan Irene. Letter to compiler. 28 April 2001.

Amborski, Leonard E. *The Last Voyage: Maritime Heroes of World War II.* Orlando, Fl: First Publish, 2001.

—. Letter to compiler. 16 August 2001.

Anderson, Bernard L. *Diary*, In *Nightmare In Bari:* by Gerald Reminick. Palo, CA: The Glencannon Press, 2001.

Auer, Robert. "Sailing Under Foreign Flags." May 2001.

Barker, Moses. "Moses Barker's talk to the S.S. *Stephen Hopkins* Chapter of the American Merchant Marine Veterans." (Audio-tape) March 2001. Courtesy of William Bentley and the S.S. *Stephen Hopkins* Chapter of the American Merchant Marine Veterans.

Bellin, Julius W. Letter to compiler. 12 March 2001.

—. "The names Christensen, Boling and Bunch have stayed in my memory for all my years. They will continue to do so." March 2001.

Benedetto, Joseph. "Murmansk." 2001.

—. "Reunion." 2001.

—. "Well done, Guisseppe." 2001.

Bennett, James J. "Aiming to Deliver – The Untold Story of the U.S. Navy Armed Guard." *Veterans of Foreign Wars*, September 1992, 28-30+.

Berry, Robert B. *Gunners Get Glory: Lt. Bob Berry's Story of the Navy's Armed Guard.* New York: Bobbs-Merrill, 1943.

Bernstein, Walter. "Night Watch." *Yale Review,* June 1944, 658-67.

Biscardi, James W. "Getting Sick." October 2002.

—. Letter to compiler. 11 October 2002.

—. "Letter to the Editor – Armed Guard gets no respect." *Intelligencer* 16 May 1996.

Blair, Clay. *Hitler's U-Boat War: The Hunters, 1939-1942.* New York: Modern Library, 1996.

—. *Hitler's U-Boat War: The Hunted, 1942-1945.* New York: Modern Library, 1998.

Bridger, Agnes and Thomas Bowerman eds. "B Member List," *WW II U.S. Navy Armed Guard and WW II Merchant Marine*, 13 March 2003 http://www.armed-guard.com/bbbb.html

—. "United States Navy Armed Guard World War I And II," *U.S. Armed Guard Veterans –Volume I,* 31 October 2002 http://www.armed-guard.com/agv1a.html

Briggs, Frank R., Jr., "Detached command – Multiple Duties of Armed Guard Officers." *United States Naval Institute Proceedings* 69 (November 1943): 1469-1470.

Britton, Beverly L. "Navy Stepchildren: The Armed Guard." *United States Naval Institute Proceedings* 73 (December 1947): 1495-1501.

Brooks, C. Wayland. "Revision of the Neutrality Act." *Vital Speeches*, 1 November 1941, 43-44.

Brown, Richard M. "Bora Bora." 2001.

—. "Buzz Bomb Alley." 2001.

—. "Glasgow: The Ideal Liberty Town." 2001.

—. "The Hot Dog Maru." 2001.

—. "I would have kissed the ship builders." 2001.

—. "July 4th." 2001.

Browning, Robert M. Jr., *U.S. Merchant Vessel War Casualties of World War II.* Annapolis, MD: Naval Institute Press, 1996.

Bunker, John Gorley. *Liberty Ships: The Ugly Ducklings of World War II.* Annapolis, MD: Naval Institute press, 1972.

Carse, Robert. *The Long Haul: The United States Merchant Marine Service in World War II.* New York: Norton, 1965.

Collins, Hansel D. "Stormy." "Mountains of Water." March 2001.

Cool, Willem. "History of the Artillery-training ship *Von Kinsbergen*," *Royal Netherlands Navy of World War II*,

30 December 2002 http://laden.tref.nl/~jviss000/Vankin_his.htm

Creswell, John. *Sea Warfare 1939-1945*. Berkeley: University of California Pr., 1967.

Culik, Anthony E. "TNT." February 2001.

Davis, Clifford N. "A Comforting Letter." 21 June 2003.

"Declaration concerning the Laws of Naval War, 208 Consol. T.S. 338 (1909)," 19 November 2002 http://www1.umn.edu/humanrts/instree/1909b.htm

Department Of The Navy – Naval Historical Center. *Naval Armed Guard Service: Convoys to Northern Russia an Overview and Bibliography*, 12 November 2002 http://www.history.navy.mil/faqs/faq104-2.htm

—. *Naval Armed Guard Service: Japanese Atrocities Against*, 12 November 2002 http://www.history.navy.mil/faqs/faq104-5.htm

—. *Naval Armed Guard Service in World War II*, 18 January 2002 http://www.history.navy.mil/faqs/faq104-1.htm

—. *Naval Armed Guard Service: Merchant Ships at Normandy during the D-Day Invasion (Operation Neptune), June-July 1944*, 8 February 2003 http://www.history.navy.mil/faqs/faq104-7.htm

Dickerman, Irving M. "A Sea Experience." *The Andover Beacon, Inc.* April 2001. Reprinted with permission of the *Andover Beacon, Inc.*

Dungan, Tracy. "Antwerp City of Sudden Death." *V-2 Rocket.Com-A4/V2 Resource Site,* 18 February 2003 http://www.v2rocket.com/start/chapters.antwerp.html

Dupra, Lyle E. "Armed Guard (Speech) at the 2000 Convention." May 2000.

—. "The New England Armed Guard Meeting (Speech)." 16 August 1994.

—. "Plaque Dedication and Installation Honoring the United States Naval Armed Guard of World War II, at Albany, New York –(Speech)." 9 June 1998.

—. *We Delivered! The U.S. Navy Armed Guard in World War II.* Manhattan, KS: Sunflower University Press, 1997.

"F.D.R. Proposal to Arm Ships Speeds Test of Neutrality Act." *Newsweek,* 6 October 1941, 14-15.

"Fact Sheet Issued On National Maritime Day, May 22, 1945." *United States Maritime Commission and War Shipping Administration,* 29 October 2002 http://www.marad.dot.gov/Education/history/facts.html

"Fangs for Freighters." *Popular Mechanics*, December 1942, 14-15.

Farias, James. "*Axtell J. Byles*." March 2002.

Fogarty, Edmund. "Atlantic Fog." June 2003.

Gailey, James J. "U.S. Navy Armed Guard WW II: First Voyage." *The Pointer,* March/April 1993, 9-10.

—. "Ibid: Ice Fields and Fog." Ibid, 12.

—. "Ibid: Other duties our crew was required to do…" Ibid, 13.

—. "Training." Ibid, 9-10.

Galati, Robert. *A Winning Team: The Armed Guard and Merchant Marine in World War II.* Irving, TX: Innovatia Press, 1995.

Gallant, Jack. *Navy & Marine Corps World War II Commemorative Committee*, 4 February 2002 http://www.chinfo.navy.mil/navpalib/wwii/facts/armguard.txt

Gleichauf, Justin F. *Unsung Sailors: The Naval Armed Guard in WW II.* Annapolis, MD: Naval Institute Press, 1990.

Griffith, John H. "Discussions Comments and Notes: Navy Stepchildren: The Armed Guard." *Proccedings of the United States Naval Institute* 77 (October 1951): 1103.

Gross, John H. "My Navy Experiences." 2001.

Gun Crew 651 – S.S. *Ralph Izard.* "A Farewell Letter -24 August 1943." *Tales of Hoffman Island Newsletter*, June 2002, 18. Courtesy James V. Shannon.

"Guns for American Ships." *Scholastic,* 1 December 1941, 6.

Hackett, Robert D. and Sander Kingsepp, eds. "HIJMS Submarine I – 12: Tabular Record of Movement," *Sensuikan: Stories and Battle Histories of the IJN's Submarines,* 11 April 2003 http://www.combined-fleet.com/I-12.htm

Hall, Tony, ed. *D-Day: Operation Overlord: From landing at Normandy to the liberation of Paris*. New York: Smithmark Publishers, Inc., 1993.

Hassard, Robert. "A Message to a Friend." July 2002.

Hayes, Charles J. "Murmansk Experiences." *The Pointer*, March-April 1996.

Helgason, Gudmundur, ed. "U-852," *uboat.net: The U-boat War 1939-1945*, 1 April 2003 http://www.uboat.net/boats/u852.htm

—. "U-594," Ibid, 3 January 2003 http://www.uboat.net/boats/u594.htm

—. "U-177," Ibid, 9 January 2004 http://www.uboat.net/boats/u177.htm

—. "U-195," Ibid, http://www.uboat.net/boats/u195.htm>

Hickam, Homer H. *Torpedo Junction: U-Boat War off America's East Coast, 1942.* Annapolis, MD: Naval Institute Press, 1989.

Hicks, William H. Letter to compiler. 12 June 2002.

Hoehling, A.A. *The Fighting Liberty Ships: A Memoir.* Kent, OH: Kent State University Press, 1990.

Hoffman, Wendell. Letter – "A Tribute to a shipmate, Channing Reeves." 20 February 1994. Courtesy of Wendell Hoffman.

Horodysky, Dan and Toni, eds. "NOTICE To All Merchant Marine Personnel Aboard," *American Merchant Marine at War*, 26 October 2002 http://www.usmm.org/diaries.html

—. "Salary Comparison U.S. Navy vs. American Merchant Marine During World War II, *Ibid*, 1 November 2002 http://www.usmm.org/salary.html

—. "U.S. Merchant Ships Sunk or Damaged in World War II," *Ibid,* 2 January 2003 http://www.usmm.org/shipssunkdamaged.html

—. "U.S. Naval Armed Guard Casualties During World War II," *Ibid,* 13 November 2002 http://www.usmm.org/armedguard.html

—. "U.S. Ships Sunk or Damaged in Approaches to Mediterranean Sea and Black Sea," *Ibid,* 23 January 2003 http://www.usmm.org/medit.html

—. "U.S. Ships Sunk or Damaged in Caribbean Sea During World War II," *Ibid,* 21 December 2002 http://www.usmm.org/carib.html

—. "U.S. Ships Sunk or Damaged on East Coast and Gulf of Mexico During World War II," *Ibid,* 21 December 2002 http://www.usmm.org/eastgulf.html#anchor474786

—. "U.S. Ships Sunk or Damaged in Murmansk Run," *Ibid,* 7 January and 8 February 2003 http://www.usmm.org/europe.html

—. U.S. Ships Sunk or Damaged in South Atlantic, Indian Ocean and Red Sea," *Ibid,* 25 March 2003 http://www.usmm.org/satlantic.html

—. "U.S. Ships Sunk or Damaged in Pacific Area During World War II," *Ibid,* 4 April 2003 http://www.usmm.org/pacific.html

Hough, Richard Alexander. *The Great War at Sea 1914-1918.* Oxford: Oxford University Press, 1983.

"House of Representatives." *Congressional Record,* Vol. 144 No. 66, 21 May 1998.

Huber, Frederick C. "Typhoon of April 1943." February 2002.

Hughes, Terry and John Costello. *The Battle of the Atlantic.* New York: Dual Press/James Wade, 1977.

Hurley, George X. "Armed Guard Song." 1946.

—. "D-Day." (Poem) 1998.

—. "Hillcrest." (Poem) 1995.

—. "I vowed if I ever came back, I'd never go near Murmansk again." 1943.

—. "Monument Poem." 1995.

—. "My Snowstorm." (Poem) 2003.

—. "Our Toast – U.S. Armed Guard." 3 December 2002.

—. "The Plaque." (Poem) 2002.

—. "S.S. *Henry Bacon.*" (Poem) 1947.

—. "Saga of the Murmansk Run." (Poem) 1944.

—. "Tom's Parade." (Poem) 2002.

Janes, J.W. "S.S. *Ezra Meeker.*" April 2002.

—. "S.S. *Meton.*" April 2002.

—. "Pacific Experiences." April 2002.

Kelshall, Gaylord T.M. *The U-Boat War In The Caribbean.* Annapolis, MD: Naval Institute Press, 1994.

Kemble, Alvin T., Jr. "34 Days." 2003.

Kitson, W.G. "The Tea Party." November 2002.

Kloenne, Donald G. "Pacific Travels." March 2001.

—. "Training." March 2001.

Knight, Telfair. Letter to Mr. Arren H. Atherton, "The Answer to the Supposed Inequity in Pay Between Merchant Seamen and Members of the Armed Forces in World War II." 1943. Courtesy of Dan and Toni Horodysky.

LaMarche, Milan. "Duty in the South Pacific on a Supply Ship." 2003.

—. "Incident in New Zealand." 2003.

Land, Emory S. *The United States Merchant Marine At War: Report of the War Shipping Administrator to the President.* Washington: DC, 1946.

Lowe, Albert. "My Voyage on the S.S. *Steel Engineer* –September 24, 1942-August 9, 1943." April 2001.

Lucarelli, John A. "The Next Morning the Harbor Was Full of Ships." 24 January 2002.

—. "There was this large flash." January 2002.

Ludlam, Albert S. "Port Elizabeth Tea." March 2001.

Martin, Marjorie H. "Growth of an Armed Guard Library." *Library Journal,* 1 November 1944, 921.

McGee, William L. *Bluejacket Odyssey: Guadalcanal to Bikini: Naval Armed Guard in the Pacific.* Palo Alto, CA: The Glencannon Press, 1997.

McLeod, Fred. "Calcutta with My Brother." April 2001.

McKenna, Joseph, Jr., "Our Day." 2002.

—. "Thank God for Joe McKenna." January 2002.

Messimer, Dwight R. "Heinz-Wilhelm Eck Siegerjustiz and the Peleus Affair," *Uboat.net: The U-boat War 1939-1945,* 1 April 2003 http://www.uboat.net/articles/index.html? article=18>

Mills, Van C. "Key West Florida – Hell Hole of the Navy." 23 August 1903.

—. "Remembering Pearl Harbor." 1 December 2001.

Montesarchio, James. "D-Day." March 2001.

—. "I never told my C.O. that ...." March 2001.

Moore, Arthur R. *A Careless Word ...A Needless Sinking* 7th ed. New Jersey: Dennis Roland Chapter of the American Merchant Marine Veterans, 1998.

Morison, Samuel Eliot. *History Of The United States Naval Operations In World War II. Vol. 1: The Battle of the Atlantic September 1939-May 1943.* Boston: Little, Brown And Company, 1966.

MultiEducator, Inc. "LST of the United States," *NavyHistory.com*, 22 February 2003 http://multied.com/navy/patrol/19.html

Muggenthaler, August Karl. *German Raiders of World War II.* Englewood Cliffs, N.J.: Prentice-Hall, Inc. 1977.

Nieri, Dante. "S.S. *John M. Clayton.*" September 2002.

"'Neutrality Act' of August 31, 1935, Joint Resolution." 49 Stat. 1081; U.S.C. 441 note, 25 November 2002 http://www.mtholyoke.edu/acad/intrel/interwar/neutralityact.htm

"Neutrality Acts 1935-1941." 19 November 2002 http://history.acused.edu/gen/WW2Timeline/neutralityacts.html

Neven, John. "*S.S. Wallace R. Farrington* August 2, 1944 - October 26, 1944." 2001.

—. "World Cruise – S.S. *Front Royal* November 21, 1944 to September 14, 1945." December 2001.

Norling, Robert. "Action in the North Atlantic." 2000.

—. "Battling Boredom." *The Drachen Foundation Newsletter: Kite Archives, Science & Culture* 4 (January 1998): 13.

—. "The Captain's Dead." 2000.

—. "Coincidences." 2001.

—. "Counting the Days." 2001.

—. "Crime and Punishment." 2001.

—. "Down the Hatch." 2001.

—. "Friendly Fire." 2001.

—. "And Grown Men Cried." 2001.

—. "Shooting Back." 1991.

—. "Some Characters." 2001.

—. "Stuka." 2001.

—. "A Thirst for Adventure." 2001.

"October 1944." *Ibiblio.org*, 2 March 2003 http://www.ibiblio.org/pha/chr/chr44-10.html

Oehlecker, William. "A Wave Floated Us High Off Our Feet." February 2001.

Paessun, Louis. "The Secret Navy of WW II." 2003.

Pavolic, George J. "Stowaway." 24 February 2001.

Peak, George A. "What a Small World." March 2001.

Pearce, Franklin H. "Sure glad that's over." July 2001.

—. "Then Everything Broke Loose." June 2001.

Pitittieri, Samuel J. "How My Trip To Bari, Italy Started." In *Nightmare In Bari:* By Gerald Reminick. Palo Alto, CA: The Glencannon Press, 2001.

Pratt, William V. "Why the U.S. Plans to Arm It's Ships." *Newsweek,* 20 October 1941, 26.

Prince, Bertrand B. *Report of Voyage, S.S.* Edmund Fanning *to Chief of Naval Operations.* 15 May 1944. Courtesy of Albert Lowe.

Public Law 105-261- The Strom Thurmond National Defense Authorization Act for Fiscal Year 1999. 17 October 1998.

Ream, Walter E. "The Patch." 1978.

Reinicke, F.G. *Voyage Report of S.S.* Edmund Fanning *to Chief of Naval Operations.* 28 June 1944. Courtesy of Albert Lowe.

Reminick, Gerald. *Nightmare In Bari: The World War II Liberty Ship Poison Gas Disaster and Cover-up.* Palo Alto, CA: The Glencannon Press, 2001.

—. *Patriots and Heroes: True Stories of the U.S. Merchant Marine in World War II; Vol. I.* Palo Alto, CA: The Glencannon Press, 2000.

—. Ibid. Vol. II. The Glencannon Press, 2004.

Riesenberg, Felix. Jr. "Communists at Sea." *Nation,* 23 October 1937, 432.

—. *Sea War: The Story Of The U.S. Merchant Marine In World War II.* Westport, CT: Greenwood Press, 1956.

Ritter, Louis V. "The First of Four Trips Across the Atlantic." March 2001.

—. Three Dynamite Sticks." March 2001.

Roosevelt, Franklin D. "The President's Anti-Neutrality Message." *Current History*, December 1941, 310-313.

"Roosevelt and Hull on Neutrality Repeal." *Current History*, January 1942, 398-401.

"Roosevelt Prods Congress Anew as He Pledges Fight to Finish." *Newsweek*, 3 November 1941.

Ross, Harlan P. "The Tug of War." (Abridged). Full Article published in *Sea Classics,* May-June 2002.

Ruark, Robert C. "They Called 'Em Fish Food." *Saturday Evening Post*, 6 May 1944, 24+.

S.S. *Stephen Hopkins* File, Timothy J. Mahoney, "Memorandum re: trip to Barra Itapoana… 24 November 1942." U.S. Coast Guard National Maritime Center, Arlington, Virginia.

Sawyer, L.A. and W.H. Mitchell. *The Liberty Ships* 2nd ed. London: Lloyds of London Press, Ltd., 1985.

Schmalenbach, Paul. *German Raiders: A History of auxiliary cruisers of the German Navy 1895-1945.* Cambridge, Great Britain: Patrick Stephens, 1979.

Schnepf, Ed. "There Shall Be No Surrender So Long As The Guns Can Be Fought: The United States Naval Armed Guards of WW II." *WWII U.S. Navy Armed Guard and WW II Merchant Marine* http://www.armed-guard.com/sc01843.html

"Sell Wartime Ships." *Business Week*, 17 July 1937, 42.

Sheridan, James E. Sr., Letter to compiler. 12 June 2003.

—. Letter to Mrs. Cournoyer's 5th Grade Class. 4 June 1998.

Sheridan, John M. "S.S. *Owen Wister*." *Linda and The Gunner's Mate*, 1985.

"*A Ships' Log: The S.S.* William Patterson *Liberty Ship, August 18, 1943-March 5, 1944*." Courtesy of Albert Lowe.

Silverman, Howard L. "Antwerp Not Ghent." December 2001.

Skinner, Harold E. "Banana Cruise." 2001.

—. Survival In A Navy Service School." November 2002.

—. "Ulithi the Mighty Atoll." 2002.

Slader, John. *The Fourth Service: Merchantmen at War 1939-1945*. London: Robert Hale Limited, 1994.

Somers, Robert L. "Diary Aboard S.S. *Knute Nelson* 29 November – 31 December 1944.

—. "My Second Voyage on the S.S. *Patrick Henry – Febraury 16, 1944 to October 1944.*

Starkey, John A. "How many guys can you fit under a mess table?" March 2001.

—. "My Trip to Russia." March 2001.

Swados, Felice. "Seamen and the Law." *The New Republic*, 9 March 1938, 124.

Toohill, Joseph V. "From Smooth Log." 31 December 1944 (excerpts to) 14 January 1945.

—. Letter to compiler. 7 March 2001.

U.S. Department of Commerce Maritime Administration. *The United States Merchant Marine: A Brief History.* Washington, DC, 1972.

United States Navy Armed Guard Veterans of World War II: A History of the Armed Guard Veterans of World War II. Dallas, TX: Taylor Publishing Company, 1990.

Wagner, Joseph V. and his Naval Armed Guard shipmates of the S.S. *Abraham Baldwin.* "The Curse of the Abraham Baldwin or Twenty Ways Not To Cross The Atlantic." (Poem) 1943.

Webb, Joe. "America the Beautiful." 2001.

Wolfe, Bernard. "Getting the Convoys Through." *Popular Science*, May 1943, 108-112.

Woods, Edward T. "A Teenager Goes to War." In *Patriots and Heroes: True Stories of the U.S. Merchant Marine in World War II: Vol I.* Palo Alto: CA, The Glencannon Press, 2000.

Woodward, David. *The Secret Raiders: The Story Of The German Armed Raiders In The Second World War.* New York: W.W. Norton & Company, 1955.

York, John. "Action On The Murmansk Run: Diary September 1944-May 1945." In *Patriots and Heroes*: Vol II. Palo Alto, CA: The Glencannon Press, 2004.

Zink, Ralph M. *Voyage Reports, S.S.* Clara Barton*, 11 June and 27 August 1944.* Courtesy of Albert Lowe.

INDEX

S

T

U

V

W

Y

Z